PRAISE FOR *TOUCH*

In the tradition of William Jame[s'] *[The Varieties of] Religious Experience*, Yvonne Kasons might well be called "The Varieties of Spiritually Transformative Experiences," and, like its predecessor, it, too, is likely to become a classic. For it is a brilliant treatment of these important spiritual experiences, both theoretically and empirically, and is chock full of fascinating illustrative cases. In addition, it contains many helpful and wise suggestions for how to deal with the challenging aspects of these experiences. For my money, it is the single most valuable resource now available both for clinicians and for those who have undergone these life-changing transcendent encounters.

— Kenneth Ring, Ph.D., professor emeritus of psychology, University of Connecticut, co-founder, International Association for Near-Death Studies, author of *Lessons from the Light*

Now comes the pioneer of the term "Spiritually Transformative Experiences" with a new revision of her previous book *Farther Shores*, that is not only updated but substantially deepened by additional material. I consider this revitalized classic the single best resource, and therefore a must-read, for anyone who has had an STE or who works with such experiencers in medical, psychological, or spiritual health-care settings.

— Janice Miner Holden, Ed.D., LPC-S, LMFT, NCC, ACMHP, chair, Department of Counseling & Higher Education, professor, Counseling Program, University of North Texas, past president, International Association for Near-Death Studies, editor, *Journal of Near-Death Studies*

This expanded version of Yvonne Kason's *Farther Shores* is dramatically revised in the light of her decade of spiritual growth since that book's last edition, with entirely new chapters and new and deeper understandings of how to nurture spiritual transformation. While

Farther Shores was a pioneering book in its day, this revision breaks new ground, reflecting Dr. Kason's incredible journey and greater insights over the ensuing years.

— Bruce Greyson, M.D., Carlson Professor Emeritus of Psychiatry & Neurobehavioral Sciences, University of Virginia, co-founder, International Association for Near-Death Studies

As President of the Board of Directors of ACISTE — the American Center for the Integration of Spiritually Transformative Experiences, an organization devoted to training professionals how to work with STEs — I believe Dr. Kason's text should be required reading for all entering the field. I have personally recommended her prior texts to my doctoral students. I have also recommended it to clients with whom I have worked and who are struggling to stay present amidst difficult spiritual crisis. Finally, I have used her book in my own life, as a guide to working through my own spiritual development.... *Touched by the Light* will no doubt be a key read for the next generation of spiritual seekers and professional helpers alike.

— Ryan Rominger, Ph.D., ACSGC, president, board of directors, American Center for the Integration of Spiritually Transformative Experiences, associate university research chair, Center for Leadership Studies & Educational Research, University of Phoenix, adjunct research faculty, Sofia University, California Institute of Integral Studies

A lucid and illuminating compendium of Spiritually Transformative Experiences by a wise and knowledgeable guide. Exploring these very common — yet poorly understood — occurrences through the lens of yogic consciousness is fascinating. Doctors should put this on their must-read list.

— Patricia Pearson, author of *Opening Heaven's Door: What the Dying May Be Trying to Tell Us About Where They're Going*

Dr. Yvonne Kason has brought together in this book an astonishing gathering of information from quoted spiritual lines, clinical understandings, and individual accounts of spiritual energies that open us to reconnect to our Divine source. Her writings will help individuals going through such dynamic experiences by giving them a way to understand and integrate happenings that are usually not understood by the mainstream. Her information can help physicians and professional practitioners ground their practices in clearer protocols that will assist these individuals as midwives in a transformative process. These individuals have been "cracked open" by the Divine and are the ones that, once reintegrated, will bring more conscious ways to benefit their local communities and the global community at large. This book is a jewel on the path to wholeness!

— Jyoti Prevatt, Ph.D., spiritual director, Center for Sacred Studies, founder, The Fountain for the Natural Order of Our Existence, author of *An Angel Called My Name*

PRAISE FOR *FARTHER SHORES*

Through fascinating case studies and her own personal experience, Dr. Yvonne Kason explores the mysterious forces shaping our spiritual and psychic lives. Provocative, well-researched, and full of practical wisdom.

— Sylvia Fraser, author of *My Father's House* and *The Quest for the Fourth Monkey*

… An exceptionally readable and useful book on near-death and other spiritually transformative experiences. Written in a popular style that will appeal to intelligent lay readers, this book is careful enough about its science to be palatable as well to physicians and scholars.

— Bruce Greyson, M.D., Bonner-Lowry Professor of Personality Studies, University of Virginia Medical School, editor of *The Journal of Near-Death Studies* and *The Near-Death Experience: Problems, Prospects, Perspectives*

Dr. Kason's … near-death experience … propelled her on a lifetime quest for answers. In discovering some for herself, she found ways of helping others deal with the kind of life-shaking events that had been routinely dismissed by orthodox medical practitioners as unbelievable, irrelevant, and bizarre.

— *Chatelaine*

What is striking about this book is the down-to-earth nature of Kason's interpretations of the data she presents ... a grounded and sensible book.

— *Canadian Book Review Annual*

As a physician, Kason is able to bring a fresh perspective to much of this material. She's able to account clinically for many of the physical symptoms of the typical experience.

— *Vancouver Sun*

... An exceptional book ... [that] takes the reader into a world where mystical happenings bring direction and healing to our everyday lives.

— Jyoti (Jeneane Prevatt, Ph.D.), former director of the Spiritual Emergence Network, author of *An Angel Called My Name*

... A major contribution to our understanding of a wide range of spiritually transformative experiences ... Kason is a wise and knowledgeable guide in these realms, and I can recommend her book with the greatest enthusiasm.

— Kenneth Ring, Ph.D., professor emeritus of psychology, University of Connecticut, author of *Heading Toward Omega* and *Lessons from the Light*

... Builds a bridge between the scientific and the spiritual, a bridge physicians will feel comfortable crossing.

— *Family Practice*

TOUCHED BY THE LIGHT

TOUCHED BY THE LIGHT

Exploring Spiritually Transformative Experiences

YVONNE KASON, M.D.

DUNDURN
TORONTO

Gopi Krishna account on pages 59–61 from *Living With Kundalini: The Autobiography of Gopi Krishna*, by Gopi Krishna, © 1967, 1970 by James Hillman. Reprinted by arrangement with The Permissions Company, Inc., on behalf of Shambhala Publications, Inc., Colorado, www.shambhala.com.

Materials quoted from *Autobiography of a Yogi* published by Self-Realization Fellowship, Los Angeles, California.

Cover image: Lake & mountain: istock.com/SensorSpot; Sky: istock.com/republica
Printer: Webcom, a division of Marquis Printing Inc.

Library and Archives Canada Cataloguing in Publication

Title: Touched by the light : exploring spiritually transformative experiences / Yvonne Kason, M.D.
Names: Kason, Yvonne, author.
Description: Includes bibliographical references and index.
Identifiers: Canadiana (print) 20190112794 | Canadiana (ebook) 20190112859 | ISBN 9781459745513 (softcover) | ISBN 9781459745520 (PDF) | ISBN 9781459745537 (EPUB)
Subjects: LCSH: Parapsychology—Case studies. | LCGFT: Case studies.
Classification: LCC BF1031 .K37 2019 | DDC 133.8—dc23

1 2 3 4 5   23 22 21 20 19

We acknowledge the support of the **Canada Council for the Arts**, which last year invested $153 million to bring the arts to Canadians throughout the country, and the **Ontario Arts Council** for our publishing program. We also acknowledge the financial support of the **Government of Ontario**, through the **Ontario Book Publishing Tax Credit** and **Ontario Creates**, and the **Government of Canada**.

Nous remercions le Conseil des arts du Canada de son soutien. L'an dernier, le Conseil a investi 153 millions de dollars pour mettre de l'art dans la vie des Canadiennes et des Canadiens de tout le pays.

Care has been taken to trace the ownership of copyright material used in this book. The author and the publisher welcome any information enabling them to rectify any references or credits in subsequent editions.

The publisher is not responsible for websites or their content unless they are owned by the publisher.

Printed and bound in Canada.

VISIT US AT

dundurn.com | @dundurnpress | dundurnpress | dundurnpress

Dundurn
3 Church Street, Suite 500
Toronto, Ontario, Canada
M5E 1M2

Dedicated to the memory of
Pandit Gopi Krishna,
and
Paramahansa Yogananda.
Lights in the Darkness

CONTENTS

AUTHOR'S NOTE

THE PERSONAL CASE HISTORIES and stories included in this book are based on actual experiences, as they were described to me by patients, colleagues, and friends. In order to protect the anonymity and confidentiality of the persons involved, I have paraphrased the stories and have changed some small details and identifying features. When individuals wished to have their identities revealed, I have left their stories in their own words.

PREFACE

I AM DELIGHTED AT how well received my earlier books, *A Farther Shore* (1994) and *Farther Shores* (2000, 2008) have been. In the years since their publication, hundreds of people from around the world have written me to thank me: for coining the phrase "Spiritually Transformative Experiences" (STEs), and for the groundbreaking framework for diverse Spiritually Transformative Experiences I presented — a framework that bridged modern psychology, psychiatry, and Western medicine, with the yogic model of consciousness and kundalini. I defined "Spiritually Transformative Experiences" in these books as an umbrella term, to include diverse types of mystical experiences, Near-Death Experiences (NDEs), Spiritual Energy/ Kundalini episodes, psychic awakenings, and inspired creativity and genius.

Many professional researchers of Near-Death Experiences and other paranormal experiences of consciousness have now begun to adopt and use this term that I first coined, "Spiritually Transformative Experiences," including in ACISTE, the American Center for the Integration of Spiritually Transformative Experiences; in IANDS, the International Association for Near-Death Studies; and in ETERNEA. I am deeply honoured that the term "Spiritually Transformative Experiences" has now been adopted and used by so many other pioneering professionals in the field. I am glad that other STE researchers find the term accurate and useful.

After what I now know was a spontaneous kundalini awakening experience in 1976, a powerful white-light/mystical Near-Death Experience in a 1979 plane crash, and a psychic awakening a few weeks later, I was propelled to research these exceptional consciousness experiences to try to understand what on earth had happened to me. Gradually over the years as I continued my personal research quest, more and more patients came to my medical office telling me stories of their own powerful STEs, and sharing horror stories of how their STEs were mislabelled by doctors, clergy, and family members as being signs of mental illness, work of the devil, or hallucinations. As I learned more about STEs, I felt increasingly called to educate others about the reality of STEs, and to advocate for and support STE experiencers. Thus in 1990 I publicly specialized my medical practice in the research and counselling of patients with diverse types of Spiritually Transformative Experiences, becoming the first Canadian medical doctor to do so.

As I describe in this book, my new medical specialty of Spiritually Transformative Experiences led me to have a fascinating career. Over the years I became a founder and board member of the Kundalini Research Network, the founder of the Spiritual Emergence Research and Referral Clinic, Canadian Coordinator of the Spiritual Emergence Network, and co-founder of the Spirituality in Health-Care Network. I became the author or co-author of four books, spoke internationally at conferences, and gave numerous radio and television interviews about STEs. I loved my medical career, and I loved counselling STE patients.

On November 8, 2003, my life changed completely. I was gravely injured in a slip-and-fall accident, and instantly died. After a profoundly beautiful NDE in the heavenly realm of loving white light, I reawoke in my previously dead body to find myself seriously injured with a traumatic brain injury (TBI). For twelve years after my 2003 TBI and NDE, I thought my previous life as a practising medical doctor and as an author and public speaker was permanently finished.

To my great amazement and delight, on February 24, 2016, while deeply meditating, I suddenly experienced a miraculous brain healing — a miracle of neuroplasticity of the brain! Suddenly and unexpectedly my writing-inspired creativity spontaneously reawoke! After twelve years of complete loss, suddenly the flow of inspiration, my creative ability to write books and give talks, reawakened as if from a deep twelve-year slumber.

I completed two new books in less than a year following my spontaneous brain healing of February 2016: this book, *Touched by the Light: Exploring Spiritually Transformative Experiences*; and *Soul Lessons from the Light*, the detailed stories of and my reflections on the five NDEs and other peak STEs I've have had over the course of my lifetime.

Both my new books are particularly special because they are testimonials — testimonials to the miracle of brain neuroplasticity, to the healing power of meditation, and to the grace of the Higher Power. My miraculous brain healing also gives hope to other persons who suffer supposedly "incurable" neurological conditions. Now, although I no longer practise medicine, my inspiration and ability to write and give talks has miraculously reawakened — and with great gusto! I feel like a caged bird finally set free, because I am finally able to express in my new books and in talks the knowledge, life experience, and insights that had been "locked in" inside my head for the past twelve years after my TBI.

Touched by the Light covers much of what I included in my last book, *Farther Shores*, but also includes many new sections, topics, and chapters. Every topic has been updated and revised, to reflect today's research and my current deeper insight and understanding about diverse Spiritually Transformative Experiences and their after-effects — long-term spiritual transformation of consciousness.

With my newly reawakened inspiration and writing ability, there are many reasons I thought it important that I write a new book on STEs, to update and expand upon what I had previously written about STEs. First, I thought this important because I have changed significantly since I wrote *Farther Shores* in 2000. My knowledge and understanding of STEs, spiritual transformation of consciousness, and the yogic model of consciousness and kundalini have deepened significantly over these years. I have now been practising yogic meditation daily for forty years. Further, my understanding of yoga science has deepened greatly since 2000, by my study of the extensive writings of the yogic saint and guru, Paramahansa Yogananda.

Second, my experiential understanding about Near-Death Experiences and other STEs has increased substantially since my earlier books were published. As I describe in *Touched by the Light*, and in even greater detail in *Soul Lessons from the Light*, many years after my 1979 plane-crash NDE that launched my quest to research NDEs and other STEs, I was blessed with two more powerful Near-Death Experiences: one in 1995, and another in 2003. With reflection, I now realize that I also had two Near-Death Experiences as a child. I thus have had a total of five Near-Death Experiences over the course of my life! I wish to now share my current deeper personal awareness of STEs.

Third, the world has changed significantly since *Farther Shores* was published. Public awareness of STEs, especially of Near-Death Experiences, has increased dramatically in the West in the last twenty years, through books, films, and other media. Further, in 2018 I became a board member of the International Association for Near-Death Studies, and a member of ACISTE, the American Center for the Integration of Spiritually Transformative Experiences. I therefore want my new books to present completely up-to-date information on NDEs and other STEs.

Fourth, exchange of ideas between the East and the West has also increased dramatically in recent years, so that yoga philosophy has become widely known in the West. Yoga and meditation are no longer considered "foreign" concepts. In fact, yoga and meditation have become widely practised. This increased awareness makes it possible for me to now share additional detail and depth of understanding about the yogic model of consciousness in *Touched by the Light*, without seeming too esoteric for the Western reader.

Fifth, I felt it important in *Touched by the Light* to bridge the innovative ideas of Gopi Krishna and his modern kundalini model, which I presented in *Farther Shores*, more deeply with the classical teachings on yogic science as comprehensively presented by "The Father of Yoga in the West," Paramahansa Yogananda. This integrated perspective more accurately reflects my current deeper understanding. Throughout this book I attempt to give a multi-faith perspective and bridge the yogic model of consciousness as put forth by these two yogic visionaries and other scholars with current Western understanding in psychology and medicine.

Finally, because I have now retired from the practice of medicine, I feel much freer to express my personal opinions and to share my personal STE experiences than when I wrote my earlier books. Therefore, in this new book I have more openly stated my personal opinions on matters, and shared several more of my own personal STE stories as case examples.

It is my sincere hope that *Touched by the Light* will both inspire and educate readers. I hope readers will come away knowing that Spiritually Transformative Experiences are real, peak experiences, signs of an expanding range of human consciousness, and are definitely not signs of mental illness or an overactive imagination, as some mistakenly contend. I also hope that as readers reflect upon the miracle of my healed writing ability, and the uplifting true stories of my own and many STE experiencers' glimpses of the Divine realm shared throughout this book, that they may feel joy, inspiration, renewed hope, and ultimately greater love for our shared Higher Power, God.

INTRODUCTION

MANY PEOPLE AROUND THE WORLD are having Spiritually Transformative Experiences (STEs). I know this first-hand — I have had many STEs myself. When I was in medical school in 1976, I had what I now know was a kundalini awakening experience. Then, when I was a medical resident in 1979, I had a life-changing mystical "Near-Death Experience" (NDE) in an airplane crash, followed by a psychic awakening a few weeks later. My struggle to understand my own extraordinary experiences propelled me on a quest, as a medical doctor and a psychotherapist, to research mystical and paranormal experiences. I wanted to discover what was known by medicine, psychology, and spiritual traditions about mystical experiences, Near-Death Experiences, and psychic phenomena, and to share this awareness with others.

Touched by the Light is the product of forty years of inner and outer research. Over the years more and more people came forward to speak to me as a doctor and psychotherapist about their STEs, especially after 1990 when I publicly specialized my medical practice on the research and counselling of persons having STEs. To this day, close to a thousand persons have shared the stories of their powerful STEs with me: mystical experiences, Near-Death Experiences, Spiritual Energy or Kundalini Episodes, inspired creative experiences, and psychic awakenings. I've studied my own STEs over this time as well, and researched the scholarly literature, exchanged insights with other consciousness researchers, and learned from teachers of both Eastern and Western spiritual traditions.

I coined the phrase *Spiritually Transformative Experiences* in 1994, as an umbrella term to encompass this broad range of experiences happening to people today, which all tend to cause a "spiritual awakening" in the experiencer — changing the experiencer's values and attitudes in a more spiritual and altruistic direction. Additionally, STEs of all types also seem to share similar long-term after-effects. STEs often seem to begin (or accelerate) a long-term process of transformation in body, mind, and spirit. As you will read, these STE after-effects, this long-term process of psychological purification, spiritual deepening, and expansion of the range of consciousness, is known of in various spiritual traditions, where it has been called the "mystical path" or "kundalini process."

Unfortunately, until now Western medicine, psychology, and society as a whole have been uninformed about Near-Death Experiences, kundalini awakening, mystical experiences and other STEs, and their prevalence among people today. At the time of my 1979 NDE, even good friends and medical colleagues invalidated my experience, and speculated that my NDE was an "electrolyte imbalance" or a "hallucination." I knew this could not be true of an experience that was so intensely positive and had such a powerful, lasting impact upon me.

My personal understanding of Near-Death Experiences was deepened dramatically in 1995 when I had another out-of-body mystical experience in a close call — another powerful Near-Death Experience. Then to my further amazement, in 2003 I had yet another life-changing white-light Near-Death Experience, when I sustained a traumatic brain injury in a slip-and-fall accident.

In *Touched by the Light* I am sharing the conclusions from my forty-year quest to understand STEs — a framework and vocabulary to define the major types of STEs and their many subtypes, and a framework to understand the after-effects — physical, psychological, paranormal, and spiritual — using many actual case stories and several of my own STE stories as examples. I am also sharing the model I have found most helpful in understanding STEs and their after-effects, the yogic model of consciousness and kundalini. This framework is based on a blend of Gopi Krishna's contemporary interpretation of ancient yogic concepts about kundalini, yogic science as recently described for the West by Paramahansa

Yogananda, and the insights of myself and other consciousness researchers. This yogic framework is universal and multi-faith, bridging Eastern and Western thought, as well as medicine and spirituality. It is the best framework I have found to understand STEs and their common after-effects — the biological, psychological, and spiritual symptoms of long-term spiritual transformation of consciousness.

This book is a guide for those people having STEs and undergoing long-term spiritual transformation. I hope that by reading *Touched by the Light* they will realize that they are not alone, that their STEs are real and are also being experienced by many people today, and that STEs have been known for millennia in the mystical traditions of the world's major faiths. I offer such individuals some practical guidelines for navigating many years of the transformation process, which may at times be tumultuous, requiring intense psycho-spiritual housecleaning, but which yields beautiful spiritual results and equipoise in the end.

Touched by the Light is also a guide for health-care professionals, clergy, and counsellors to whom STE experiencers may turn for help and support. My hope is to give professionals a framework for understanding STEs and their after-effects, so they can better assess and assist their clients.

I also hope this synthesis of both my personal STE experiences and forty years of clinical experience and research will stimulate other STE researchers. Large numbers of people are having STEs and are undergoing spiritual transformation of consciousness. I think it essential that more research be done to better document and understand these experiences, and to learn how to best assist and support persons having them. Professionals and the public need to become better informed about STEs, so that we stop mislabelling and pathologizing STE experiencers!

Finally, I sincerely hope that everyone reading this book will come away knowing that Spiritually Transformative Experiences are very real experiences — experiences that reveal to us that we are truly spiritual beings, not just physical bodies — spiritual beings incarnated here in physical bodies in order to grow, learn, and expand in our capacity to love.

PART I

DEFINING SPIRITUALLY TRANSFORMATIVE EXPERIENCES

I

MY 1979 PLANE-CRASH
NEAR-DEATH EXPERIENCE

MANY PEOPLE AROUND THE WORLD today are having "Spiritually Transformative Experiences" (STEs), remarkable experiences of consciousness that have a strong positive psychological and spiritual effect on the individual. STEs tend to change the experiencer's values and beliefs in a more spiritual and more altruistic direction — a powerful STE causing what is often called a "spiritual awakening." A person's entire world view and their ideas, values, priorities, and beliefs may change. I have often heard people say after a powerful STE that their perception of reality — and their whole personality — has been transformed and propelled in a far more spiritual direction. For this reason I have come to call these powerful transforming experiences "Spiritually Transformative Experiences" (STEs), a phrase I coined in 1994.

I speak from personal experience. In 1979, when I was twenty-six years old, I had a powerful Spiritually Transformative Experience, a Near-Death Experience, which would change the course of my life forever. My childhood was fairly ordinary. My father and mother were both European immigrants who came to Canada to seek a better life after the brutality of the Second World War. I was born and raised — along with a sister and two brothers — in the pleasant, upper-middle-class suburbs of Toronto. Raised a Christian, I participated in Sunday School and, as a teenager, in the church choir of my local United Church of Canada. I believed in a God both because I had been taught to do so and because the belief gave me hope that the world — and humankind — might somehow survive its history of senseless violence and repeated wars.

Because I was considered academically "gifted," I was placed in a special accelerated school program, Etobicoke Advancement Classes. One benefit of this was that I developed a tremendous love of reading. In high school during the late 1960s to early 1970s, I listened to the music of the Beatles, was introduced to the writings of Alan Watts and Timothy Leary, and became fascinated with their discussions of the so-called mystical states of consciousness that could be glimpsed through the use of hallucinogenic drugs such as LSD. But it quickly became clear to me that people should be able to reach these mystical states — if they did indeed represent some type of union with the Divine — without the use of drugs. This thought led me, like many others of my generation, to explore Eastern philosophies, meditation, and yoga.

During university and medical school I began to practise hatha yoga and to read books on positive thinking. In my last year of medical school, I took a meditation course that claimed that regular meditation would help me relax, study better, and get better grades in my exams. Being a dedicated medical student, I was eager to do well in my final examinations. I began to meditate daily. I took to meditation immediately. It felt natural to me, as if I were a duck being introduced to swimming on water for the first time.

In December 1976, after a few months of regular twice-daily meditation, I had an initial experience with consciousness expansion during a deep meditation that I did not understand fully until much later in life. I now know that this was my first adult Spiritually Transformative Experience — a kundalini awakening experience. I will describe this experience in chapter 4 on Spiritual Energy/Kundalini Episodes. Following this kundalini awakening, however, I returned the focus of my attention to my medical-school studies and exams, and for the time being put aside thoughts about my extraordinary meditation experience.

Then on March 27, 1979, during the final year of my medical residency, I had another, much more powerful STE, my first adult Near-Death Experience. This experience was so transformative that I could not push it to the back of my mind. It changed my life forever. In retrospect, I wonder if perhaps my meditation-induced kundalini awakening in some way helped prepare my consciousness for the powerful Near-Death Experience I had a couple years later. This 1979 plane-crash NDE marked the beginning of a profound spiritual transformation in my life.

The Plane Crash

In the spring of 1979, as part of my residency in Family Medicine at the University of Toronto, I was assigned for one month to a small, rural hospital in Sioux Lookout that provided service for a number of isolated First Nations villages in remote areas of Northern Ontario. On March 27, 1979, my supervising physician designated me to accompany an Indigenous woman, Jean Marie Peters, who had measles encephalitis, on a medical air evacuation from Sioux Lookout to Winnipeg, Manitoba. She needed the more specialized medical facilities there to treat her rapidly deteriorating condition.

During the flight, I was required to supervise her care, giving her the intravenous drugs needed to stabilize her condition and manually pumping a breathing bag, at regular intervals, that would send oxygen directly into her lungs through an airway tube that was inserted through her mouth.

The plane, a six-seat, twin-engine Piper Aztec, was packed. The patient was strapped onto a stretcher directly behind the pilot's seat where two of the original six seats had been, with the oxygen tank wedged behind the seat normally used by a co-pilot. Sally Irwin, a nurse who had also been assigned to the flight, and I were seated beside the patient.

When the plane lifted off the runway, I was so busy tending the patient that I didn't notice a heavy snowstorm had begun. But by the time we had flown for thirty or forty minutes and were about twenty miles from Kenora, a town on Lake of the Woods, the storm had become a near-blizzard. Suddenly, I noticed a change in the sound of the twin propellers. I looked up and saw that the right propeller had stopped. The pilot, Gerald Kruschenske, was vigorously pushing buttons and pulling levers. Something was obviously wrong. Shouting over the roar of the engine, I asked what was going on. He shouted back that everything was all right. About ten seconds later I was reassured when the right propeller started again. Everything seemed to be back to normal, and I returned my attention to the patient.

A few minutes later the left propeller started sputtering. Looking up, I saw that the right propeller was still working but the left propeller had now stopped. Alarmed, I shouted again at the pilot Gerry to find out what was happening, but he didn't answer. He was desperately pushing buttons, pulling levers, and pumping handles in an attempt to restart the left engine. I noticed we were flying quite low over the trees and hills. Unbeknownst to the nurse Sally and me, Gerry had been in radio contact with the Kenora airport for some time and was trying to make an emergency landing there. He had already made one attempt, but, flying with only one engine in the howling wind, he couldn't manoeuvre the plane into proper position. The airport then tried to direct him to a landing strip on the frozen lake. Through the raging snow, he saw what he thought was the landing strip and made an attempt to come down, but again he couldn't get the plane into proper position. As he fought to pull the sluggish plane up again and take another try at the landing, he saw a hill near the edge of the lake and realized instantly that the plane would never clear it. Taking his only option, he cut the sputtering right engine and headed down, praying the ice would hold.

Although Sally and I realized something was wrong, I had no idea how desperate the situation was — until I looked out the window and saw the second propeller die. Both engines were gone.

"Oh my God," I thought, "we're going to crash!" A wave of intense fear and panic overtook me. "God, help! I'm going to die!" I mentally cried out.

Then, immediately after my mental cry for help, I suddenly felt a wave of profound peace and calm descend upon me. With the descending calm, I heard an inner voice comforting me. Verses from the Bible — verses that I didn't know by heart and wasn't consciously trying to remember — flowed through my mind, as if they were being poured into my consciousness by some external force: "Be still, and know that I am God."* "I am with you, now and always."** As the words penetrated the depths of my soul, I became flooded with a sense of peace, and the presence of God. I was no longer afraid. It felt like a force field of peace had descended upon me and pushed away all of my fear. My mind was still. I knew that God was there, and somehow I knew with absolute certainty something I had never known before: there was absolutely nothing to fear in death. I felt enveloped and protected by God's peace.

As the plane continued to tumble toward the ground in violent air turbulence, I turned again to tending the patient Jean. She had regained

---

*   Psalms 46:10.
** Matthew 28:20.

consciousness and was frightened by the turbulence and atmosphere of tension in the plane. Her eyes looked into mine, pleading for help. Filled with a paranormal peace, calm, and bliss that had somehow come upon me, I was able to reassure her. "Everything will be all right," I comforted her, somehow knowing this to be true whether we lived or died. Just then Sally suggested that we turn off the oxygen tank. Agreeing, I turned off the tank and freed Jean so she could breathe on her own, and then continued to calmly reassure her with absolute conviction: I knew somehow, to the core of my being, that no matter what happened, there was nothing to fear.

Gerry managed to steer the powerless, falling plane and crash-landed it onto the ice of a semifrozen lake. But just as the plane touched down on the ice, Gerry saw that the plane was skidding toward a huge stretch of open water. Knowing the plane would never stop in time, he forced its nose down into the ice to slow our skid. The nose dug in and, by some miracle, the plane stopped just at the edge of the ice beside open water.

But, as soon as the plane stopped and the full weight of the plane settled, the ice began to break and the plane quickly started to sink into the freezing water. Gerry jumped out of his front door, stood on the left wing, and started radioing an emergency message.

Meanwhile, icy water was filling the floor of the plane, and I was struggling without success to open the co-pilot's door in front of me on the right. The water rose rapidly. I shouted to the pilot, Gerry, to assist me but he was still frantically trying to radio for help. The freezing water was pouring deeper and deeper into the plane. Although I was still in a mystical, peaceful state, I knew we urgently needed to get out of the sinking plane. I turned to Sally: "Help me lift the stretcher and we'll float it out." Again I shouted to Gerry. "Help me open the door!" Dropping the radio, he finally grabbed the co-pilot's door handle, found it was jammed, and banged with his fist and foot until he finally managed to force it open.

I stepped out through the door onto the right wing of the plane and found myself up to the groin in freezing lake water. Though I pulled with all my might and weight at patient Jean's stretcher, I could not pull it out of the door. I called to Gerry for help. Just as I did, he shouted, "Get back! The plane is going down!" I bent into the plane and quickly pulled Sally out from behind the stretcher and, together, standing on the sinking plane wing, we desperately tried to pull Jean, floating, strapped to her stretcher, out of the co-pilot's door. But it was impossible. Then I remembered that the stretcher had been loaded through the cargo hatch at the back of the plane, and that there was simply no way to get the stretcher out of the front co-pilot's door. Before we could even think about trying to unstrap her, the plane suddenly tilted radically, nose-dived, and sank. There was no way to dive after Jean; the plane had sunk without a trace into deep, pitch-black water.

Gerry, Sally, and I suddenly found ourselves floating in freezing water about two hundred yards from the closest land, an island. Open water with a strong, swiftly moving current separated us from the shore. Above us a fierce winter storm raged, pelting us with snow and howling wind. Behind us the rest of the lake appeared to be frozen, but we had no way of judging the thickness of the ice. Later, I learned that we had crashed on Lake of the Woods at a place called "Devil's Gap," a spot so named because of the treacherous, strong current, which causes the ice to never freeze in winter.

As I kicked and struggled to keep my head above the water, I quickly began to tire. My soaked arctic parka was heavily dragging me down, and my insulated winter boots were starting to feel like lead weights pulling me down into the water. I tried to take off the heavy parka, but discovered my hands were already so close to frozen that I had lost my sense of touch and couldn't manipulate the zipper. I knew we had to get out of the water, and fast. I looked across the black, icy water and heard a voice in my head say, "Swim to shore!"

Being new to intuitive experiences and higher guidance, I did not listen to the inner voice, but in my mind argued with it. My rational mind remembered what I had been taught in childhood swimming lessons for water safety: "Never try to swim to shore!" "It's always farther than it seems." "You'll drown if you try," I had been taught. Meanwhile Gerry repeatedly shouted, "Try to get on the ice!" I therefore ignored the inner voice's instructions and instead turned away from shore and swam toward the ice. I then tried to climb up on it.

Each time I attempted to kick and pull myself up onto the ice, the ice beneath my arms would break off in large chunks and sink. Again and again I tried, struggling and kicking my feet vigorously, becoming more exhausted with each unsuccessful attempt to pull myself up. The voice in my head repeated, "Swim to shore!" Sally was clinging tightly to Gerry. I later learned that she could not swim. Together they persisted in desperately trying to get onto the ice. But the ice was too thin to support anyone's weight. "Swim to shore," the inner voice repeated strongly in my mind, for the third time. Finally I surrendered to the inner voice's guidance. "The ice is too thin," I shouted to Gerry and Sally. I then turned from the ice and began swimming through the fast-moving open water toward the island shore. It was a long and very difficult swim.

I was perhaps halfway to shore the first time my body went under in sheer exhaustion. My throat filled immediately with icy lake water. Instinctively I struggled with all my strength and willpower to kick my way back up to the surface. I coughed, sputtered, and gratefully gasped a breath of air into my lungs as I reached the surface again. I then continued my desperate struggle, stroke by stroke, inching my way slowly closer to shore.

Going Out-of-Body Into the Light

Suddenly, as I struggled through the frigid water, I heard a low-pitched whooshing noise, something like the rushing of a large bird's wings. At the same time, I felt my consciousness abruptly rise up out of my body and found myself looking down at my body struggling through the water below. It seemed as if my awareness, or what I think of as "I," had expanded to fill a much larger space than it had before, and my point of perception had risen twenty feet or so above my physical body. The sense of peace and calm I had been feeling intensified, and then I rose further, to a space filled with bright light and a sense of intense unconditional love.

In this light-filled space I felt like I was "HOME," that I was being embraced and permeated by profound unconditional love, a love that I immediately knew emanated from the infinitely loving Higher Power behind the universe. I also knew, somehow, that this loving Higher Power was infinitely intelligent, underlying all of creation — past, present, and future. This was not an intellectual knowledge; it was a certainty that went to the very core of my being — a soul-knowing. The embracing presence of this loving intelligence enveloped and permeated me. It was

13

the most profoundly beautiful, blissful experience I have ever had in my life. I was in loving, joyous ecstasy. I knew that everything was unfolding as it should.

The light of the light realm was not brilliant and blinding, but was soft and diffused, glowing beautifully. It appeared somewhat like the soft sparkling light that you can see all around you from a plane window just before a rising plane breaks through the top of clouds into bright sunshine above.

I briefly saw a luminous face of light in this light realm, gazing at me gently from the soft cloud-like perimeter, then the face faded from view. I did not recognize this benevolent-appearing face, and still wonder about it to this day. The masculine face appeared kind, emanating gentleness and love. I did not disclose that I saw this face in the light for many years because it felt so extraordinary and sacred to me.

Consciousness Two Places at Once

From above in the light realm, I watched with detachment and blissful curiosity as my physical body swam to shore. My body was still alive, aggressively struggling to swim to shore. But somehow my awareness seemed to be two places at once. A small part of my awareness was still in my physical body, but most of my awareness — say 95 percent — was out of my body, floating above my body and looking down, watching the drama unfold below me. I sometimes compare this experience to feeling as if I were perceiving my life as two images at the same time on a split-screen TV. The bigger picture, 95 percent of my awareness, was the perception of bliss/ecstasy in the loving light. The smaller picture, as in the upper corner of a split-screen TV, was the tiny portion of my awareness that was still in my body. I was aware of both realities at the same time. However, most of my awareness was in bliss and ecstasy in the loving light.

As my body struggled to reach the island shore, I sank again into the icy water from sheer exhaustion and the weight of my waterlogged clothes. Again icy lake water filled my lungs. As I watched from above, I saw myself sputter, cough, and struggle back to the surface. A few minutes later, when my body was completely exhausted, about to go under for the third and final time, the split-screen images of my awareness flipped, and my consciousness seemed to slip mainly back into my body for a while. I found myself looking toward the shore through my physical eyes. It was only about twenty feet away, but there was a strong current pulling me to the right and I could swim no farther. I was still in that mystical state of bliss and ecstasy, and I knew with absolute certainty in this state that death held nothing to fear. I knew that "I" would live on whether my body lived or died. I felt only an intellectual curiosity, and can remember thinking, "Oh, I see, I am meant to die here," and "It is true, you do drown the third time you go down."

Fearlessly and blissfully I surrendered to the Divine and what I thought was my death. But just at that moment, as I was about to go down for the final time, I saw — once again, through my physical eyes — that a tall, fallen pine tree lay in the water, extending out from the island shore. The tree was to my right, and the current was rapidly carrying me toward it. Suddenly I realized that if I could swim just two more strokes, the current would carry me right to the top of the tree. In my expanded state of consciousness, I could see an etheric rescuing hand superimposed upon the tree, beckoning and reaching out to help me.

Somehow I was given the strength to swim those last few strokes. When my frozen hand struck the fallen tree, I felt nothing, no sensation at all. I looked down at my completely numb hand holding the tree, saw that it was bright red, and felt surprised. My rational, medically trained mind pierced my blissful state of consciousness, telling me my hand should be white if it were frozen, since blood vessels constrict to save body heat. Later I learned that, in the latter stages of freezing, the body loses the ability to constrict blood vessels and the white frozen hands become red. Death usually comes fairly quickly after this if the body isn't warmed.

Mechanically, I pulled myself along the tree to the island shore and clambered over some piles of ice onto the land. I immediately turned to the lake and shouted out to Gerry and Sally: "Swim to shore! You can make it!" I urged them. Gerry by that time had helped Sally grab a piece of frozen wood and ice that was keeping her afloat. It wouldn't hold them both, so he turned and started swimming to shore. He eventually made it in and crawled to my side. Then the lake was silent. The nurse had stopped crying for help. I believed that she, like our patient Jean, must have drowned.

Still both in paranormal and normal consciousness, I asked Gerry if he knew how to light a fire without matches. He didn't. Deathly cold, I started vomiting repeatedly, perhaps because my body was trying to get rid of the dirty lake water I had swallowed. A strong desire to sleep came over me, almost overwhelming me, but my inner voice screamed, "No!" Somehow I knew that, even though my consciousness was in bliss and peace, floating out of my body, I must not let my physical body fall asleep. If I went to sleep, I knew I wouldn't wake up again. Instinctively, I crouched into a full squat and tucked my frozen fingers into my armpits to try to warm them. I told Gerry to do the same. The bitter, freezing cold was beyond description. Then I felt my consciousness shift and move away from my physical body again. I knew that we could not survive long in the snowstorm, the subzero weather, and in our wet, nearly frozen clothes. We were freezing to death. My consciousness hovered above my freezing body in light and love.

The Rescue

We almost certainly wouldn't have been rescued in time if it hadn't been for an amazing series of coincidences. The snowstorm was so severe and the terrain so hilly that our final distress signal could only have been picked up by a plane flying almost directly overhead. Just at the critical moment, one was. An Air Canada flight, on its way from Edmonton to Ottawa, picked up the signal and radioed our crash location to the airport in nearby Kenora.

Still, we were a long way from rescue. We had crashed in a remote region. Because of the mix of ice and open water, the island was not accessible by road, boat, or snowmobile. Nothing but a helicopter could reach us, and normally none were located in the region. But, by chance, one was being ferried that day from Edmonton to Val d'Or, Quebec, by a pilot named Brian Clegg. Concerned by the snowstorm, Brian had hoped to land at Kenora Airport but had been forced to come down at a small Ontario Ministry of Natural Resources base about five miles from where our plane had crashed.

When Brian had first landed, he had gone into the base and met with a Ministry staff pilot, Bob Grant, who had also been grounded by the storm. As they were talking, the phone rang: Kenora Airport was relaying a distress message from the pilot of a twin-engine Aztec that was flying in the area and having serious engine trouble.

Brian Clegg sensed that his helicopter might be needed. He rushed out, began removing its protective weather coverings, and turned on his radio. He then heard the emergency crash message relayed from the Air Canada jet, and immediately started his engine. He called to Bob Grant and, without any thought for their own safety, the two headed into the storm, to search for us.

As they flew, Kenora Airport directed them to the general area of the crash. The two pilots searched frantically for the large pieces of wreckage they thought would be visible on the ice or among the trees, but, hampered by the snowstorm, they could not see Gerry and me huddled under the trees on the island or Sally floating like a human icicle, clinging to a piece of ice-caked wood in the lake. After making a rapid sweep of the area and finding nothing, they decided to take a closer look at Devil's Gap, where they thought they might have seen something floating in the open water. Coming down low, they spied a seat cushion — then they spotted Sally, who was unconscious.

Brian hovered the helicopter a few feet above her in the icy water, while Bob climbed out and, hanging on to a strut, tried to pull her rigid, ice-covered form out of the water. Again and again she slid from his grasp. When all else failed, Brian tried to balance the helicopter right on the water, a dangerous manoeuvre since the least shift in weight could cause the helicopter to crash. Fearlessly Bob — a non-swimmer — straddled the skid, dangled his legs in the icy water, and managed to grasp Sally and, eventually, get one of her hands around the skid. With Sally hanging and Bob pressing her hand onto the skid, the helicopter carried them to a spot where the ice was thick enough to hold Sally's weight. Then, as the helicopter hovered a few feet above the ice, Bob balanced on the skid and tried in vain to push all of her rigid, frozen body through the doorway and onto the seat. Finally, he managed to wedge in all but her legs. Using his body to brace her in, Bob stood outside the helicopter on the ice-caked skid while they flew to Kenora hospital.

Gerry and I watched Sally's rescue from shore, waving our arms above our heads in the hope that the helicopter pilots would see us. When the helicopter flew away with Sally, the lake became deadly silent again. "Do you think they'll come back for us?" I asked Gerry. He shrugged uncertainly. We both waited glumly in the bitter cold, hoping desperately that the helicopter would come back to rescue us, too.

Thankfully, about twenty minutes later the two men did return in the helicopter, checking for other survivors. They finally spotted us there on the island shore, but couldn't find a place to land. The island was fully forested, covered with trees, and bordered by fast-moving water. They were on the verge of despair when they noticed a small inlet where the water was protected enough from the current to have frozen solid. Brian managed to land the skids of the helicopter on this small piece of ice, but the patch of ice was so small that the rear propeller was spinning over open water.

Our rescuers gestured to us to walk over to the helicopter. Gerry was able to stumble over a small hill to the helicopter, but I was only semiconscious and unable to walk that distance. Without hesitation, Bob jumped out and — not knowing if the inlet ice beneath his feet could support the additional weight — came to get me. He carried and pulled me over the hill, across the patch of ice, and helped me into the helicopter. Once in the helicopter, they asked me, "Is there anyone else?" "Yes," I responded. "One more, but it is too late for her." With that, I lost consciousness, floating in the loving light.

Coming Back Into My Body

When we arrived at Kenora hospital, the helicopter landed on the hospital's driveway. My consciousness was floating above my body, watching. I was taken out of the helicopter, placed on a stretcher, and wheeled into the hospital. I felt completely at peace and had no fear of what seemed to be my impending death. As I watched from above, a nurse covered me and my wet, frozen clothes with a thin, loosely woven cotton hospital blanket. Another nurse tried to take my temperature and was puzzled that she couldn't get a reading. My body temperature was so low the thermometer could not measure it! As I watched I felt myself start to float further and further away from my body. I knew that I was dying, and I was at peace.

Suddenly I heard a voice say, "Boy, could I use a hot bath!" Hovering above, I was surprised to realize the voice had come from my own physical body. Later I discovered that rewarming the body by submersion in hot water is an excellent emergency treatment for advanced hypothermia. However, I hadn't been taught this in medical school — and I have no idea why or how my body uttered these words.

Thinking I was regaining consciousness and making a brave attempt at humor, the nurses laughed initially. But then one nurse grew serious and suggested that the hot water might help revive us. The nurses then quickly wheeled our stretchers to the physiotherapy department, pulled off our ice-encrusted clothes, and slid our frozen bodies into the hot whirlpool baths.

It was while I was in the hot whirlpool bath that I finally felt my consciousness reenter my body. As my body was submerged in the hot water, I suddenly heard a loud whoosh and felt pulled down, abruptly shrinking from my expanded state above, and pulled through the top of my head, down into the small confines of my body. The sensation was similar to what I imagine a genie might feel when it is forcibly sucked back into its tiny bottle. I heard a loud whoosh, felt a strong downward pulling sensation, and was suddenly aware of being totally back in my body again. I rubbed my numb hands along my arms and legs in the hot water, and exclaimed with joy, "I'm back! I'm back! I'm going to live! I'm going to live!" And I knew that it was true.

Even though I was quite ill with severe frostbite on my face, neck, and hands, and a wrenching cough from the dirty lake water I had aspirated into my lungs, I felt wonderful emotionally. I was basking in bliss, with joy at being given another chance at life, and with awe of the spiritual nature of my experience. Peace, joy, and love flowed through me.

That night, Sally and I were put in the same hospital room. She also seemed to be strangely blissful and at peace. At one point she turned to me and said, "I don't know why it happened, Yvonne, but we have both been saved. Maybe we are going to do something important in our lives one day." I just smiled in agreement. I sensed that she, too, must have had some sort of intense spiritual experience while close to death.

In May of that year Brian Clegg and Bob Grant were publicly acknowledged by the government of Ontario for their courage and, in September, the Governor General of Canada awarded them both the Star of Courage, one of Canada's highest awards for civilian valour. Two months later they received an international award for outstanding valour — a Silver Medal from the Carnegie Hero Fund Commission. And, when an inquest on the accident was held, our pilot, Gerald Kruschenske, received a commendation for the quick thinking and skill that undoubtedly kept us from all dying when the plane first went down.

The Transformational Impact

The day after the crash, I was released from Kenora Hospital. I returned to Toronto but was unable to work for about four weeks. The frostbite on my hands was so severe that I couldn't even hold a pen or fork and I had absolutely no feeling in my fingertips. This meant I couldn't use my hands to examine patients or write on medical charts at work. For a while I coughed and was feverish, but eventually my lungs managed to clear the bits of residue from the lake water that I had inhaled.

The month I had off work helped me recuperate physically but, more important, gave me time to begin to integrate the overwhelming emotional and spiritual impact of the experience into my daily life. Using terms from my Christian upbringing, I could have said that I had experienced a miracle, or the grace of God. Still, I had no idea what to call what had happened to me, what I now know was a Near-Death Experience.

For some time after the NDE I was "love-intoxicated," bubbling love constantly. I remained in a state of awe. I wept with joy at the thought of being alive and at having been given a second chance. When I looked at the world, a wave of love flooded out of me toward everyone and everything. My heart swelled with love when I looked at squirrels running in my yard. Watching neighbourhood children playing would make a wave of intense love toward them pour out of my heart. Any song that mentioned God, romance, children, parents, animals, or righting any type of social injustice made me weep tears of joy and triggered feelings of intense bliss and love.

I felt a powerful, personal connection to our totally loving Higher Power, the intelligent loving force behind the universe, what I call God. I knew to the core of my being that every other person on the planet was also connected and loved by our loving God in the same way, whether they knew it or not. I also had a new strong inner conviction that the God that I had glimpsed was the same one loving mother/father God of all religions.

My Near-Death Experience had awakened an intense spiritual hunger in me. I developed a new, strong yearning to read from the Bible daily, as well as to study other religions' holy books. I knew we were all striving to understand the same one God. I developed the impulse to regularly "talk to God," to pray earnestly to my God, who now felt very real and very close to me. I had an intensified desire to meditate deeply and regularly.

I lost my fear of death after my Near-Death Experience. I had a new inner knowing based on my own personal experience, a knowing that I was not just the physical body, but I was a soul living in a physical body, a soul that would live on after death of the body. I had a deep intuitive understanding of the sacredness of life, and knew life to be a precious opportunity. Somehow I knew intuitively that it was spiritually incorrect to end one's life prematurely, by suicide. Many years later I learned through my clinical research that, as an after-effect of the mystical type of Near-Death Experiences, most experiencers emerge with similarly transformed spiritual convictions.

I soon became aware that the experience was affecting other areas of my life, too, and having a profound transformational effect on me psychologically. I realized it was time to come to grips with and heal some of the unresolved psychological issues in my life. After the NDE, suppressed childhood memories began to surface spontaneously. One involved my father: He and I had been feuding since I was a child, and we hadn't spoken for about two years. In a moment of clarity shortly after my NDE, I realized much of the anger I had directed at him stemmed from witnessing a heated argument between my mother and him when I was a child. As the memory resurfaced, I realized how traumatic the experience had been for me as a child, and that I had been angry at him from that moment on.

Immediately I telephoned my father, and in my love-filled state post-NDE told him for the first time, ever, that I loved him, and asked if we could talk. We had a truly meaningful discussion about how my parents' marital difficulties had negatively influenced our father-daughter relationship. Somehow, the intense love and clarity that stayed with me in the weeks after my mystical NDE enabled me to effortlessly let go of my resentment.

The anger I had harboured toward my father for twenty-one years seemed to evaporate, and he and I made peace. Then I went to the rest of my family, and told them how much I loved them.

A transformation also seemed to occur in my emotional maturity and strength. With this new-found maturity I seemed to be able to see things more clearly than before, and I became aware of another piece of psychological business that needed to be resolved. At the time of the plane crash, I belonged to a small meditation group where I had learned some basic meditation techniques. But after the crash I clearly realized in my soul that for many reasons this particular group was not my spiritual path. With my new strength, clarity, and intensified spiritual convictions, I left this group. I felt clearer emotionally than I ever had in my life.

The months of transformation that occurred after my Near-Death Experience left me feeling psychologically strong, clear, and centred. I felt tremendous inner strength and the courage to speak honestly and lovingly. This Near-Death Experience still remains a source of tremendous spiritual inspiration forty years later. More important, it began a process of personal transformation that has continued to this day.

When I finally returned to work, I had regained much of the feeling in my fingertips and I felt physically and emotionally well — but I still didn't know I had had a Near-Death Experience. I talked excitedly to many of my friends and medical colleagues about floating out of my body, the light, the profound unconditional love, and feeling as if I had come "HOME," been in the presence of the loving power behind the universe — glimpsing God. No one could offer me an acceptable explanation. Some of my physician friends said it was a hallucination brought on by low blood sugar, an electrolyte imbalance, or the effect of cold on the brain. Only one person — a physician who was also a devout Christian — gave me an acceptable explanation: He called it, simply, a mystical experience. Thus when I spoke of my plane-crash experience for many years I said I'd had a mystical experience while I was near death. Now I know that what I underwent that day was a Near-Death Experience, a type of Spiritually Transformative Experience.

As I came to terms with my plane-crash experience, I certainly didn't know an NDE could leave one's mind open to psychic input. Imagine my shock when, several weeks after the plane wreck, I had my first psychic experience.

My Psychic Awakening

After work one evening, I was driving to visit a friend, whom I will call Susan. As I was stopped at a red light, a vivid, bright, and almost glowing image popped into my mind's eye: a brain coated in pus. The image was so clear I was stunned.

I was certain the picture I saw represented meningitis — an infection of the surface lining of the brain. I was also sure that it was Susan's brain. Initially, bewildered by the experience, I decided not to mention it to anyone. But, when I arrived at Susan's house, I asked her how she was feeling. She told me she had been suffering from a severe, unusual headache — a classic symptom of meningitis — for several hours. I didn't want to alarm her, but, just to make sure, I asked her about other common symptoms of meningitis. Even though she didn't have any of them, the image of the horrible pus-covered brain haunted me, and I felt I had to say something. Hesitantly, I told her about the vision and what I thought it represented. She thought for a moment and then asked how she could tell if her headache did indicate early meningitis. I explained meningitis symptoms to her, and we agreed that, in the event these symptoms developed, she would go to the local emergency department and explain that a friend who was a doctor had suggested she be tested for meningitis.

Later that evening, Susan did become increasingly ill. When she went to emergency, the doctors confirmed that she had developed a rare, often fatal type of meningitis. The early diagnosis allowed the doctors to treat her successfully, and she was able to return home in two weeks.

Although I didn't realize it at the time, I now know that the image I saw in the car that day was a type of psychic experience known as a clairvoyant vision. It was a symbol that represented a physical reality that I could not possibly have known about. As amazed as I was by this experience, I was reluctant to mention it to others — especially other doctors — for many years. I was afraid that I would be disbelieved or ridiculed, even though I knew in my heart how real and powerful the vision had been.

Over the years I learned a great deal more about psychic experiences, but only in 1990 when I met Dr. Kenneth Ring, the eminent NDE researcher and author, did I learn that scientific research existed to show that many people who have NDEs have similar psychic awakenings afterward.

In addition to triggering an acceleration in my own personal spiritual transformation process, my 1979 NDE intensified my desire as a medical doctor to discover more about mystical and paranormal phenomena and how they relate to both personal transformation and long-term spiritual transformation of consciousness. As you will see in the following chapters, my personal and professional search led me to the teachings of spiritual masters of diverse traditions and the writings of great scholars and scientists. Eventually, it also led me to specialize my clinical practice in counselling people who are undergoing Spiritually Transformative Experiences, helping them understand, heal, and grow on their spiritual journeys. Looking back, I can see that my 1979 Near-Death Experience accelerated my own spiritual journey.

Since that NDE, I have been blessed with many other Spiritually Transformative Experiences, and many symptoms of long-term spiritual transformation are now part of my daily life. But I have no grandiosity about this. Through my research and clinical work, I know that STEs are happening to thousands, perhaps even millions, of people of all ages, and of all faiths, around the world today. I share the stories of many fascinating and inspiring STEs had by my patients, colleagues, and friends throughout this book.

I was blessed with two more Near-Death Experiences in the years following my NDE in the plane crash … one in 1995, and another in 2003. These two later NDEs confirmed and deepened my convictions about Near-Death Experiences and Spiritually Transformative Experiences that I share in this book. I describe my other NDEs in chapter 5, on Near-Death Experiences, and in greater detail in my other book, *Soul Lessons from the Light*.

The process of spiritual transformation of consciousness is never completely smooth. Indeed, at times it can be very challenging. But it is possible to minimize and deal effectively with challenges and difficulties and to enhance the spiritual transformation process. This is particularly true if STE experiencers understand that the transformation process they are going through is long-term, and they start to use strategies to promote a healthy spiritual transformation process — balanced in body, mind, and spirit, as described in detail in the following pages. As you will see through many inspiring STE case stories I share, we can all ultimately glimpse or even reach beautiful states of joy, peace, and expanded spiritual awareness.

2

TYPES OF SPIRITUALLY TRANSFORMATIVE EXPERIENCES

OVER THE YEARS, in the process of trying to better understand my own plane-crash Near-Death Experience, I began to gather a great deal of information on what I have come to call Spiritually Transformative Experiences: Mystical Experiences, Near-Death Experiences, Psychic Experiences, Spontaneous Inspired Creativity, and Spiritual Energy/Kundalini Episodes. I have also learned a great deal through counselling close to a thousand persons having diverse types of STEs.

In the following pages I am going to consider each of these STE categories, and using moving, true-case examples, look at how they have affected some of my patients, colleagues, friends, and even myself. I'll also take a closer look at how extremely intense or very dramatic STEs may be mistaken for — or possibly contribute to — some types of mental or emotional problems. In addition, I'll examine the strategies and techniques that have helped people integrate their STEs into their daily lives, and deal with the tremendous change and upheaval they may cause. Beyond this, I'll explore the long-term process of spiritual transformation of consciousness itself.

After years of study and research I have come to think that STEs are part of an ongoing transformation and expansion of consciousness in which we sometimes get glimpses, or become intermittently capable of perceiving, other levels of reality, including what we might consider mystical or paranormal dimensions. STEs may cause a spiritual awakening, propelling experiencers to engage much more deeply in their personal spiritual search and spiritual practices. STEs often appear to be signs that spiritual transformation of consciousness may be starting, or accelerating.

Spiritually Transformative Experiences can differ greatly in intensity. Some are relatively mild; others, which I call STE peaks or STEPs, are extremely powerful. A STEP is a discrete, time-limited STE episode that is intensely absorbing or even overwhelming, and powerfully transformative in impact. STEP seems a particularly appropriate name: when people have one of these peak spiritual experiences they often take a major step forward along their spiritual journey.

Sometimes the changes in our consciousness are gradual, allowing us time to adjust our view of reality slowly and thoughtfully. But with STEPs, changes in understanding can occur abruptly or rapidly. STEPs can cause reality as we had known it to shift before our very eyes. They can challenge our thinking on almost every subject, cause a major shift in our world views, and force us to question much of what we have based our lives on.

When this happens we need to know we are not alone. We need to know that STEs and STEPs are normal, and, while in some ways uniquely our own, are also universal. Great scholars and thinkers have, in fact, been writing about such STE experiences for centuries.

Mystical Experiences

References to mystical experience — the transcending of the self and the union with the Divine or absolute — abound in all the world's major religions. Many can be found in the Bible. In the New Testament, there is the classic story of St. Paul on the road to Damascus, where he was blinded for three days by a white light from heaven and converted to Christianity (Galatians 1:15–16). The Catholic canon is filled with stories of saints who spoke candidly of their experiences of union with the Divine. In the Old Testament, Moses's profound mystical experience is described, in which the Ten Commandments were revealed (Exodus 20). Yogic sacred texts describe mystical experiences as "samadhi" experiences. Buddhist texts speak of mystical states as enlightenment and nirvana.

Psychic Experiences

References to Psychic Experiences are more common in the great religious traditions than one might expect. In Buddhism, psychic abilities are called iddhis or wonderful gifts. Although their development is considered a natural part of the spiritual journey, seekers are taught to turn away from them so that they are not distracted from their true goal, enlightenment or union with the Absolute. Hindu yogis call these powers siddhis and view them much as the Buddhists do. In early Christianity, references to the psychic phenomena of gifts of tongues, prophecy, and healing were common, and although many modern Christians tend to think of them as evidence of miracles from earlier days, St. Paul and the Apostles spoke of them as simple realities for those who had been baptized in the Holy Spirit.

Near-Death Experiences

Numerous Christian authorities accept the reality of Near-Death Experiences — and many feel the stories told by Near-Death Experiencers give added credence to the concept of life after death. The scholar and Anglican priest Tom Harpur writes in *Life After Death*, "I now believe that the near-universal, ancient human belief in personal survival after death is the result of ... experiences of contact with another reality [i.e., Near-Death Experiences]." Harpur also points out that NDE experiencers describe scenes that are remarkably similar to the descriptions of the Bardo — the Buddhist between-life state — that are found in *The Tibetan Book of the Dead*.

Spontaneous Inspired Creativity and Genius

At first glance, Spontaneous Inspired Creativity and Genius might seem to have little to do with spiritual experiences or world religions. But, interestingly, inspired creativity has been experienced by many saints and spiritual masters. St. Francis of Assisi wrote beautiful, inspired poetry and songs. The little-educated nun St. Hildegard of Bingen spontaneously wrote poetry, composed music, and painted beautiful pictures. Lal Ded, the most beloved Hindu yogini and saint of Kashmir, wrote poetry that transformed the Kashmiri language. And the poetic writings of many Sufi saints — including Rumi and Rabiah — are considered great literary works.

Spiritual Energy/Kundalini Episodes

Spiritual energy experiences are well described in the yogic tradition, known as the awakening of kundalini, a latent, spiritual energy mechanism in the human body. When this energy is awakened people experience a sensation of energy rushing up the body, travelling upwards from the base of the spine to the brain. Associated with inner light and inner sounds, it can bring about paranormal expanded states of perception and, ultimately, mystical union. The awakening of kundalini is a phenomenon described in yoga and Hinduism, but similar spiritual energy processes are also described in other religions, in particular Taoism, Tibetan Buddhism, Christian mysticism, Judaism, Sufism, and shamanism.

Spiritual Energy Cross-Culturally

From these examples it is clear that STEs are well known in the mystical traditions of the world's major religions. Many of the esoteric teachings within these religions go even further: they allude to a spiritual energy that seems to be associated with — or perhaps underlie — many or all the types of Spiritually Transformative Experiences. Although the vocabulary differs, the common premise within all the traditions is that this spiritual energy or force, when active within an individual, is associated with new development of STEs, or rarely of more prolonged, sustained spiritual states of expanded consciousness. This spiritual energy or force is almost always symbolized by light or fire.

In the Hindu yogic tradition, the spiritual energy is called kundalini. Paramahansa Yogananda stated, "Kundalini is the subtle energy lying dormant in the muladhara chakra [coccyx chakra at the base of the spine — see chapter 9].... Kundalini is awakened and ascends the sushumna [astral spine channel] freeing the consciousness from the senses and worldly attachments, and unifying the self with the Self."

In Tibetan Buddhism, the spiritual energy is called candali or Dumo fire. Chayim Barton, in his Ph.D. dissertation thesis, directly compares kundalini to the Tibetan Buddhist concept of igniting the inner fire, the "gtum mo" (Dumo).

In Taoism, spiritual energy/kundalini is a higher spiritual aspect of chi or the Circulation of Light. Dr. Phillip Lansky and Dr. Shen Yu, two experts in Taoist Chi Kung, propose that the esoteric techniques of "Bone Marrow Chi Kung" are advanced practices aimed to create spiritual energy movement and, thereby, stimulate spiritual transformation of consciousness, equivalent to how kundalini awakening stimulates spiritual transformation of consciousness.

Dr. Bonnie Greenwell concludes in *Energies of Transformation* that the Taoist equivalent to kundalini is the "Circulation of Light." Dr. Greenwell goes on to document many other cross-cultural references to a spiritually transformative energy like kundalini — in Eskimo shamans, Hopi Indian traditions, !Kung Bushmen of Africa, Jewish Kabbala, Gnostic gospels, and in alchemy.

Kundalini is also known in the Sufi tradition, according to Irina Tweedie in *The Chasm of Fire*. She quotes her teacher, a Sufi master, as saying: "… kundalini is … As a rule the energy at the base of the spine is more or less dormant. By our system it is awakened gently … When it reaches the heart chakra: it means peace, bliss, states of expanded consciousness."

In the German Kabbalistic tradition of Judaism, the mystic seeks to transform his or her soul by uniting with the Divine light and fire known as Shekinah, the female aspect of God. Swami Kripananda cites Carlo Suares in *The Cipher of Genesis,* who stated that in certain Kabbalistic traditions the name of the serpent in the Garden of Eden is "Kundalini."

A number of Christian theologians have examined the parallels between the yogic concept of kundalini and the concept of the Holy Spirit in Christianity. Philip St. Romaine wrote in *Kundalini Energy and Christian Spirituality* that some types of experiences of the Holy Spirit are kundalini experiences.

Charles Fillmore, the American mystic whose teachings led to the founding of the Unity Church, also described spiritual energy/kundalini within Christianity. *Holy Spirit Regeneration,* a Unity School of Christianity text, states, "Prayer and meditation may awaken the fire energy (Kundalini) of the Holy Spirit. This energy is the great purifier of Spirit which begins a subtle inner process which ultimately leads to a state of union with the Christ. As the result of this awakening, you may experience physical sensations of rocking, shaking, or automatic breathing (pranayama) … There may be burning sensations as the fire of the Holy Spirit purifies the energy centers in the body," and "There may be distinct sensations in the chakras as purified energy moves through to open them to the higher energies of the Self."

It is not the purpose of this book to attempt a detailed comparison of different religious traditions' views on spiritual energy/kundalini. However, I think it is important to realize — as strange as it may seem to us at first — that the awareness of the existence of some type of spiritual energy or force in the body, and the associated STEs and spiritual transformation of consciousness, has been around for centuries and has appeared in many cultures.

Understanding Yoga and Kundalini

Although the yogic model of consciousness and the spiritual energy/kundalini are discussed in detail in chapter 9, we need to take a brief look at the subject before we go on to the case histories of people who are having STEs today. Although the term "kundalini" may sound foreign to the Western ear, I have chosen to use it for two reasons. First, it comes from the yogic tradition, and today almost everyone — regardless of their religious background or spiritual orientation — has some familiarity with and respect for yoga. Second, the descriptions of a spiritual transformative energy and its workings in the astral brain and body, and on consciousness, are more detailed and accessible in yoga than they are in other traditions.

When most people in the West think of yoga, they think of hatha yoga, the physical exercises or postures known as asanas. However, these are just one aspect of yoga. Yoga is, at its roots, a system of discipline and practices designed to stimulate kundalini and spiritual transformation of consciousness in a healthy way, so that the practitioner would ultimately experience the realization of his or her union with the Divine.

The word "yoga" means "union," and comes from the Sanskrit "yuj," which means "to yoke" or "to bind together." The *Yoga Sutras of Patanjali*, written about 300 BCE, provides an eightfold system for personal development and spiritual deepening to ultimately reach samadhi or union with the Divine, "The Eight Limbs of Yoga." The spiritual seeker was taught by a guru, or spiritual teacher, to assiduously follow the disciplines involved in each of the Eight Limbs of Yoga.

Kundalini is held to be the mechanism, a kind of biological, psychological, spiritual force, which, when activated, speeds up the spiritual transformation of the brain, astral brain, and consciousness, so that the realization of one's union with the Divine is more rapidly possible. The word "kundalini" means "coiled up" in Sanskrit and in the ancient yogic texts was symbolized by a serpent that sleeps, coiled three and a half times, at the base of the spine. By following the mental, physical, and spiritual disciplines of the Eight Limbs of Yoga, the student prepares herself in body, mind, and spirit to "awaken" the kundalini, resulting in STEs and more expanded states of consciousness.

Most yogic traditions teach that it requires many years of sincere devoted effort in self-development and regular spiritual practice, as well as the grace of the Divine, before a spiritual aspirant may experience the awakening of the spiritual energy/kundalini. The awakened spiritual energy/kundalini is said to rise up the astral spine, passing through the chakras, the energy centres that exist along the astral spine and brain. When kundalini is fully awakened it reaches the astral brain, enabling the yogi to have a mystical experience, or "samadhi." Usually, after a few moments, the spiritual energy/ kundalini descends again to a lower chakra, often the one at the base of the spine. With persistent spiritual practice and moral development, a yogi may become able to maintain the ongoing upward flow of the spiritual energy/ kundalini to the astral brain for increasing lengths of time, thereby attaining more expanded states of consciousness and deeper levels of samadhi. The advanced yogi may ultimately reach the extremely rare sahaja state, nirbikalpa samadhi, ongoing mystical communion, or "nirvana."

STEs and the Yogic Model of Consciousness

It is easy to place each of the five types of Spiritually Transformative Experiences within this framework. The terms "mystical experience" and "samadhi" are often used interchangeably in the yogic literature to describe various glimpses of the Divine or Absolute. A great saint or mystic with a fully awakened kundalini can manifest all of the types of STEs.

Psychic experiences have their place in the framework, as well. One of the four books of Patanjali's *Yoga Sutras* is devoted to the subject of siddhis or psychic abilities. The development of these abilities is considered a normal part of the spiritual transformation process. Many of the phenomena associated with Near-Death Experiences are also recognized in the yogic tradition and thought by some modern yogis to be associated with some degree of transient awakening of kundalini.

Development of inspired creativity is also mentioned in the ancient yogic texts and is believed to be a gift granted to some who have awakened kundalini to some degree. For example, in *Panchastavi*, a book from circa 800 CE, part of the Shakti doctrines of India, we find these words in praise of kundalini: "Thou art also the origin of all speech and (hence) art ... the sphere of Thy surpassing beauty ... becomes the means of granting ... the talents of a poet [to Thy devotees]."

Given the fact that the five types of Spiritually Transformative Experiences discussed so far are recognized within the framework of yoga and kundalini, it is not surprising that many people who are having diverse types of STEs are also reporting the symptoms of kundalini awakening. However, not everyone who has an STE experiences spiritual energy/kundalini activation. Some yogic traditions also describe STEs happening to individuals due to a "chakra activation" or limited brain centre activation without any kundalini awakening. Other persons have described mystical experiences that clearly felt as a descent of the Divine from above, or a gift of grace from the Divine Higher Power. For this reason, I have added Spiritual Energy/Kundalini Episodes as a separate category of STE. Throughout the book I use the term "spiritual energy/kundalini" in a general way to refer to the spiritually transformative energy that is given many different names in many different spiritual traditions, but when I discuss Spiritual Energy/Kundalini Episodes I am referring to a Spiritually Transformative Experience in which an individual experiences all — or several — of the traditional signs of kundalini awakening as they are discussed in yoga.

From this description, it is easy to see that there are certain overlaps between Spiritual Energy/Kundalini Episodes and the other STEs. If kundalini is indeed the spiritual energy mechanism to accelerate spiritual transformation of consciousness, we would expect to find that STE experiencers with signs of kundalini activity tend to have more than one type of STE, and recurrent or ongoing STEs. The research I was involved in shows that this is indeed the case.

Multiple STE Experiencers — STEs Recur and Vary

It is important to realize that a wide range exists in the intensity — and profundity — of STEs. There is, for example, a tremendous difference between a fleeting psychic sensing, and a STEP in which the experiencer loses all sense of ego self, and remains in communion for days, weeks, months, or years. My clinical experience also indicates that few people have just one STE in their lifetime. Many people become "Multiple STE Experiencers." Most people having one psychic experience go on to have recurrent psychic experiences, just as those with inspired creativity go on to have recurrent inspirations.

However, when an individual has a spiritual energy/kundalini awakening, or a mystical experience or mystical NDE, which is generally accompanied by a kundalini awakening, this often heralds the beginning of a long-term process of spiritual transformation of consciousness, punctuated with many, and different types of, STEs. Once the process of spiritual transformation has begun, it may go on for the rest of the experiencer's life. And, although I believe every human being is on a spiritual journey, it may be that those who are having STEs and long-term transformation are on an accelerated journey. Those who have many STEs on their spiritual path may or may not reach their ultimate spiritual goals faster than anyone else. The ancient yogis warned us that many potential pitfalls exist along the spiritual path.

Now that we've considered the major types of Spiritually Transformative Experiences, we'll look at each type of STE in detail, and hear fascinating and inspiring stories of some people who are going through these experiences.

3

MYSTICAL EXPERIENCES

AFTER MY DRAMATIC MYSTICAL Near-Death Experience in the 1979 plane crash, I began to search for more information on the subject. I wanted to know how mystical experiences were viewed by theologians from different religions, and — because of my medical training — especially by the scientific and scholarly communities.

I wasn't disappointed in my search through the world's religions. Even though in my own church I had never heard mystical experience spoken of as something that could happen to the average person, I found many descriptions of the phenomenon itself in both the Old and New Testaments of the Bible and in the lives of the Catholic saints. In the Eastern religions I examined, I found that mystical states of consciousness were outlined in detail. In Hinduism, texts such as the *Yoga Sutras* and Upanishads describe mystical states of consciousness and ultimately liberation, in which the individual soul realizes union with Brahman or the Absolute. I found similar references to mystical experience and ultimate liberation, or nirvana, in the Buddhist teachings and works such as *The Tibetan Book of the Dead*.

My search for scientists and scholars who wrote about these experiences led me to the noted philosopher and psychologist Dr. William James. In his classic work *The Varieties of Religious Experience*, I found stories of many average people who had experienced — just as I had — a sense of union and communion with the Divine. Reading James also helped clarify my own understanding of the experience itself. He identified four main characteristics of what he called "mystical states":

1. *Ineffability.* Mystical experiences "defy expression"; it is essentially impossible for the experiencer to convey their importance, grandeur, or profundity to another; they have to be experienced to be fully comprehended.

2. *Noetic quality.* Although mystical experiences are similar to states of feeling, they are also states of knowing. The experience contains "revelations," "illuminations," and "insights into depths of truth."

3. *Transiency.* Except in rare cases, mystical experiences cannot be sustained for long. Even though their quality can usually only be "imperfectly reproduced in memory," they may bring about a continual development in "inner richness" in the experiencer from one recurrence to another.

4. *Passivity.* Although the occurrence of mystical states may be facilitated by certain practices, once the state has begun "the mystic feels as if his own will were in abeyance" or "as if he were grasped and held by a superior power." After such experiences, a profound sense of their importance remains and they "modify the inner life of the subject" between recurrences.

My search also led to the works of a number of other medical doctors and psychiatrists. One was the Swiss psychiatrist Dr. Carl Jung, who called the mystical experience an experience of the "numinous" and saw it as a powerful, positive force in the process of individuation, or the ultimate realization of self. I was fascinated to discover that he had experienced a wide range of paranormal phenomena during his lifetime, including mystical visions and a Near-Death Experience. He had also researched and lectured on kundalini.

Psychologist Dr. Abraham Maslow also wrote about mystical experiences. He called them "peak experiences" and placed them at the very top of a hierarchy of human growth and development leading to a state of health and wholeness he called "self-actualization."

An even earlier account of mystical experience was written by Dr. Richard Maurice Bucke, a Canadian psychiatrist. After having a profound mystical experience himself, Dr. Bucke began studying the lives of many religious leaders, saints, and creative geniuses. In 1902 his book *Cosmic Consciousness* developed his well-supported theory that human consciousness was evolving and that, as it did, humans were developing an increasing ability to perceive a new, vastly expanded state of consciousness. Bucke believed the human race was moving slowly, but inexorably, toward the time when everyone alive would attain what he called cosmic consciousness. Within this framework, individuals who had profound mystical experiences represented — in vastly varying degrees — harbingers of this future state. Bucke made it clear that there was a tremendous difference between someone like himself who had what he called a fleeting "taste of Brahmic splendor" and someone like Buddha who existed in a perennial state of cosmic bliss.

As I found more and more evidence that leading thinkers in theology, psychology, and psychiatry accepted the reality of mystical experience, I became less reticent to speak with my colleagues about my personal experiences. After almost twelve years of my personal research, and after a strong "calling" mystical experience in 1990 (which I will share later in this chapter), I began to speak openly to my professional colleagues and to the public about my personal Near-Death Experience and my research. As a result, I was asked to speak about my NDE at many professional meetings and public conferences, and to the media — newspapers, magazines, radio, television, and on the internet. Many patients were referred to me who had had mystical or other paranormal experiences, and many other STE experiencers sought me out.

Over more than twenty years in my medical practice, I worked professionally, counselling close to a thousand persons who had had a wide range of Spiritually Transformative Experiences. Of these, most felt they had had some type of mystical experience at some point in their lives. This is not as surprising as it might seem. A 1989 Gallup poll found that one of every three Americans believed he or she had had some type of mystical experience. I believe, in fact, that every person in whom the spiritual energy/kundalini is active and who is involved in a process of spiritual transformation of consciousness will eventually begin to have mystical experiences. These experiences may occur spontaneously or may be stimulated by certain activities such as intense heartfelt prayer, intense meditation, focused contemplation on a deity or a spiritual concept, deep soul-searching, or intense yogic practices.

The people who have discussed their mystical experiences with me come from a variety of educational backgrounds, cultures, and religious traditions. In some cases, the experience takes a form that is related to the person's own cultural and religious background. In others, it seems to cut across cultures and arise out of a tradition that is foreign to the experiencer. When this happens, the experience often causes a change or broadening in religious convictions or spiritual beliefs. During my own mystical Near-Death Experience, for example, I perceived God to be an omnipresent, omnipotent, universal force of love, light, and intelligence. I found this broadened my previous concept of God considerably.

Types of Mystical Experiences

Though mystical experiences take many different forms, in my clinical work and research I have found that they generally fall into seven main categories. Even though any one mystical experience might contain elements from several different categories, one of the categories usually seems to stand out and be useful for identifying the experience or giving it a name, a vocabulary — a simple process that often helps people integrate STEs into their daily lives.

1. *Unitive experiences.* A feeling of union with God, the Divine, the universal consciousness, or with the universal life force; an experience of merging into the oneness of all things; a feeling that one's self is united with the entire universe, or connected with all creation.
2. *Ecstatic or Bliss episodes.* Experiences of profound bliss, joy, ecstasy, all-encompassing love, awestruck wonder at the profundity of the universe, or overwhelming feelings of devotion to the Divine, all of which may be accompanied by spontaneous tears of joy.
3. *Mystical visions.* Visions of deities, saints, gurus, spiritual archetypes, or important figures from the world's religions, such as the Buddha, Jesus Christ, Krishna, Mohammed, Moses, and/or the Virgin Mary; usually accompanied by a

powerful feeling of unconditional love, compassion, healing, and/or guidance.

4. *Expansive episodes.* A sense of dramatically expanded consciousness in which the individual point of perception seems to expand from its normal to a much greater size; the sense of expansion may stop at a few feet beyond the head or move outward until it seems to encompass the entire earth or even the whole cosmos.

5. *Spiritual rebirth/Religious conversion/Purification.* A sudden, profound spiritual awakening; a spontaneous religious conversion; a dramatic reorientation of spiritual beliefs; a sense of being purified or chastened followed by a profound spiritual upliftment or heart-opening; a sense of "dying," hitting bottom, facing past errors, or having a shamanistic type of encounter with the dark side — followed by a profound experience of spiritual rebirth, illumination, ecstasy, or union with the Divine.

6. *Revelation/Illumination.* A sudden, profound insight into the nature of the universe or absolute truth; a spontaneous intellectual revelation that is beyond the bounds of normal, analytical reason and that brings with it new spiritual insight or new knowledge for humankind; a spontaneous revelation regarding one's life purpose, or life's meaning.

7. *Dissolution experiences.* An experience of the complete dissolution, dissolving of the small ego self into the Cosmic All, the Absolute, the Infinite, the stillness. Deep dissolution is indescribable.

All of the above types of mystical experience may be accompanied by strong perceptions of light or luminosity. Very often mystical experiences include perceptions of a soft bright "White Light," and/or white luminous "beings of light." Other mystical experiences may include an inner visual perception of a deep dusky-blue colour, like immersion in a deep, expansive, blue ocean of peace/love.

A Unitive Experience

The following story was told to me by a patient whom I will call Courtney. Born and raised in Montreal, Canada, with a weekend family home in the mountains north of the city, Courtney had her first STE, a unitive mystical experience, when she was a teenager.

Ever since I was a child, I loved to wander through the fields behind my country home. I loved the smells of the earth, the plants, and the trees. I loved the beautiful play of colours in nature, how they changed through the four seasons, and I loved to watch the colours of the sky at sunset, how they highlighted the mountains in different hues. Somehow, even as a child, I felt close to God up there, like I was watching his paintbrush at work.

One autumn day, when I was twelve or thirteen, I went for a long, leaf-viewing walk along a local country road. At one point I came to an opening between the hills and suddenly an amazing vista of brilliant orange, scarlet, and golden leaves garlanding the rolling hills blazed into my full view. The sky contrasted a dazzling, deep-blue hue. The view was breathtaking. I gasped, and in my heart spontaneously cried out an inner prayer: "Oh! Thank you, God!"

With this prayer, I suddenly noticed a change begin in me. The colours started to become brighter and more luminous. Overcome with the beauty, tears of awe rolled down my cheeks. Then, I began to feel as if I was expanding until, suddenly, I felt as if I'd merged with and filled the whole scene. I was one with the trees, one with the hills, and one with the sky. I felt totally connected with it all and with the love behind the Universe. I have no idea how long I stood there, riveted to the spot, merged into the beauty of God's creation.

After some time my awareness returned to my body, standing on the road, my face covered in tears. Although that feeling of union had gone, I still felt a strong direct connection to the loving Higher Power. Inspired by this experience, I went home and began to draw vigorously. I tried to somehow capture on paper the blazing colours, the luminosity — the God in nature that I had felt.

Being raised an Anglican, I had, before this experience, thought that God was a power to be feared, a power who sat in judgment, ready to punish me for my shortcomings. But after this experience, I knew this to be incorrect. I just knew, somehow, to the core of my being that God was a loving God, and that I and all people were loved by him at all times.

This experience had a profound, transformative effect on Courtney. Her spiritual convictions dramatically shifted and deepened afterward. Although she found, unfortunately, that she could not talk openly about this unitive mystical experience either in her church or in her family, she remained convinced of its reality and sacredness. She continued to go to her local church, and although she disagreed with some of the pastor's interpretations of the Scriptures, she enjoyed the time for prayer and spiritual contemplation. In her adult life she became very active in community service and charity activities in the church parish. Over the years, Courtney has gone on to have other STEs, most notably in her thirties when she began to have symptoms of spiritual energy/kundalini awakening. But she looks back on this first experience as the one that set her on her spiritual path.

A Spiritual Rebirth

The following is an example of spiritual rebirth. The experience occurred to Dr. G. Graham-Cumming, a highly respected, successful Canadian medical doctor who had been ordained as a minister earlier in his career and later came to reject all religious teachings. The experience changed the course of his life. He worked under difficult and sometimes dangerous conditions in a number of countries. In a letter he wrote to me in 1991, he shared this story:

At age thirty I had become rather a bitter debunker of all "Faiths" and, having been theologically trained and ordained, rather a potent one. Going home one evening in May 1937, I came to a crossroads I crossed every day, habitually veering to the right although it did not really matter which way I went. Both roads took me home if by very different routes. Just as I was striding off as usual that evening, however, I was jolted to a halt as if by a physical barrier and "heard" ringing in my head like a bell, "You must choose NOW!" What I had to decide was whether I would live believing life to be purposive and significant or merely the aimless accident of evolution I professed to believe it. It dawned on me it would make a considerable difference in how I would live, but it was not a matter I cared to debate, let alone decide, just there and then. Trying to dismiss the challenge, I attempted to proceed but found myself unable to move — paralyzed by indecision, I suppose. I've no idea how long I stood there twisting and turning in my head. Eventually I elected to consider life to be purposive, if to what purpose I had no idea. I was startled to find myself exclaiming, "I will believe. Help my unbelief!" At once the paralysis holding me relaxed and I went home in some mental turmoil.

It was a bright moonlit night. I went out into the moonlight to wrestle with my mental tumult. Suddenly the moonlight seemed to start swirling round me, swathing me in opalescent veils that began to obscure vision and restrict movement. Just as I was beginning to get a bit scared, it seemed to me that someone out there was tearing away those smothering veils and I felt a great relief — but, as the last was stripped from me, I found myself in the Presence of an unseen but overwhelming Power, irresistible, undeceivable and inescapable. That was when I discovered sheer terror! My only wish was not to be, but that was denied. I was and had to face the essentiality of existing. Grovelling on my knees, I cried out, "Go away! Go away! I am evil!" But that "Voice" like a bell rang, "Rise. I will enable you." I did, shakily, hardly able to believe I was being accepted, even commissioned for service. It was shown to me that those "veils of light" blinding and binding me symbolized my misconceptions and imperfect scientific and religious "knowledge," all of which had to be set aside, not denied but set aside pending further enlightenment. Seeking enlightenment is what I've been doing ever since …

The transformative impact this experience had on Dr. Graham-Cumming is clear. His working life became dedicated to humanitarian efforts. After retirement he remained involved in social causes. His spiritual focus was stronger than ever, and he wrote beautiful transcendental poetry that he received through inspiration.

Mystical Visions

Mystical visions are another type of mystical experience that I came across fairly frequently in my patients. The next story is a more "visual" type of mystical vision. It was told to me by a man I'll call Jack. At the time of the experience, Jack was in university working on his Ph.D. He was actively involved in his church, where he sang in the choir.

We had just finished choir practice in the church basement. We had been practising the "Hallelujah Chorus," and I felt uplifted and serene. I went up to the chapel to pray before I set off for home. I felt overwhelmed by Jesus's love for humanity and by God's love for us all. Strains of the "Hallelujah Chorus" still rang through my head.

Suddenly, in the middle of a heartfelt prayer, I felt the strong urge to look up at the chapel altar. I opened my eyes and saw, to my amazement, Jesus Christ glowing with dazzling light standing by the altar. I knew it was Him.

> The look of love in His eyes penetrated my soul. I heard
> Him say, "Come to me!" I burst into tears of joy, and the
> vision of the Christ was gone.

The vision had a great effect on Jack's life. His faith in God grew stronger and he became certain, in a way he had never been before, that God and Jesus are there for each and every person who calls upon them for help.

Jack's experience provides a good example of how mystical visions often occur. However, the way Jack reacted after the experience is also significant: He was afraid to tell anyone — even the people in his own church who shared his deep faith and religious convictions — what he had seen. In spite of his own unshakable certainty that the experience had really happened, he was afraid people wouldn't believe him or, worse, that they would think he was insane. Even when he finally shared the experience with me a few years after it had happened, he did so only in strictest confidence.

Such fears are extremely common with people who have STEs. Many mystical and other paranormal experiences are kept secret. Although some people choose not to share their experiences for personal reasons, many others keep silent out of fear of ridicule. One of my hopes in sharing these stories is that they will help other STE experiencers realize that they are not alone. As I explain in detail in chapter 17, "Strategies for Living with Spiritual Transformation," they can find appropriate, supportive people who are willing to listen.

Mystical visions, like all types of mystical experiences, can take many forms. Although a vision, by definition, is in some sense a visual experience, it may also involve other kinds of "perception" of the presence of a religious or spiritual figure including scent, sound, touch, taste, or emotion.

Visions can also cross religious and cultural boundaries. Although Jack, who was a Christian, saw a vision that was very much part of his tradition, this is not always the case. A Christian can have a mystical vision of Buddha, or a Hindu can have one of St. Francis. A story that illustrates this was told to me by an extremely successful businesswoman whom I'll call Jeneane. Her experience also illustrates, as was mentioned earlier, how the categories we are using to define mystical experience — and the categories of other STEs — are somewhat arbitrary and often overlap. This experience, for example, contains elements of a "perception" of a spiritual figure as well as elements of a type of unitive experience that represents, if not a union with the divine principle of the universe, a deep feeling of oneness with a holy or spiritual presence.

> My experience occurred after I had been involved in yoga and meditation for a few years. I had been raised as a Roman Catholic and my faith was extremely important to me. In fact, I had become rather well known for my views on the importance the teachings of Catholicism held for those who had been raised in the tradition, and I did a great deal of public speaking on the subject.
>
> When I was in my midforties, the man I was very much in love with and had planned to marry suddenly left me for another woman. In an attempt to cope with my pain and disillusionment, I threw myself more deeply than ever into my career and began to work extremely long hours.
>
> One Sunday, as I came home after spending most of the day at the office, I paused on the doorstep. As I put the key in the door, a slight shift seemed to occur in my consciousness. An inner voice seemed to be telling me that I had to quit punishing myself and begin to nurture myself more. With this in mind, I walked up the stairs, poured myself a hot bath, and filled it with scented oil. As I settled into the soothing water, I began to slip into a deep meditative state.
>
> Quite suddenly, I perceived an image of an East Asian woman. Although I didn't recognize her, I was certain that the woman was a holy person or saint of an Eastern religion. The woman radiated profound love and compassion.
>
> As the experience continued, I felt my consciousness meld with that of the saint's. I felt enveloped in the woman's love and compassion and even one with the woman herself. As this occurred, I was overwhelmed with emotion

and felt my frustration, disappointment, and anger with my former fiancé begin to evaporate and fade away.

I remained in this deep state of union with the saint for about twenty minutes. When I arose from the bath, still in a meditative state, I even had a physical sensation of my own limbs moving with the supple grace and graciousness the saint had moved with.

The immediate effects of the experience stayed with me for twenty-four hours and, even when it began to fade, I felt a profound closeness to the saint and had a feeling that the woman was watching over me and protecting me. I felt a great sense of peace and realized that I was never alone.

The experience also had a tremendous spiritual and emotional healing effect. I was able to forgive my fiancé and wish him well. I was even able to reach out and emotionally embrace the woman he had left me for. I had received such a gift of grace, love, and compassion that I felt it flowing out of me and back to the world.

Sometime later, Jeneane happened on an exact likeness of the holy woman from her experience and learned that the woman was a Buddhist enlightened being — or Bodhisattva — named Quan Yin. Jeneane discovered that, according to tradition, Quan Yin is said to have been "born of the tears of the Buddha" and is known as the goddess of compassion.

Saved by a Mystical Vision

Although mystical visions often occur during times of meditation and contemplation, they — like other types of paranormal experiences — can also occur after a heartfelt plea for guidance or help. The following events happened to a young woman whom I'll call Julie, who had been raised as a Roman Catholic. At the time, she was about twenty years old and in university studying social work. Her story is an unusual and an extremely disturbing tale, but the vision that she saw had such a direct effect on her very survival that I have decided to include it.

One evening I attended a friend's graduation and, to celebrate, went with a group of friends to a local pub after the ceremony. One of the group was a young man I had been acquainted with for a few years. After we had a couple of drinks, "Alex" offered to drive me home. Since I'd known him for a while I couldn't see any harm in the suggestion and accepted. But instead of driving me home, he parked the car behind a dark, deserted factory. When I explained I wasn't interested in "parking" and wanted to go home, he became angry. Before I could get away, he grabbed me and began to accost me, ripping my dress and forcing himself on me.

As I struggled against him and shouted "No!" he became completely crazed, violently raped me, and brutalized me, even ripping hair from my body. Then, as I continued to fight, he began to scream that I was a bitch and that he was going to kill me. He reached under the seat with one hand and began to search for something, yelling about a knife. As he did, I managed to slip from his grasp and run from the car.

Bleeding and wounded, I began to run through the wooded area behind the factory. I was gripped with terror, certain that Alex really would kill me if he caught me, and I tried to run as fast as I could. But the area was pitch black, and I was extremely weak. I crashed through the woods, stumbling over rocks and branches and into trees. I could hear Alex behind me, gaining on me, and I knew I had no hope of outrunning him.

In utter desperation, I threw myself on the ground and began to pray to the Virgin Mary for help. Suddenly, a woman bathed in a radiant light appeared before me and said, "Take my hand, I will help you." The light emanating from the woman seemed to illuminate the dark forest floor. The woman led me along, pointing out the way to go, and motioning when I should duck down or be completely silent. As the radiant woman led me out of the woods, Alex thrashed through the trees looking for me in vain. Once out of the woods, the woman continued to lead me through backyards and laneways, until I suddenly realized I was very near a friend's house. The woman then disappeared, and I ran to my friend who took me in and helped me get the medical treatment I desperately needed.

Totally traumatized, Julie was unable to report the rape for some time. And, tragically, because the event occurred long before "date rape" was recognized as the horrendous crime it is, Alex was not charged when she finally did report it.

Over time, Julie recovered with the help of supportive friends and family. But even though these people knew the story of the rape, she shared the story of the vision with no one. She believed in her heart that the Virgin Mary had appeared to her and saved her life, but she also believed that people would think she was crazy if she told them. Still she longed to tell someone and be reassured that the experience was not a symptom of mental illness.

Then one day Julie, who had been a patient of mine for some time, read an article in the *Toronto Star* about my Near-Death Experience. She began to hope that, because I had had a paranormal experience, I might be able to understand what had happened to her. Soon after this, while she was in my office for a routine physical, she suddenly blurted out her story. When she was finished, I explained that I knew many people who had had mystical visions and that I believed, as she did, that hers had appeared in answer to her prayers. She was immensely relieved to be able to tell someone about the vision and be reassured that she was not "crazy." Overwhelmed with emotion, she sobbed for some time.

A few years later, Alex was arrested and convicted of the rape and murder of an elderly woman whose home he had burglarized. It seems Julie's vision really did save her life.

A Revelation Experience — My "Calling" Experience

A revelation/illumination type of mystical experience may suddenly and spontaneously reveal to the STE experiencer new knowledge, or a new and deeper spiritual purpose and meaning for their life. This happened to me in 1990, in what I refer to as my "calling" mystical experience. Prior to 1990, I had been "in the closet" about my mystical 1979 Near-Death Experience and my 1976 kundalini awakening, and rarely spoke of them to anyone. I felt inwardly propelled to privately research mystical states of consciousness and the yogic model of consciousness and kundalini, but I felt very reluctant to share my personal experiences publicly or with my professional colleagues. From 1979 to 1990 I only spoke privately about my STE experiences to a handful of individuals and small groups. This changed dramatically after my "calling" mystical experience in 1990, which led me to "come out of the closet," to share what I had learned about STEs, and ultimately to write my books on STEs. Here is the story of my "calling," revelation-type mystical experience.

I was walking on the sand dunes in Monterey, California, the day that this occurred. I was contemplating what I had experienced over the course of the last three days. I had been attending the Spiritual Emergence Network's annual conference, which was focusing on kundalini awakening that year. I had agreed to the request to be one of the facilitators for an impromptu meeting of conference participants who thought they were experiencing kundalini. I, and the other volunteer facilitators, did not know how many, or even if any, conference participants would come to this informal gathering.

To my amazement and deep surprise, close to a hundred persons arrived. The large group divided into smaller groups so that participants could share their stories within a group with their facilitator.

I started by telling my randomly assigned group of twenty or so that I was a medical doctor, and that I had personally experienced a kundalini awakening and also a Near-Death Experience. My personal sharing had the effect of a floodgate opening. One after another the participants in my group shared their moving personal stories of the intense challenges they had endured after their kundalini awakenings. Many told of their tragic experiences of being falsely labelled as mentally ill by doctors and psychologists. Others shared equally tragic experiences of being labelled by clergy as delusional, imagining it, or self-inflated. Many persons present openly wept tears of relief, and expressed deep heartfelt gratitude to me, that I, as a practising medical doctor, had disclosed my own kundalini and NDE experiences. Many exclaimed that this was the first time, after perhaps five, ten, or even twenty years of being ridiculed or pathologized for their STEs, that they could share the story of their STEs with a medical doctor who believed them, who validated their lived experience, and did not automatically label them as crazy.

I was deeply moved by this sharing event and the outpouring of gratitude toward me as a medical doctor.

I went for a walk afterward at the nearby sand-dunes park, to contemplate this moving event. Suddenly, I felt as if the heavens opened and a brilliant white light descended upon me from above. I felt like I no longer had a top to my head, that my head had opened up like a flower bud opens when it blossoms, and that the open top of my head had become a brilliant beacon of light — brightly radiating white light in all directions. I felt as if the Light of the Higher Power had cracked me open in body, mind, and spirit, and I was now completely exposed to the Divine above. I felt an indescribable, exquisitely beautiful, divine nectar drip in my throat.

While basking in the purity, expansion, and wonder of this Light and Divine ambrosia, I somehow instantly knew something that I had not known before. I knew what I must now do with my life. Without any words having been heard or spoken, I instantly and spontaneously knew, as if it had been revealed by the Light somehow, that I must publicly talk to doctors, patients, anyone who would listen, to declare that mystical experiences and spiritual energy/kundalini awakenings were real, and to proclaim that these mystical experiences were NOT mental illnesses. I knew this to be sacred knowledge, and a TRUTH, a Truth that I had glimpsed within my own being by Divine grace, for whatever unknown reason in God's Divine plan. I knew that Spirit/the Higher Power was now calling me to action. It was time for me to openly speak my Truth, to share what I had learned.

The Light and expansion slowly faded after several more minutes. I then returned to my normal state of awareness. I was trembling inside. I felt in my soul that the knowledge about kundalini and other STEs that the Divine had given me was a precious and sacred gift. I realized that the Divine had now given me a responsibility with this gift — a clear calling for my life. It was my moral and sacred obligation to share what I had learned and experienced.

From that day forward, I began to speak openly and publicly about my 1979 Near-Death Experience and my research into all types of STEs. I felt "called" to urgently spread awareness that STEs were real "peak" experiences, and not a sign of mental illness, as was all too frequently mistakenly thought. After my "calling" experience, it felt to me that by synchronicity life started opening many doors, by giving me opportunities to speak at conferences, on television, on radio, and to newspapers and magazines. I intuitively knew that my spiritual work was to heed my "calling," and to have the courage and clarity to walk through the opening doors, to speak my truth publicly, even before somewhat skeptical audiences.

Many STE experiencers have told me over the last thirty-plus years that it was tremendously helpful and reassuring to them to hear me, a then practising medical doctor, publicly admit to having had a Near-Death Experience and other STEs. Now that I have retired from medical practice, I feel much more comfortable sharing more of my personal STE stories. Therefore here in *Touched by the Light,* I am sharing the stories of some of my other STEs, such as my 1990 "calling" mystical experience, my 1995 NDE, and my 2003 NDE. I kept these latter STEs private until now, as they felt sacred to me. But now, as I'm getting older, I feel it important that in addition to sharing many of my patients' STE stories, I share my own story of multiple STEs over the course of my life.

As I said in chapter 1, I am not trying to inflate myself by sharing my STE stories, but rather I humbly hope that other STE experiencers, including other multiple STE experiencers, will feel empowered and normalized by knowing that a medical doctor like myself could have a long successful medical career and a happy, grounded personal life, and at the same time be undergoing long-term spiritual transformation of consciousness that included several STEs and STEPs.

Every person I have met who has had a mystical experience that might be classified as a STEP has been deeply moved by it. All of them have developed strong, personal convictions about the reality of a Divine universal intelligence. Their experiences have been uplifting, and the memory of the moment has remained a continual source of inspiration over the years. In a sense, mystical experiences are the "highest" type of STE or STEP. They are so alluring that many people yearn to have them again and again, and spend the rest of their lives trying to regain the moments of transcendence. I believe this yearning is an irresistible force that is drawing us, as a race, toward a higher state of consciousness.

4

SPIRITUAL ENERGY/
KUNDALINI EPISODES

THE SIGNS OF SPIRITUAL ENERGY/KUNDALINI awakening
have been described in sources that range from the ancient texts on yoga, to
books by modern yogic gurus and teachers, to the works of contemporary
philosophers, psychologists, and psychiatrists. As described in chapter 2,
the mystical traditions of the world's major religions allude to a spiritual
energy or force that can produce bodily symptoms, and activate STEs and
long-term spiritual transformation of consciousness. My first awareness
of both spiritual energy/kundalini and the awakening of kundalini came
through meeting Gopi Krishna in India in 1977, and later meetings, correspondence, and reading all his works. Pandit Gopi Krishna was an Indian
yogi, philosopher, and scholar.* He ultimately became a mentor to me, urging me to do kundalini research. When he died in 1984, Gopi Krishna left
a large body of published material on the subject of kundalini that included
eighteen books and scores of essays and articles.

Gopi Krishna was born in a small Kashmiri village in 1903. He began to practise meditation when he was seventeen years old, rising every
morning before dawn and meditating for three hours. He followed this
routine devotedly until one December morning, at age thirty-four, he had a
profound mystical experience with strong spiritual energy sensations in his
body. Although this initial experience was temporary, for the next twelve
years he alternated between states of expanded consciousness and periods

---

*   Pandit is an honorary Indian title given to some wise and particularly respected
    individuals.

of tormenting physical pain and fluctuating mental states that included anxiety and depression.

Struggling to discover what was happening to him, Gopi Krishna began to study the ancient yogic texts. Eventually, he came to the conclusion that he had awakened kundalini — but that the process had not occurred exactly as it should have. Further study of the ancient texts and modern translations such as Arthur Avalon's classic work *The Serpent Power* helped him discover how to correct what had gone wrong with his awakening and how to moderate the influences of this overwhelming energy. By the time he was forty-six, the fluctuating psychological states and distressing physical sensations had receded and he entered a perennial state of expanded consciousness.

Although he had previously had no writing ability, he was suddenly able to write exquisitely beautiful poetry. This poetry came to him through a process of inspiration, both in languages he knew and ones he had never heard or seen before. A rational, practical man, he was amazed by his new ability and began to search even more thoroughly through the yogic mystical literature to discover more about the transformative process he was experiencing. After many years of study — and objectively observing his own transformative process — he concluded that the kundalini mechanism was the driving force behind the evolution of the human race to a higher level of consciousness, and that its awakening created a potential for an accelerated transformation of the body and brain that could lead to and enable states of what he called "higher consciousness."

After becoming respected around the world as one of the foremost authorities on the subject, he did much to convince the West that kundalini is a very real biological-psychological-spiritual mechanism. Although he was often urged by would-be disciples to become a guru, he refused. He knew that he was not a guru. Instead, he spent the rest of his life researching and writing about kundalini and the evolution of consciousness. He tried to convince the Eastern and Western scientific and medical communities of the importance of serious scientific research on spiritual energy/kundalini as the biological basis for the evolution of the race to higher levels of consciousness and the expanded paranormal states that would accompany it.

A number of contemporary Western scholars have also written about kundalini awakening. One of the most widely respected is Swiss psychiatrist Dr. Carl Jung, whose seminars on kundalini are compiled in *The Psychology of Kundalini Yoga*. Jung's research on kundalini is considered a milestone in the bridging of Western psychology of individuation with the Eastern model of kundalini-driven development of higher consciousness. A second respected kundalini scholar is Mircea Eliade, former chair of the Department of History of Religions at the University of Chicago. In his classic work *Yoga: Immortality and Freedom*, Eliade attempted to bring to the West some understanding of the relationship between yoga, the awakening of kundalini, and mystical states of consciousness.

Psychiatrists writing on the subject include Dr. Lee Sannella and Dr. Stanislav Grof. Dr. Sannella has become widely known for his books, in which he documents a number of cases of individuals in the United States who were experiencing kundalini awakening. Eventually, he opened a clinic in California that specializes in the assessment, support, and treatment of people undergoing this process. Dr. Sannella supported Gopi Krishna's idea that there was a biological basis for kundalini-type symptoms and worked with the late Dr. Itzhak Bentov studying the changes in the electromagnetic fields of long-time meditators and persons undergoing kundalini awakening.

Dr. Stanislav Grof and his wife Christina Grof — a writer and former yoga teacher who has undergone her own kundalini awakening — have written a number of books on what they call "Spiritual Emergence Syndrome" and the part they believe kundalini awakening plays in the process of spiritual growth and transformation.

One excellent study of kundalini was written in 1990 by Dr. Bonnie Greenwell, a California psychologist. In *The Energies of Transformation* she reviews the works of many important yogis, examines the ideas of various schools of yoga, and details her experience as a counsellor working with people who are having kundalini experiences.

The yogi and guru Paramahansa Yogananda (1893–1952) wrote in his classic book *Autobiography of a Yogi* what I consider to be the best comprehensive description of the yogic model of consciousness, including references to the role of spiritual energy/kundalini, which he called "lifeforce" in the spine. Yogananda described spiritual energy/kundalini in even greater detail in his book *God Talks with Arjuna: The Bhagavad Gita — The Royal Science of God-Realization*.

Signs of a Spiritual Energy/Kundalini Episode

Based on the ancient Tantric yoga texts and on his own experiences, Gopi Krishna outlined the main characteristics of a classical kundalini episode as:

1. *Energy rushes.* Sensations of energy, heat, and/or light that rise up the spine or rush up through the body toward the head. The energy may feel like something rushing, flowing, trickling, exploding, jumping, vibrating, burning, piercing, or like an electrical current, and may cause physical movement or pulsation of the body. And one or more of:

2. *Light.* The perception of inner light, liquid light flowing in the body, inner luminosity, outer luminosity, or the sensation of being engulfed in a brilliant white light; and/or

3. *Inner sounds.* The perception of inner sounds often likened to the rushing of wind, the distant roar of a waterfall, the rushing of wings, rumbling of a motor, or humming, the ringing of bells, the buzzing of bees, the chirping of crickets, or "music of the spheres"; and/or

4. *Sexual-like sensations.* Sometimes sensations of upward-moving energy activity in the genital area are felt, or unusual sexual arousal or a penile erection that is not associated with normal sexual stimulation; rarely, spontaneous orgasms that seem to be directed inward and upward rather than outward; and/or

5. *Experiences of paranormal consciousness.* The above physical sensations are associated, ultimately, with an expansion of consciousness, mystical experience, revelation, psychic experience, or spontaneous experience of inspired creativity.

In my work I have come across a great many people whose most dramatic and prominent STE has been what I refer to as a Spiritual Energy/Kundalini Episode — a distinct, time-limited experience of two or more of the above signs. For many, the process begins quite suddenly, and the experience almost always represents a STEP. In these sudden, dramatic awakenings the signs experienced are pronounced. I think — as Gopi Krishna did — that all types of STEs can be experienced at various levels of the awakening of kundalini. However, in my clinical experience and research, I have found that not all people having STEs experience the symptoms of a spiritual energy/kundalini activation. There are a number of reasons for this.

First, some people experiencing STEs do not have a spiritual energy/kundalini activation at all. In the yogic tradition it is believed that an isolated STE may occur by Divine grace, or by a "chakra opening" without any kundalini arousal. It is also thought that psychic abilities may be present from birth or be developed through specific mental practices, without any kundalini activation. This perspective is supported by my clinical experience.

Second, the awakening of kundalini and its subsequent activity occur on a continuum. According to the yogic tradition, only a small proportion of spiritual aspirants would ever awaken this spiritual energy/kundalini, and usually only after many years, and often after many past lives, of sincere spiritual striving. The few who do have the spiritual energy/kundalini awaken generally have a temporary and/or partial awakening at first, resulting in temporary mystical experiences, what are called "sabikalpa samadhi." Only a very small number of these individuals would then, following many more years of continued spiritual effort, have undergone the expansion and purification of their consciousness to the point where they have the capacity to hold the flow of kundalini energy permanently at the crown chakra and brain, to have an ongoing state of mystical consciousness, what is called "nirbikalpa samadhi," or "liberation." According to the yogic tradition, this extremely rare state of nirbikalpa samadhi, or ongoing cosmic consciousness while fully able to function in the world, was manifested in the world's great spiritual Masters, such as Jesus Christ, Bhagavan Krishna, and the Buddha.

I think of the "awakening" of the spiritual energy/kundalini as the first stirrings of this latent spiritual force that exists in all of us, the beginning of a long spiritual transformation process. At the other end of the vast continuum is the person in perennial cosmic consciousness — one of the illuminati. Along the continuum are people who are experiencing varying degrees of ongoing kundalini activity and varying degrees of spiritual transformation of consciousness. Thus, some people may have STEs but be aware of only minor stirrings of the energy and experience very few of the classic signs.

Third, the awakening of kundalini is not always sudden and dramatic; it can occur slowly and increase gradually in activity over a long period of time. When this occurs, according to Gopi Krishna, the gradual increase in kundalini activity — and the accompanying signs — can be so subtle that the individual does not even notice the minute and ever-increasing changes in his or her perception.

Finally, a few rare individuals are born with an awakened kundalini. In these cases, the individual experiences all the classic signs of spiritual energy/kundalini activity but is not aware that his or her experiences are different from anyone else's. Alternatively, the individual's body may be so prepared for and accustomed to the flow of this energy that he or she does not experience the bodily symptoms that tend to be so noticeable in sudden awakenings. A person born with an awakened kundalini would, however, exhibit the signs of higher consciousness at a very young age. Guru Nanak was an example of this type of awakening. According to tradition, he wrote inspirational poetry before he attended school, could discourse on spiritual questions while he was still a child, and went on to found the religion of the Sikhs.

In the literature, definitions and vocabulary on spiritual energy/kundalini vary, and there is sometimes inconsistency between sources. In some yogic traditions, the term "kundalini awakening" is reserved for the very first Spiritual Energy/Kundalini Episode that an individual has. Any subsequent increases in kundalini activity would in those traditions be referred to as a "kundalini rising," that is, rising to a higher level of functioning than before, and/or rising to a higher chakra than previous. In other traditions "kundalini awakening" is used to refer to any strong kundalini activation, episode, or STEP, even in a person who already has an active kundalini. However, I think our current knowledge of spiritual energy/kundalini is far too limited for us to make these finer distinctions. For clarity, and to avoid confusion in terminology, I will use the term "Spiritual Energy/Kundalini Episodes" to refer to both the initial spiritual energy/kundalini awakening, as well as the subsequent spiritual energy/kundalini risings.

In my work, I have found that STEPs that take the form of Spiritual Energy/Kundalini Episodes occur most commonly in people who have been involved in intense spiritual practices such as meditation, hatha yoga, pranayama (breathwork), or extremely focused prayer.

Gopi Krishna's Kundalini Awakening

Since I had the honour of knowing Gopi Krishna personally, and attending a number of his talks at scientific and scholarly symposiums, I would like to start with his story as it is recorded in his book *Kundalini: The Evolutionary Energy in Man* (later republished in an expanded form as *Living with Kundalini: The Autobiography of Gopi Krishna*). This account has become widely recognized as one of the most comprehensive, descriptive accounts of kundalini awakening available.

> One morning during the Christmas of 1937 I sat cross-legged in a small room in a little house on the outskirts of the town of Jammu … I was meditating with my face towards the window on the east through which the first grey streaks of the slowly brightening dawn fell into the room. Long practice had accustomed me to sit in the same posture for hours at a time without the least discomfort, and I sat breathing slowly and rhythmically, my attention drawn towards the crown of my head, contemplating an imaginary lotus in full bloom, radiating light.
>
> I sat steadily, unmoving and erect, my thoughts uninterruptedly centered on the shining lotus, intent on keeping my attention from wandering and bringing it back again and again whenever it moved in any other direction. The intensity of concentration interrupted my breathing; gradually it slowed down to such an extent that at times it was barely perceptible. My whole being was so engrossed in the contemplation of the lotus that for several minutes at a time I lost touch with my body and surroundings.…
>
> During one such spell of intense concentration I suddenly felt a strange sensation below the base of the spine, at the place touching the seat, while I sat cross-legged on a folded blanket spread on the floor. The sensation was so extraordinary and so pleasing that my attention was forcibly drawn towards it. The moment my attention

was thus unexpectedly withdrawn from the point on which it was focused, the sensation ceased…. Again I fixed [my attention] on the lotus, and as the image grew clear and distinct at the top of my head, again the sensation occurred. This time I tried to maintain the fixity of my attention and succeeded for a few seconds, but the sensation extending upwards grew so intense and was so extraordinary, as compared to anything I had experienced before, that in spite of myself my mind went towards it, and at that very moment it again disappeared.

… After a while I grew composed and was soon as deep in meditation as before. When completely immersed I again experienced the sensation, but this time, instead of allowing my mind to leave the point where I had fixed it, I maintained a rigidity of attention throughout. The sensation again extended upwards, growing in intensity, and I felt myself wavering; but with a great effort I kept my attention centered round the lotus. Suddenly, with a roar like that of a waterfall, I felt a stream of liquid light entering my brain through the spinal cord.

Entirely unprepared for such a development, I was completely taken by surprise; but regaining self-control instantaneously, I remained sitting in the same posture, keeping my mind on the point of concentration. The illumination grew brighter and brighter, the roaring louder, I experienced a rocking sensation and then felt myself slipping out of my body, entirely enveloped in a halo of light. It is impossible to describe the experience accurately. I felt the point of consciousness that was myself growing wider, surrounded by waves of light. It grew wider and wider, spreading outward while the body, normally the immediate object of its perception, appeared to have receded into the distance until I became entirely unconscious of it. I was now all consciousness, without any outline, without any idea of a corporeal appendage, without any feeling or sensation coming from the senses, immersed in a sea of light simultaneously conscious and aware of every point, spread out, as it were, in all directions without any barrier or material obstruction. I was no longer myself, or to be more accurate, no longer as I knew myself to be, a small point of awareness confined in a body, but instead was a vast circle of consciousness in which the body was but a point, bathed in light and in a state of exaltation and happiness impossible to describe.

After some time, the duration of which I could not judge, the circle began to narrow down; I felt myself contracting, becoming smaller and smaller, until I again became dimly conscious of the outline of my body, then more clearly; and as I slipped back to my old condition, I became suddenly aware of the noises in the street, felt my arms and legs and head, and once more became my narrow self in touch with body and surroundings.

My Kundalini Awakening

In retrospect, I think my first adult STE, which occurred in 1976, was actually a Spiritual Energy/Kundalini Episode. Initially, I did not realize what had happened to me, and I did not become aware that it was a Kundalini Episode until several years later, after my 1979 Near-Death Experience. Here is my story:

In October 1976, when I was twenty-three years old, I took a meditation course, and then began a daily practice of meditation. I found that meditation came easily to me, almost like second nature. I meditated for at least thirty minutes every weekday morning, and longer many evenings and on weekends.

In December 1976, after about two months of regular meditation practice, I participated in a three-hour-long group meditation session in an auditorium. While in a deep meditative state, I was visualizing myself sending love and light out from my heart to the others in the auditorium. After about twenty minutes, I suddenly heard a noise like the roar of a waterfall, I felt a wave of energy rush up my spine, and simultaneously I felt my consciousness rise above my body and expand. I felt as if my consciousness had filled with light and had now expanded from the size of my head, to the huge size of the auditorium. I felt intense and powerful feelings of love and bliss. It was as if I had become love itself! I remained in this state of expansion, light, and bliss until the meditation ended. After the meditation my consciousness contracted to its regular state, but I felt an afterglow of inner peace, radiance, deep joy, and love.

I did not talk to others about what had happened, because in my naïveté I thought it probably happened regularly to all the more experienced meditators. I did not want to reveal that it had taken me a few months to "finally" figure out how to meditate correctly. I thought, "No wonder people like to meditate — it feels great!" Following this blissful expansive episode, I started intermittently feeling rushes of energy going up my spine, often associated with spiritual insights.

It was only several weeks later, after I discovered that I was not able to reproduce the blissful episode during subsequent daily meditations, that I quietly asked an experienced meditator what I was doing wrong. Only then did I discover that these experiences did not occur regularly to others.

I had no way to label my meditation experience, or the energy rushes that I felt afterward, until a few years later, when I read some of Gopi Krishna's books on kundalini. I was then relieved to have found a name for what I was experiencing. This is one of the reasons why labelling Spiritually Transformative Experiences can be so useful. Giving an unusual experience a non-pathological name — and learning that it has parallels in many cultural and spiritual traditions — helps us integrate it into our lives.

A Canadian Doctor's Story

Gopi Krishna's experience fits the description of kundalini awakening described in the yogic tradition so closely that you might think such a classic awakening could happen only to someone steeped in the Indian culture, but this is not the case. In my work I have found that Spiritual Energy/ Kundalini Episodes cross all cultural and religious boundaries and occur to people who have never practised yoga or heard of any type of transformative energy. One of the most interesting stories I have heard was that of a young doctor whom I'll call Gwen. She had a dramatic spiritual energy/kundalini awakening during her third year of medical school. Prior to her experience she had never done yoga, meditated, or practised any Eastern or Western spiritual discipline. She did, however, have a strong innate spirituality and spent hours and hours in extremely deep concentration — an activity that may mimic in some ways the highly focused concentration and meditation called, respectively, dharana and dhyana in the Eight Limbs of Yoga (described in detail in chapter 9). Here is Gwen's story as she told it to me:

> I had just had a relaxing supper with a close friend one Saturday evening. I had been studying and in a very intense state of concentration for most of the day. In fact, throughout my university education, and especially during medical school, I studied very intensely, and frequently went into almost trance-like states of absorption during my studies. I think all this intense absorption and concentration is what inadvertently stimulated my kundalini.
>
> That evening, after the supper, I discovered that I had an intense pressure headache. My friend suggested that he try giving me a head massage to relieve the headache. I sat down in a comfortable position, and he began to massage my scalp.

Suddenly, my whole body started shaking uncontrollably. I felt rushes of energy coursing up my body to my head, and my whole body jerked with the pulses of energy. My back, arms, and legs all jerked repeatedly as the energy pulses raced upwards. I could not stop the shaking. My body was rocked and shaken by these energy pulses from about 9:30 p.m. until 3:30 a.m. I was fully conscious the whole time, and was acutely aware of what was happening in my body.

I was very frightened during the shaking episode. I had no idea what was going on. I could not control my body; I could not stop the jerking movements of my body and limbs. I shouted out to my friend, asking what was happening. He did not know, and he just sat with me to comfort me. I knew it could not be a seizure, because I was fully conscious throughout the whole episode. Later I found it interesting that my headache had disappeared as soon as the energy pulses began. When the energy rushes and body shaking finally stopped, I felt overwhelmingly fatigued, as if I had experienced a tremendous release of some sort. I crawled into bed and went to sleep immediately.

In the morning when I awoke, I felt as if I had been reborn. When I opened my eyes, the world seemed to have become a magical place. I felt as if I were in love with the world, and that the universe and I were making love to each other. It seemed as if the world was filled with light; all the colours and dimensions of objects seemed clearer and more beautiful. Every sensation was enhanced. It was as if I was breathing in the life-energy of the universe with each breath. I felt as if my consciousness had expanded to immense proportions, and I felt totally at one with the entire universe. I felt the oneness of all things, and I felt that all was well in the Divine plan of the universe.

As I basked in this blissful state, I started to spontaneously recite scriptures that I had not yet read from the

Koran and from the Bible. I started to spontaneously go into yoga postures and do yoga mudras, or hand movements, even though at that point I had never studied yoga.

In the weeks that followed, I remained in an expanded, mystical state of consciousness. I felt a tremendous physical energy during this time. I could easily run at full speed for four miles, even though I had not previously jogged. I seemed to suddenly have great psychic energy also, and I had spontaneously developed new psychic abilities. I was clairsentient, and could perceive emotional and physical problems in others. Several people told me that they experienced a healing of their pain when I would lay my hands on a painful part of their body. And when people needed help with emotional problems or pain, I would seem to automatically know what to say. I was also able to see auras around people and to perceive the energy of other things — plants, trees, rocks, everything.

I felt as if I had undergone a complete rebirth. The experience created a childlike innocence in me. I developed an utter trust in the wisdom of the intelligent power behind the universe. I felt a real sense of grace, of surrendering to a higher power. I felt as if my physical body had become an open vehicle for the life force to express itself through.

I also seemed, spontaneously, to develop tremendous new understanding of the realities behind the universe, and answers to the paradoxes of life and the universe. I could see the wisdom within the folly around us.

The blissful expanded mystical state of consciousness lasted for six months, then my consciousness contracted until it seemed to reach a state that was only somewhat larger than my original state of consciousness. It remains in this state today.

This entire experience changed me totally. It actually seems to have left me more intelligent than I was previously. I can think more clearly and more perceptively. After the experience I developed the urge to meditate daily on the Divine. I have retained some telepathic abilities and remain psychically open, although not to the extent that I was during the six months of expanded consciousness. Although I never experience violent body jerking the way I did that first evening, I still experience recurrent energy surges that rush up my body toward my brain. I perceive this as the life force surging through me.

Immediately after her experience, Gwen found the changes in her perception and the expansion of her consciousness so overwhelming that she decided to take a year off school. She spent the time travelling, learning about different spiritual traditions, and meeting people with similar interests around the world. After a while she managed to integrate the experience and what she learned from it into her daily life. She returned to medical school, completed her studies, and has become an excellent, dedicated physician.

Kundalini Awakening and Breathwork

In *The Stormy Search for Self,* Christina Grof describes her kundalini awakening. It clearly has several of the characteristics of the Spiritual Energy/ Kundalini Episode. One of the things that makes Christina Grof's story so interesting is that she may have inadvertently stimulated her kundalini through the combination of a long-time practice of hatha yoga and Lamaze childbirth-breathing techniques. These techniques are similar to some pranayama exercises — the breathing techniques used by yogis to stimulate kundalini. Christina's case is, of course, unusual. Most women do not need to worry that practising either Lamaze or the gentle yoga stretches appropriate for pregnancy could have such dramatic results.

Christina Grof's kundalini awakening occurred during the birth of her first child.

Lying on the delivery table, I glanced up at the immense surgical lamp and the kind, curious faces of the doctor, the assisting intern and nurses, and my husband. After only a few hours of labor, my son was suddenly and rapidly making his way into the world as I enthusiastically co-operated. As the people around me encouraged me to "push ... push ... nice and hard, remember to breathe," I felt an abrupt snap somewhere inside of me as powerful and unfamiliar energies were released unexpectedly and began streaming through my body. I started to shake uncontrollably. Enormous electrical tremors coursed from my toes up my legs and spine to the top of my head. Brilliant mosaics of white light exploded in my head, and instead of continuing the Lamaze panting, I felt strange, involuntary breathing rhythms taking over.

It was as though I had just been hit by some miraculous but frightening force, and I was both excited and terrified; the shaking, the visions, and the spontaneous breathing were certainly not what I had expected from all of my months of preparation. As soon as my son was delivered, I was given two shots of morphine, which stopped the whole process. Soon, the wonder faded and I became embarrassed and fearful. I was a restrained, well-mannered woman who had a strong sense of authority over my life, and now I had completely lost control. Very quickly, I pulled myself together.

During the birth of her second child, Christina had an even stronger Spiritual Energy/Kundalini experience. This time she was given tranquilizers that stopped the experience, just as the morphine had during the birth of her first child.

Even though she had studied yoga, Christina did not know exactly what had happened to her. The fact that heavy medication stopped both experiences added to her feeling that what she had undergone was a sign of illness.

Four years later, her spiritual journey began in earnest when she had another powerful experience while meditating with an Indian guru. After this her life changed radically. As with many people who experience continued "high-voltage" kundalini activity, she had periods of anxiety and depression as well as periods of spiritual awareness and bliss. Eventually she met her future husband, Dr. Stanislav Grof, who helped her see her experiences as part of a process of personal growth and transformation. The Grofs' work is discussed further in chapter 15 on spiritual emergencies and psychoses.

Spiritual Energy/Kundalini and Alcoholic Recovery

In my clinical experience, some people involved in the intensive psychological and spiritual healing work of recovering from addictions may experience a spiritual energy/kundalini activation. This may happen at any point in their recovery, including when they "hit bottom," and from this mental and spiritual abyss desperately cry out for help to the Divine. In my opinion, this was true of Bill Wilson, the co-founder of Alcoholics Anonymous, whose "hot flash" or "white-light experience" has many clear signs of a Spiritual Energy/Kundalini Episode. Here is the description of Bill Wilson's experience as described in AA's book *Pass It On*:

> ... he and Lois were waiting for the end. Now, there was nothing ahead but death or madness. This was the finish, the jumping-off place. "The terrifying darkness had become complete," Bill said. "In agony of spirit, I again thought of the cancer of alcoholism which had now consumed me in mind and spirit, and soon the body." The abyss gaped before him.
>
> In his helplessness and desperation, Bill cried out, "I'll do anything, anything at all!" He had reached a point of total, utter deflation — a state of complete surrender. With neither faith nor hope, he cried, "If there be a God, let Him show Himself!"
>
> What happened next was electric. "Suddenly, my room blazed with an indescribably white light. I was seized with an ecstasy beyond description. Every joy I had known was pale by comparison. The light, the ecstasy — I was conscious of nothing else for a time.

"Then, seen in the mind's eye, there was a mountain. I stood upon its summit, where a great wind blew. A wind, not of air, but of spirit. In great, clean strength, it blew right through me. Then came the blazing thought, 'You are a free man.' I know not at all how long I remained in this state, but finally the light and the ecstasy subsided. I again saw the wall of my room. As I became more quiet, a great peace stole over me, and this was accompanied by a sensation difficult to describe. I became acutely conscious of a Presence which seemed like a veritable sea of living spirit. I lay on the shores of a new world. 'This,' I thought, 'must be the great reality. The God of the preachers.'

"Savoring my new world, I remained in this state for a long time. I seemed to be possessed by the absolute, and the curious conviction deepened that no matter how wrong things seemed to be, there could be no question of the ultimate rightness of God's universe. For the first time, I felt that I really belonged. I knew that I was loved and could love in return. I thanked my God, who had given me a glimpse of His absolute self. Even though a pilgrim upon an uncertain highway, I needed to be concerned no more, for I had glimpsed the great beyond."

Bill Wilson had just had his 39th birthday, and he still had half his life ahead of him. He always said that after that experience, he never again doubted the existence of God. He never took another drink.

... he often referred to his enormous, intense, mystical, life-changing spiritual experience as a "hot flash." He did this so often that other A.A.'s began using the same term, never realizing that Bill was deliberately "deflating" his own experience (and his own ego) by describing it thus.

Bill Wilson's experience had several clear and classic symptoms of a Spiritual Energy/Kundalini Episode: an energy movement in his body that he described as the spiritual wind blowing through him, strong heat sensations, inner sounds of wind blowing, intense white-light perceptions, and the associated mystical experience. This experience had a profound, spiritually transformative impact on Bill Wilson. Not only did he never take another drink of alcohol, he also became less materialistic, more service-oriented, and developed deep, unshakable spiritual convictions. The experience also opened him to other STEs. He became convinced of the reality of past lives and had both psychic and inspired creative experiences in the months and years afterward. In my clinical work I have met several other recovering alcoholics who have had similar, if perhaps less dramatic, spiritual energy/kundalini awakenings when hitting bottom and pleading to the Divine for assistance. These awakenings propelled them forward into their journey of recovery and healing.

Downward-Flowing Spiritual Energy

Not everyone who experiences a Spiritual Energy/Kundalini Episode experiences sensations of energy moving upwards through the body. In fact, some people report powerful Spiritual Energy/Kundalini Episodes where it feels like the energy is coming down from above and descending into the experiencer. These types of experiences are sometimes referred to in Christian traditions as the "descent of grace" or "descent of the Holy Spirit." They are usually accompanied by the other signs of a Spiritual Energy/Kundalini Episode — perceptions of light, inner sounds, energy rushes (sometimes downwards), vibrating, jerking, or spiralling, plus the associated mystical or paranormal experience.

Jyoti, a friend and fellow kundalini researcher, describes such a downward-flowing kundalini episode in her autobiography, *An Angel Called My Name.*

> On the evening of April 30, 1983, I was taking a shower when a loud buzzing noise began. It became so loud I felt sure that everyone else could hear it … The loud buzzing seemed to reach a peak at which point a bright Light appeared above me. A beam shot down from it and poured into the top of my head, traveling throughout my

entire body. My body seemed to be drawn forward. I felt totally nurtured and the process went on for quite some time. I fell deeper and deeper into an altered state of consciousness. After a while, I returned to a more functional state, but I still felt altered in some way ... decided to meditate ... The energy was extremely strong, and again the loud buzzing returned. The Light returned, hovering over my head. As it descended, a sense of calmness and beauty seemed to fill the room in an all-encompassing, ever-present glow. I felt great empathy with it. Four figures in white-hooded robes appeared, one on each side and two at the end of the bed. Their form was wavy like heat coming off a road, but their appearance was distinct. They stood quietly and serenely, as if in a ceremony ...

Richard and I lay down on the bed ... Again the energy returned. I visualized it as a white light that drew a circle around us encompassing our bodies. The energy seemed to flow across both of us. I found myself in a white swirling tunnel that had a bright red sphere at the other end. Its light radiated out and filled the tunnel with a red glow. People were standing in the tunnel. They disappeared leaving only one man, who began to walk toward me and then motioned with his arm to come ... The scene changed, and I was looking into the corner of a living room with a couch, a chair, and a lamp. The scene changed again and I saw a city street scene. It appeared to be European with trees lining the area between the street and the sidewalk. It was a busy street with cars rushing to and fro. Each scene seemed so distinctly different that no connection could be made. Again the scene changed, displaying a beautiful, sunny landscape. The sun began to shine more brightly and filled the scene with such a brightness and intensity that only the silhouette of a tree in the center remained.

Following this scene, I found myself flying over a terrain of rolling hills. I enjoyed the sensation so much that

I began to indulge in it, flying closer to the ground — up and down and over the hills. Suddenly, something pulled me up. I realized that I was in outer space looking down upon what appeared to be the planet earth. How in the world did I get out here? Outer space wasn't dark, but rather produced a sense of clarity. The earth was breathtaking in her hues of blue and green.... I had the distinct feeling that I would soon realize my true origin. At that moment I sensed my concentration being broken

I got up ... My head was confused and my heart full. I sobbed for hours not knowing why. Upon returning to ordinary reality, I was filled with completeness, fullness and total commitment.... I am not sure I will ever be able to verbalize the intense meaning this evening held for me ... I can only say that Spirit shook my world once again and impregnated me with an overwhelming sense of love and wholeness.

Jyoti has continued to have repeated Spiritual Energy/Kundalini Episodes over the years, and is in a process of long-term spiritual transformation of consciousness.

Kundalini by Any Other Name

Many — if not most — people who have Spiritual Energy/Kundalini Episodes are not aware that they have had what is called a kundalini awakening in the yogic tradition. Others simply choose to give the experience another name, such as "Holy Spirit" or "White-Light Experience." Dr. William Brugh Joy, a California doctor who specialized in internal medicine, has had many profoundly moving spiritual experiences in his life. He has become a well-known and highly respected speaker at conferences on spiritual subjects and has written a number of books. This story of one of Dr. Joy's STEs in *Joy's Way: A Map for the Transformational Journey* contains most of the elements of a Spiritual Energy/Kundalini Episode:

In a morning meditation in February 1976, I had the sensation of a motor turning on in my chest area, and then I saw a momentary flash of blinding white light. In each subsequent meditation, and each night just after I went to bed, I experienced the same blindingly intense flash of light; it was far more intense than looking at the sun or at any other brilliantly lighted object I had ever seen. I began to try to hold the light in my awareness, but I could not do it. The light was just too bright. A second was more than I could stand.

The experience, sometimes skipping a few days but always of the same quality, continued until November 1976. Then, one night, I was lying in bed, just about to fall asleep, when the motor came on; but this time it was not the usual motor. This time it was like a Diesel truck. Its vibration shook not only me, but also the kingsize bed. It was first centered in my chest area, then moved into the lower abdomen, then up toward my head. On came the superbrilliant light. It was not just a flash, and it did not stop. For a moment, I was terrified. Then I heard a voice say, "What do you think you have been preparing for?" I accepted it and relaxed into the experience. It lasted for about six hours: intense, intense, intense white light and the quaking of my whole body.

William Brugh Joy's experience is typical of many of the stories I have heard. Often people having a Spiritual Energy/Kundalini Episode have no prior knowledge of kundalini and have no idea what is happening to them. Some are terrified initially. Others think that they are dying or going crazy. Some even think an alien force or UFO is causing the intense energy experience. Still others think it is a normal, blissful, meditation-related or prayer-related experience. It is reassuring to know that most people who have Spiritual Energy/Kundalini Episodes tend to function quite normally between them and, although the physical symptoms sometimes continue, they generally do so at fairly low intensity between the peak episodes.

The many people I have met who have had Spiritual Energy/Kundalini Episodes have eventually become tremendously uplifted and inspired by the experience. Once they had a name for their episode, a framework in which they could understand this very physical yet paranormal experience, they could relax and grow from the profound energetic opening. I think it is essential that awareness of kundalini awakening and its associated physical symptoms be spread throughout the Western world, so that persons experiencing it will have such a framework, and will also be given appropriate guidance and support throughout this dramatic spiritual awakening. Further, as I mentioned earlier, I think a Spiritual Energy/Kundalini Episode heralds the beginning of a journey of long-term psychological and spiritual transformation of consciousness. In the same way as mystical experiences, Spiritual Energy/Kundalini Episodes create an intense spiritual yearning in the experiencer, which draws them to strive to complete this journey, to reach transcendence, God-consciousness, enlightenment, liberation.

5

NEAR-DEATH EXPERIENCES

THE TERM "NEAR-DEATH EXPERIENCE" (NDE) was coined by Dr. Raymond Moody, M.D., an American psychiatrist, to describe a phenomenon he documented in his groundbreaking 1975 book, *Life After Life*. In his medical practice, Dr. Moody had observed that a surprising number of people reported having an out-of-body experience and/or a white-light mystical experience while very near death, or when clinically dead and later resuscitated. After he documented more than one hundred cases in his book, Near-Death Experiences began to receive attention.

At the time of my 1979 plane-crash NDE (described in chapter 1) that launched me on my quest to research NDEs, there was very little awareness about Near-Death Experiences either within the medical profession or in the public eye. When I started talking publicly about my Near-Death Experience in 1990, I was, in fact, the first Canadian medical doctor to speak about having had an NDE. I was also the first Canadian medical doctor to begin to research and to specialize in counselling patients who had NDEs. Fortunately, there has now been a big increase in public awareness of NDEs, mainly through the media. For example, in George Lucas's epic 1980 film *Star Wars Episode V: The Empire Strikes Back,* which was re-released in 1997, the hero, Luke, has an NDE while freezing to death. In Luke's quite accurately depicted NDE he has a mystical vision of a "being of light," the spirit of his deceased mentor Obi Wan. Obi Wan gives Luke an important life-message in the NDE, as often occurs during NDEs. Director Joel Schumacher's 1990 film *Flatliners* depicts a group of young people experimenting with inducing Near-Death Experiences. Several other documentaries and films have now reenacted some NDE experiencers' stories. In fact, my own NDE has now been re-enacted on *Sightings* and in two television documentaries. Patricia Pearson wrote about my NDE in her acclaimed 2014 book *Opening Heaven's Door.* The popular film based on the 2010 bestselling book *Heaven is for Real,* by Todd Burpo and Lynn Vincent, recounted the dramatic story of the childhood NDE of Burpo's then three-year-old son. Several Near-Death Experiencers have recently written bestselling books about their NDEs, including Dr. Eben Alexander, Anita Moorjani, and Dr. Mary Neal. All this media attention has vastly increased public awareness of NDEs.

Doctors and psychologists from around the world have also begun to increasingly tell of similar reports made by their patients, and several books have since been written on the subject. One of the most significant of these books is *Heading Toward Omega* by Dr. Kenneth Ring, an eminent American research psychologist and co-founder of the International Association for Near-Death Studies (IANDS). More recently, Dutch cardiologist and researcher Dr. Pim van Lommel wrote *Consciousness Beyond Life: The Science of the Near-Death Experience.* Another significant book is *The Handbook of Near-Death Experience,* edited by Dr. Janice Holden, Dr. Bruce Greyson, and Debbie James. Current NDE researchers have gone beyond merely documenting the existence of NDEs, and have also focused on the positive changes in values, attitudes, and behaviour occurring in people's lives after such experiences. Dr. Ring and American psychiatrist Dr. Bruce Greyson, M.D., a fellow co-founder of IANDS, have gone even further, postulating kundalini awakening as a possible mechanism underlying NDEs. I support this hypothesis, and will expand on my own ideas about kundalini and NDEs in chapter 9, on the Yogic Model of Consciousness and Kundalini.

Theologians have been as fascinated with the subject as are doctors and psychologists. In his book *Life After Death* Tom Harpur, a scholar, ordained Anglican priest, and respected Canadian author, analyzes NDEs as one of a number of subjects that are relevant to the question of life after death. Harpur examines the historical perspectives and surveys much of the material that has been published on NDEs since Moody's book. Harpur concludes that expanding exploration and research in the field is "one of the most exciting developments of our time" and that he finds himself increasingly, if cautiously, "positive about the validity of the NDE as a witness to invisible realities beyond."

Even though there are still skeptics who believe that NDEs are caused by everything from overactive imagination to lack of oxygen in the brain, the number of people interested in the subject is rapidly growing. IANDS, the International Association for Near-Death Studies, founded in 1978 and of which I am a long-time member and current board member, facilitates dialogue and research on NDEs. Both are clearly needed. More and more children and adults are reporting NDEs. One reason for this might be that improvements in technology — from emergency rescue equipment to medical resuscitation techniques — mean that far more people survive close brushes with death.

Still, not everyone who is near death and then resuscitated has an NDE. Statistics on the percentages of people who do vary greatly. According to the research of Nancy Zingrone and Carlos Alvarado, in *The Handbook of Near-Death Experiences,* between 17 and 35 percent of persons who are questioned after returning from a close brush with death report an NDE. This also means that 65 to 83 percent of persons who return from near death do not have an NDE. In addition, individuals who have been close to death on more than one occasion may report no NDE at all with one brush with death, and then a clear NDE with another close call. According to yogic philosophy as explained by Swami Yukteswar in *Autobiography of a Yogi,* sometimes after the death of a body, a soul "... remains for the most part in the deep stupor of the death-sleep and is hardly conscious of the beautiful astral sphere. After the astral rest, such a man returns to the material plane to learn further lessons ..." We do not yet know why some people have NDEs and others do not, or why the same person may have an NDE with one brush with death, and not with another.

We do know, however, that NDEs are Spiritually Transformative Experiences. They transform experiencers, changing their values and attitudes in a more spiritual and altruistic direction. It is one point that researchers and writers like Ring, von Lommel, Greyson, Holden, Harpur, and I agree on. It is something I have found to be true both from people I have counselled and from my own personal experience. I have been blessed with five Near-Death Experiences over the course of my lifetime, three in my adult life and two in my childhood. My personal NDEs combined with my outer clinical experience and research have convinced me that NDEs and other Spiritually Transformative Experiences are very real, peak human experiences.

Characteristics of Near-Death Experiences

One of the most interesting things about NDEs is how similar the pattern of different people's experiences are. People often interpret the experiences differently, based on their cultural and religious perspectives, but the actual experiences are virtually identical in all cultures. Although every person's NDE is unique, slightly different from other persons' NDEs, Dr. Moody identified fifteen general features that are common to NDEs. These features have now become the standard identifying factors used by most researchers in the field.

Although most NDEs do not contain all the fifteen NDE features Moody lists, it is usual for NDEs to have at least eight of the fifteen. The features usually occur in the general order listed below. My work with NDE experiencers seems to indicate that the number of NDE features people experience tends to increase with the length of time they were unconscious, close to death, or clinically dead before being resuscitated. Although I have modified and expanded on a number of the points using my own experience and terminology, the following features are similar to the ones listed by Dr. Raymond Moody in *Life After Life*.

1. *Ineffability.* NDEs have dimensions and aspects that are beyond words and cannot be adequately conveyed, expressed, or described to others.
2. *Auditory awareness.* Clear and accurate recall of what others were saying while the experiencer was unconscious or clinically dead.
3. *Strong feelings of peace.* A feeling of peace, comfort, and tranquility; fear either dissolves or is completely absent.
4. *Unusual inner sounds.* An internal sense of "hearing" buzzing, ringing, roaring, whistling, wind, distant wind chimes, or even "celestial" music, "music of the spheres."

5. *Floating out of the body.* An out-of-body experience. The individual's "point of perception"— or the spirit body — rises, allowing the experiencer to observe his or her physical body and the surroundings; the spirit body may also travel to other locations, often to observe loved ones.

6. *Dark tunnel.* A sensation of moving away from the physical body through a long, dark passage or tunnel with a bright light at the far end.

7. *Meeting spirits.* Mystical visions — seeing "beings of light." Contact with loving spirits who are usually seen as youthful and/or shining white figures. They are often luminous spirits of departed loved ones, relatives, or friends, or they may be visions of saints, an angel, or a spiritual Master, such as Jesus. Communication may occur through telepathy or thought-transference, usually delivering a strong life-message, or a spiritual concept.

8. *White-Light Experience.* A Mystical experience. Encountering or being immersed in indescribable white light that emanates a powerful aura of intense love and unconditional acceptance. This mystical aura of love may be overwhelming, and may inspire awe, devotion, and/or a willingness to repent and to surrender to the Divine. The White-Light Experience is sometimes perceived as an immense, intelligent, loving force, a "formless being of light," which may be interpreted by the experiencer as God, or the formless spirit of Jesus, an angel, or another religious figure. Mystical revelations and/or an illumination may occur, with new knowledge, life-messages, or spiritual teachings being revealed, or even prophecy of future events being shown.

9. *Life-review.* A review or rapid reexperiencing of emotional or significant life events, including ones that may have been forgotten or repressed. There may be the opportunity to learn a soul lesson from the life-review, which is usually to be more loving and kind to others.

10. *Life barrier.* The perception of a barrier or border that the spirit body cannot cross if it wants to return to the physical body.

11. *Abrupt return to the body.* A sensation of rapidly travelling back down through the tunnel and/or of being suddenly pulled down, sucked down, or being sucked back into the physical body, often through the top of the head; the sensation of suddenly re-entering the physical body, sometimes with a jolt.

12. *Conviction of the reality of the experience.* An absolute certainty that the experience was real and not a fantasy or a dream — even in the face of disbelief or ridicule. Experiencers usually have a clear memory of the experience, which may remain exceptionally clear for many years.

13. *Transformational impact.* A life that is changed in one or more ways: (a) psychologically — the person may mature rapidly, abandon self-destructive habits, adopt a more positive and compassionate outlook, appreciate life more, feel enriched, gain new insights about life or lifestyle, or rapidly or spontaneously resolve psychological issues; (b) spiritually — he or she may gain new insights into the nature of the universe, become convinced of the reality of a Higher Power, learn important lessons about love, the basic unity of the world's religions, or other spiritual matters, or become stronger, more courageous, or more willing to speak the truth as they see it; (c) psychically — he or she may notice the development of intuition or psychic abilities or an increase in these faculties.

14. *New views of death.* The loss of fear of death and an increase in the certainty that the spirit lives on after death of the physical body.

15. *Independent corroboration.* Veridical perceptions. Events observed on the physical plane during the out-of-body experience are corroborated by other people or evidence.

Some confusion may occur at times because in the last few years some persons have begun to loosely call any close call or brush with death a "near-death experience," even when no NDE occurred as defined by Dr. Moody's NDE features. However, throughout this book I will use the term "Near-Death Experience" in accordance with Dr. Moody's NDE criteria as listed above, as are used by other NDE researchers today. I will use the term "Near-Death Experience" to refer only to an out-of-body and/or mystical experience with five or more of the above NDE features, which occurred to a person when they were dead or near death.

A Young Judge's White-Light Mystical NDE

Some Near-Death Experiences very closely follow the list of Moody's NDE features. The following story was told to me by a young female lawyer whom I'll call Sylvia. She was extremely successful in her work and had held a position as a judge for two years before her NDE. Sylvia's Near-Death Experience includes almost all of the classic features of an NDE listed above.

> I was driving home late one night after work along a dark, winding desert road. The evening seemed quite usual. As I drove, I was looking forward to getting home, greeting my husband, and spending some time playing with my two-year-old son. Suddenly, a huge transport truck raced around a bend, pulled into my lane, and faced my small car head-on.
>
> My immediate reaction was to panic; I realized that I could not avoid crashing into the truck. I thought, "I'm going to die!" In a flash, I felt my consciousness leave my body and float above the car as I watched the accident happen below. I saw my body become cut and battered by the impact of the collision, but I felt no pain or fear, only a sense of peace and calm.
>
> Then I suddenly found myself at the entrance to a long, dark tunnel, with a bright light glowing at the far end. Progressing along the tunnel, I began to experience an instantaneous replay of the events of my life. Once the "life-review" was finished, I found myself in the dazzlingly brilliant white light at the end of the tunnel and perceived a number of loving beings who seemed to be made of light. Although I was not certain who they were, I sensed they might be deceased family or friends who loved me. They greeted me with warmth, acceptance, and love. I felt I was

enveloped by the loving light of God, or the intelligence behind the universe. It was the most intensely beautiful and uplifting feeling I had ever had.

Quite suddenly, I felt myself being pulled away from the light. It seemed as if my "soul" was sinking down into a darker, smaller space. With a sudden jolt, I found myself waking up in my battered body. Groggy and aching all over, I discovered I was in a hospital emergency department where, I learned later, I had been brought by an ambulance and resuscitated.

Sylvia was profoundly moved by her experience, but she was also confused. She had never heard of Near-Death Experiences, and she did not know what to make of what she had undergone. Thinking that the doctors would not understand, she did not tell them of the experience. Her husband was the first person she told. But he thought she had imagined the whole thing, and he became angry whenever she wanted to talk about it.

Wanting desperately to understand what had happened to her, Sylvia remained preoccupied with the experience. Her husband became increasingly hostile about her fascination with it, and eventually they separated. They are now divorced.

In her search for understanding, Sylvia also tried to talk to the pastor of her local fundamentalist church. He told her that the experience must have been the work of the devil and that she should repent. Unwilling to agree with this interpretation, Sylvia went to her medical doctor, a physician who had never heard of Near-Death Experiences. He recommended that she see a psychiatrist, which Sylvia did.

The psychiatrist was also unfamiliar with NDEs. Observing Sylvia's emotional intensity when she talked about the impact of the experience, the psychiatrist suggested that an unresolved emotional conflict had triggered the "delusion." He suggested that she uncover the conflict and resolve it through long-term psychotherapy and that, once this was done, the delusion would be eliminated. He then suggested she take some tranquilizers for the "anxiety" she was experiencing. Sylvia decided not to take the medication or try his psychotherapy.

Sylvia began to feel very confused and alone. Although she sensed she had undergone some type of mystical experience, no one around her seemed to think there was any validity to her story. Still, she was aware of many positive changes in her life. She had lost her fear of death and came to see God as the loving, intelligent divine force driving the universe rather than the vengeful judge she had once conceived of. She also came to believe that the founders of all the world's religions were trying to understand the same truth. Sylvia steadfastly refused to believe that such wonderful spiritual insights could have come from a delusion or a figment of her imagination.

Sylvia recovered physically from the accident, returned to her work as a judge, and adjusted to life as a single mother. She didn't become familiar with the concept of Near-Death Experiences until many years later when she came across Kenneth Ring's book *Heading Toward Omega*. What she read there confirmed the reality of her own experience and helped her understand why and how it had transformed her life.

Out-of-Body NDEs

Not all Near-Death Experiences have as many classic NDE features as Sylvia's did, and, notably, not all include the white-light mystical experience component. Many people have reported NDEs that were primarily an out-of-body experience, where they felt their point of awareness floated up out of their body, and they could observe their injured, dead, or dying body from above. In my clinical experience, often brief NDEs consist of just an out-of-body experience associated with a feeling of peace, while longer NDEs may begin with an out-of-body experience and then as time progresses include travelling through a dark tunnel, a life-review, mystical vision encounters with beings of light, and/or a white-light mystical experience.

"Paul," a thirty-eight-year-old engineer, had an out-of-body NDE in his midtwenties when he came extremely close to drowning.

> I was canoeing with an inexperienced friend in Canada in early spring just after the ice melted on the lakes. The canoe accidentally overturned, and we fell into near-freezing water. We were both wearing heavy parkas and boots, and

my partner could not swim. Panicking, my friend tried to climb on top of me and pushed me under the water.

After struggling underwater for a few moments, I felt certain I was going to drown. Suddenly, I felt my consciousness float up, out of my body. I became very peaceful and calm. As I looked down from above, I saw a motor boat appear out of nowhere, race over toward us, and pull us out of the water a few moments later. When our rescuers pulled my head out of the freezing water, I gasped for air and was instantaneously aware of being back in my body.

Paul was never actually unconscious during his Near-Death Experience, and it lasted only a brief time. Following the pattern I've noticed in brief NDEs, he experienced only five of the typical features of NDEs: an out-of-body experience, a deep feeling of peace, an abrupt return to his body, independent corroboration, and, later, an unshakable conviction concerning the reality of the experience.

My Childhood Out-of-Body NDEs

As my research and understanding of the diversity of NDEs deepened over the years, I slowly came to the realization that I had, in fact, also had two NDEs when I was a child. I did not realize this for most of my life because as a child aged five and then eleven when my NDEs happened, I did not label the experiences as anything unusual. I just accepted my out-of-body experiences during close calls as normal childhood experiences. I also didn't recognize my childhood NDEs at first because they were both out-of-body type NDEs, very different from my adult NDEs, which were all mystical/white-light experiences, experiences that were much more powerfully transformative than my childhood NDEs. Thus for many years I did not link the experiences together. It was only recently with reflection that I realized that my two childhood out-of-body experiences were, in fact, childhood NDEs.

My first childhood NDE happened when I was five years old, during the summer before kindergarten, while I was travelling with my parents in

Switzerland. I clearly recall that on this day we were waiting for a train at a station, standing on a train platform. As I describe in greater detail in *Soul Lessons from the Light*:

> As we waited at the train station, I saw a station attendant jump down off the platform onto the railway tracks, then quickly climb up onto the next platform at the far side of the tracks. "Oh that looks like fun!" I thought to myself. I decided to do the same thing, and leaned forward beginning to jump onto the railway tracks.
>
> Suddenly it felt like time stood still. It was as if the movie in a theatre had frozen at one frame. My thoughts continued to flow, but the world around me seemed to have stopped, frozen in time. I suddenly found myself floating above my body, viewing the scene below me. I could now clearly see what I had not realized when I began to jump, that I was jumping onto the tracks directly in front of a rapidly oncoming train arriving at the station. Strangely, although it appeared that the train was about to hit me, I did not feel any fear. Somehow I felt a powerful peace and stillness. I felt calm and unafraid. "Oh, I see. I'm about to be hit by a train," I thought calmly.
>
> The next instant the "movie" of my life started moving again, and an adult's hand appeared out of nowhere, pulling me rapidly back up onto the platform. Suddenly I was back in my body again, standing on the station platform as the oncoming train pulled into the station in front of me.

When I was eleven years old I had my second childhood NDE, when I was involved in a car accident where I sustained a serious head injury and became unconscious. Since the time of this childhood accident, I have always remembered floating above my unconscious body, feeling completely peaceful and calm. As I describe in greater detail in *Soul Lessons from the Light*:

My last worldly memory of this car accident at age eleven was the sensation of a sudden sharp jolt of the fully loaded car as we sped along a highway. My whole family was in the car that day, my dad driving, mom in the front passenger seat, and myself and my three siblings crowded in the back seat. This was before the age of seat belts. The rear of the station-wagon was packed full with family luggage. Evidently during the accident as the car rolled off the road down a steep embankment, my young body was thrown into the rear of the vehicle and I had sustained a head injury.

My next memory is of being out-of-body, my spirit and point of perception floating above the car wreckage immediately after the accident. My unconscious body was nearby, buried under the luggage in the rear of the mangled station-wagon. I clearly recall glimpsing my injured father from above, while he lay injured at the roadside. I witnessed my father calling out for me, as from above I heard him cry out, "My daughter, my daughter!" [My body had not yet been found by the rescuers.] It felt to me as if my soul somehow knew that Dad was calling out for me, and this call from his soul had drawn my out-of-body spirit to move to him briefly.

My next clear memory is of my spirit and point of perception floating up by the ceiling above my unconscious body in the emergency room of the nearby hospital where we had been taken by ambulance. I watched from above as my body lay motionless on a surgical table. Below me, I could clearly see the shiny metallic curved top surface of a large disc-shaped operating room light which hung over the table. I watched from above as two men, doctors I presumed, bent over my unconscious body, examining it and trying to revive me. I felt no pain or distress. I felt still, completely peaceful, and totally unafraid.

> I clearly recall the moment that I regained conscious-
> ness a few days later. I remember suddenly waking up,
> to find myself in a bed in a children's ward of a hospital.

As a child at the time of the car accident, I did not realize that I had experienced anything out of the ordinary while I was unconscious, and thought my out-of-body memories to be a normal experience for someone who had been unconscious. Now I realize that my two childhood out-of-body experiences both fall within the broad spectrum of out-of-body Near-Death Experiences.

Transformational Impact of Out-of-Body NDEs versus Mystical NDEs

I and other NDE researchers have found there is a significant difference in the degree of transformational impact of an out-of-body type NDE, as compared to the impact of a white-light mystical type NDE. Mystical white-light NDEs tend to have a much greater and sometimes dramatic spiritually transformative impact on the experiencer, as compared to the impact of NDEs that include only an out-of-body experience. Mystical white-light NDEs may completely change experiencers' world view and cause a sudden spiritual awakening, shifting their values and beliefs in a far more spiritual direction. Additionally mystical NDEs tend to leave the experiencer more open to further mystical experiences as well as to new psychic abilities.

Still, most persons who have an out-of-body type NDE also report they were transformed in some ways by their experience. Although some seemed unchanged, many find themselves susceptible to other out-of-body experiences and more open to other types of psychic experiences. Some find the out-of-body NDE opened their mind to the reality that their spirit is separate from their physical body, causing a more subtle spiritual awakening. And in some cases an out-of-body NDE can begin a long-term process of spiritual transformation as an after-effect, similar to what occurs to most mystical white-light NDE experiencers.

Life-Review in NDEs

Some NDE experiencers report a life-review as part of their Near-Death Experience. This life-review can vary from fleeting glimpses of highlights of their lives, to very long and detailed reviews.

Dannion Brinkley had a very long and detailed life-review in his dramatic NDE at the age of twenty-five, which he describes in great detail in his inspiring book, *Saved by the Light*. Dannion's life-review had an extremely spiritually transformative impact on him, and provides an excellent example of this aspect of an NDE. Here is a brief summary of the life-review portion of Dannion Brinkley's NDE:

> After being struck by lightning, Dannion Brinkley found himself out-of-body, with a being of light in front of him. He immediately began to experience a replay of his whole life, somehow feeling and seeing everything that had ever happened to him over the course of his life. He describes his life-review as not pleasant. Starting from events in his childhood, he saw incidents where he had been unkind to others. He then found himself in the bodies of those he had been mean to, and he felt the emotional pain that he had caused them. This perspective continued through every negative incident of his childhood that came to mind. Sometimes he would also feel, in addition to the pain that he had caused others, the pain this had inflicted on the next person they reacted to. He saw the chain of emotional reactions — how we deeply affect one another.
>
> This life-review, including feeling the emotions of persons he had hurt or harmed, continued into his adult life, including his years in the military during the war in Vietnam. He relived incidents where he killed North Vietnamese soldiers, and he felt their sadness and confusion at suddenly dying. Dannion then felt the rest of the chain reaction — the sad feelings of the soldiers' families when they learned of the deaths. Dannion relived all the

kills he made during the war in this multiperspective fashion. In some cases he even felt the loss the death he caused would make to future generations.

When Dannion Brinkley's life-review in his NDE was over, he felt sorrow and shame. He expected some sort of cosmic rebuke or reprimand, but the being of light radiated only nonjudgmental compassion and love. The being of light telepathically communicated to him, "*Who you are is the difference that God makes ... and that difference is love.*" With these thoughts revealed, Dannion felt a spiritual blessing as the burden of guilt lifted from his soul.

Dannion Brinkley went on to have a much longer NDE with many visionary experiences and revelations while in the Light, before he later awoke in his once-dead body. Dannion Brinkley's NDE and life-review transformed him profoundly. He has dedicated his life afterward to helping others, working with the sick, elderly, and dying, and sharing his wonderful, inspiring NDE story and its message of love with people everywhere.

My 1995 NDE with Life-Review

I, too, had a very powerful NDE that included a life-review on February 27, 1995, my second adult NDE. My 1995 NDE occurred at a time when I thought I was facing imminent death in a near-miss plane incident, when I psychologically faced what I thought was certain death. My life-review was different from that of Dannion Brinkley, as it included peak positive experiences I had in my life. To not overload this book with my own personal STE stories, I will only share the key points of this story here. I describe my 1995 NDE and its powerful after-effects in greater detail in *Soul Lessons from the Light*. Here is my story:

I was flying in a large Air Canada commercial plane that day, and we had flown into a bad winter ice storm. The plane was buffeted by strong winds, and a visible layer of ice had frozen on the plane's wings. We were descending and approaching our landing at Toronto International airport, when the pilot suddenly aborted the landing just before touching down, about fifty feet or so above the runway. I later learned that the pilot had seen a pack of coyotes obstructing our runway.

The pilot slammed the wing flaps back, and the engines screamed as the pilot urgently tried to get the heavy plane to regain enough airspeed to start ascending again, to avoid crashing into the animals. The plane shook violently with air turbulence. It looked like we were going to crash. The other passengers in the plane started screaming and crying out loud in fear.

I immediately thought, "Oh, I see. I was meant to survive the other plane crash [in 1979], so that I would write my book on NDEs, but I am going to die today, in this plane crash." I had learned from yoga that the most auspicious way to die was consciously, striving to go high into the Light of Spirit, so I closed my eyes. I prayed for God to look after my young son, then I quickly went into deep meditation.

Instantly I felt my spirit leave my body. I found myself moving rapidly upwards through a dark but calm and peaceful space. As my spirit travelled upwards I experienced a life-review where I briefly re-experienced three peak mystical experiences that I had in my life. It felt as if I travelled back in time, and that each STE was briefly happening to me right now, one after the other.

First I found myself back in my 1979 NDE, at the point of time while I was swimming to shore and I had risen out of my body into the heavenly realm of the profoundly loving white light. I felt as if I was actually back in that experience again. I felt the powerful unconditional love. I could see the white light surrounding me. I could feel the strong sense of being safe, of being *home*. I re-experienced my knowing that there is nothing to fear in death, that "I" would live on even if my physical body died in the worldly drama unfolding in the lake below me.

Then suddenly I jumped through time to my 1990 calling mystical experience that I had in Monterey, California. I seemed to be there exactly at the moment that I had the highest peak of this mystical experience. I relived, as if it were happening to me right now, the profound expansion of my consciousness. I perceived the brilliant white light radiating from my head, seemingly illuminating my surroundings with light. I once again felt the ecstasy, the joy, the revelation.

After a few moments it seemed that I suddenly jumped in time to the peak moment of another powerful mystical experience I had while meditating in 1994. I saw and felt all the images, joy, and bliss as if they were occurring to me right now. It was totally experiential. I relived these three experiences again seeing all the visual images and again feeling all the blissful emotions.

Just as suddenly as it began, my life-review ended, I found my spirit continuing to move upwards through the darkness of space. The darkness around me had now developed a very deep-blue colour, and it had started to become brighter, more filled with light.

Suddenly, a luminous being of light appeared in front of me. The body of this being of light seemed to be made of translucent blue light. Its body looked half male and half female, with four arms held in unusual postures, and one leg raised forward. It looked a bit like statues of the "dancing Shiva" that I later saw. The being of light radiated a Divine loving aura and it felt to me that he/she was a saint, or an angel sent to meet me. He/she then spoke to me mentally, through telepathy or thought-transference. "It is not your time," he/she lovingly but firmly stated.

Immediately, I found my spirit back in my physical body again, sitting in the plane. The pilot eventually landed the plane safely at Toronto International Airport, but I remained in an extraordinary state of consciousness. I felt like I had no skin, no boundary between myself and the world around me. The next morning when I awoke, I found myself in a blessed state of ongoing mystical communion, which lasted for about two months.

Although I was never dead or even physically injured during this near-miss plane incident, my 1995 NDE had eleven of Dr. Moody's features of a classic NDE. The after-effect of ongoing mystical communion was the most profound after-effect of any of my multiple NDEs.

It is interesting to note that of the five Near-Death Experiences that I have had over the course of my life, this is the only NDE in which I experienced a life-review. This supports my clinical observation that every Near-Death Experience is unique — with differences in detail between different individuals' NDEs, and differences in detail between multiple NDEs had by one person over the course of their lifetime.

Anyone Can Have an NDE

It is important to realize that people of all ages, of any educational background or level of intelligence, can have NDEs. Several NDE researchers have documented hundreds of cases of children who have had them. In my clinical experience, I have encountered people who ranged in age from early childhood to their nineties when they had these experiences. NDEs can be triggered by any type of life-threatening illness or accident, even attempted suicide.

One of the most moving experiences that I have ever heard occurred to a forty-three-year-old mentally challenged woman with chronic schizophrenia who I'll call June. Her NDE occurred after an attempted suicide. This is the story as she told it to me:

> It was just after Christmas. I was very depressed. My family did not want to see me at Christmas and I was all alone. I knew that there was something wrong with my brain, and people called me crazy and retarded. I knew

I could never have a normal happy life like you see on TV so I decided to kill myself. I took my whole bottle of antidepressant pills and drank a whole bottle of vodka. Somebody had told me that would kill me.

When I passed out, I remember floating up out of my body and looking down at my body passed out on the floor. I felt sorry for my body. It was all covered in vomit. I must have thrown up and then passed out on it. I felt very calm, though, and I looked up and saw a dark tunnel with a light at the end of it. I went through the tunnel, and I came out at the most wonderful place you could ever imagine. There was this really bright light, and I saw my grandparents and other relatives who had already died around me. I felt love coming from everywhere, from everyone. I felt like I was being hugged by God. It was so beautiful. But my relatives told me that it was not my time to die. They told me in the nicest, loving way, that I should not try to kill myself, that I should go back. Suddenly I was back in my body again, and I woke up, covered in vomit on the floor.

I don't think I will ever try to kill myself again. But I know that there's nothing to be scared of when you do die. It's nice. But somehow I know that in the big plan of things I am supposed to live in this body with a retarded brain. Maybe I will teach somebody something ... maybe there is something good I am supposed to do, even in this messed up head and body.

June's experience highlights that NDEs can happen to anyone, including people with chronic psychiatric disorders. Her description of her NDE is extremely clear, and stood out as distinctly different from the auditory hallucinations she suffered from with her chronic schizophrenia. June's experience was also typical of many people who have an NDE while attempting suicide: They discover that they need to come back and deal with their lives to the best of their ability.

Distressing or Frightening Near-Death Experiences

Unfortunately, not all NDEs are positive. Tom Harpur cites Margot Grey's research that reports that up to one in eight of NDEs is perceived by the experiencer as negative or distressing. The reasons for this are not yet understood — and probably will not be until more research is done. Here is the story of a distressing NDE told to me by a woman I'll call Anna, a survivor of a Nazi concentration camp:

> I was about twenty years old when the experience occurred. I had been captured and put into this concentration camp three years earlier. I had seen both of my parents die of starvation. They had insisted upon giving me some of their food because we were not being given enough to eat. They thought that out of the three of us, I had the best chance to survive. The winter after they died, some sort of infectious diarrhea struck the camp. Sanitation was poor, and therefore the infection spread quickly. Many people died from the effects of the diarrhea.
>
> I became so weak from the fever and the diarrhea that I was unable to leave my cot. As I became severely dehydrated, I became too weak to eat or drink. I remember feeling my consciousness fade, my vision grew black. Suddenly I felt myself slip up, out of my body. I was floating above my unconscious body, looking down on it. I felt terrified. "No! No!" I screamed inwardly. "I do not want to die too!" I felt overwhelmed with fear and panic. I wanted desperately to get back into my body and wake up. I do not know how long I stayed out of my body, but it was the most horrible, terrifying sensation I ever had. The next thing I remember is waking up in my cot the next morning. My fever had come down during the night.

Anna's NDE was clearly not an inspiring or uplifting event, but as yet we do not know why. One fact Dr. Ring has discovered in his research, however, is that there does not seem to be any relationship between the precipitating event and whether the NDE is pleasurable or distressing. In other words, people who have very similar accidents or illnesses can have very different NDEs.

One factor contributing to a distressing NDE that I have observed is the dying person refusing to surrender to or turn to God. Several persons who recounted terrifying NDEs told me that they resisted going to the light, they resisted the NDE, or they refused to turn to God. Anna certainly fought against the experience. Her thoughts did not turn to God and she did not surrender to the Near-Death Experience.

A thirty-eight-year-old housewife, whom I'll call Lucille, also had a terrifying NDE, which she described to me as follows:

> I was at home one Saturday afternoon when I suddenly developed an excruciating headache. I called out to my husband and my daughter as I collapsed onto the kitchen floor. I lost consciousness. My husband dialed 911, and an ambulance came and took me to the hospital. The doctors discovered that I had suffered a severe brain hemorrhage, and I had to undergo emergency surgery in order to save my life.
>
> At some point after I lost consciousness, I felt myself float out of my body. Suddenly I was up by the ceiling, and I could see my husband and daughter, worried, huddled over my unconscious body. "No! I am not going to die!" I screamed inside my soul. I saw a tunnel with a bright yellow-white light at the end. I felt myself being pulled down the tunnel, toward the light. "No!" I screamed. I fought against the pull toward the light. Somehow I knew that the light was God, and I thought going to the light would mean death on earth. I desperately struggled against the pull toward the light. I thought constantly of my daughter, and I vowed that I would let nothing take me away from her. The struggle to resist the pull was horrible. I felt as if I was desperately clawing my way, swimming against a very strong

current in a river. I struggled to stay away from the light. I felt anger and fear. "No!" I kept saying to myself.

Finally, I regained consciousness in my body. I was now in the recovery room of the hospital, following my brain surgery. I was glad to still be alive, but I felt terribly upset by the ordeal I had been through.

Clearly, Lucille resisted the urge to turn to the light in her experience, and in fact, it seems that this resistance was what made her NDE nightmarish. When I asked her if there was anything unpleasant about the light, or the tunnel itself, she stated that there was not. In fact, she said the light radiated a very intense feeling of love. It was by this intense radiation of love that she recognized the light to be God. In tears, she admits that she just was not prepared to surrender to God, that she desperately wanted to stay alive, to be with her daughter.

In my clinical experience, there seem to be three subtypes of negative NDEs: 1) a lack of surrender to the Higher Power and resisting the pull out-of-body; 2) lower astral experiences of dark tormenting entities; and 3) nightmare-like distortions and confusion — which may be related to drugs or toxins affecting the brain and not actual NDEs.

Sometimes other experiencers describe their NDE as negative not because it was unpleasant or distressful in itself, but because they did not want to return to their body! They would have preferred to stay in the beauty, love, and peace of the light. Several people have told me that they felt angry about the NDE experience for this reason. They were living in physically abusive and/or psychologically destructive home situations at the time of their NDE. They felt angry at God after the NDE for sending them away from the loving light and back into their abusive situations.

A Frightening NDE Turns into a Positive NDE

One of the most dramatic negative NDE stories I have ever heard is the one told to a fellow International Association for Near-Death Studies researcher, Dr. M. Taylor Bach, and recorded on his video *A Message of Hope*. Pastor Howard Storm describes his NDE, which began as frightening and distressful but then shifted into a profoundly positive experience. His NDE began as what I call a lower astral experience, which later shifted to a mystical experience when he turned to God. Howard Storm was a businessman and atheist at the time of the NDE. I have paraphrased his description.

> About five years ago, I almost died from a bleeding ulcer. I recall lying in my hospital bed, awaiting emergency surgery, when I felt myself go faint, slipping into darkness. I tried to call out or move, but I could not. Suddenly I found myself standing at the side of my bed, looking down at my unconscious body. I tried to call out to the nurses, but I was unable to make any noise. I felt I was in a dark, heavy space. I thought that I must have died. The thought crossed my mind that I should pray, but I did not. I had been a vehement atheist for the last forty years of my life, and I was not about to change now.
>
> The darkness grew heavier. I felt myself go out of the room and down what seemed like a dark hallway, into a very dark and uncomfortable space. Slowly I became aware that there were dark presences in the shadows of the darkness. These presences started taunting me, poking my body and saying rude things using offensive language. I shouted at them to go away. Once again I had the thought that I should pray, but I did not. The taunting voices became louder, and their pokes started feeling as if their hands were claws and they were ripping my flesh. I was in agony and terrified. I begged them to stop hurting me, but they laughed and kept jeering at me and tearing at my flesh. Finally I felt completely destroyed. I was writhing in agony, crying out in physical pain and emotional devastation.
>
> Once again, the thought crossed my mind to pray. This time, I thought, "What do I have to lose?" However, I didn't know how to pray. Suddenly I recalled a phrase from a hymn I had sung in my childhood, "Jesus loves

me, this I know." I began to sing "Jesus loves me," making up words in parts where I had forgotten them. The taunting voices shouted at me as I sang, "Stop that! It's no use! There's nobody to hear you!" But as the voices ordered me to stop, I continued to sing, and then I started to pray, with heartfelt sincerity. "Please, Lord Jesus," I prayed, "if you really are out there, please help me!" As I continued to pray and sing, the dark entities seemed to move away. "Stop that, the light is hurting us," they said. I continued to pray earnestly.

Suddenly, I noticed a speck of light, far away, like a shooting star, moving toward me through the darkness. As the light moved closer and closer, the dark presences seemed to disappear, or dissolve in the light. As the ball of light drew near, I felt as if I was lifted out of the darkness and raised into the protection of this loving bubble of light. Although no words were spoken, I immediately sensed that this loving light was a spiritual being — Lord Jesus. The being of light carried me up through space, and into a phenomenally immense, even more brilliant light, which I recognized in my heart as God. As we moved into the light, I felt my soul embraced by God's infinite love.

I wept. I felt myself unworthy of such love, of such compassion. I felt ashamed of my many years of having maligned those with spiritual faith. I trembled, saying to the Divine light that I was unworthy, that there must have been some mistake. Without words, the light — God — informed me that there are no mistakes, that all are deserving of Divine love. I wept with joy and ecstatic bliss.

When my body was resuscitated in the hospital, I abruptly returned to the earthly plane. I was bursting with joy at this profound spiritual awakening, and I could not wait to share this story with all who would listen. I changed my life work, and am now a pastor, eager to tell everyone about God's love!

Howard Storm's story demonstrates that it is possible for a negative low-astral type of NDE to be turned into a positive white-light one through turning to God. This once again supports my hypothesis that a critical element in many distressing NDEs is the failure or refusal of the individual to turn to or surrender to God.

When I counsel people who have had a distressing NDE, I first try to understand which aspect of the NDE seemed frightening or distressing to them — the experience itself, the possibility of death, or the return to life. Then I try to help the person understand what psychological and spiritual lessons can be learned from this negative reaction to the NDE. Usually, I have found that persons who have had a distressing NDE can transcend the negative impact by trusting in the Divine wisdom of the loving light if they encountered it, and/or by addressing whatever psychological and/or spiritual issues need to be addressed — here on the earthly plane. Persons with nightmare-like distortions/confusion can be comforted by knowing the experience was drug or toxin induced.

The issue of frightening or distressing NDEs is complex and deserves a great deal more research.

Death NDEs

A fascinating group of Near-Death Experiences are those that occurred to persons when they were clinically dead for a period of time and later revived or resuscitated. In my research I have found that Death NDEs tend to be very powerful and dramatic in their impact on the experiencer. Of all the types of NDEs, I find Death NDEs tend be the most spiritually transformative.

Three dramatic death-type NDEs that have been vividly described in books written by their experiencers are Dannion Brinkley's Death NDE described in *Saved by the Light*, Betty Eadie's Death NDE described in *Embraced by the Light*, and my own 2003 Death NDE, in *Soul Lessons from the Light*. I was privileged to have had the opportunity to speak with both Dannion Brinkley and Betty Eadie in the past, and I have also heard the stories of several other Death NDEs from persons who were clinically dead during their NDE.

My 2003 Death NDE

Having had three mystical/white-light Near-Death Experiences as an adult and two out-of-body NDEs as a child, looking back, the NDE that felt the deepest to me was my most recent, 2003 NDE, when I died completely for a period of time. This happened on November 8, 2003, at Niagara Falls, Canada, when I slipped on some black ice, fell backwards hitting my head hard on rock pavement, and instantly died from a traumatic brain injury with a brain hemorrhage. Here is my story, which I describe in greater detail in *Soul Lessons from the Light*:

> After viewing Niagara Falls for the last time that evening, I turned and started walking along the walkway toward my car in the parking lot. Suddenly I slipped on an invisible patch of black ice, and fell backwards. My head hit the rock pavement hard. At the moment of impact I felt intense searing pain, like an axe chopping into my brain. My spirit instantly left my body. I found myself rapidly moving upward through the dark evening sky. Within a few seconds I completely lost awareness of my physical body, which now lay lifeless on the ground below me.
>
> The darkness of the evening sky quickly disappeared, and I found my spirit entering a place brightly radiating with white Light, the realm that I had seen in my 1979 NDE. Once again I felt permeated with profound unconditional love, the unconditional love of the omnipotent Higher Power underlying all creation, what I call God. The white Light was not blinding, but was soft and diffused, similar to the sparkling white luminescence one can view from an airplane as the plane rises through the bright glistening top layer of clouds, just before the plane breaks into the sunny sky above.
>
> I immediately saw two luminous beings of light, joyously welcoming me into the heavenly White-Light realm. I instantly recognized them. They were two great saints

whom I loved and revered and considered my Gurus, Paramahansa Yogananda and Mahavatar Babaji in their light bodies. I felt in awe in their holy presence.

The beings of light, my Gurus, telepathically informed me that I had died, that my "work" in the body of Dr. Yvonne Kason was finished now. There was a feeling of great joy in the Light, as if a joyous graduation celebration was being held in my honour. All communication was telepathic or intuitive, speech was not necessary. I felt indescribable joy, ecstasy, and Divine communion.

I then shifted into a blissful state of pure thought, pure consciousness, a plane glimpsing the infinite stillness and wisdom of the Absolute, with no visual images. Much was revealed to me during what seemed to be timeless time. Information was not communicated to me linearly, one fact at a time, but rather all at once in an "a-ha" experience, or revelation. It felt as if my expanded consciousness in the heavenly realm was now able to integrate vast amounts of information all at once. It felt as if while I had been incarnated in my physical body, the memory of my soul's experiences across many lifetimes had been obscured from my mortal view by a dark cloth or veil. Now in the Light realm it seemed as if the obscuring cloth or veil had been pulled away, and I could now see the big picture all at once. Many of my past lives were instantly revealed to me, and I could see the interconnectedness of my many experiences over many lifetimes. With this revelation, many aspects of my life as Dr. Yvonne Kason suddenly made sense to me.

Somehow the passage of time in the Light realm did not seem to correspond with the passage of time on the earthly plane. Past, present, and future all seemed to co-exist, or be beyond time.

At some point, after a period of timeless time, my beloved Gurus reappeared to me, spoke to me intuitively or telepathically again. "You may now choose whether to return to the maimed body of Dr. Yvonne Kason, and/or to reincarnate in the body of a baby, to further serve the Divine Mother."

Before my mind had time to think, my soul responded. It felt as if my response came out of my heart rather than out of my head. My bliss-filled heart devotedly responded, "Masters, please guide me. What is the higher choice? I want to do God's will."

Paramahansa Yogananda's loving inner voice floated through my soul with an exquisite sweetness, telepathically saying, "It will be more difficult, but to return." Before I had time to think, and without hesitation, my heart and soul instantly responded, "I accept."

Faster than the speed of thought, between the thoughts "I" and "accept," I suddenly found myself gasping a breath of life into my body. Returning to my previously dead body felt like suddenly waking up inside an ice cube. I immediately became aware of intense physical cold and an excruciating severe headache.

I have observed that Death NDEs, such as my 2003 NDE, differ from other "near-death" NDEs in certain ways. Death NDE experiencers usually report being welcomed, ushered into the afterlife by loving beings of light. This was true for Dannion Brinkley, Betty Eadie, and myself. The welcoming beings of light seem to be sent by the loving Higher Power to help the experiencer understand and adjust to their death transition. The beings of light may telepathically explain that the experiencer has died and their spirit has now entered the afterlife. Other times the experiencer somehow immediately knows that they have died.

During Death NDEs, often much is learned in the time spent in the heavenly realm of the loving light. Sometimes this learning occurs in revelations such as I experienced — with large amounts of information somehow being revealed all at once. Other times a large amount of detailed information is conveyed through elaborate "lessons" including complex visual experiences and instruction, which occurred to both Dannion Brinkley and Betty Eadie. In yoga philosophy, these differences are explained as experiencing "astral heaven," with powerful visual perceptions of white light realms, beings of light, and feelings of profound universal love and wisdom; versus experiences of the more subtle, casual plane of stillness and pure thought, permeated with the infinite wisdom and bliss of the Higher Power.

It is interesting to note that some NDE experiencers who were never clinically dead but were unconscious during their NDE have similarly reported learning elaborate "lessons" during their near-death time in the realm of white light. This phenomenon was recently reported by NDE experiencers Dr. Eben Alexander and Anita Moorjani.

Time Incongruence in NDEs

Many Death NDE experiencers report that the passage of time in the heavenly realm of Light does not seem to correspond with the linear passage of time as experienced here on earth. Past, present, and future may seem to coexist, or bend, as it seemed during my 2003 Death NDE. Some feel a difficult-to-describe sense of "timeless time," that somehow time is not moving forward in a linear fashion during the NDE. Some report that they felt they had a much longer experience in the light realm than the length of time passed according to earthly clocks. It is as if time can loop or bend in the NDE realm of light, to enable a long Near-Death Experience in a shorter earthly time frame. This was true of both my 1995 and 2003 NDEs.

Other NDE experiencers report a much shorter NDE than the length of time they were dead or unconscious. This was my experience in my childhood NDE at age eleven in the car accident, where my NDE memories are much shorter than the two or three days I was unconscious.

Yet another fascinating time phenomenon that some NDE experiencers report is that earthly time seemed to stand still during their NDE. As I recounted in my train station near-miss NDE at age five, some NDE experiencers report that although their consciousness felt like time was moving forward during the NDE, the events in the physical world around them seemed to stop, frozen in time, for the duration of the NDE.

Another time/space incongruity in some NDEs is the phenomenon of the experiencer feeling that their consciousness was two places at the same time during the NDE — both out-of-body in the white-light realm, and at the same time in their body to some degree. We currently have no explanation for these fascinating time incongruities reported to occur during NDEs.

Facing-Death NDEs

Technically, when Dr. Moody and other pioneering NDE researchers first began to refer to Near-Death Experiences in the 1970s and 1980s, they were limiting the definition of Near-Death Experiences to the out-of-body and mystical experiences that occurred when persons were clinically dead then later resuscitated, or when persons had a serious injury or illness and came very close to physical death. However, in my work I have come across many people who had NDEs when they had a close call and thought they were about to imminently die, when they were psychologically and emotionally facing their death, whether or not they actually became injured later.

Now I and many other doctors and NDE researchers have expanded our definition of Near-Death Experiences to include those NDEs that happen to persons who have a close call and think they are about to imminently die: Facing-Death NDEs. In my experience people who report Facing-Death NDEs often describe only a few of the typical features of an NDE, although they may report multiple features the same as a "near-death" type of NDE.

Several former soldiers have told me stories of Facing-Death NDEs, having an out-of-body experience on battlefields, seeing their lives flash before their eyes, or feeling the presence of protective, loving spirits when they were in situations so dangerous that they were convinced they were about to die. One elderly World War II veteran, whom I will call George, told me the following story about his Facing-Death NDE during that war.

> I was in the air force during World War II. On this particular day I and my co-pilot were flying with a small squad of bombers. We were flying somewhere over either France or Germany. Suddenly we were taken by surprise by a group of enemy fighter planes. The planes began to battle and fire

on each other. After several tense minutes of shooting, my plane was hit. A fire started burning on one of the engines, and my airplane started spiralling out of control, falling toward the ground. I was certain I was going to die.

Suddenly I felt a profound feeling of peace and calm come over me. I felt my consciousness leave my body, and I found myself back at my home in America with my wife, floating above her on the ceiling, it seemed. I watched her from above, as she sat by the fireplace reading, like she often did. I felt that I was saying goodbye.

Then abruptly my awareness jumped back into my body in the falling plane. My co-pilot had managed to pull the airplane out of its free fall. We were alive and safe! We then managed to safely fly the damaged aircraft to an allied landing strip.

From that day onwards, I never doubted that my soul would live on after death. The memory of this experience still gives me spiritual comfort, over fifty years later.

Although George was never actually dead or injured, George was convinced that he was facing imminent death during his NDE. George's Facing-Death NDE had five features of a typical NDE. It seems clear that his experience — even though he was not unconscious or physically harmed in any way — falls within the spectrum of NDEs.

Another moving Facing-Death NDE was told to me by a Vietnam war veteran, whom I will call Arthur.

I was serving in the U.S. army during the war in Vietnam. One day my platoon was engaged in a nasty firefight with a group of Viet Cong. At one moment I saw a grenade land on the ground two feet in front of me. "I'm going to die," I thought.

Suddenly I heard a strange roaring sound, and felt myself go out of my body. I seemed to go up a dark tunnel to somewhere high above my body into a large, light-filled space. It was indescribable — peaceful, quiet, and full of love. I began to flash through memories of significant events of my life, as if I was both remembering the events and briefly reliving them. Then I suddenly found myself back in the USA, back at my home, floating on the ceiling somehow, and watching my wife and children sleeping in their beds at home.

Abruptly I felt myself return to my body in Vietnam, with my buddy nudging my shoulder, urging me to move on. The grenade had been a dud, and had not exploded. I was safe.

Although I did not die that day, my experience changed me. My love for my family became much more important to me than it had been before. I remember the experience clearly to this day. I never spoke about it to my army buddies, because I thought they would think me crazy. But this experience absolutely convinced me that my soul will live on after death, whenever that actually comes.

Even though Arthur was never actually dead or even injured in this incident, his Facing-Death NDE had ten features of a classic NDE. Arthur was very grateful to be able to share the story of his NDE with me, and to receive my confirmation, as a medical doctor, that this indeed was a type of Near-Death Experience, even though Arthur had never actually been injured at the time.

Other Death-Related STEs

Facing-Death NDEs like those of Arthur, George, and me raise questions about what exactly triggers an NDE. The spiritual experiences of some other — and very different — groups that are close to death makes the question even more intriguing. Some persons who are close to death have "Deathbed Visions" — experiences that may parallel classic NDEs but that occur hours or days before they actually die.

Other persons may have powerful STEs when they are at no risk of death themselves, but rather relating to the death of somebody else, somebody that they are close to. When an STE happens at the moment of death of another, this is called a "Death-Watch Experience." When an STE happens weeks or months after the death of a loved one, where it seems the departed loved one is attempting to communicate, this is called an "After-Death Communication." I will discuss Death-Watch Experiences and After-Death Communications in the next chapter.

Deathbed Visions

Deathbed Visions are strong spiritual experiences that may be similar to NDEs, and which occur to people several hours or even several days before the actual moment of their death from a terminal illness, old age, or even an unexpected accident. Various researchers refer to these experiences as "Deathbed Visions," "deathbed experiences," "nearing-death awareness," or "end-of-life experiences." I will use the term "Deathbed Visions."

In my work as a family physician, I have dealt with many elderly patients with illnesses that will ultimately cause their deaths, and many younger persons with terminal illnesses such as cancer. On several occasions these dying persons have told me about having a vision or extraordinary dream that relates to their impending death. Many of my medical colleagues' patients have related similar accounts.

Deathbed Visions often have a number of typical NDE features. They may include a sense of peace and calm; a loss of fear of death; a mystical vision of beings of light — the luminous spirits of deceased loved ones who come to reassure them or accompany them; seeing a long, dark tunnel with a loving white light at the far end; and/or a mystical vision of a prophet or important figure from the dying person's religion, such as Christ or Moses. Sometimes Deathbed Visions are described as an experience wherein the veil separating the heavenly realm of the afterlife and our earthly reality becomes extremely thin, and the experiencer becomes able to see glimpses of the other side, or to talk with departed loved ones on the other side.

I and other health-care providers have found that people who have these Deathbed Vision experiences often interpret them as a clear sign that they will be dying soon. They are often considerably changed by the experience; they usually seem to accept their impending deaths much more calmly than before, and become more deeply at peace, more serene. Frequently, they may use their remaining time to tell their family members that they love them, to reassure them that they are ready to die, and to urge them not to grieve deeply. They will often reassure their friends and family that they are not afraid to die. Sometimes they even say that they welcome death.

One striking Deathbed Vision was told to me by an elderly woman whom I will call Marta. Marta's Deathbed Vision occurred in a dream she had shortly before her death at the age of eighty-nine.

> I had the strangest dream last night. I dreamt that I was somewhere beautiful, talking with my dearly beloved departed husband [he had died two years earlier] and my dear sweet father [he had died twenty years earlier]. They were both very happy to see me, and were welcoming me and embracing me. They looked wonderful, like they were both young and healthy again. Their bodies seemed to glisten and radiate light.
>
> Then my father spoke to me. He said "Marta, you belong with us now." I felt in my soul that this was true.

Marta confided in me about her Deathbed Vision, and that she thought it meant that she was going to die soon. Marta said that she felt ready to die, she felt at peace, and that she had lived a long, good life. She said she looked forward to seeing her husband and her father again, when the time should come. Marta died peacefully several weeks later.

The dying person's loved ones may also feel deeply reassured if they are told about the Deathbed Vision. One of the most striking examples of this I have ever heard was told to me by a woman whom I'll call April, who had lost two young sons at different times.

> My son Billy got leukemia when he was seven. He had been taking chemotherapy, and he seemed to be doing

well. The doctors were optimistic, and we didn't expect him to die.

Then one morning Billy told me that he had had a dream the night before. He said that in it his brother Bruce had come to see him and that he knew now that he would be dying soon. Billy wanted me to know that he knew everything would be all right.

Billy then turned to me and said, "Mom, why didn't you ever tell me I had a brother named Bruce, who died?" I was so overcome, I didn't know what to say. When Billy was an infant his brother Bruce had died in a car accident, and somehow we had never been able to tell him about it.

The next day Billy died, too. Although losing Billy was very hard, I held on to the idea that he and Bruce were together now, and somebody, somewhere was taking care of my two babies.

Even though the loss of her sons had happened years before, April was in tears as she told me this story. Still, she said again and again how much Billy's Deathbed Vision dream had reassured her and helped bring her some sense of peace.

I think Deathbed Visions are a blessing, a death-related STE, which by Divine grace occurs shortly before death, to prepare individuals for their final transition into the Light at the time of their actual physical death. I have heard several reports of persons having a Deathbed-Vision-type experience, even when they had no idea that they would be dying shortly.

I have become further convinced of this possibility because I had a beautiful mystical Deathbed Vision on November 8, 2003, starting a few hours before my slip-and-fall accident when I died [for a period of time] due to a traumatic brain injury and brain hemorrhage. I had no idea that I was about to "die" a few hours later that day.

The evening of November 8, 2003, I visited Niagara Falls, Canada, and meditated for a while on the platform at the base of the falls, as I had done several times before. I loved to meditate there because the roar and vibration of the massive waterfalls reminded me of the inner OM vibration. I could enter a deep meditative state very quickly there.

While meditating, about three hours before I unexpectedly died in the sudden slip-and-fall accident, I slipped into a beautiful state of ongoing mystical communion. I finally felt that I had found my way back "Home" again.

In this mystical state, with eyes wide open I saw a vision of a welcoming being of light whom I recognized immediately. It was the great saint Mahavatar Babaji, in his light body. I felt as if the veil separating earthly reality and the heavenly realm had disappeared almost completely. I was able to perceive both realities at the same time — the outer physical realm and the inner spiritual realm. I remained in that state of ongoing mystical communion for about three hours, while I resumed my worldly activities. In this ongoing mystical communion I ate dinner at the restaurant overlooking the falls, had a lengthy dinner conversation with my friend, and walked around viewing the falls.

Three hours after my Deathbed Vision began I had a slip-and-fall accident, suffered a traumatic brain injury and died, immediately slipping into a powerful Death NDE [which I described earlier]. The same being of light, saintly Mahavatar Babaji, again appeared to me after I died, this time accompanied by the saint Paramahansa Yogananda — both welcoming me into the loving white-light realm of the afterlife.

In my case, it seems that my November 8, 2003, experiences started with a Deathbed Vision a few hours before I died. Then, after my accidental death, I slipped seamlessly into a death transition. When I agreed to return to my previously dead body, this experience changed in nature to become a death-type NDE.

Terminal Lucidity

Another interesting phenomenon, that may sometimes occur during a Deathbed Vision, is called "Terminal Lucidity." During an episode of Terminal Lucidity, the medical condition of the dying person seems to temporarily dramatically improve. The dying person may become unexpectedly alert and coherent. They may use their lucid period to communicate some warm messages to their loved ones. I have been told several accounts in which Terminal Lucidity was so pronounced that a person suffering from dementia or Alzheimer's disease suddenly spoke clearly and coherently shortly before their death, even if they had not been mentally lucid for days or even months. Generally the period of Terminal Lucidity is temporary, and the person thus blessed usually dies the next day or so.

A Continuum of Experiences

From a research standpoint, my own 1979 NDE that I described in chapter 1 is interesting because it contained elements of both a Facing-Death NDE and a classic NDE. My Facing-Death NDE began before the plane crashed, immediately after the second engine on the plane failed and we rapidly began to lose altitude. As soon as I thought I was about to die and, in fear, the words "Oh God, I'm going to die" came into my mind, when I psychologically faced death, my NDE experience began. Later, as I was near drowning and my body began to freeze, I became physically close to death. I then experienced a deepening of my NDE, and more of the classic features: an inner roaring sound, floating out-of-body, going into the light, and a mystical experience — feeling a powerful loving force which I intuitively knew to be our Higher Power, God.

Based on my own multiple NDEs and on my clinical and research work, I have come to suspect that individuals who have had Facing-Death NDEs might well have gone on to have deeper NDEs if their experiences had lasted longer, or if they had come physically closer to death, as I did in 1979. It seems logical to me that the different types of NDEs we have been discussing all exist along a continuum.

NDEs and Transformation

Although some skeptical scientists still question the validity of Near-Death Experiences — and the role of kundalini awakening in NDEs still needs further study and scientific verification — few people can deny the transformative impact NDEs have on experiencers. In some ways NDEs are the most clear-cut type of Spiritually Transformative Experience. The moment of death or near death is usually so clearly defined and dramatic that experiencers can see distinctly the differences in their values and attitudes before and after the event. Betty Eadie, Dannion Brinkley, Dr. Eben Alexander, Dr. Mary Neal, and Anita Moorjani are some of the NDE experiencers who have become famous from their books, in which they describe their NDEs and the dramatic spiritual transformations they each experienced afterward.

In my own case, transformation occurred in several areas of my life after my 1979 NDE. I noticed immediate psychological changes in me. The NDE seemed to have a "growing-up" effect on my psyche. I noticed an immediate improvement in my relationships with my parents, and I healed my previously estranged relationship with my father. The NDE launched me to begin my personal healing and recovery work. My capacity to love and forgive increased, my spiritual convictions became greater, and my commitment to standing up for the truth became stronger.

This NDE also transformed me psychically. As I described in chapter 1, a few weeks after my 1979 NDE I had my first clear-cut psychic experience, or what is called by some researchers a "psychic awakening." Over the years, the number of different types of psychic experiences I have has increased gradually, my sensitivity has increased, and a gradual change in my consciousness has occurred.

Spiritually, the 1979 NDE transformed me greatly, as well. I developed a much greater urge toward prayer, meditation, yoga, and reading spiritual books. I felt drawn to reading daily from the Holy Scriptures, something I had never done before. My NDE absolutely convinced me of the reality of our Higher Power, God — not because I had read it from a book, but because I had personally experienced a glimpse of God, and knew the Higher Power to be a reality! I also totally lost my fear of death. I became convinced that our souls live on after death of the physical body, and this conviction has remained with me for the rest of my life, strengthened by my later NDEs and STEs.

In the years following my 1979 NDE and continuing to today, I also noticed a number of unusual physical sensations that I now realize are related to some degree of ongoing spiritual energy/kundalini activity. For example, episodically I feel rapid rushes of energy up my spine. These rushes might occur with STEs, during and after long meditations, or at any time when I receive a sudden spiritual insight or intuitive flash. I have also felt periods of unusual burning pains in my lower back, usually during times of intense spiritual concentration.

Recurrent inner sounds is another unusual body sensation I noticed after my 1979 NDE, again possibly related to ongoing kundalini activity. Initially, the inner sounds would occur mainly when I was meditating or deeply contemplating a spiritual topic, but the inner sounds became more frequent, then constant. At first the inner sounds sounded like the chirping of crickets, or sometimes like a large motor rumbling. After several years my inner sound changed into a constant "music of the spheres," a sound like distant wind chimes or tinkling bells, sometimes accompanied by a low-pitched roaring sound. According to the yogic tradition, these inner sounds are the astral sounds of the chakras, which are sometimes perceptible after the chakras have been awakened or activated by the spiritual energy/kundalini.

As I have shared, my life has been punctuated with several other powerful STEs over the years. From my clinical work and research, I now know that a similar long-term spiritual transformation process occurs to many people who have had powerful STEs or STEPs, including Near-Death Experiences.

Multiple NDE Experiencers

A new fascinating phenomenon that is emerging is that of the multiple NDE experiencer — persons who have experienced more than one NDE over the course of their lifetime. Dannion Brinkley now reports having had three NDEs over the course of his life. The pioneering IANDS researcher P.M.H. Atwater has written about having three Near-Death Experiences. I, in fact, have now had five Near-Death Experiences over the course of my life.

As I shared in this chapter, in the years following my 1979 Near-Death Experience I had two more adult NDEs. On February 27, 1995, I had a transformative Facing-Death NDE. Then, on November 8, 2003, I was blessed with my most powerful NDE of all, my Death NDE. All three of my adult NDEs transformed me tremendously — psychologically, psychically, and spiritually. Each NDE propelled my life forward, in an even more spiritual direction. Although each NDE was unique, different from the others in many ways, they also had many commonalities. They all confirmed the reality of the loving Higher Power, and confirmed the immortality of the soul, that the soul lives on after death of the physical body.

As I reflect upon the multiple NDEs and STEs that I have had over the course of my life, I wonder if my two childhood NDEs and/or my 1979 kundalini awakening somehow predisposed me to more NDEs and other STEs later in life. I think it very likely that persons who have had an NDE or another type of STE, a "spiritual awakening," and are subsequently undergoing the long-term spiritual transformation process, are indeed more susceptible than the average person to further STEs, especially if they are stimulating their spiritual process through regular meditation and spiritual living. Another fascinating possibility (for those who believe in reincarnation), is that perhaps multiple NDE/STE experiencers came into this lifetime predisposed to having STEs, including NDEs, because of spiritual efforts made in past lives.

Future research will be needed to determine whether or not having one NDE makes a person more susceptible to having future NDEs in a near-death situation. If my impression is correct, with the current advances in medicine and resuscitation techniques, multiple NDE experiencers may become more and more common in the future.

The vast diversity of NDEs, and the emerging phenomenon of multiple NDE experiencers like Dannion Brinkley, P.M.H. Atwater, and myself, are intriguing and fascinating topics for continued research!

6

DEATH-WATCH EXPERIENCES AND AFTER-DEATH COMMUNICATIONS

DEATH-WATCH EXPERIENCES (DWE) and After-Death Communications (ADC) are two very common types of STEs that occur to persons who are not close to death themselves. Rather, these types of experiences may happen to persons who are close to somebody else who dies. Basically, a Death-Watch Experience is an STE that happens to people at the time of someone else's death. An After-Death Communication is an STE which seems to be a message from a deceased loved one's spirit that occurs days, weeks, or months after a loved one's death.

I coined the phrase "Death-Watch Experience" (DWE) in 1995, and used it in my book *Farther Shores* (2000), because I couldn't find a name for these types of moment-of-another's-death spiritual experiences. Such a large number of people have told me about their Death-Watch Experiences and After-Death Communications that I decided it was important to add a chapter in *Touched by the Light* focused exclusively on DWEs and ADCs. Other researchers sometimes refer to Death-Watch Experiences variously as "Shared-Death Experiences," "End-of-Life Experiences," "Shared Crossings," "Deathbed Communications," or "Deathbed Coincidences." I will use my original terminology of "Death-Watch Experiences."

Types of Death-Watch Experiences

A Death-Watch Experience is an STE that happens to people who are not close to death. Rather, Death-Watch Experiences happen to persons when someone else dies. They are more likely to happen to persons who are in close physical proximity to someone who dies, and/or who are emotionally close to somebody who dies, or both. Although a Death-Watch Experience usually occurs at the time of the other person's death, it can also occur shortly before or shortly after the exact moment of death. On rare occasions a Death-Watch Experience can be shared by several people at once.

Although I have found that DWEs are more likely to happen when a person is physically at the bedside of the dying person, DWEs can also happen to individuals when they are at a distant location from the dying loved one. All types of Death-Watch Experiences can happen without the person being aware that their loved one is dying. After having a Death-Watch Experience, the experiencer often intuitively knows that the person has died, even if they had no awareness that they were in ill health.

Most persons having Death-Watch Experiences feel that they have glimpsed or felt another person's spirit during their death transition. These glimpses can be extremely varied. Some DWEs can be remarkably similar to a Near-Death Experience. Other Death-Watch Experiences may be brief visions of the spirit of their dying loved one, at around the time of their death. The departed spirit may seem to give a final blessing of love, or lovingly say goodbye. Other DWE experiencers hear their departed loved one's voice delivering a message. Some DWEs experiencers report they developed bodily pains or symptoms of a sickness they don't have, that turn out to be identical to the symptoms that their dying loved one had at their time of death. For others, a mystical experience is the most marked feature of their Death-Watch Experience, as if they were brushed by the Divine energy of an angel, who was helping their loved one cross over at their time of death. Still other DWE experiencers report being spontaneously pulled out-of-body, seemingly to help usher the spirit(s) of a departed person or persons toward the Light.

NDE-Like Death-Watch Experiences — Shared-Death Experiences

Some Death-Watch Experiences very closely resemble a classic NDE, and the experiencer feels they have shared in their loved one's death and crossing-over experience. I sometimes call these Shared-Death Experiences. Such was the case of a woman I'll call Louisa, who told me the following beautiful story of her Death-Watch Experience at the time of her husband's death:

My beloved husband Jim was diagnosed with advanced lymphoma about twenty years ago. Jim's condition deteriorated very rapidly. About three months after his cancer diagnosis, as I sat at Jim's bedside, a wonderful feeling of peace and calm somehow filled the room. The bond of love between us was gloriously open and strong. It was as if our hearts were joined as one. Although we never spoke the words, I felt we both knew intuitively that today would be the last day of his life.

We spent the day in deep, loving conversation. We talked about the many years of our marriage, and settled all the leftover bits of misunderstandings that we each had. We came to a point of intense, clear, unconditional love and mutual acceptance. Somehow, in this powerful atmosphere of peace and love, I could accept his approaching death, and I carefully listened to my beloved as he told me his last wishes. I felt as if God had cast a magical spell of love and clear thinking upon both of us that day, a spell that allowed us to clear all our unfinished business and to get to a place of pure love and forgiveness with each other.

When Jim had finished talking, we both became silent. I tenderly held Jim's hand in mine as he lay resting in his bed. I felt totally connected to him, in love, and at peace. Suddenly, I felt myself rise above my body, and I felt myself and Jim moving upwards. We were rapidly moving together up through a dark tunnel, toward a bright light. The light was radiating intense love. I could still feel myself holding Jim's hand. We glanced at each other. His face looked young and healthy, radiant with love, and he seemed to glow with an inner light. Somehow we were both floating upwards, being gently pulled up through the dark tunnel toward the beautiful white light at the far end. We both wanted to go to the loving light.

Suddenly, partway up the tunnel, I felt myself stop moving toward the light, as if I'd been stopped by an invisible force field. I felt Jim's hand slip out of mine as he kept on moving upwards in the tunnel toward the light. For an instant he stopped and turned his head to look at me. Jim's face beamed a smile that radiated a wave of love toward me, as if to say goodbye, then he turned his face away and continued to move up toward the light. I wanted to go with him! I struggled to push myself up toward him. The next instant I was aware that I was in my body, back in the bedroom sitting at Jim's bedside, holding his now lifeless hand. Jim had died. I wept.

Now, many years later, I can never forget that precious day of grace, and the experience that I believe was glimpsing and sharing in Jim's death experience. Although I miss Jim tremendously, I take comfort in the fact that I know that he is at peace. He has gone home to the loving beautiful light, to what I call God. Sharing in Jim's death experience helped give me the strength to carry on after his death. I know we will be together again one day.

Louisa was in tears when she told me this story. She had been holding this extraordinary experience as a secret in her heart for almost twenty years. She had never told anyone about her Death-Watch Experience, because she had been afraid that they would label her as crazy or dismiss her experience as a flight of imagination. Talking with me was the first time that she had felt comfortable to describe her experience to anyone. Louisa was grateful when I reassured her that she was not crazy or imagining things, and that I had heard many stories similar to hers. She was happy that I could finally give her experience a non-pathological name, a Death-Watch Experience.

Although Louisa felt a tremendous loss at the death of her beloved husband, she said that her Death-Watch Experience, her sharing in Jim's going to the loving light of God, has been a great comfort to her throughout her grief. Louisa had not been a particularly religious person before Jim's death, but after the DWE, Louisa became convinced of the reality of Spirit, and that the soul lives on after death. She said she now knows that there is nothing to fear in death — that a loving God awaits us when we turn to the light. Louisa's story is, in my opinion, a classic and very beautiful NDE-like Death-Watch Experience.

Body-Symptom Death-Watch Experiences

Some Death-Watch Experiencers report that they had bodily pains or symptoms of a sickness at the time of their loved one's death, that turn out to be identical to the symptoms that their dying loved one had. A woman whom I will call Daisy told me of such a body-symptom Death-Watch Experience that she had at the time of her father's death. Daisy was at home in Toronto, Canada, on the day that her father died. Her father was a great distance away, travelling in Europe, at the time of his death. Here is Daisy's story:

> On the day that my father died, I was at home with my husband and children, doing my usual morning routine. I knew my father was out of the country, travelling in Europe for a few weeks. I thought he was healthy, and I had no idea that he was having any serious health problems.
>
> Without warning, while I was washing the dishes in the kitchen I suddenly developed severe, crushing chest pain. I felt overwhelmed. My head was spinning. I felt like a vise-grip was squeezing my chest, and I could hardly breathe. I doubled over in pain, and sank down onto a chair, gasping for air. I wondered if I was having a heart attack!
>
> Suddenly I had a vision of my father's face, radiant with light. He seemed to beam me love. Simultaneously, the chest pain I had been having disappeared, and I could now breathe freely again. The vision of my father's face lingered for a few seconds, then disappeared.

I immediately wondered if my father had had a heart attack in Europe. A few minutes later the phone rang. I received the phone message confirming that my father had indeed collapsed a few minutes earlier with severe chest pain and shortness of breath. Before the ambulance could arrive, my father had died, with what was later confirmed as a massive heart attack.

Daisy had her body-symptom Death-Watch Experience at the exact time of her father's heart attack and death, even though she was thousands of miles away from him at the time, and even though she was not at all consciously aware that her father was ill and dying. I have heard many DWE reports from people who were miles away from their loved one who died. I think that it is the bond of love between people that links them in consciousness, enabling persons to sometimes experience their loved one's body symptoms, glimpse aspects of their loved one's spirit, or glimpse aspects of their loved one's death transition, in a Death-Watch Experience.

Death-Watch Visions

Death-Watch Visions are the type of Death-Watch Experience that have been reported to me the most frequently. Death-Watch Visions may be of many types. Often brief visions are seen of what appears to be the spirit of the dying loved one, at or near the time of their death. The vision may be a glimpse of the departed loved one's luminous face, which seems to radiate a final blessing of love or a goodbye.

The Death-Watch Vision may occur when an experiencer is awake, as it did to Daisy at the end of her body-symptom DWE, or it may occur when the experiencer is asleep, in the form of a clear and lucid vision that feels more vivid than a dream. This was true for me, when my beloved grandfather died unexpectedly in 1991. My grandfather's spirit appeared to me in my sleep, to say goodbye. Here is the story of my Death-Watch Vision when my grandpa died:

My grandfather and I were very close, although he lived in Switzerland and I lived in Canada. One night while I was sleeping at home in Canada, I had a clear and vivid "dream" in which my grandfather appeared to me. His face was as I had never seen it — the face of his youth. Grandfather's youthful appearance surprised me, because I had never known him when he was young. I had always seen and known my grandfather as an older man! Grandfather's now youthful face was radiant, and beamed love toward me.

There was no verbal communication between us in this vision. But, I somehow knew that my grandfather had died, and that he had come to say a loving goodbye to me. I woke up from my sleep, with a clear vivid memory of the experience. About half an hour later my telephone rang. I knew immediately what the message was that I was about to hear: Grandpa had died.

Some persons sitting at a dying loved one's bedside report a Death-Watch Vision of seeing an orb of light, or the spirit, leave their loved one's body at the time of death. Others report seeing a being of light or an angel at the bedside, which at the moment of death accompanied the spirit of their loved one as it departed their body and rose out of the room. These Death-Watch Visions seem to be brief visual glimpses of the loved one's spirit crossing over to the "other side" at the moment of death. This was true of the Death-Watch Vision I had in 2009, at the time of my beloved mother's death. I was sitting at my eighty-five-year-old mother's hospital bedside when it occurred.

My mom was dying of severe pneumonia. I had been praying over mom and reading to her from the Bible, which had been her dying request of me. At her moment of death, I was sitting at her bedside holding her hand and singing a hymn to her, "The Lord is my Shepherd."

In the middle of my singing, I suddenly felt as if a wisp of energy slipped out of mom's hand held in mine.

The next moment in my mind's eye I saw a radiant white image of my mom's spirit above her body. She looked young and beautiful. She was dressed in a radiant white ball gown, as if she were going to a formal dance like she and my father loved to do when they were young. Then the radiant white image of my long-deceased father appeared above her. Dad looked young and handsome, as he did as a young man. Dad was dressed in an elegant suit, appropriate for a formal dance. Dad held out his arms to embrace my mother, and I saw them waltz up together, arm in arm, into the Light.

My vision ended abruptly. I finished the hymn I was singing, although mom's body had now stopped breathing. A nurse entered the room a few minutes later, and confirmed what I already knew. My mother had died.

The memory of my Death-Watch Vision, of seeing my father welcoming my mother into the Light, gave me great joy and comfort during my time of loss, and continues to uplift me to this day. Despite my grief at the loss of my beloved mother, I take great comfort in knowing that Mom and Dad are together again, reunited in the bliss and love of their youth.

Others not at the bedside when their loved one dies have reported Death-Watch Experiences consisting of seeing their loved one's face appear in a mirror at the time of their death. This Death-Watch Vision in a mirror was told to me by a man in his forties whom I will call Bruce. Bruce recounted:

My mother had been unexpectedly hospitalized with a massive stroke in a city that was a drive of several hours away from me. I immediately phoned my sister who lived close to me, and together we quickly packed our things and started the long drive to mother's hospital.

When we were still about an hour away from the hospital, I suddenly saw my mother's face clearly in the rear-view mirror. She was just looking at me, smiling. I could see her face clearly for several seconds, then it slowly disappeared.

"I don't think we are going to make it in time." I told my sister. "I think mom just died." Sure enough, when we finally arrived at the hospital we were given the sad news. Our mom had died about an hour before we arrived, exactly at the time that I saw her face in the rear-view mirror.

Auditory Death-Watch Experiences

Death-Watch Experiences are sometimes auditory, and may include hearing the dying loved one's voice speaking a parting message, asking a question, or even asking for help. The fascinating story of an auditory DWE that occurred at the time of death of a complete stranger was told to me by a paramedic ambulance attendant whom I will call Michael. Here is Michael's story:

I was working as a paramedic in an ambulance the day that I had this experience. The ambulance was called to the scene of a high-speed car accident on a country highway. When my ambulance arrived at the scene, we discovered that the driver of one car had walked away virtually unbruised, but the driver of the second vehicle, a young woman who apparently had not been wearing her seat belt, had been mortally injured. We attempted unsuccessfully to resuscitate her, but she remained vital signs absent.

As I began to cover up the young woman's lifeless body, I was surprised to hear a woman's voice in my head crying out, "Help me, please!" she cried. "What's going on? I can't move my body." The young woman's cold, deceased body lay on the pavement below me. "Help me!" her voice in my head repeated.

I mentally said to the woman "You've been in a serious car accident." She mentally responded "Yes, I know." I went on mentally, "You were very seriously injured, and we can't resuscitate you." "I'm scared!" she replied, "What am I supposed to do?" I remembered what I had heard about NDEs and the light that souls go to after death. I therefore said, "Look around you. Do you see a light?" After a brief pause her voice mentally responded "Yes, I can see a light now." "Go to the Light" I urged her. "It is so beautiful" she responded. Then there was silence.

Her soul went into the light, I believe.

Michael said that he had been beside many people when they died, as part of his professional work as a paramedic. However, this incident was the only time that he had a spiritual or paranormal experience at the time of a patient's death. It remains a mystery as to why at times DWEs occur, and at other times they do not.

Brushed-by-an-Angel Death-Watch Experiences

For some experiencers, a mystical experience is the most marked feature of their Death-Watch Experience. Several people have told me that they felt as if they had been brushed by an angel, at the time of their loved one's passing. They experienced an exquisitely beautiful spiritual transmission, as if they were touched by and blessed by the loving energy of a higher spiritual being, or an angel, who was helping their loved one's spirit cross over at their time of death. A colleague whom I will call Harry, a long-time meditator and student of yoga, told me of his DWE, which included a mystical experience and the perception of an angelic being at the time of his father's death. Here is Harry's beautiful DWE story:

> My elderly father was hospitalized for the last two weeks of his life. The doctors had told us that he was dying, so I and the family were prepared for his impending death. Because we had been raised Roman Catholic, I thought it important that I pray and meditate at father's bedside each day when I came to visit. On the day that father died, I was in his hospital room, praying at his bedside.

I began to notice something was different from before, as a wonderful aura of peace and stillness began to fill the room. The vibration of the room seemed to somehow become sweetly spiritualized. I opened my eyes, and to my surprise I could see the hazy image of a radiant light-being standing at my dying father's bedside. The being had the form of an angel. The angel exuded an aura of profound unconditional love. I saw the angel reach out its hand to my father. I watched as my father's spirit lifted out of his physical body, and saw father's spirit take the angel's outstretched hand. Suddenly the two moved upwards together. The angelic being brushed me, as they moved away and disappeared.

Upon receiving the brush from the angel, I suddenly went into a deep mystical state of ecstasy. I went into a profound state of expansion, of peace, of bliss. I remained in that expansive mystical state for a long time. I was roused to awareness of my body again when a nurse doing her usual rounds came into the room to check on my father's condition. She confirmed what I already knew, that my father had died quietly in his sleep.

Another time when people have frequently reported mystical experiences at the time of another's death, a "brushed by an angel" type of Death-Watch Experience, is upon the death of a saint. Sri Daya Mata, an advanced disciple of Paramahansa Yogananda, stated in the film *Awake: The Life of Yogananda*, that, while present at Yogananda's side in 1952 at his moment of death, she felt a tremendous spiritual transmission permeate her soul.

I heard a similar account from a fifty-five-year-old deeply spiritual man whom I will call Francis. He recounted a mystical brushed-by-an-angel Death-Watch Experience when at the bedside of a yogic saint when she passed away.

I had the good fortune of being in the room when an elderly female saint that I revered passed away a few years ago. I was visiting her together with a few nuns and monks of her lineage. During the last hour of her life, her room was profoundly peaceful. She lay silently in her bed with her face beaming with joy, as she gazed, eyes half opened, up into the heavens it seemed. We visitors were all sitting quietly in her room, praying or meditating. As her death approached, the vibration in the room became increasingly powerful and uplifting. It felt like we were all sharing in her dying experience of the veils getting thinner between our realm and the astral heavens.

The intensity of the light and the spiritual vibration kept getting stronger, until at her moment of death a pulse of intense spiritual energy hit all of us in the room, like a strong wave. It felt to me like she had brushed us all with her spirit, and had blessed us with her spiritual energy at the moment of her crossing to the other side. I was instantly cast into a deep, expansive, mystical state of consciousness. I stayed in that deep ecstasy, peace, and bliss for almost an hour after her passing. Others in the room shared with me later that they too were blessed with a deep mystical experience when the beloved saint passed on. This mystical experience had a profound and lasting impact on me, and I am sure it did for others too.

Ushering Death-Watch Experiences

Another fascinating type of Death-Watch Experience reported by STE experiencers is an ushering type of DWE. In this type of Death-Watch Experience, experiencers report being spontaneously pulled out-of-body, seemingly to help usher the spirit of a departed person or persons toward the Light. This may occur with persons that the experiencer knows, or with complete strangers.

Ushering DWE with strangers has been reported to me by several people, related to major world disasters. These experiencers stated that at the time of some major natural disasters and/or catastrophic world events, at the exact time when many people died suddenly, they spontaneously felt themselves swept out-of-body and they found their spirit above the scene of the disaster somehow. They could see the spirits of many confused souls of persons who had died, hovering around their now dead physical bodies in the wreckage. The experiencers felt instinctively or intuitively prompted to help the confused souls find their way up into the Light.

I have heard several powerful accounts of ushering Death-Watch Experiences that happened to different people on September 11, 2001, at the time of collapse of the two World Trade Center towers in New York, during the terrorist attack. I was one of them. Here is the story of my DWE on September 11, my first ushering type Death-Watch Experience:

> During the terrorist attacks on the World Trade Center in New York on September 11, 2001, I was watching the events on television as they unfolded. I watched in horror as the two towers collapsed. I began to pray for the victims.
>
> Abruptly, I felt as if my breath had been sucked out of me and I was swept into a deep meditative state. I was immediately out of my body, and found my spirit thousands of miles away, hovering above the wreckage at the collapsed World Trade Center in New York. I could see hundreds of spirits departing their newly dead bodies and rising rapidly up into the light.
>
> I could see some spirits of newly dead persons, including some deceased children, who seemed to be confused. They remained low to the ground in the thick darkness around the wreckage.
>
> Instinctively, I somehow knew that I must try to help the confused souls understand that they had died, and help them find their way into the light. It seemed that other spirits were there also helping some of the newly deceased to find their way up into the light. With that thought, my spirit was suddenly down with the group of confused spirits. "Go to the light," I repeatedly urged them. "God

will look after your families. You have passed over now. Go to the light," I mentally repeated. Several souls seemed to hear my mental message and indeed looked upwards, then rapidly moved up into the light.

I saw the spirits of two young children, who seemed to be stuck in the darkness, clinging to the worldly wreckage, looking for their parents. As a mother, my heart leapt out to these young children's spirits. Instinctively, my spirit went down to them, and took them both by the hand. "Come with me," I comforted them. "You will be safe with me. I'm a Mommy. I will take you to the light." The two young spirits came with me, finally looked up, saw the light above, and I released their hands as they floated up into the light.

I had never previously had such an experience related to any worldly disasters. In retrospect, I simply interpret my ushering Death-Watch Experience as happening because I was a person of faith, and God called me that day to help some of these suddenly deceased souls cross over into the light. I also sensed that many other people were brought there in spirit by God as well, to help souls cross over into the light.

Many persons' stories of ushering Death-Watch Experiences, when they felt intuitively drawn to help confused, newly deceased souls cross over into the light, seem to confirm the wisdom of many religious traditions, which encourage clergy and relatives of the newly deceased to pray over the body, to read out loud from holy scripture, and to sing hymns beside the body. DWEs suggest that these sacred prayers, readings, and hymns may perhaps be perceived by the newly deceased spirit, and may actually help them in their death transition to realize they should turn to God in their consciousness, to cross over into the light.

As extraordinary as these and other Death-Watch Experiences might seem at first glance, I have heard so many of these types of stories told to me in confidence, by healthy, well-adjusted people, that I have become convinced of the reality of this type of STE. I am especially convinced because I have had Death-Watch Experiences myself! Unfortunately, up until now, most people who have had Death-Watch Experiences have been afraid to discuss their experiences openly. This is largely due to the lack of public awareness of all STEs, including Death-Watch Experiences, and due to the tendency in the last century for many doctors and psychologists to misinterpret spiritual and paranormal experiences as hallucinations and a sign of mental illness. As a result, most Death-Watch experiencers, like other STE experiencers, have remained secretive, in the closet, afraid to publicly talk about their powerful experiences.

I am hoping that by my spreading awareness about Death-Watch Experiences and other STEs in this book, and by my sharing the stories of some of my own STEs, it will help more people have the courage to come out of the closet and talk about their own experiences. I think as more people speak openly about their STEs, it will help increase spiritual awareness on our planet. As I will discuss further in chapters 19 and 20 on meditation and finding our way home, I believe that increased spiritual awareness is very important to the future of our planet, to help all people realize that we are truly spiritual beings, incarnated here on earth to learn and grow, and to help promote a greater sense of the love and connectedness between all peoples, to ultimately help promote world peace.

After-Death Communications

An After-Death Communication (ADC) is an STE — a spiritual or paranormal experience — in which it seems that a deceased loved one's spirit is communicating a message to a living friend or family member, and which occurs days, weeks, or months after a loved one's death. To be defined as an ADC, this message from the deceased loved one must be received directly and spontaneously, without the use of any intermediaries like psychics, mediums, rituals, or devices of any kind.

In my clinical experience, ADCs are quite common. Bill Guggenheim and Judy Guggenheim, authors of *Hello from Heaven: A New Field of Research — After-Death Communications — Confirms that Life and Love Are Eternal*, have been doing extensive research on ADCs. They have documented over three thousand cases of ADCs, and estimate that 20 to 40 percent of the population of the USA have had one or more ADCs. Further research will be needed confirm the actual prevalence of ADCs as well as other STEs. Jan Holden, Ed.D., has conducted fascinating research on ADCs as well, including their spiritual and psychological impact.

Many ADCs occur within a few days after a loved one has died. They may include a brief vision of what seems to be the deceased loved one's spirit. A young woman whom I will call Flora told me about two separate vision-type ADCs that she experienced after her father's death.

I was heartbroken when Papa died a few years ago. We had been extremely close. I grieved intensely. At Papa's funeral four days after his death, I was despondent with intense grief as I gazed at his lifeless body in the open casket. Prompted by a strange inner urge to look up, I was amazed to see the spirit of my father standing at the head of his coffin. Papa's spirit was radiant, lovingly looking at me. I heard his voice in my head, gently speak "Do not grieve so. I am fine."

Papa's spirit remained there at the head of the coffin for some time. I took my seat in the chapel and watched Papa's spirit as he observed his friends and relatives who streamed by to view his lifeless body in the open casket. I have no idea if anyone else was aware that Papa's spirit was there that day. Finally, Papa's spirit disappeared from my view.

I still grieved the death of my father, but I felt comforted by seeing his spirit at the funeral. About ten days later, when I was at work at my job at the local bakery, suddenly, for no apparent reason, I once again saw the spirit of Papa! This time he was standing a few feet away from me, in the bakery. His face looked young and radiant. He said nothing to me this time, but I felt in my heart that he was saying a loving goodbye. His image disappeared from view, and I have not seen Papa's spirit since.

Physical After-Death Communications

Other persons have reported ADCs that involve physical experiences related to their deceased loved one, such as sounds, smells, objects moving, or radios and TVs turning themselves on at symbolic times. An elderly widow whom I'll call Penelope told me the following story of her physical ADC, which occurred after her beloved husband died:

> I felt empty and missed Burt terribly after he died. We had been married for over sixty years, so the majority of my life had been spent together with him. I found evenings to be the time I missed him the most. We had been in the habit for many years of sitting together in front of the fireplace in the evening after dinner. Burt would sit in his favorite rocking chair and smoke one cigar. I would sit in the easy chair and do my knitting or read a little.
>
> About a week after Burt died, as I was sitting in my easy chair knitting after dinner, I started to clearly smell the strong aroma of Burt's cigar. I glanced into his ashtray by the rocking chair to see if perhaps some cigar ash had somehow lit up, but the ashtray was washed clean and empty, just as I had left it. As the strong aroma of Burt's cigar smoke continued to surround me, I noticed that Burt's rocking chair started to rock. *Oh Burt, it is you*, I thought with delight. I knew in my heart that Burt's spirit was around me, and that he was letting me know in a way that only I would recognize, that he was still alive in spirit, and that he was fine.

Physical ADCs can sometimes be perceived by several people at the same time. It seems to those who report this type of ADC that their departed loved one wanted the whole group or whole family to know that they are fine, and still living on in spirit. One man whom I will call Jerry told me of a striking physical ADC that happened to him in the presence of his wife and his father.

> Mother passed away with breast cancer several years ago. Her death hit the entire family very hard, especially my

father. My father came to live with my wife and myself for a few weeks, so that we could offer him some support through his time of loss.

About one week after mother's funeral, while the three of us were sitting around the kitchen table eating lunch, suddenly the radio on the kitchen counter turned itself on.

The song "Amazing Grace" was being played on the radio. We all looked at each other in astonishment as we listened to "Amazing Grace." This song had been one of mother's favorite hymns, so much so that we arranged to have it sung at mother's funeral. At the end of the song I went and turned the radio off. We were all deeply moved. We all believed in our hearts that mother's spirit had come to us that day. She made her presence known to us in a way that we were clearly able to understand, by her spirit somehow turning the radio on, at the exact moment that her favorite hymn, "Amazing Grace," was being played.

Messages in After-Death Communications

Another fascinating type of After-Death Communication is one in which the spirit of the deceased loved one seems to communicate an important message, or some unfinished worldly business, to their living friend or family member. A middle-aged woman whom I will call Marianne told me about her ADC in which her departed mother seemed to urgently wish to communicate an important message to her. Here is Marianne's story:

Mom died a few years ago, after suffering with dementia the last three years of her life. I loved mom dearly, but we had been unable to have any deep conversations for some time, due to her worsening dementia. About two weeks after mom's death, I suddenly had a vision in which I could see my mother's face. I could also smell the strong scent of her favorite perfume.

Mother's voice spoke clearly to me in my mind. She seemed mentally clear and sharp, as she had been before her dementia began. "Please forgive me! I was deceived," she urgently told me. Mentally I responded, as tears of joy streamed down my face, "Mom, there is nothing to forgive. I love you!" But the image of mother's face intensified in my mind, and her voice repeated in my mind, "Please forgive me! I was deceived!"

At that time I was not aware of anything mother had done while alive that might lead her spirit to ask for my forgiveness. However, due to the urgency and insistence in mother's voice, I offered mom my forgiveness, even though I did not know for what reason. "Okay mom, I forgive you! I love you!" I mentally said to her. We both radiated love toward each other, then slowly the image of my mother's face disappeared from view, as did the scent of her perfume.

It was a couple months later that I finally discovered the reason mother wanted my forgiveness. As I was striving to get mom's financial affairs in order, I discovered that she had been swindled out of most of her life savings by a dishonest conman. Mom had signed a contract a few years earlier without my knowledge, which was very unusual for her. She had invested most of her life savings in the conman's fraudulent business scheme. The bulk of mother's lifetime savings had now disappeared, and could not be recovered, despite my efforts to collect mom's invested funds through legal action.

I think that after mom died her dementia was removed from her, and then with her renewed mental clarity mom realized that she had made a big mistake in agreeing to put her money into the conman's fraudulent business scheme. Her spirit seemed to feel guilty that she had not consulted with me first, as she probably should have, and also that the bulk of my inheritance funds had now been lost through the swindle. I am convinced that my mother was indeed deceived by the smooth-talking conman, as her spirit told me. In my heart I absolutely and completely forgive my mother. I see her as the victim of crime, the victim of elder-abuse and fraud.

I am very grateful and take comfort in the fact that mom's spirit came to me in this vision, and that I forgave her spirit. I now know that mom and I are at complete peace with each other in our hearts, despite the big financial loss.

After-Death Communications and Death-Watch Experiences offer us a message of love and hope. The stories of Death-Watch Experiences and After-Death Communications, like NDEs, confirm what the world's major religions have taught us, that our souls live on after death of the body. We are truly immortal spiritual beings, here on earth having a bodily learning experience. Further, Death-Watch Experiences and After-Death Communications can sometimes cause a spiritual awakening, or, like other STEs, sometimes propel the experiencer into a process of spiritual transformation of consciousness.

7

PSYCHIC EXPERIENCES

A TREMENDOUS AMOUNT OF RESEARCH has been done on intuition, psychic abilities, and psychic phenomena over the last few decades. And although not everyone believes they exist, and some people share the perception that psychic phenomena are not real but rather are based on deception or trickery, many respected scientists, psychiatrists, doctors, and psychologists do think some psychic phenomena are genuine. Dr. Stanislav Grof, Dr. Kenneth Ring, and Dr. Carl Jung are among those who have written about paranormal phenomena and have been convinced of their reality.

Psychic Awakening — or psychic opening — has become a generally accepted term for describing the onset of psychic experiences in a person who has not previously had them, or the development of new, different, or more powerful experiences in a person who has already had some type of psychic or milder intuitive experiences. In general, the term Psychic Experience can refer to almost any type of paranormal experience in which the experiencer perceives something that cannot normally be perceived by the five senses.

In my clinical experience I have found that Psychic Awakenings and Psychic Experiences are extremely common in people who have had mystical experiences, Classical Kundalini Episodes, and Near-Death Experiences, and I have become convinced that they are a natural part of the process of spiritual transformation of consciousness. In fact, almost every person I have ever counselled who has had an STE has noticed either the onset or the development of enhanced intuition and psychic abilities at some point after their STEs began. Extremely powerful Psychic Awakenings and Psychic Experiences can also be STEPs. As mentioned in chapter 4 on Spiritual Energy/Kundalini Episodes, the opposite is not true. Not everyone having psychic experiences is undergoing spiritual transformation.

Some unique individuals are born with the gift of certain psychic abilities, such as clairvoyance or clairaudience. Such individuals, sometimes called "indigo children," have been portrayed in many popular movies and television series as mediums, who can see and/or communicate with the spirits of dead persons. These individuals psychically gifted from birth are not the focus of this chapter. Rather, I am focusing on individuals who spontaneously develop new psychic abilities/episodes while adults, as an STE.

Psychic experiences, of course, take many different forms, and they are defined in a variety of ways. For these reasons, I have made a fairly extensive — but not exhaustive — list of common psychic experiences and provided definitions based on those developed and used by the Academy of Intuitive Studies in California, with additions based on my clinical experience.

Types of Psychic Experiences

1. *Abstract intuition.* Automatically knowing the answer to a problem without having to go through the logical steps of thinking and learning.
2. *Astral travel.* Episodes in which the spirit (sometimes called the astral body or spirit personality) seems to leave the physical body and travel to another place, time, or dimension.
3. *Automatic writing.* Writing or some other creative endeavour done without conscious thought by the experiencer; it is often assumed that a "spirit guide" connects in some way to the experiencer's hand or arm and uses it to write messages, paint, draw, or play a musical instrument.
4. *Clairaudience.* Mentally perceiving or actually hearing sounds or voices that are beyond the range of natural hearing.
5. *Clairsentience.* The ability to feel and know the true feelings of another, including the ability to locate pain in another, by sensing it in one's own body.

6. *Clairvoyance.* (1) The ability to see auras, subtle energy fields, or chakras; (2) the ability to see meaningful colours, patterns, or symbols that are not normally visible; (3) the ability to see objects or events that are concealed or beyond the natural range of sight, including seeing spirits of the deceased, and remote viewing of worldly events.

7. *Psychic or spiritual healing.* The ability to heal others by touch (also called "the laying on of hands"); the related experience of being healed by the touch of another, or being healed through prayers or focused thoughts.

8. *Out-of-body experiences.* Episodes in which the spirit seems to leave the physical body, but remains within sight of or in the general location of the physical body.

9. *Past-life recall.* The ability to know, see, or clearly sense what seems to be previous-life incarnations.

10. *Precognition.* The ability to see, know, or emotionally sense the future; this includes having premonitions, prophetic dreams, and premonitory visions.

11. *Psychometry.* The ability to receive intuitive information about a person or object by touching either the person or the object with one's hands.

12. *Communication with spirit guides.* The ability to communicate with what seems to be a spirit helper, guardian angel, or guide by seeing, hearing, feeling, knowing, or smelling their presence.

13. *Telekinesis.* The ability to move objects by thought or mental influence (also called psychokinesis).

14. *Telepyrokinesis.* The ability to start fires by thought or mental influence (also called pyrokinesis).

15. *Telepathy.* The ability to send and/or receive thoughts or mental images to or from another person.

16. *Trance channelling.* A phenomenon in which the experiencer's own personality seems to step aside, and another seemingly disembodied spirit personality uses the experiencer's physical body to communicate.

17. *Mediumship.* The ability to hear, see, and/or feel spirits of what seem to be disembodied deceased souls.
18. *Materialization.* The ability to make solid objects or persons appear out of thin air. Includes stigmata.
19. *Bilocation.* The ability of an individual to appear in physical form at two distinct places at once.
20. *Transdimensional experiences.* (1) Episodes in which the experiencer temporarily enters what seems to be another dimension; or (2) seeing beings or encountering entities which seem to originate from another dimension. Transdimensional experiences may be associated with a discontinuity or an incongruence in the passage of time, such as missing time, or a lengthy experience occurring in a very short earthly time frame.

Sudden Psychic Awakenings are sometimes confusing or disrupt the experiencer's life. This is particularly true when the awakening is a powerful one. However, the onset of the mildest psychic abilities can be disruptive — or even frightening, especially if the experiencer is convinced psychic phenomena do really not exist or believes they are bizarre or somehow connected with "the devil" or "dark forces."

Even people who believe in psychic abilities can be unsettled by their own experience of them, and may even try to block them. Since so many scientists and doctors still scoff at the existence of psychic phenomena, some experiencers wonder for a while about their own sanity. Others think that these abilities belong only to a few rare and gifted individuals, and may be afraid that their imaginations have run wild.

A Psychic Awakening of Clairvoyance

The clairvoyant ability to see spirits of deceased persons has become well known to the public through popular TV shows such as *The Ghost Whisperer* and contemporary movies like *The Sixth Sense.* However, this psychic phenomenon is not a fantasy, and does indeed sometimes occur to STE experiencers.

The following is the story of a woman I'll call Dagmar, a child-care worker whose Psychic Awakening and first STEP was a clairvoyant vision of her deceased father. She was initially quite confused by it, and by the other psychic experiences that followed.

All my life I was a very intuitive person, but I had never had any clear psychic experiences. When I was thirty years old, my father died of pneumonia in our home. I was very saddened by the loss of my father because I had loved him very dearly.

About one week after he died, I was thinking about him while I was at work, and suddenly I saw my father standing there, in the corner of the room! My first reaction was delight. "Dad! It's so good to see you!" I thought. In a second or two, I realized he wasn't physically there, that he had died — but I could still see him as clear as could be.

I sensed in my mind that my father was telling me that he was okay, that death was nothing to fear. The vision lasted for about ten minutes, then slowly disappeared. I was very happy to have had a chance to see my father again. But I was very confused because I didn't know how or why it had happened. And even though I knew on one level it was real, I started to wonder if I might have been seeing things or if I was losing my mind. I didn't tell anybody about this for almost a year, because I was afraid that they would think I was crazy.

After that I started having many types of psychic experiences. They have included psychic visions, psychic dreams, and premonitions. One of my most dramatic psychic visions had to do with another death. About one year ago, my neighbour's son died. He was only three years old. The entire family was grieving deeply over their tragic loss. At the funeral, suddenly I could see the little boy standing there, behind his family, watching the funeral service. I could also see that he was not alone; he was accompanied by a number of beautiful beings that seemed to be made of light. He looked directly at me and smiled.

I thought about it carefully and decided to tell the boy's mother what I had seen. Right after the funeral I spoke with her and simply told her that I was absolutely sure her son was at peace and that others were caring for him. I was surprised at how much comfort she seemed to find in my words and, perhaps, by the conviction I felt. Later, when we were alone, I told her in detail about the psychic vision. Since then she has thanked me over and over for telling her.

Experiences like this continue to happen to me. I have no idea why I suddenly started having them. At first, I was worried and was afraid I might be going crazy. Now I think these experiences are a gift and a part of my spiritual unfoldment.

In adjusting to her psychic experiences, Dagmar went through what seems to be a fairly typical pattern. At first she found them unsettling and confusing. She was convinced, on the one hand, that they were real and, on the other, that her "seeing things" might indicate some type of mental problem. She was also very reluctant to tell others about them for fear they would say she was "crazy." Over the past few years Dagmar has become far more comfortable with her psychic abilities. She has come to accept them as part of her own particular spiritual journey. Whenever she has a psychic experience, she prays for help in understanding its significance and for guidance about what she should do with the information she has gained. Dagmar now understands that she can have these visions and still be a completely normal, mentally healthy individual. Although she has learned to respect her psychic impressions, she knows not everyone believes in the paranormal, so she tends to keep her experiences relatively private and share them only with those who will understand. She also keeps them in proper perspective and views them as a sidelight rather than the main focus of her spiritual journey.

An Experience of Clairsentience

Psychic experiences take so many different forms that even people who are aware of most types can be troubled or caught off guard when they have an experience that they are completely unfamiliar with. In my work, I have found that a surprising number of people experience clairsentience even though they have never heard of it. Since this particular type of psychic experience often involves sensing or feeling another person's pain in one's own body or emotions, it can be particularly distressing until the experiencer discovers exactly what is happening to him or her. The following story provides a good example of this. It happened to Jeneane, the businesswoman whose mystical experience was described in chapter 3. After her experience of perceiving the Bodhisattva Quan Yin, Jeneane began to have an increasing number of spiritual experiences. Still, when her first experience of clairsentience occurred, she wasn't sure what was happening to her.

About two years after I began my regular practices of hatha yoga and Jungian dream analysis, I had an extremely unusual experience one day during a meeting with a regular client. While we were speaking, I suddenly felt a strong pressure-like pain in the middle of my chest. A few moments after this occurred, my client broke into tears and confided to me that his wife had left him a few days earlier.

I sensed that the pain in my chest might be somehow related to my client's "heart pain," but I wasn't sure, and the pain in my own chest did not stop for one full hour, until after the client had left my office. Concerned, I went to my doctor for a checkup and tests on my heart later that week. The doctor told me that my heart was fine and that the transient chest pain could have been caused by gas or muscle tension.

Although it reassured me to know there was nothing wrong with my heart, I couldn't accept the doctor's explanation. I was especially puzzled since I had begun to notice that this intense pressure and pain returned to the middle of my chest whenever I was with a person who was experiencing emotional pain. Eventually, each time the chest pain returned I asked the person I was with if something was bothering him or her — and I almost always got an affirmative response.

Over the next few weeks, I began to notice another unusual physical sensation: a painful pressure in the centre of my forehead. I soon discovered this sensation was occurring when I was around people who were angry or in mental turmoil. This pain would sometimes become agonizing for me when I was in a crowded public place like a subway train.

Even though Jeneane eventually developed a good sense of what was happening to her, she had no idea what to call it. After learning of my interest in the paranormal she approached me, described her experiences, and asked if I had ever heard of such a thing. She found it reassuring when I was able to provide her with a label for the experience, clairsentience, and tell her that this and other types of Psychic Awakenings were common for those who were on the spiritual journey. She also found it helpful to learn that there were techniques (see chapter 17, "Strategies for Living with Spiritual Transformation") which would help her block, ease, or eliminate the pain she was "picking up" from others.

Telekinesis

Telekinesis is the ability to move objects by thought, and has been graphically portrayed in many current films, such as in George Lucas's *Star Wars* films. In each film, the "Jedi Masters" are portrayed as having the psychic ability to move their "light saber" and other objects through the power of thought. This phenomenon is not limited to Hollywood fantasy films. Many STE experiencers have told me accounts of experiencing objects around them physically move or break for no apparent physical reason. Eminent psychiatrist and NDE experiencer Dr. Carl Jung reportedly experienced psychokinesis of objects around him.

In my clinical experience, spontaneous psychokinesis tends to occur most frequently to STE experiencers when they are emotionally upset or under great duress. Objects around them may suddenly move or break, as if they were invisibly jostled by the STE experiencer's intense, tumultuous mental energies. This happened to me on one occasion when I was preparing to make a public presentation before a very hostile audience. As I strived to calm my anxiety in a room adjacent to the crowded auditorium, suddenly, and for no apparent physical reason, a coffee mug sitting on a table more than a foot away from me moved several inches to fall off the table and onto the floor. My immediate intuitive impression was that my intense emotional stress combined with my intense efforts to focus my mental energies somehow created a shock wave of jostling mental energy.

In my opinion some poltergeist phenomena where household objects move for no apparent reason may be truly due to psychokinesis unknowingly caused by the room's inhabitants. Other times however, poltergeist phenomena do seem to the experiencers to be physical evidence of unseen spirits at work.

Materializations

Several STE experiencers have told me of witnessing first-hand the psychic phenomenon of materialization — the appearance of a solid object out of thin air. According to the yogic tradition some very advanced adepts are said to be able to materialize objects.

Sai Baba, the contemporary yogic saint of India, is renowned for his materialization of many objects, including food, precious gems, "vibuti" (holy ash), and religious objects. Several of my highly credible STE patients have reported witnessing some of Sai Baba's materializations in India.

Paramahansa Yogananda also documents the phenomenon of materialization as possible for spiritually advanced yogic adepts, in his renowned book *Autobiography of a Yogi*. He describes the now famous story of how the very advanced yogic saint and guru Mahavatar Babaji materialized an entire ornate palace to aid completion of the karma of his exalted disciple, Lahiri Mahasaya. According to Paramahansa Yogananda, an impeccable source, this manifestation was thus explained to Lahiri Mahasaya:

"Yonder light is the glow of a golden palace, materialized here tonight by the peerless Babaji. In the dim past, you once expressed a desire to enjoy the beauties of a palace. Our master is now satisfying your wish, thus freeing you from the last bond of your karma." ...

[Lahiri Mahasaya asked] "... this structure surpasses the bounds of human imagination. Please explain to me the mystery of its origin."

... "There is nothing inexplicable about this materialization. The whole cosmos is a projected thought of the Creator ... In tune with the infinite all-accomplishing Will [of the Divine], Babaji is able to command the elemental atoms to combine and manifest themselves in any form. This golden palace, instantaneously brought into being, is real — in the same sense that the earth is real. Babaji created this beautiful mansion out of his mind, and is holding its atoms together by the power of his will, even as God's thought created the earth and His will maintains it." He added, "When this structure has served its purpose, Babaji will dematerialize it."

Lahiri Mahasaya reportedly enjoyed the beauty of the materialized palace for many hours, and ate materialized food in it, in the presence of his exalted guru Mahavatar Babaji. Babaji later dematerialized the palace.

In the extraordinary cases of these advanced yogic adept saints materializing physical objects, it seems the purpose was to assist and help speed the spiritual transformation of the observing spiritual aspirant, and/or to stoke their faith in the infinite power of the Divine Source and show a glimpse of the vast potentials and possibilities of Higher Consciousness.

Stigmata

Stigmata is another fascinating materialization phenomenon that is rare, but very well documented. Stigmata is the spontaneous appearance of wounds, often discharging blood, which appear in locations that generally replicate the wounds of Jesus Christ on the cross. In my opinion stigmata is a type of materialization psychic phenomenon.

The first recorded stigmatic was St. Francis of Assisi, a great Christian saint of impeccable reputation. More recently stigmata was experienced by St. Padre Pio, an Italian monk who died in 1968.

Many stigmatics (persons who develop stigmata) also enter into a mystical state of consciousness while they are having the stigmata. As recorded by Paramahansa Yogananda and others, Therese Neumann, the contemporary German stigmatic (1898–1962), reportedly would enter a mystical visionary experience during the appearance of her stigmata, during which time she would inwardly witness the passion and agony of Jesus Christ on the Cross. Thus stigmata may be a combined mystical vision experience and psychic materialization phenomenon.

Bilocation

Bilocation is another type of materialization experience that has been repeatedly documented in the yogic tradition. Paramahansa Yogananda, in *Autobiography of a Yogi*, describes a dramatic incident of bilocation of a saint that he witnessed at the age of twelve years. This occurred when young Yogananda was visiting Banaras, India, the home of the advanced yogi Swami Pranabananda.

After Yogananda had sat at Swami Pranabananda's side for about one hour, a family friend arrived at the door, stating that Swami Pranabananda had met him about thirty minutes earlier and asked him to please come to his home to meet young Yogananda as soon as possible. Yogananda recounts:

> "Sir, how do you happen to come here?" I felt baffled ...
> over his inexplicable presence.
>
> [The friend replied,] "Everything is mysterious today!
> Less than an hour ago I had just finished my bath in the
> Ganges when Swami Pranabananda approached me. I
> have no idea how he knew I was there at that time."
>
> "[Yogananda] is waiting for you in my apartment"
> [Swami Pranabananda] said. "Will you come with me?" I

gladly agreed. As we proceeded hand in hand, the swami in his wooden sandals was strangely able to outpace me, though I wore these stout walking shoes.

…"I have something else to do at present." He [Swami Pranabananda] gave me an enigmatical glance. "I must leave you behind. You can join me in my house where [Yogananda] and I will be awaiting you."

Before I could remonstrate, he dashed swiftly past me and disappeared in the crowd. I walked here as fast as possible.

… [Yogananda responded] "I cannot believe my ears! … Swami Pranabananda, has not left my sight a moment since I first came about an hour ago."

Paramahansa Yogananda goes on to state that, in retrospect, he thinks Swami Pranabananda's demonstration of the psychic phenomenon of bi-location that day was done in an effort to stir spiritual ardor in Yogananda's young heart.

Encounters with Unidentified Flying Objects

A UFO Encounter (UFOE) is generally defined as an experience in which an individual actually sees and communicates with — or has some other type of close contact with — beings that appear to come from another dimension or planet. The UFOE experiencer sometimes has the impression that he or she was taken to an alien spaceship or was transdimensionally moved to other places or dimensions. It may be perceived as an abduction, in which the experiencer is medically examined or taught spiritual lessons. Simple UFO sightings of lights or strange space craft in the sky do not fit into this category of experience.

UFO Encounters are the paranormal phenomenon that I am least familiar and least comfortable with. But in my work I have spoken with several people who believe they have had this type of experience. And, of course, the question of the existence of alien life forms opens up a whole range of spiritual and scientific issues that are beyond the scope of this book. Still, I think it is important to include UFO Encounters because they frequently seem to have a profound transformational effect on the experiencer.

Dr. Kenneth Ring conducted a carefully controlled research project on this subject and reported on it in his third book, *The Omega Project*. During his research Dr. Ring discovered that individuals who reported having close UFO Encounters or abductions also scored very high on a scale he devised to rate kundalini activity. He also found that a UFO Encounter often had the same type of transformational impact that a Near-Death Experience had.

Further evidence that the UFO Encounter can precipitate spiritual transformation is given in an essay by Keith Thompson, "The UFO Encounter Experience as a Crisis of Transformation," that appeared in the Grofs' book *Spiritual Emergency*. Thompson discusses in depth how the perceptions of those who report UFO Encounters are changed, and says that, perhaps, the UFOE — like NDEs, mystical visions, and other paranormal phenomena — acts like a prod that pushes us on to the next level of consciousness.

A Classic UFO Encounter

One of the most classic and best-documented cases of a UFO encounter is the story of Betty Andreasson, which was published in the book *The Andreasson Affair*. Andreasson was taken to another "place" by UFO beings, subjected to what seemed to be a medical examination, taught a number of spiritual lessons, and then returned. She did not recall her experience immediately after it happened, but only after she was hypnotized during therapy some time later.

This gradual recall is common among UFOE experiencers and seems to follow a fairly consistent pattern: at first, the experiencers do not recall anything about the experience. They are, however, aware of a period of time that they can't account for or for which they have no memory. Then, over time, memories of the encounter begin to surface, sometimes more and more rapidly, until finally the experiencers are able to reconstruct much, if not all, of the encounter. Often this process of remembering occurs in dreams, during hypnotic regression, or in what the experiencers describe as flashbacks. The following is a classic example of one type of UFO encounter that fits this pattern. It was told to me by a medical doctor whom I'll call Shawn. She was in her midthirties when it occurred, and had been meditating regularly and in the process of spiritual transformation for several years. Even though she had had a number of mystical and psychic STEs, she was extremely skeptical about UFO experiences before this experience.

One summer weekend I was driving to a medical conference that was being held at a retreat centre in the country. As I was driving along a fairly remote road, I was contemplating some spiritual concepts I had recently been discussing with friends. I wasn't in any particular hurry, because I was only about a half hour from the site and the conference wasn't due to begin for more than an hour. Suddenly, I felt as if I had just "dropped" into my body. I had had this sensation sometimes when I first woke up in the morning, and it seemed as if my spirit had left my body while I was sleeping and then suddenly dropped back into it when I awakened. But I certainly had never had it when I was already awake or driving. After feeling this marked sensation, I looked at the surrounding countryside — which I had driven through many times before — and felt totally disoriented. I had a feeling of *jamais vu*, as if I had never seen the area before. I didn't recognize anything, and I didn't know where I was. Glancing at the clock on the dashboard, I saw that it was almost time for the conference to begin. I assumed that I must have been so absorbed in my thoughts that I'd been driving on "automatic pilot" and that I must be very close to the conference. Just then I rounded a corner and came through a small town that I recognized. Amazed, I realized that I was still a good twenty minutes from the conference. More than half an hour had elapsed, and I had no memory of what had happened during that time.

At first I pushed this out of my mind and concentrated on the conference. But the next day there was an occurrence that, in retrospect, made me think something unusual might have happened to me. One of the presenters at the conference, a psychologist, mentioned the subject of UFO abductions. The moment he did, I found waves of intense fear washing over me. This was a very unusual reaction for me to have in any circumstance, let alone the one I was in.

About a week later, I was going about my busy daily life when I began to have flashbacks. At first they were flashes of images of what seemed to be alien beings and of being examined by them. The flashes were so disconcerting that I began to meditate and pray each day, asking for Divine guidance to help me understand exactly what these flashes were. I was beginning to sense — although I wanted to deny it — that they might be a memory that was trying to resurface, and I needed to know if this was the case or if they were simply flights of my imagination. As I continued to pray and meditate on this over the next few days, the images became clearer, additional details began to fall into place, and then the memory of what had occurred coalesced into a whole.

I have a clear visual image of being asked telepathically to lie down on a table. I was in some sort of strange room with illuminated control panels on some of the walls and with subdued lighting that was a shade of royal blue. The beings communicating with me had faces shaped like upside-down pears and huge dark eyes. I noticed that the irises of their eyes were pigmented; some had brown eyes, others had blue or hazel green. They also had eyelids and they blinked. My medically trained mind seemed to make a particular note of this. Several years earlier, I had seen the movie *Communion*, which had similar-looking beings whose eyes were portrayed as eyelidless, black pools.

An overpowering, invisible force seemed to push my body onto the examining table, and I felt frightened. As I began to silently pray to God to protect me, one of the aliens looked down at me, smiled as I prayed, and said telepathically, "Do not be afraid. We do not want to hurt you. We just want to see how you are doing." This alien exuded an aura of gentleness and love. The eyes gazing down at me were dark blue and looked compassionate.

I was subjected to some sort of physical examination that I have only vague memories of — there may have been some sort of rectal probe and some sort of thin wire-like probe that was inserted through my umbilicus or my lower abdomen. When the examination was over, I was released from the table, taken to what looked like a television or computer screen, and made to look at some information on the screen. Although I do not recall the content of the material, I do know that it was written in a language that I do not currently understand. It had symbols that looked like three-dimensional drawings and a little like broad hieroglyphics.

The appearance of the aliens was slightly different from the impression I had gained from reading and hearing about the subject. The skin that I could see on their reverse-pear-shaped heads had a texture that was slightly heavier than human skin, rather porous and leathery looking. It was paler than human skin and had a slight milky-grey undertone. Their noses had little prominence; they were small and fine and had narrow nostrils. Their mouths were small with very thin lips. They spoke to me and each other telepathically and did not move their lips to speak.

I clearly recall one of the alien's hands: he or she had very long fingers with spatulate ends and fleshy, ruddy coloured fingernails. There seemed to be one long thumb and only two, or perhaps three, fingers.

The aliens were about four and a half feet tall. They wore loose-fitting clothing and had some sort of boots or shoes on their feet. They walked about but also seemed to be able to levitate.

Through a doorway at the far right end of the room, I could see another room. In it was another being who seemed to be looking at an illuminated screen and who looked different from the others. Although I don't recall communicating with him, he seemed to be taller and looked more like a human/alien mixture.

Just before I was sent back, the being who examined me sent me a telepathic message: "Keep up the good work!"

The impact of remembering this incident was shattering. I was a respected medical doctor who had always considered these types of experiences questionable. I wondered if I was becoming mentally ill. I was afraid to tell anyone about it in case they might think I was losing my mind. I was also afraid for my children and began to pray daily to protect them from an alien abduction.

Shawn's experience has some features typical of psychic experiences: for example, she reported feeling as if she had returned to her body after an out-of-body experience, and being communicated with telepathically. After the episode, Shawn had a marked increase in other types of psychic experiences. As you read on you will discover some possible reasons for this.

Another Type of Close Encounter

The stories of UFO Encounters I have heard have convinced me that these experiences are often STEPs and overlap in many ways with other types of Spiritually Transformative Experiences. Here is the story of a patient of mine whom I will call Lisa:

My experiences started early, I think around the age of three. I remember lying in bed one night, waiting to fall asleep. Suddenly I saw two little men wearing hooded cloaks standing at the foot of my bed. They didn't scare me. They didn't do anything, they just looked at me. I looked back at them. These little men — the "little monks," I called them — appeared in my bedroom many evenings.

I told my mother about them, but she didn't believe me. Eventually, I stopped trying to tell her. But I continued to see these "little monks" in my bedroom on and off for years. It made me think I might be partially crazy or something, so I never talked about it and just tried to live my life normally.

From a very early age I also remember having spontaneous spiritual insights. I can remember reading the Bible as a child and thinking that my church (Roman Catholic) had gotten things all mixed up and missed the point of what Christ was trying to say. Also, when I was about seven years old I spontaneously came up with the concept of reincarnation. I didn't know what to call it, but I thought that it explained the immortality of the spirit. I also believed that reincarnation was what Christ was really talking about when he discussed eternal life. About fifteen years later, I was reading some Eastern philosophy for the first time and was surprised to discover that others had the same idea and that they called it reincarnation.

When I was around twenty, I got interested in meditation and began to meditate regularly. A few years later, my most intense contact with the "little monks"— I now think of them as aliens — occurred. As I was meditating one day, I suddenly got the feeling that the little men were in my room, so I opened my eyes. Sure enough, there they were. This time they seemed to be staring at me with incredible intensity, and the room seemed to be filled with a very bright white light. I felt as if they were trying to take me somewhere with them, and I started floating out of my body. The aliens just seemed to glide through the air. But I knew I did not want to go with them and I fought against it. At the same time, I felt as if my head was going to explode and I was aware of a terrible burning pain in my back, as if my whole spine was on fire. All the while I fought to stay in my body, and I kept telling the little men to go away.

Finally they just disappeared, and I felt totally back in my body, in my room. I had an intense splitting headache for three days afterward, together with this weird burning back pain. Eventually, both these pains went away. I never told a doctor or anyone else about this because I thought they'd think I was crazy.

It never occurred to me that the little monks could be aliens or that they could have anything to do with UFOs, until I read an article in *Scientific American* three years ago that described the experiences of people who were abducted by UFOs or saw aliens. One of the descriptions of a type of alien that was commonly seen was identical to the little monks that I had been seeing since childhood. After reading the article, I began to wonder if I had ever been abducted by aliens from a UFO, but just couldn't remember it. Then I thought that maybe they were trying to abduct me that day I had such a powerful experience, but that they couldn't take me because I fought back.

A Tentative Hypothesis for UFOEs

It is interesting to note that some of Lisa's symptoms were suggestive of a Spiritual Energy/Kundalini experience: the burning pain in her back, the pressure and pain in her head, the sensation of floating out of her body, and the perception of the white light. This is especially interesting given the fact that Dr. Kenneth Ring has found such a high correlation between UFO Encounters and signs of kundalini awakening on his rating scale.

Although this possible relationship may seem strange at first, there may be a number of logical explanations for it. In some cases, people who are unknowingly having the sensations and paranormal experiences associated with kundalini activity may have no idea how to interpret their experience. And, in their struggle to make sense of their experience and to find a way to describe it, they fit it into the framework of the UFO Encounter. For example, a person who is sitting in a forest one night and suddenly sees a blinding white light may later tell people that he has seen a UFO because he has no other way to identify or label the experience.

Considering the vastness of the universe, it is very conceivable that other sentient life forms live on other planets and in other galaxies. It is also possible that some of these beings may have a technology more advanced than ours and may have physically observed or visited our planet. I think that some UFO sightings may be due to these visitors. These UFO sightings do not have a spiritually transformative impact on the viewer.

It is my clinical hypothesis that some other UFO Encounters, however, may be a type of transdimensional psychic experience. Many physicists today believe that we live in a multidimensional universe even though we can normally perceive only three of these dimensions with the physical eye (height, width, and depth). For hundreds of years, trance channels and mediums have claimed that they could communicate with beings or entities living in other dimensions. When the activity of kundalini begins to bring about the changes in consciousness that result in an increased ability to perceive other levels of reality, the mind may begin to glimpse these other dimensions and the life forms that fill them. It is possible that UFOE experiencers may perceive contact with "aliens" in another dimension — or place — clairvoyantly, or that they might be astral travelling there. In other cases, it may be that the beings associated with UFOs are astral travelling here, or moving between dimensions to make contact.

Although my clinical experience of people having UFOEs is limited, my observations have led me to develop two further hypotheses: First, persons experiencing other types of STEs may be, in their transforming consciousness, more receptive to transdimensional experiences than others. Second, it may be that the transdimensional contact with extraterrestrial beings in itself stimulates certain chakras, opens psychic and intuitive capacities in the brain, and/or stimulates the kundalini mechanism in some way. This idea is not as far-fetched as it first might seem. It has long been held in the yogic tradition that saints with a highly awakened kundalini can sometimes awaken the kundalini in another. This phenomenon is called shakti pata or shaktipat. In a similar way, contact with the intense psychic energies of inter-dimensional extraterrestrial beings may stimulate the psychic chakras, intuitive brain centres, and spiritual energies of the person having the experience, making him or her temporarily more psychically open and, thus, able to perceive the other beings and/or dimensions. This stimulation may leave the experiencer more psychically open as an after-effect. Many UFOE experiencers describe a dramatic psychic opening after the encounter.

The story of Shawn provides an excellent example of this. She had been undergoing spiritual transformation for years and had had many intuitive psychic and paranormal experiences. Thus, she was already psychically open or, in a sense, receptive to a transdimensional psychic experience. The experience itself also seemed to further stimulate her psychic capacities, resulting in a marked increase in her intuitive and psychic experiences after her UFO Encounter. It is interesting that during the two years before her experience she had been having a number of signs of kundalini activity, including sensations of heat and energy in her spine and visions of inner light.

Psychic Experiences Are Not Always Positive/Spiritual

I think it important to state here that psychic experiences are not always spiritual or positive in nature. In my clinical experience, many persons have reported that some psychic experiences were frightening or intrusive, like the UFO encounters that I described above. Other distressful or negative psychic experiences that may occur include painful or excessive clairsentience, excessive clairvoyance, psychic assault, possession states, negative or frightening NDEs, and walk-ins.

In yoga it is well known that psychic experiences may sometimes be negative or distressful. Yoga philosophy contends that there are many levels of the astral planes of consciousness, high heavenly astral planes, intermediate astral planes, and low or dark astral planes. During mystical experiences, the STE experiencer's consciousness is believed to open upwards, to briefly perceive the high heavenly astral planes, or sometimes the even more refined and subtle causal plane of consciousness. During most psychic experiences however, the experiencer's consciousness is opening sideways rather than upward, to perceive the intermediate astral planes, and sometimes to even perceive lower astral planes. Such a perception of the lower astral planes may include perception of dark entities of low spiritual development.

I will discuss negative or distressful psychic experiences in more detail in chapter 14 on Spiritual and Paranormal STE After-Effect Symptoms, in the section entitled *Distressing Psychic Symptoms and Psychic Disorders*.

Adjusting to Psychic Abilities

In my clinical practice I have observed that people who have a psychic awakening and continue to have psychic experiences adjust in stages to their new abilities. First, they are often puzzled, confused, or frightened. They question the nature of what they have experienced; they wonder where the experiences have come from and why. At this stage, experiencers are usually very reluctant to tell others their experiences, because they believe people will think they are crazy. However, as the psychic experiences keep occurring, most experiencers try to talk to friends or family about them. In some instances, they are rebuffed or ridiculed and find it extremely difficult to speak about their experiences again. In other cases they discover people who are eager to talk about psychic phenomena. Although this can be helpful, psychic experiencers often pick up a good deal of misinformation in this way. One of the most common problems is that they begin to get an inflated idea of themselves or the uniqueness of their abilities. In general, I have found four common problems that people have in adjusting to new psychic gifts:

1. They may become self-inflated, thinking that they have a rare gift and that they are special, or they inflate the importance of the abilities themselves.
2. They may incorrectly believe that their psychic information is infallible and always correct.
3. They may lack restraint and immediately blurt out psychically received information when they receive it.
4. They may lack judgment and indiscriminately share psychic information with anyone, or at inappropriate times or places.

One of the clearest cases of a lack of judgment was a man I worked with, whom I'll call Daniel.

A highly educated and extremely successful business-man, Daniel had started his own company and become wealthy at an early age. When he was in his early thirties he began to receive channelled material. In a one-year period, he received the material for three books that dealt with the spiritual nature of humanity, the need for humanity to reconnect with nature, and the importance of taking immediate action to save the environment. However, Daniel also began to believe he had a mission to save all the endangered species, and he developed a strong desire to communicate telepathically with whales.

These latter experiences were unusual, and when Daniel came to me as a patient it became apparent that he was exhibiting some signs of delusion. Still, a good deal of the information he was receiving psychically was, in fact, correct. Further, Daniel functioned quite normally most of the time. During these periods of normal functioning, however, Daniel exhibited some of the typical problems adjusting to his new psychic gift, all of which involve a lack of clear judgment.

After receiving channelled material for a while, Daniel came to believe that he had been in some way "chosen" as the person who would ultimately save all the whales. After receiving some information that was shown to be accurate, he began to think that all the information he channelled was accurate, and that he was special and having experiences that were far beyond anyone else's.

He began to lose the ability to discern when it was appropriate to talk about his experiences. Once, during a meeting of a non-profit — but not environmental — group, Daniel insisted that "save the whales" be added to the list of organizational goals that were being discussed.

More and more he would bring the information that related to his channelling up at business meetings and try to get his fellow board members to make investments and commitments based on it.

Ultimately, he began to discuss his psychic experiences indiscriminately. He talked about them with his accountant, his secretary, his housekeeper, and people he met in restaurants or bars.

A Balanced Perspective on Psychic Gifts and Intuition

Daniel exhibited a number of the problems that many mentally healthy individuals exhibit after they begin to develop paranormal abilities. In counselling people who have started to have psychic experiences, I have found that these difficulties are, in fact, quite common.

In order to help people put their experiences in perspective, I encourage them to look at psychic gifts as an extension of intuition and point out that some people have much stronger intuition than others but that this does not make these people special. It is also important for them to realize that both intuition and psychic experiences can be coloured a great deal by a person's emotional makeup, thoughts, and feelings: wishful thinking is often misinterpreted as psychic or intuitive information.

Since psychically received information, just like outwardly received information, is not always correct, I point out that well-adjusted, highly intuitive people have learned to balance intuition and intellect; they use their intellectual skills critically to examine and judge the information they receive through intuition or psychic experiences. They have learned that psychic information is only a tool — one of several sources of information that need to be considered in making well-informed, rational decisions.

When I had my own first psychic experience after my 1979 NDE, I can remember being so startled that I paused and prayed for guidance. This guidance helped me correctly handle the information I received. When I clairvoyantly saw the image of my friend Susan's brain covered in pus and realized that the picture somehow symbolized meningitis, I tried to balance this "psychic information" with the reality of the situation. Using my logic, I gathered information from Susan about her medical condition. When I found she had a few of the symptoms of meningitis, I didn't jump to the conclusion that my psychic information — or my interpretation of it — must have been 100 percent correct. I simply outlined the symptoms for her and advised her to get tested for meningitis if any more of them developed. As it happened, this approach had a very positive effect: Susan got early treatment for her disease and was cured. If, however, I had become fanatical about what I had seen in my vision and insisted on her going to the emergency department immediately, the result might not have been so favourable. Had she done so, the doctors almost certainly would not have tested her for meningitis: her symptoms were simply not clear enough. She would probably have been sent home, and then been very reluctant to return when her symptoms worsened — and this could have led to tragedy.

How Yogis See Psychic Abilities

Since ancient times, yogis have considered psychic gifts or siddhis to be a natural byproduct of progress along the spiritual path of yoga. However, these gifts have also been held to be potential distractions from the true goal of yoga — the realization of oneness with God or Brahman. It has long been believed that these psychic gifts should never be sought in themselves. If they do occur, they are to be acknowledged, learned from, but not dwelt upon excessively. It is held that the yogi who focuses excessively on psychic gifts may lose sight of the true spiritual objective and thereby become nothing more than a "magician," never obtaining ultimate realization.

There is also a long tradition among respected psychics that one should not try to use these gifts to gain personal power or wealth. Although this is an ethical consideration, it also has its practical side. Following the initial experience, psychic episodes often recur only irregularly and unpredictably, and even highly psychically open experiencers find they can't always make the abilities appear consistently.

Almost all the individuals who have become known and respected as actual "psychics" say that they do not, ultimately, control their abilities. Even though they can often put themselves in a frame of mind that makes a certain psychic experience more likely to occur, they cannot force it to happen. This is perhaps how some stage psychics get into trouble: they become overconfident of their psychic abilities, then when they are required to produce abilities on demand, and they can't, they resort to trickery.

There are also people who try to use their psychic powers to harm or manipulate, or play "psychic games" of some kind. Although some researchers believe it is simply not possible to use psychic abilities for harmful purposes, others disagree. I will discuss the topic of psychic assault in chapter 14, on spiritual and paranormal STE after-effect symptoms.

Clearly, we need to gain a far greater understanding of psychic phenomena. In the meantime, I hope that anyone who is developing psychic abilities as part of the process of spiritual transformation will be cautious, use discernment, and pray for guidance as to how to use their insights for the highest good. It helps to keep Psychic Experiences in proper perspective by realizing that they are a common sidelight on a journey whose actual purpose is the process of spiritual transformation of consciousness.

8

INSPIRED CREATIVITY
AND GENIUS

IN MY WORK WITH PEOPLE WHO HAVE had STEs and are undergoing spiritual transformation, I have found that many of them notice an increase in their creativity. They begin to feel an urge to keep journals or write poetry or stories, to draw or paint, to express themselves through music, to give talks, or to write books. I have found that this increase in the creative urge is common regardless of the types of STEs the person is experiencing. Although most people do not generally produce works that are masterpieces, their new-found or increased creative expression does seem to be very much a part of their spiritual unfolding.

In a few cases, the creative experience can be so powerful or so deeply intertwined with a mystical or paranormal element that it becomes a STEP in its own right. For some people, these creative inspired experiences are their most prominent type of STE. In some yogic traditions it is said that a partial flow of the kundalini to the brain yields inspiration, rather than liberation. The yogis also warned that such inspiration may hold great truths, but sometimes may be mixed with half-truths due to the impurities in the consciousness of a partially realized individual. Discernment is needed when contemplating the truths in inspired works, just as with intellectual works.

"Inspired creativity" is a particularly apt name for this type of experience since, in its theological sense, the word "inspiration" refers to the influence of the Divine on the human mind or soul. Some people who experience profound inspired creativity produce writings, musical compositions, or artwork that is outstanding or remarkable in some way. Others may spontaneously develop creative gifts or abilities in areas in which they previously had no talent whatsoever. The STE category of Inspired Creativity and Genius is not limited to artistic inspiration. This phenomenon can also manifest itself as profound intellectual insights or discoveries, or the development or advancement of theories in the sciences, humanities, or philosophies.

The relationship between creativity and spiritual experiences may not at first be clear. However, one only has to look back in time to discover many examples of an overlap between creativity or genius and profound spiritual experiences. Many saints and mystics have created wonderful works of art, poetry, music, inspirational writing, or made significant contributions to science. And many geniuses from both the arts and the sciences have had mystical experiences and have said that their great works were Divinely inspired.

Hildegard of Bingen — Mystic with Inspired Creativity

One of the classic examples of a mystic who had a tremendous capacity for inspired creativity was the Catholic saint Hildegard of Bingen, born in 1098. Hildegard, even in childhood, had a spiritual nature. When she was eight years old her parents sent her to be educated in a Benedictine convent. When old enough, she took her final vows and became a cloistered nun. Although she had visions and psychic experiences from an early age, her life in the cloister proceeded fairly normally, and she eventually became head of the convent.

Five years later, she had a mystical experience more profound than anything she had ever experienced. She wrote later that the "heavens were opened" for her, and she received a prophetic calling. She soon began to write extensively, to paint, and to compose music. In much of her writing she tried to describe her visions and capture their symbolic beauty and meaning. But she also wrote poetry, several books on natural history and medicine, a morality play, and composed music. She began to paint her visions, and her paintings have been likened to those of William Blake. Music she composed is still sung and played today. Some of her herbal remedies are also still in use.

Hildegard once wrote that she constantly experienced a vision of what she called "a reflection of the living light" that was "far, far brighter than a cloud that carries the sun." On rarer occasions, she even experienced directly what she called the "living light" itself. The scope of Hildegard's creative output went far beyond her education, and she made it clear that the material for it came from inspiration: "as the sun, the moon, and the stars appear in water, so writings, sermons, virtues, and certain human actions take form for me and gleam within."

Paramahansa Yogananda — Mystic with Inspired Creativity

Another example of a mystic who had a tremendous capacity for inspired creativity was the yogic saint and guru Paramahansa Yogananda, formerly known as Swami Yogananda. Born in 1893 in India, he was highly spiritual from his childhood, and had many visions and spiritual experiences from an early age. He sought out monastic life in his teens, and Yogananda met his guru, Swami Sri Yukteswar, when he was seventeen. Swami Sri Yukteswar came from a lineage of illumined gurus, including his guru Lahiri Mahasaya, whose guru was the revered Mahavatar Babaji. Yogananda trained in "Kriya Yoga," the Eightfold Path of Yoga and meditation, at Swami Sri Yuktewar's ashram, while completing his high-school and college education.

In 1920 Paramahansa Yogananda travelled to the USA to teach yoga to the West. Except for a one-year return visit to India in 1935, Paramahansa Yogananda remained in the USA, living there and teaching Kriya Yoga meditation around the country, until he died in Los Angeles in 1952. Yogananda is considered by many to be "The Father of Yoga in the West." He founded "The Church of All Religions," which he later renamed as "Self-Realization Fellowship," a religious movement that is still flourishing today.

During his thirty-two years in the West, Paramahansa Yogananda was extremely busy. He lectured to large audiences across the country, gave sermons regularly, taught Kriya Yoga meditation to thousands, and began a yogic monastic order. Despite his extremely busy schedule, Yogananda was highly creative, and wrote prolifically. He wrote and published a three-year-long series of "Lessons," an innovative correspondence course, which allowed interested persons to learn about yoga philosophy and Kriya Yoga meditation techniques through printed lessons delivered twice a month by mail to their home. Three books have been published of Paramahansa Yogananda's collected essays and talks made across the USA.

Paramahansa Yogananda also wrote a total of seventeen books, including his famous *Autobiography of a Yogi*, which is a bestseller to this day. This book is the best all-round introduction to yoga philosophy that I have read, and has been highly recommended by such prominent persons as George Harrison (formerly of the Beatles), Ravi Shankar, and Steve Jobs.

Two of Yogananda's books consist of inspired poetry, and one book consists of inspired songs and chants, which he called *Cosmic Chants*. Paramahansa Yogananda's other books include inspirational writings, and instructions on healing affirmations and meditations. His most extraordinary inspired books are his three voluminous yogic interpretations of sacred scriptures and writings: *God Talks with Arjuna: The Bhagavad Gita* (a new translation and commentary); *The Resurrection of the Christ Within You* (a revelatory commentary on the original teachings of Jesus); and *Wine of the Mystic: The Rubaiyat of Omar Khayyam* (a spiritual interpretation).

Like Hildegard's, the scope of Paramahansa Yogananda's creative output went far beyond his education. He too often attributed the inspiration of his writings as coming from the Divine source. In the 2014 film *Awake: The Life of Yogananda*, Deepak Chopra called Paramahansa Yogananda "a spiritual genius, who had access to a much larger spiritual domain of awareness that most people don't have access to."

Some Geniuses Had Mystical Experiences

Many individuals who have been known primarily for their creative genius rather than their mystical natures speak about inspiration in similar terms. The great composer Johannes Brahms called upon his Maker when he felt the urge to compose and would sometimes receive his music from divine inspiration:

> I immediately feel vibrations that thrill my whole being ...
> These are the Spirit illuminating the soul power within,
> and in this exalted state, I see clearly what is obscure in my
> ordinary moods; then I feel capable of drawing inspiration

from above, as Beethoven did. Above all, I realize at such moments the tremendous significance of Jesus's supreme revelation, "I and my father are one." Those vibrations assume the forms of distinct mental images, after I have formulated my desire and resolve in regard to what I want — namely, to be inspired so that I can compose something that will uplift and benefit humanity — something of permanent value.

Straightaway the ideas flow in upon me, directly from God, and not only do I see distinct themes in my mind's eye, but they are clothed in the right forms, harmonies, and orchestration. Measure by measure, the finished product is revealed to me when I am in those rare inspired moods.

Clearly, for Brahms the creative experience was also a deeply spiritual or mystical one. Similar examples can also be found in the world of scientific genius. Nikola Tesla, who is considered by many to be the greatest inventor of the twentieth century, received detailed plans for many of his inventions in blinding flashes of light. He developed a deep spiritual awareness of reality, and recognized that his abilities and ideas came to him from a reality beyond the physical.

Albert Einstein, too, saw the relationship between the spiritual experience, inspiration, and genius. Although he did not speak publicly about any spiritual experiences he may have had himself, he often wrote about what he called the "cosmic religious experience." Further, he wrote about it in a way that makes it almost certain that he was speaking from some type of personal mystical experience. In *Living Philosophies*, he noted: "It is enough for me to contemplate the mystery of conscious life perpetuating itself through all the universe which we can dimly perceive, and to try humbly to comprehend even an infinitesimal part of the intelligence manifested in nature ... The most beautiful thing we can experience is the mysterious. It is the source of all true art and science."

In *The World As I See It*, Einstein wrote, "I maintain that the cosmic religious experience is the strongest and noblest incitement to scientific research." He added that the most important function of both art and science was "to awaken this feeling and keep it alive in those who are capable of it."

STEs and the Creative Experience

Historical cases of creative genius such as St. Hildegard, Einstein, Brahms, and Paramahansa Yogananda show a definite relationship between profound spiritual experience and creative inspiration. Of course, not everyone who has STEs of Inspired Creativity becomes a creative genius or creates works of the calibre of a St. Hildegard, Yogananda, or an Einstein.

As is the case with other types of STEs, experiences of Inspired Creativity occur along a continuum, varying in intensity and in the quality of the creative material produced. Some individuals who have this type of STE create works of great quality or even genius, but this is rare. For the rest, the experience centres not so much on the creation of works of genius as on the sudden, spontaneous development of a particular creative ability where none was present before.

Creativity and Altered States

The following is the story of a woman whom I'll call Ellen whose experience of Inspired Creativity was a STEP that changed her life completely.

Until she was nearing middle age, Ellen worked as an engineer. She was extremely well educated, had obtained a Master of Science degree in engineering, and had risen to the top of a field in which it was extremely difficult for women to succeed at that time. She was married to another equally successful engineer. The two of them had worked on important projects around the world and had earned a high income. Although Ellen's most dramatic STEP occurred when she was about forty, her process of spiritual transformation began a few years earlier. Here is the story she told me about her experiences and their tremendous transformative impact:

> When I was in my late thirties, I began to feel discontented and to sense that something essential was missing

from my life, even though I had no idea what it might be. By most socially accepted standards, I should have been happy with my life: I had a good marriage, a great deal of money, and a highly successful career. Confused and troubled by my discontentment, I began Jungian analysis.

During this process I kept a journal, recorded my dreams in detail, and spent far more time in introspection.

One morning, shortly after arising, I was overcome with fatigue and felt I had to lie back down on my bed. I had begun to drift off when, without warning, sensations of energy began to stream up my body and into my head. Suddenly, I seemed to be immersed in a beautiful, intensely brilliant, white light. For a moment, I felt myself merge with what I can only describe as the intelligence behind the universe, the cosmic power, or the cosmic white light. When the experience ended I felt overwhelmed and profoundly moved.

Shortly after what I have come to call my "white-light experience," my dreams became more vivid. They also seemed to be providing me with clear images of paintings and directions on exactly how these paintings could be done. At the time, this seemed extremely strange to me. I had never had any artistic talent or any interest at all in drawing or painting. Still, I recorded the dreams carefully, as I was in the habit of doing.

Eventually I began to draw or paint these dreams. Over a period of time, the urge to spend my time painting grew. Ultimately it became so strong that I quit my job in engineering and enrolled in art school. Once in art school, I mastered techniques with amazing speed. After only a year in the program, my professor took me aside and told me that I had learned all I possibly could from the school and that it was time for me to leave and get on with my artwork.

While I was studying art, I had continued to record my dreams and had been attempting to paint the images.

Although I didn't fully realize it at first, I came to understand that my dreams were providing me not just with images but with information on innovative techniques and unusual materials that would be needed to reproduce the images.

Since leaving art school six years ago, I have worked full-time as an artist and have continued to paint my dream images. I have created a tremendous volume of high-quality work and, in fact, have produced enough material to have six separate, individual showings of new work put on in five years — an accomplishment that is remarkable among even the most talented and prolific artists.

In spite of the success of my work, I feel a great deal of humility about my art. Rather than thinking of myself as the creator, I like to consider myself simply a "receiver" or an instrument who brings the dream images into physical reality. I strongly believe that I receive my ability and my inspiration from a source beyond myself.

Except for Ellen's "white-light experience," Inspired Creativity has been the main feature of her transformative process — and the process has clearly been a spiritual one. Many of the paintings are symbolic depictions of transformation and growth. A number of them represent such clearly spiritual subjects as kundalini awakenings. Many others give the viewer a powerful sense of the oneness of all things, and some seem to resonate with a life force of their own.

As soon as the creative process began, Ellen's life also began to develop an increasingly spiritual focus. She continued to delve deeply into the works of Jung, but also began to seek out others who wrote on spiritual subjects. She became extremely interested in works such as Bucke's *Cosmic Consciousness* and began to read avidly the works of Gopi Krishna. She now feels that this has helped her to integrate her experiences into her life and to understand that kundalini drives the tremendous transformation she is undergoing.

Like many people's spiritual journeys, however, Ellen's has been in some ways a difficult one. Even though she has adjusted to the tremendous creative urge that now takes up so much of her life, her family has not. Ellen's husband and the other members of her family initially ridiculed her decision to give up her financially successful career and the lifestyle that went with it.

The differences between Ellen and her husband grew until they finally divorced. Fortunately, the rest of Ellen's family has been able to accept the change and support her new direction in life. In spite of the difficulties that Ellen has had to work out, she is confident that she made the right decision. Her painting brings her tremendous satisfaction, and she knows she is doing what she was meant to do. She has finally discovered the dimension that was missing from her life.

When Ellen is painting her dream images she often finds herself in a trance-like state that she feels allows her to become a conduit for inspiration. Many of the great artists, composers, writers, philosophers, and scientists have described this type of experience. Truly inspired creative episodes often seem to be experienced in an intensely absorbed, paranormal state of consciousness that has mystical overtones. Composer Richard Wagner once wrote that inspiration came from "universal currents of Divine Thought vibrating the ether everywhere" and that "[when I am] in that trance-like condition, which is the prerequisite of all true creative effort, I feel that I am one with this vibrating Force, that it is omniscient, and that I can draw upon it to an extent that is limited only by my capacity to do so."

Many of the people I have known whose STEs included Inspired Creativity have spoken of similar experiences. One is a woman I'll call Gail, who has a doctorate in neuroendocrinology. Gail was involved in research at a respected private university. Widely published, she had received a number of awards and grants and seemed to be on the fast track to academic success. Her colleagues were certain it was only a matter of time before Harvard or another top university invited her to continue work there. However, when she was in her midforties her direction in life radically changed.

> I developed a flu-like illness, which left me profoundly exhausted. After almost two years of visiting specialists, the illness was diagnosed as severe Chronic Fatigue Syndrome.

In my case the illness left me not only terribly exhausted, but also unable to concentrate. Even though I tried to battle the disease physically and mentally, I was eventually forced to quit my work at the university.

At some time during the first year of the illness I began to have dramatic sensations of light and of energy coursing through my body. Although the sensations were very powerful and unfamiliar, I was not worried about them: I thought they might be the result of my body's efforts to fight the illness. I even wondered if the illness might not have somehow stimulated some type of latent healing power in my body.

At about the time the experiences of light and energy began, I developed a tremendous urge to draw. I found this strange because I had never had any artistic tendencies. After a time, however, I decided to enroll in a part-time art course as I was still unable to work. On the second evening of the course, the instructor took me aside and told me that I shouldn't be taking the course, I should be teaching it. I was astounded; I had no idea how I had developed the artistic ability I suddenly seemed to be exhibiting. The instructor, also a woman, was fascinated by what I told her and suggested that we try working together.

When we did get together, we decided to experiment by working on the same canvas. As soon as we stood in front of the canvas and began to paint, a strange thing happened: both of us spontaneously entered an altered state of consciousness, and we began to paint in a manner so synchronized that we almost seemed to be two arms of one painter.

For the past three years, my instructor and I have continued to paint jointly in this altered state of consciousness. Before we begin a new painting, we look at sketches we have made of our dreams and other subjects and at photographs we have taken. Eventually an idea for a painting will seem to grab both of us. With nothing more than this vague idea in our minds we begin to paint — usually on an extremely large canvas. Immediately it seems as if we are somehow taken over and we become completely absorbed in our work. We become like two halves expressing one energy. We often work in this state for days with very little rest or sleep. Often, when a painting is completed, we collapse in exhaustion.

Gail and her former instructor sometimes paint as many as two to three huge canvases a month in spite of her continued chronic fatigue. Many of these paintings have deeply spiritual themes. Vibrant with colour and vitality, they are considered by many to be exceptionally good. No one looking at them can tell they were done by two people, one a trained, professional artist and the other a scientist who had no training or artistic ability until she was forty-five years old.

For Gail, her periods of Inspired Creativity have gone hand in hand with her spiritual growth. She spontaneously developed a strong desire to meditate and has joined a network of people interested in similar subjects. She is determined to continue her spiritual journey and work as an artist. Like Ellen, Gail has found that these decisions have met with a great deal of resistance from her family. Her husband became incensed with her intense focus on painting. They have since separated. Some other members of Gail's family believe that she is mentally unbalanced. Still, Gail has a number of new and old supportive friends who care for her and believe in her. She feels confident that she is living her life as she should. In fact, one of the most fascinating aspects of Gail's story is that her long illness seems to have impaired her ability to concentrate on scientific material or focus her intellect for any length of time — and yet her creative ability has developed and flourished.

Creativity and Intense Absorption

Often people like Ellen and Gail who experience Inspired Creativity talk about entering what they describe as an altered state of consciousness. In many STEs involving Inspired Creativity, a strong feature is the intensity of experiencers' absorption in this altered state. A man I'll call Edward provided one of the best examples of this I have ever seen. Although Edward held a doctorate in social work, he had been painting for years and his artwork was an extremely important part of his life. Here is his story:

> My desire to paint began spontaneously when I was an adolescent. When I paint, I feel myself going into an altered state of consciousness that is almost a trance. I become virtually oblivious to external stimuli and lose track of night and day and times for meals and sleep.
>
> I have also found that I cannot make these creative periods begin. My friends often try to commission work from me, but I am unable to begin a painting at will. It seems that the creative urge has to surface out of my innermost self and then propel me into the altered mental state that is necessary before I can express my creativity.
>
> Once one of these states begins, I go into a compulsive, highly energetic mode that I call my painting frenzy. I become extremely irritated if something interrupts me, and I resent it when someone tries to remind me of worldly schedules or commitments.
>
> I am able to paint only when I am in one of these trance-like states. I am also aware that my creative periods have a mystical quality. Although my paintings are all scenes from nature, I have been told they have a transcendental quality. I try to capture an otherworldly luminosity that I see in scenes of nature when I am in one of my altered states.

It is interesting to note that Edward, like so many other people who experience Inspired Creativity, has felt rushes of energy up his spine for years.

Gifted Children and Creativity

A number of the people who are undergoing the process of spiritual transformation report powerful inspired creative experiences as children. Two of them could be considered child prodigies. Although the term "child prodigy" is sometimes associated with child geniuses such as Mozart, it is often used in the scientific literature to refer to any child who has produced original, high-quality music, writing, scientific insights, or artwork before the age of fourteen. One of the people who fits this category is a man I'll call Martin. He is now thirty and is working on his Ph.D. in physics. As a child, Martin showed an inspired ability to create and compose music that was closely related to mystical experiences. Here is his story:

> From a very young age I felt that I did not fit in — that I was different. I went to the Roman Catholic church with my parents, and I heard talk there about mystical states, and how only Jesus, the apostles, the saints, and the Virgin Mary ever experienced them. I remember at the age of seven thinking that the church was wrong, because I went into these incredible states of bliss and awe whenever I surrendered to the inner music I felt pouring through my soul.
>
> At a very young age I learned to play guitar and piano, and I used to sit and play the music I heard resounding inside my head. I discovered that if I opened up to the Divine I would experience feelings of bliss and ecstasy and I would hear extremely beautiful music pouring through my soul. The music I heard and played in this way was original. I had no sheet music for it, and I had never heard it before. It was simply flowing through me.
>
> I tried to talk to my parents about what I was experiencing, but they told me not to talk about such nonsense. They agreed I seemed to like music, but they thought that my talking about mystical experiences and bliss was the work of the devil or something evil. Slowly, I started to believe that there must be something wrong or something bad about the blissful state I went into when I played. And, finally, when I was around ten I became convinced that what my parents were saying was true. One of the

reasons for this was that the experiences felt too good — and I had learned by then that life wasn't supposed to feel that good. I started to actively suppress the music and not allow myself to go into the mystical states.

I managed to keep them suppressed until about three years ago when I was working on my Ph.D. Suddenly I felt as if something inside of me cracked or exploded and I couldn't keep this incredible creative urge down anymore. It terrified me, because I didn't know what it was.

Martin's story is similar to those of many people I have worked with who were exceptionally creative as children. Often parents and even teachers don't recognize exceptional creative talents of this type because they don't fit within the boundaries dictated by the rigid, linear thinking so common in our schools and society. At the urging of his parents, Martin succeeded in suppressing his mystical/creative urge for many years. But this creative force could not be held down forever. The same was true in the case of a woman I'll call Sheila, who had an amazing gift for writing when she was a child. She told me her story when she came to me for counselling:

When I was about ten years old I began to write complete novels. While I was writing I would fall into an almost mystical state which was characterized by intense absorption and wonderful bliss. Unfortunately, my ability was never recognized by my parents, who refused to read anything I ever wrote. I felt a deep inner urge to become a writer when I grew up, but my family scoffed at the idea, saying I would never earn a reasonable income.

I excelled in school, and my parents urged me to become a lawyer. Many of my teachers agreed, and I eventually became convinced that going to law school would be the best thing I could do with my intellectual abilities. Still, although I kept it hidden from my parents, I continued to write.

Once I entered law school, however, I found I no longer had time to write. This situation continued until I had worked as a lawyer for three years. By this time I found that I was profoundly depressed. I felt my life was empty, even though I had worldly success. As a result of counselling, I decided to cut down on my workload and give myself time to write. Once I began to give vent to the powerful creative urge I felt and to write again, my depression lifted, and I began to find meaning in my life.

Child prodigies are rare, and my work with them has been limited. However, the stories of Martin and Sheila are typical of my experience: Both felt their creative experiences had a strong mystical component, and neither of them was able to completely suppress the creative force that flowed within them. Further, both Martin and Sheila grew into adults who have a very strong spiritual focus. Of course, further research would be needed to determine whether this is typical of all child prodigies and to discover exactly what the relationship might be between this type of mystical/creative experience and the process of spiritual transformation.

Milder Inspired Creativity and Poetry

Many cases of Inspired Creativity are much milder than those experienced by Ellen and Gail. Few people suddenly develop the outstanding degree of talent that they did or are able to begin new careers with so little training. However, the spontaneous development of milder forms of Inspired Creativity is very common in people involved in a process of spiritual transformation. Most of the people I have seen who have STEs — if not STEPs — involving Inspired Creativity have either been involved in spiritual pursuits for a long time or have become highly spiritually focused soon after the experiences begin. Further, in many cases, the creative material produced — whether it was scientific insights, philosophy, art, poetry, prose, or music — had a spiritual or transcendental quality.

A very common form of milder Inspired Creativity in STE experiencers is inspired poetry. Many STE experiencers have told me of suddenly beginning to write inspired poetry, sometimes multi-page epics! One case of this type is that of a woman I'll call Cassandra, who was a housewife and mother.

> Since my twenties, I have been actively involved in my own spiritual journey. It began when I took a course in meditation, in which I had a mystical vision. That abruptly changed my life. I began to practise meditation, prayer, and self-reflection regularly. Soon the pursuit of spiritual understanding became the main focus of my life. Eventually I began to do yoga and martial arts.
>
> I steadfastly continued my meditation and spiritual practices for years, without feeling that I had any further spiritual experiences. When I was in my late thirties, however, I developed strong kundalini symptoms: heat, piercing back pain, energy rushes, and sometimes I went into spontaneous yoga postures. I suddenly developed an overwhelming urge to write poetry. I found that rhyming couplets relating to spiritual themes would float into my consciousness. As I wrote them down, more and more would flow into my mind. Eventually a poem — pages in length — would take shape. Sometimes the process of producing a poem occurred rapidly; at other times parts of the poem would come to me over several weeks. Gradually the poem took the form of a lengthy epic.
>
> I was amazed by this development. I had never thought of myself as a person who had any ability as a poet.

Cassandra has found that she has little or no control over writing this poetry. She says it simply "comes to her" and seems to flow with little intellectual effort on her part. Although these inspired poetry experiences are not as dramatic as the artistic transformation of someone like Ellen, it seems clear to me that they represent a common feature of transformation of consciousness on the spiritual journey.

One of the most fascinating things about the people I've met who experience STEs with Inspired Creativity is that they all talk about going into some type of altered state when they have their experiences, and they all agree that there is a mystical component to the experience itself. I have also found that almost everyone who is having any type of STE tends to experience a noticeable — and sometimes extreme — increase in the urge to be creative. Surely this indicates that the relationship between Inspired Creativity, genius, mystical experience, and kundalini will be a fertile and fascinating area for future research.

PART 2

RESEARCHING THE YOGIC MODEL OF CONSCIOUSNESS, KUNDALINI, AND STEs

THE YOGIC MODEL OF CONSCIOUSNESS AND KUNDALINI

IT SHOULD BE CLEAR FROM THE CASE HISTORIES related in the first section of this book that many people are undergoing the types of extraordinary spiritual and paranormal experiences I call STEs. However, very little Western scientific research has been done to learn more about them in general and to discover whether the striking similarities and parallels found in these experiences might not be explained by some common denominator.

In the East, yogic sages, mystics, and the Masters of the Himalayas have studied and documented STEs and spiritual transformation of consciousness for thousands of years. Their scientific research method was to practise lifelong disciplines of yoga and meditation, and to make inner and outer observation of the self, with comparison to the observations of other yogis. These eons of yogic research discovered that the kundalini is a mechanism in the body and brain, said to normally lay dormant at the base of the astral spine, that, when activated, can accelerate a person's spiritual transformation of consciousness. Although agreeing on major points, diverse yogic traditions have developed slightly different understandings and slightly different vocabularies of the spiritual energy/kundalini and spiritual transformation of consciousness, just as diverse world religions have developed slightly different understandings of the spiritual energy active in mystics!

My first introduction to the yogic model of consciousness and the kundalini mechanism came from my meetings with Gopi Krishna from 1977 to 1983 and from my study of his writings and theories. His model made sense to me, and helped me understand STEs and assist others with STEs. Therefore, I will describe Gopi Krishna's kundalini model in detail. Later, my deeper understanding of the yogic model of consciousness and kundalini came from studying many yogic texts, especially from studying the writings of the contemporary yogic saint and guru, Paramahansa Yogananda.

Although Swami Vivekananda came to the USA for a short time, 1893 to 1897, and 1899, introducing yoga in the USA, as I mentioned in chapter 8 on Inspired Creativity and Genius, Paramahansa Yogananda was the first Indian guru to come to North America and make it his home, for thirty-two years, from 1920 until his death in 1952, travelling nationwide teaching the philosophy and science of yoga, plus yogic techniques of meditation. Thus he earned the title of "The Father of Yoga in the West." I found Paramahansa Yogananda's extensive writings to be the most comprehensive and in-depth overview of the ancient science of yoga, written from a multi-faith perspective and very accessible to a Western reader. Therefore, I will also outline the yogic model of consciousness and kundalini as described by Paramahansa Yogananda, in some detail.

Proposed Scientific Research into Kundalini

Pandit Gopi Krishna proposed a hypothesis or starting point for Western scientific research on kundalini and its relationship to Spiritually Transformative Experiences and spiritual transformation of consciousness. A synopsis of Gopi Krishna's hypothesis is as follows: kundalini, when awakened, is the biological-psychological-spiritual mechanism responsible for Mystical Experiences, Classical Kundalini Episodes, Psychic Awakenings, Near-Death Experiences, Inspired Creativity and Genius, and, when unhealthy, some types of mental illness with mystical features.

My clinical experience suggests that this hypothesis provides an excellent starting point for research. It would help explain the commonalities found in various types of STEs and provide a platform for future research that might come closer to determining the exact nature of the spiritual energy that mystics have described for thousands of years. Current Western scientific theories about the nature of the universe and human consciousness cannot explain STEs. The yogic model of consciousness and kundalini provides a missing link: a plausible theory to explain spiritual transformation of consciousness.

His modern interpretation of the ancient yogic teachings on consciousness and kundalini was first put forward by Gopi Krishna in 1967, in his still-popular book *Kundalini: The Evolutionary Energy in Man*, and was described in increasing detail in his other seventeen books. Gopi Krishna theorized that the spiritual energy/kundalini was the biological-spiritual mechanism driving human evolution, transforming humanity's consciousness, and making it possible for us to attain the tremendously expanded states of awareness that he called "higher consciousness." He developed his ideas by researching the ancient yogic texts, by interpreting them in light of modern knowledge about the human body, by observing the workings of kundalini in his own body, and through inspired creative insights and revelations that he received as part of his spiritual transformation. The last forty years of his life were spent working to promote awareness of kundalini and to convince the Western scientific community to seriously investigate kundalini and its transformative effect on consciousness.

Gopi Krishna proposed that spiritual energy/kundalini could be researched scientifically in a number of ways: (1) literary research, which would involve researching the lives and writings of great mystics and geniuses of the past to see if evidence of kundalini awakening could be found, and collecting information from the vast literature on kundalini from the oral and written yogic traditions and other esoteric mystical traditions; (2) developing a questionnaire that would examine the experiences of people living today who are undergoing the profound paranormal experiences characterized as STEs in this book; (3) carrying out detailed medical and biochemical analysis of hormones and body fluids in individuals experiencing profound kundalini awakening and in people experiencing mental illness with mystical features; and (4) developing a project in which selected people would begin a disciplined attempt to arouse kundalini while being scientifically and medically monitored. In addition to these worldly research strategies, Gopi Krishna also recommended that every person do kundalini research in the crucible of their own consciousness — by following the Eight Limbs of Yoga, including right living and daily meditation.

Although no full-scale scientific investigation was ever launched during his lifetime, Gopi Krishna's hypothesis did attract the attention of some leading scientists and scholars. One was Dr. Carl Friedrich von Weizsäcker, physicist and former director of the Max Planck Institute for Research of Living Conditions in the Modern World. In his foreword to Gopi Krishna's *The Biological Basis of Religion and Genius*, Professor von Weizsäcker reveals his deep respect for Gopi Krishna's ideas and calls him "an eyewitness to the truth he represents."

Another avid supporter of Gopi Krishna was Dr. Karan Singh, a medical doctor who was the Minister of Health and Welfare for Indira Gandhi's government in India. Dr. Singh even gained approval and funding for a massive scientific project to test the kundalini hypothesis, but the Gandhi government fell just before the project was to begin.

A number of Kundalini Research Institutes and Associations have formed around the world, and some of the literary research Gopi Krishna proposed has begun, conducted by myself, as well as by other kundalini researchers. In 1990 a major step was taken when an international group of scientists, doctors, and researchers — myself included — met at the home of Dr. Bonnie Greenwell, a clinical psychologist and former director of the Counselling Center at the Institute of Transpersonal Psychology, near San Jose, California, to discuss the possibility of collaborating on scientific research into spiritual energy/kundalini. Those present came from a variety of backgrounds, represented diverse spiritual traditions, and held widely different ideas about kundalini, but all agreed on the importance of scientific research into the possible relationship between the spiritual energy/ kundalini, mystical states of consciousness, and other STEs.

At the meeting the Kundalini Research Network was formed as a coalition of individuals and organizations whose top priority would be to increase the awareness of kundalini and its associated phenomena in the Western scientific and medical communities as soon as possible. For this reason, the KRN Questionnaire Research Project was begun. I was a member of the original project committee. In 1991, I became chairperson for the project, a position I held until 1998. In the same year, under my supervision, the KRN Questionnaire was developed and a pilot study completed. Shortly thereafter, the principal study was launched. A number of intriguing findings have been made. However, before we go on to consider them, we need to look more deeply at the basic concepts of the ancient yogic model of consciousness and spiritual energy/kundalini. We also must examine how the awakening of kundalini might function as the biological-psychological-spiritual basis for Spiritually Transformative Experiences.

Underlying Principles of the Yogic Model

Paramahansa Yogananda stated that the true goal of Yoga, and the true goal of life, is liberation, oneness with God, self-realization. The basic premise underlying the yogic model of consciousness and kundalini is that the next goal of human evolution is for all individuals to gradually manifest an expanding range and higher states of consciousness, which will ultimately include mystical and paranormal perceptions. This expansion of consciousness will occur as a result of the activation of one or more presently dormant brain/astral brain centres or functions. When through persistent spiritual self-effort and with the grace of the Divine the spiritual energy/kundalini mechanism is awakened in an individual, this evolutionary transformation of consciousness can be accelerated.

According to Gopi Krishna, a healthy kundalini awakening causes two distinct changes in the body and astral body. One is that the body is stimulated to supply potent fuels to the transforming brain and astral brain. Two psychic fuels, prana/life-energy and ojas/sublimated sexual energy, are transported, rush, or flow up the spine/astral spine to the brain/astral brain. This may be perceived as a movement and flow of energy up the spine. The other is the stimulation of a normally dormant region of the brain/astral brain known as the brahma randhra in yoga. He postulated that as this area is stimulated into activity, it makes possible the expanded perceptions that are presently thought of as mystical and paranormal states of consciousness.

Similarly, Paramahansa Yogananda described awakening of the kundalini mechanism to cause the prana/life-energy to reverse direction of flow. Rather than the prana/life-energy flowing in its normal downward and outward direction from the astral spine to vivify the body parts and physical senses, instead with a kundalini awakening the prana/life-energy flows inward from the body, and upwards through the astral spine's "sushumna" channel to the astral brain. Further, Paramahansa Yogananda went on to state that because consciousness is focused where the life-energy is focused, with a kundalini awakening and the inward and upward flow of prana/life-energy, the individual's consciousness focus also flows inwards and upwards. The upward-flowing consciousness is thereby freed from its entanglement with the outer physical senses, worldly emotional attachments, and limited ego consciousness. This allows the individual's consciousness to rise up to the astral brain, to experience union with the Soul. Thus mystical experiences and ultimately self-realization or liberation become possible.

Circulation of Potent Prana — The Intelligent Life-Energy

According to the yogic model of consciousness, we are all actually immortal Souls, unique sparks or rays of the one infinite source, Divine Spirit, God. Our immortal Souls are encased in three progressively denser bodies; first the "causal body," thus named because it causes the other two denser soul encasements; next the "astral body"; and finally the physical body. As Paramahansa Yogananda describes in detail in *God Talks with Arjuna,* the causal body is the thought/consciousness body encasing the Soul, and which consists of thirty-five ideas or thought-forces. The causal body's thought-forces create the denser astral light body of intelligent life-energy/prana, which consists of nineteen elements and powers. The powers of the astral/life-energy body are what build, maintain, and enliven the yet denser physical body. The centres of life and consciousness from which the astral powers function in the body are located in the astral brain or "thousand-petal lotus of light," and in the astral spine or "sushumna," which contains six subtle centres or "chakras."

According to the yogic tradition, "universal prana" is an extremely subtle, super-intelligent cosmic life-energy — as yet unidentified by Western science — that fills all of creation. Each living body contains "individual prana," known in China as chi (qi), in Japan as ki, and in the West as bio-energy, or life-energy. According to the yogic tradition, the astral body is composed of individual prana, and forms a very subtle, biochemical sheath permeating and surrounding our physical bodies. The astral body is sometimes referred to as the etheric body or subtle body. The yogic literature describes five subtypes of individual prana, according to their functions in the body. However these subtypes are beyond the scope of this book, and I will group all subtypes together as "prana."

The individual prana, which acts to vivify each being, acts on all the cells and tissues of the body, and is continuously affected and replenished by universal prana. Paramahansa Yogananda said that universal prana/astral life-energy recharges individual prana by being absorbed into the body through a region in the brain around the medulla oblongata. Individual prana/life-energy circulates through the body in astral channels called the "nadis" — a complex system believed by some to include or be superimposed upon the nervous system. Individual prana is also identified with the psyche or the individual personality.

Although prana and the nadis have been written about in detail in many yogic texts, including the Tantras and Paramahansa Yogananda's *God Talks with Arjuna,* Gopi Krishna's writings propose another way how individual prana might function in terms of what we currently know about the body and nervous system. He thought that individual prana is also produced by certain cells of the body as a part of their normal functioning, and that prana is also absorbed from the air we breathe and from the food we eat. Whatever the sources, yogic traditions state that once prana/life-energy is absorbed from outside the body or is produced internally, it is transported by the astral spine and astral nadis or nerves. Prana stimulates and is used for healthy functioning of the body and brain, and is used as "psychic fuel" for the functions that are carried out by our consciousness. Prana can also be stored in the central nervous system or in the sexual organs.

Gopi Krishna thought that with the activation of the kundalini mechanism, however, body cells are stimulated to produce a more refined, more potent form of prana and in greater quantities. The nervous system is also stimulated into a higher degree of activity than normal in order to extract greater quantities of prana from the cells and from the prana stores in the nerves and the sexual organs, and to send it to the transforming brain/ astral brain. He thought the flow of this highly potent form of the prana/ life-energy could sometimes be perceived as energy flowing up the body and spine, and/or an inner luminosity as it pours into the brain.

Ojas — Sublimated Sexual Energy

In the yogic tradition, the sexual organs are believed to be the main source of "ojas," or sublimated sexual energy, another potent fuel for the transforming brain/astral brain. It is believed that when the sexual secretions are sent downward or outward in the act of procreation, ojas, in its grosser form, is the vital principle that vivifies the egg and sperm. With the healthy awakening of the kundalini mechanism, however, ojas is believed to be sublimated and transmuted into a finer form, and to travel up through the spine/astral spine into the brain. Ojas functions as a potent, nutritive tonic with rejuvenating properties for the transforming brain/astral brain as new brain functions develop, and possibly the previously dormant brahma randhra region activates. Sometimes the upward flow of ojas creates an exquisite sensation as it rises to the brain. Gopi Krishna believed it to be the "soma," "nectar," or "ambrosia" that is so often referred to in treatises on kundalini.

Ojas can also travel up the spine/astral spine and out through the major nerve plexuses, or chakras, and irrigate the body organs. When ojas enters the body organs, it nourishes them, to help prepare and tone the organs for the increased prana production that is now required because of the tremendously increased activity of the brain and consciousness.

In yoga, this transmutation and upward flow of ojas/sublimated sexual energy, from the sexual organs to the brain/astral brain, is called "urdhva-retas" — literally translated as the upward flow of the semen. This process may be a deeper, more biological interpretation of what is called sublimation of the sexual energy in modern psychology. The important role of ojas/sexual energy in the transformation of consciousness is thought to be one reason why so many spiritual traditions recommend abstinence or, at least, sexual moderation for spiritual aspirants. It should be added that, although retas literally means semen, it is not semen, but sexual energy that is transmuted. Gopi Krishna, for one, made it clear that there is a parallel process in the female body and that women are as likely as men to achieve the awakening of kundalini, and successful spiritual transformation of consciousness. In my clinical experience, I have found that this is indeed the case.

Stimulation of the Brain's Dormant Regions

According to the yogic model of consciousness and kundalini, activation of dormant regions and functions of the brain/astral brain occur during spiritual transformation of consciousness, to ultimately enable God-realization. Awakening of the kundalini mechanism is considered essential for this transformation to be successful. As the kundalini mechanism streams increased quantities of potent prana/life-energy and nutritive ojas/sexual energy up the spine/astral spine to the brain/astral brain, normally dormant regions and functions of the brain and/or astral brain are being stimulated and activated. Recently, pioneering Western brain researchers including Dr. Norman Doidge and Dr. Andrew Newberg have confirmed, through neuroplasticity research, that under certain circumstances the physical brain is indeed capable of activating dormant regions.

Gopi Krishna proposed the brain region that becomes activated by the kundalini to be what is known in yoga as the "brahma randhra." (In Hinduism, Brahma is God, the Creator; randhra means aperture.) The brahma randhra is sometimes called the "cavity of Brahma." Although the exact location of the brahma randhra is not known, some yogic traditions say it is near the centre of the brain/astral brain, directly above the palate — but it probably does not correspond directly to either the pituitary or the pineal glands, as is sometimes supposed.

With continued spiritual effort, Divine grace, and healthy balanced lifestyle in body, mind, ethics, and spirit, the kundalini mechanism may remain active, the brain and astral brain may continue to be stimulated with upflowing prana and ojas, one or more new brain functions or centres may activate, and new channels of perception begin to develop. In other words, the transformation in consciousness that occurs with kundalini activity slowly makes it possible to perceive mystical and/or psychic realities, the levels of reality that are glimpsed in STEs. As we have seen earlier in this book, these changes in perception can occur in a variety of ways. With a healthy, slow, gradual transformation in which the brain and astral brain continue to be supplied adequately with potent prana and ojas, the transformation begins in only a limited way. The new perceptual abilities may occur in brief flashes or in somewhat longer, but still transient, episodes.

With time, as the transforming brain centre(s) activate more fully, and if the individual continues to purify and expand their consciousness through regular meditation practices, if they heal their emotional, mental, and spiritual impurities, which are blocks to the clear flow of kundalini (see chapters 17 and 18 on Psycho-Spiritual Housecleaning), and if they live a moral, principled, spiritual life, their consciousness may continue to expand to the point that they become able to perceive with greater frequency or intensity the subtle spiritual realities that are normally beyond our perception. At first, these mystical states generally occur briefly, usually during periods of meditation, prayer, deep absorption, or concentration. They are transient mystical states called sabikalpa samadhis. Eventually, the mystical states may begin to occur at any time and, finally, become more and more a part of the experiencer's normal daily functioning.

The profound change of perception in consciousness that allows one to see spiritual-paranormal dimensions of reality has been given names in various mystical and esoteric traditions. In yoga and Hinduism, it has been called the "opening of the tenth door," "shedding the veils of Maya," "freeing from delusion," or "liberation."

As explained in some detail in chapter 4 on Spiritual Energy/Kundalini Episodes, spiritual energy/kundalini activity occurs on a continuum. I think that the degree and intensity of STEs may correspond with the level of spiritual energy/kundalini activity the person is experiencing. Once the kundalini is active, these episodic, variable experiences of expanded states of consciousness may continue for the rest of the person's life.

It is important to always remember that the yogic model of consciousness and kundalini describes a physiologic mechanism associated with a deeply *spiritual* transformation of consciousness. Individuals cannot control this process. The Higher Power, God, the intelligence behind the universe, underlies spiritual transformation of consciousness and the spiritual energy/kundalini mechanism. Spirit inwardly guides and teaches the individual how to surrender to and work with this spiritual transformation process. According to the yogic tradition the Divine Higher Power will also invisibly draw sincere spiritual seekers to a spiritual teacher or later to an illumined guru, as required to assist and guide the devotee through the spiritual transformation process.

I wish to mention here that some students of classical yoga have in the past disagreed with the yogic model of consciousness and kundalini and the many case examples of spiritual energy/kundalini awakening that I present in this book, arguing that, according to the classical teachings of their particular tradition, the kundalini mechanism cannot awaken spontaneously, stimulated by meditation or by an NDE, but can only be awakened with the assistance of an illumined guru/spiritual Master. In response to this perspective, I point out that yoga philosophy universally includes the concept of reincarnation, that Souls incarnate in many lifetimes to progressively evolve and learn their Soul lessons. It is quite possible that individuals who spontaneously awaken kundalini in this lifetime, like Gopi Krishna, or even myself, may have had their initial kundalini awakening in a past life, while they were indeed under the guidance and blessings of an illumined guru/spiritual Master.

The Chakras and the Astral Spine

Before going on to consider expanded states of consciousness in more detail, we need to take at least a brief look at the concepts of the astral spine and the chakras, for they are mentioned repeatedly in the yogic literature on prana and kundalini. Yogic science contends that just as the physical body has a brain, spinal cord, and nerves spreading throughout the body from the spine, the astral body also has an astral brain, an astral spine, and numerous astral channels/nadis extending to the entire astral body. It is thought that the astral body both encases and interpenetrates the physical body, with the astral body components interpenetrating the equivalent anatomic counterparts in the denser physical body. The prana flowing through the astral body is believed to be what vivifies and animates the physical body.

The main astral spine, or sushumna, overshadows and interpenetrates the physical spine, and is said to have three progressively subtler layers, each with progressively subtler functions. Within the sushumna, the next subtler layer of the astral spine is called the "vajra nadi," which is said to run from the sacral/second chakra to the astral brain. Within vajra nadi is the yet subtler "chitra nadi," which is said to also run up to the astral brain. The third, and most subtle, spinal layer is said to be the causal spine, which is called the "brahmanadi."

Yogic science contends that like the astral body, the more subtle causal/thought body has a causal brain and a causal spine. The causal body is said to be the intelligence behind the existence and function of the astral body, the physical body, and consciousness. The causal brain is the seat of spiritual wisdom, and sits at the top of the causal spine/brahmanadi. Paramahansa Yogananda explains that the brahmanadi is made up of a strong current of pure consciousness. Although the brahmanadi/causal spine is commonly described as being inside the chitra astral spine, it is actually subtler than the astral spine rather than physically inside it. Pure consciousness is subtler than prana/life-energy.

Two main astral nadis/channels are said to be located on either side of the sushumna/astral spine, on the left "ida," on the right "pingala." Ida and pingala are said to constitute the astral sympathetic and parasympathetic nervous systems, which in turn control those of the gross physical body.

According to the yogic tradition, when the spiritual energy/kundalini mechanism is activated, prana and ojas spontaneously begin to flow up the sushumna/astral spine channel to the brain and astral brain, opening the sushumna channel. By practising diverse yogic meditation techniques, meditators may also stimulate the upward flow of prana through the sushumna/astral spine by their self-efforts, and thereby also help stimulate or awaken the kundalini mechanism.

The spinal chakras, astral centres along the sushumna/astral spine, each connect to many nadis. The upward flow of prana and ojas through the sushumna/astral spine, from the root chakra at the base of the spine to the crown chakra at the top of the brain, may be blocked or distorted at lower chakras by mental, physical, or spiritual impurities, including our past-life karma (unlearned Soul lessons) and our samskaras (habits and tendencies).

As previously mentioned, the word "chakra" literally means "wheel," and, in yoga, the chakras are said to be energy centres or vortices along the astral spine and in the brain. Although the chakras are described in great detail in some yogic and Tantric texts, different esoteric traditions have widely varying views about them. A few believe them to be merely symbolic aids to meditation. Most believe they exist, but only in the astral body. Some people believe the chakras exist only in the physical body and are simply the major nerve plexuses. Another view, which Paramahansa Yogananda and many yogic traditions uphold, suggests that the spinal chakras represent points of communication between the physical body, the astral body, and the causal body, between the major nerve plexuses on the physical body, the major nadi plexuses on the sushumna/astral spine, and the spiritual centres on the brahmanadi/causal spine. Yogananda stated that the physical, astral, and causal bodies are knitted together at the spinal chakras, uniting the three bodies to work together.

The exact number and location of the chakras is also debated in various traditions. Some Buddhist schools, for instance, hold that there are ten major chakras; others say five. In most yogic traditions, however, there are thought to be six spinal chakras plus a seventh chakra in the astral brain at the top of the head. The yogic tradition has an anatomic map of the seven major chakras, and has given each a Sanskrit name. In ascending order they are:

1. The first and lowest spinal chakra, or "muladhara chakra," is located at the base of the spine, in the coccygeal region. It is sometimes called the root chakra.
2. The second chakra, or "svadhisthana chakra," lies a couple inches higher along the astral spine, in the sacral region.
3. The third spinal chakra, or "manipura chakra," is higher still, in the lumbar region opposite to the navel.
4. The fourth spinal chakra, or "anahata chakra," is in the dorsal region, behind the heart. It is often called the heart chakra.
5. The fifth spinal chakra, or "vishuddha chakra," is in the cervical or neck region, at the base of the throat and neck. It is often called the throat chakra.
6. The sixth chakra, or "ajna chakra," is located at a point on the forehead just above and between the eyebrows. It is sometimes called the third eye, the spiritual eye, or the Christ Consciousness centre. Some traditions say the ajna chakra is connected to the medulla oblongata at the back of the brain, as well.
7. The seventh chakra, or "sahasrara chakra," is located at the crown of the head. It is sometimes called the thousand-petaled lotus, or the crown chakra.

Some traditions hold that an additional three chakras may exist in the astral body above the crown and that there are smaller, minor chakras on either side of the heart and on the hands and feet.

Despite the debate about exactly what the chakras are, one thing is clear: many long-time meditators, serious students of yoga, and people who are undergoing STEs begin to experience sensations in the areas in which the chakras are generally thought to be located. Some also begin to perceive, perhaps clairvoyantly, such things as colours, patterns, or energy flows in these areas. It often seems as if the chakras become increasingly active energetically, and more prominent with time, following a kundalini awakening.

Many people having STEs today report that they are able to see a white, shining energy body or aura that seems to exist around their own or others' physical bodies. Others also report seeing coloured auras. Further, many report that they feel as if their bodies are tingling with energy or that energy is flowing along their arms and legs or up their spinal column. These sensations and perceptions may be related to the tremendously increased production of prana in the cells and the increased activity that occurs in the nervous system — and/or nadis — as it transports the larger amounts of more potent prana and ojas to the brain/astral brain when the kundalini mechanism is active. Some say they can see the circulating prana as a beautiful, glistening, silver luminescence that circulates through the organs and travels upwards along the nervous system. Some say that they perceive ojas flowing in the spine and brain as a beautiful, luminescent gold.

NDEs and Kundalini Awakening

An example of how the yogic model of consciousness and kundalini could explain many symptoms of STEs and their transformative after-effects can be found by examining the relationship between NDEs and kundalini awakening. NDE researchers and co-founders of the International Association for Near-Death Studies Dr. Kenneth Ring and Dr. Bruce Greyson have both postulated Kundalini activation as a possible underlying factor in NDEs. Gopi Krishna strongly held this view.

Paramahansa Yogananda explained that according to the yogic model of consciousness, at conception the soul, encased in the causal body and astral body, enters the nucleus formed by the union of the sperm and ovum. It later descends into the developing embryo via the medulla oblongata of the developing brain and descends down the developing spinal cord. Individual prana of the astral body, guided by the faculties of the soul, vivifies the embryo and guides its development into a fetus, then into a human baby. The life-energy/prana of the astral body emanates outwards from the astral spine into the physical spine and physical body, vivifying it. At the moment of death, the reverse occurs. The soul, encased in the astral and causal bodies, withdraws from the physical body into the astral spine, and ascends the astral spine, or sushumna, to exit the body through the head/astral brain. By this model, this withdrawal of the astral body and soul up the astral spine, heading toward the astral brain, would also occur during a Near-Death Experience.

In some branches of yoga it is also believed that at the time of death, the kundalini energy awakens at the root chakra and rises up the spine through the astral sushumna channel to the head, enabling the soul encased in the astral and causal body to leave the physical body through the third-eye or crown chakras of the head. Additionally, Gopi Krishna thought that in the near-death situation, the kundalini mechanism may sometimes activate in an attempt to protect the hypoxic brain from damage. He thought an arcane yogic practice called "Kechari mudra," a technique claiming to sometimes induce a kundalini awakening, was actually an ancient technique to try to induce a Near-Death Experience — and kundalini awakening. In Kechari mudra, the yogi would place the tip of their tongue as far back as possible on the palate, to ultimately block the nasal cavity and block airflow to the lungs.

It seems to me that one way of understanding the order of progression of the typical symptoms in a Near-Death Experience as identified by Raymond Moody is to compare them to the symptoms of chakra activation, in order of progression starting from the base of the spine to the brain, that occur during a kundalini awakening. Typically, one of the first sensations during an NDE is the loss of fear, a feeling of great peace and calm, a certainty that there is nothing to fear, that all is right with the universe. In the yogic tradition, these feelings are typical of those experienced when the kundalini and consciousness rises above the first/root chakra, which is the seat of fear. When the kundalini and/or consciousness reaches the second/sacral or third/lumbar chakras and stimulates them, a psychic awakening can occur, with clairaudience (hearing what is being said around your unconscious or dead body).

As the NDE continues an out-of-body experience occurs. In an NDE, this experience of floating above the unconscious or clinically dead physical body and accurately viewing what is happening below almost invariably occurs after the feeling of peace begins. According to diverse yogic traditions, an out-of-body experience may occur either when the kundalini and/or consciousness reaches the third/lumbar chakra or the fifth/throat chakra. In either case, the out-of-body experience is psychic, not mystical in nature. There is no experience of the light or of the loving Higher Power in the out-of-body experience.

If the NDE continues to deepen, a dark tunnel with light at the end is often perceived. Some yogic traditions think this dark tunnel is the perception of the opening of the third-eye chakra, and the soul/consciousness moving through the third eye, through lower astral dimensions to the high astral realm of heaven. Other yogic traditions think the dark tunnel is perceived while the kundalini and soul/consciousness is ascending the astral spine/sushumna to the brain.

As the NDE continues, whether or not a dark tunnel was seen, the kundalini and/or consciousness may rise up the astral spine to the third-eye chakra, or even to the crown chakra. The classical yogic symptoms of the kundalini reaching these upper chakras in the head is a mystical experience of some type: seeing the light of astral heaven, expansion of consciousness, mystical visions, mystical union, and/or mystical revelations. This corresponds to such typical elements of mystical NDEs as seeing visions of departed loved ones in their light bodies, having mystical visions of saints, gurus, or deities, and feeling surrounded and immersed in the loving light of the Higher Power. Mystical experiences in an NDE may progress from astral perceptions in the realm of loving light and astral light beings, to casual plane perceptions of pure thought and infinite wisdom/bliss, as it did in my 2003 NDE. In the yogic tradition this is understood as an astral samadhi progressing to a deeper and more subtle causal samadhi or causal mystical experience. Kundalini awakening is also associated with hearing an inner sound, another symptom frequently described by Near-Death Experiencers.

According to many yogic traditions, once the kundalini mechanism is initially activated or awakened, it rarely turns off completely. Although the kundalini usually returns to the root chakra after an initial awakening, and after an NDE, the kundalini mechanism may continue to be active, though only slightly. Further, once the astral body and consciousness have ascended the astral spine's sushumna, the astral sushumna channel has become opened, and remains partly open up to the chakra level that the consciousness and/or kundalini reached.

This can explain the observation made by many NDE researchers, including myself, that NDE experiencers who see the light — by this model who had an upper-chakra mystical experience — are usually greatly spiritually transformed after their NDE, with a loss of the fear of death, conviction of the reality of a Higher Power, and an increase in spiritual focus, while those who had an out-of-body NDE only, generally do not experience this same degree of spiritual transformation as an after-effect.

Because the astral sushumna pathway to the astral brain has been opened by an NDE and does not close down completely afterward, in the years following an NDE there may be some degree of ongoing kundalini activity, flowing prana up the partially opened sushumna to the level of the upper chakra to which the kundalini once rose. This may stimulate further out-of-body and psychic experiences for all NDE experiencers, and further mystical experiences for mystical NDE experiencers, with gradual ongoing transformation of the brain/astral brain. This ongoing kundalini activity or upward pranic flow may range in intensity from virtually imperceptible, to intermittent spurts, to strong and dramatic.

In my clinical experience, for those persons experiencing some ongoing kundalini/spiritual energy activity after an NDE, the level of activity and the intensity of the symptoms tend to increase over time. These kundalini symptoms may gradually become perceptible to the NDE experiencer as ongoing or recurrent inner sounds, intermittent light perceptions, or intermittent rushes of energy up the body and/or the spine. The gradual stimulation of the transforming brain/astral brain may result in more frequent psychic experiences, recurrent mystical experiences, and/or the development of inspired creativity.

Because it is much easier to reopen the sushumna once it has been previously opened, those NDE experiencers who further stimulate their kundalini through individual spiritual effort, including regular practices of meditation, heartfelt prayer, intense concentration, yoga, or other spiritual disciplines, are likely to notice a more rapid increase over time in these kundalini/spiritual energy symptoms and their spiritual transformation of consciousness.

Perennial Cosmic Consciousness — The Sahaja State

According to the yogic tradition, with Divine grace and the blessings of an illumined guru/spiritual Master (either incarnate or ascended), combined with the spiritual seeker's regular and deep meditations, self-development, and balanced lifestyle, after many years of stimulation by the kundalini mechanism the brain/astral brain may reach a level of stabilized expanded conscious functioning that allows a person to exist in a perennial state of mystical union while fully concentrating on external worldly realities at the same time. Such a person would live in a state of higher consciousness, constantly living in direct connection with the Absolute, the Divine intelligence behind the universe, and yet still be able to fully participate in and concentrate on daily, worldly activities. Such a person lives and walks in two worlds, the mystical and the physical. This state is known in yoga as the sahaja state, sahaja-samadhi, nirbikalpa samadhi, or the turiya state. In Christian mysticism this is called ongoing mystical communion, or Christ Consciousness. In Buddhism it is called enlightenment or nirvana.

It is an extremely rare condition. For centuries, the hundreds of thousands of spiritual seekers who embarked upon the path of yoga were told that only a handful would reach final liberation. In the *Bhagavad Gita*, the Hindu saint Bhagavan Krishna says, "Among thousands of men, scarce one striveth for perfection, and of the successful strivers, scarce one knoweth me in essence."

The term sahaja means "co-emergent," and describes the coexistence of two states of consciousness: mystical union and normal worldly mental functioning. It is also known as "Buddha consciousness" or "Christ consciousness," because it is held that both the Buddha and Jesus Christ were able to function in the world while at the same time existing in a state of ongoing mystical union with the Absolute. Dr. Richard Maurice Bucke, a Canadian psychiatrist, described this state as being "permanently endowed with the cosmic sense" or with "Cosmic Consciousness." Dr. Kenneth Ring calls it "Omega," using Teilhard de Chardin's term for what Teilhard believed was the goal for the evolution of consciousness. Bucke, Ring, and Gopi Krishna all hypothesize that perennial cosmic consciousness is the next major evolutionary step for the entire human race. Paramahansa Yogananda stated that to realize and experience our oneness with God, to achieve ongoing mystical union or nirbikalpa samadhi, perennial cosmic consciousness, is the true purpose of life.

The yogic tradition also contends that the human race will evolve over the next many ages, or "yugas," to manifest more expanded, spiritual states of consciousness. Further, yogic traditions state that this spiritual transformation and expansion in consciousness can be accelerated through practice of the Eight Limbs of Yoga, right living, and scientific techniques of meditation, which can stimulate or awaken the kundalini mechanism.

The Eight Limbs of Yoga

The Eight Limbs of Yoga, also known as the Eightfold Path of Yoga, were described by the ancient yogic adept Patanjali in the *Yoga Sutras*, often referred to as the *Yoga Sutras of Patanjali*. These sequential disciplines form the basic step-by-step foundation for a spiritual seeker, to help ensure an ultimate healthy awakening of the spiritual energy/kundalini, and a healthy long-term spiritual transformation of consciousness.

The first four limbs represent the physical, psychological, and spiritual disciplines that are needed for success in yoga. Through practising the first four limbs, the spiritual seeker learns to purify their psyche, body, and prana, so that they become physically, mentally, and spiritually fit and prepared for the gradual development of expanded, transcendental states of consciousness. Once this preparation is complete, often after many years of dedicated practice, the aspirant can begin to add on the practice of the last four limbs, including meditation, which were designed to slowly bring about spiritual transformation and expanded states of consciousness.

Patanjali's Eight Limbs of Yoga are as follows:

1. *Yama (Moral Conduct, the "Don'ts")*. The avoidance of immoral actions and observances of moral practices, which are the basis of spiritual discipline. The main five listed in the *Yoga Sutras* are: do not harm others, truthfulness (do not lie), do not steal, chastity (sexual continence), and greedlessness (do not covet). Other yogic texts also prescribe sympathy, rectitude, patience, steadfastness, moderation in diet, and cleanliness.

2. *Niyama (Discipline, the "Dos")*. The five practices listed in the *Yoga Sutras* are: purity of body and mind, contentment in all circumstances, self-discipline, self-study or contemplation, and devotion to God and guru. Other texts include practices such as charity, affirmation of the existence of the Divine, listening to scriptures, hospitality, modesty, being of service to others, the repetition of prayers, and performing spiritually motivated sacrifices.

3. *Asana (Right Posture)*. Patanjali says simply that "the posture should be steady and comfortable. It is accompanied by the relaxation of tension and the coinciding with the infinite." Paramahansa Yogananda said of asana that "the spinal column must be held straight and the body firm in a comfortable position for meditation." Other references to asanas are found throughout Hindu and yogic literature and were well systematized in hatha yoga. Hatha yoga teaches asanas/postures that are designed to keep the body strong and flexible and to purify it. Many asanas facilitate keeping the spine straight, the head and neck in correct alignment, and/or the prana smoothly flowing through the spine when the spiritual energy/kundalini is awakened. Some asanas are believed to stimulate certain chakras, and thereby stimulate the kundalini mechanism.

4. *Pranayama (Control of Prana via the Breath)*. Exercises for controlling the breath and thereby influencing the flow of prana/life-energy into and throughout the body. Certain pranayama techniques are believed to open the astral sushumna in the spine and stimulate the spiritual energy/kundalini.

5. *Pratyahara (Sense Withdrawal)*. Interiorizing the mind, and withdrawal or detachment of the outer senses; withdrawing the

mind into itself; developing the ability to enter, at will, a state of intense inner-mindedness.

6. *Dharana (Concentration)*. Developing the mind's capacity for inner concentration. In the *Yoga Sutras*, dharana is referred to as binding consciousness to a single locus. Traditionally, yoga aspirants learned to concentrate more and more deeply by meditating on a point, a mental image such as that of a deity, a mental chant or mantra, or on an internalized sound.

7. *Dhyana (Meditative Absorption)*. Deep yogic meditation; progressively deeper levels of intense, single-pointed concentration. May be focused on the silence between thoughts, on the inner "AUM" sound, or an attribute of the Divine. Paramahansa Yogananda said true dhyana is "*cosmic consciousness, endless spherical expansion of blissful awareness, perception of God as the Cosmic AUM reverberating throughout the whole universe.*"

8. *Samadhi (Ecstasy)*. The final limb of yoga, sometimes described as self-realization, oneness of the individualized soul and the Cosmic Spirit, or mystical union. The *Yoga Sutras* call it the condition in which consciousness shines forth as the intended object; the Upanishads say it leads first to wondrous consciousness and later to liberation. In Vedanta, samadhi is sometimes referred to as the union of the psyche with atman or the transcendental Self.

If thinkers like Dr. Bucke, Dr. Ring, and Gopi Krishna, and the yogic tradition with sages like Paramahansa Yogananda, are correct in their belief in the evolution of consciousness, it means that an ever-increasing number of people may begin to experience kundalini activation and mystical states of consciousness, until the final goal of evolution is reached. Although reaching this goal might take many lifetimes or millennia, Gopi Krishna predicted that, as a reflection of the rapid pace of evolution of consciousness occurring on our planet at the present time, we would begin to see evidence of increased kundalini activity and the accompanying paranormal phenomena in a growing number of people. This is borne out by what I have seen in the last forty years, and by what my colleagues around the world have seen.

One of the reasons Gopi Krishna worked so hard to encourage scientific research into kundalini was his concern that lack of understanding of the biological-psychological-spiritual basis for the experiences I call STEs would mean that the people experiencing them would be misdiagnosed and not be able to get help in learning how to integrate them into their daily lives. Beyond this, he believed that the medical and psychiatric communities must be prepared to deal with the types of extreme difficulties he experienced with his own awakening. They could not do this, he knew, if they did not know about or believe in the reality of the spiritual energy/ kundalini mechanism, STEs, and spiritual transformation of consciousness.

Gopi Krishna's Long-Term Kundalini Transformation

Since Gopi Krishna's own experience is widely considered the most dramatic and well-reported case of kundalini awakening recorded in our times, it would be helpful at this point to look at it in more detail, in terms of both the difficulties he experienced and the state of higher consciousness that he eventually reached. His own account of his initial kundalini awakening was included in chapter 4 on Spiritual Energy/Kundalini Episodes. He describes his life in detail in his autobiographies *Living with Kundalini* and *Kundalini: The Evolutionary Energy in Man.*

After his explosive kundalini awakening at age thirty-four, Gopi Krishna began to notice dramatic changes in both his physical body and his consciousness. For several months these changes were extremely distressing. He had digestive problems and lost interest in food. He felt an intense burning up his spine, and sensations of heat and flame replaced the incredibly beautiful silver "liquid light" he had experienced during the awakening. He was plagued with insomnia and spent many nights completely unable to sleep. He found himself subject to labile emotions and fluctuating moods. He would find himself experiencing inexplicable and unprovoked episodes of anxiety, fear, anger, and depression, which would well up spontaneously and would disappear as suddenly and inexplicably as they had begun. His deep and abiding love for his family even began to disappear, and it seemed to him as if he had actually lost the capacity to love. He also began to lose his ability to concentrate, as well as his interest in meditation, work, and conversation.

Although he had been a practitioner of yogic meditation for years, he had no guru or spiritual teacher, and he knew very little about kundalini. He began to read about it with what little concentration he could muster, and eventually became convinced that his first experience tallied very closely with the descriptions in the ancient texts of kundalini awakening. He could not, however, find any information on the persistent distressing, negative sensations that had followed it.

In his search he came across two pieces of information that he credits with saving his life. One was a line translated from a yogic text that he found in Arthur Avalon's book *The Serpent Power*. It said that the yoga student who managed to awaken kundalini should never let his stomach become completely empty, but should eat a small meal every two to three hours. The other piece of information came from his brother-in-law, a student of yoga, whose guru had once told him that problems could arise if kundalini was awakened through any other nadi than the sushumna. The guru had said that if kundalini was aroused through the pingala, the astral channel to the right of the sushumna, which is associated with heat, mental imbalances and sensations of unbearable heat could occur. The guru had painted such a bleak picture that Gopi Krishna immediately sought other advice on the subject; but, unfortunately, he found none.

Over the next several weeks, his condition worsened. He had become almost completely unable to eat, and the sensations of heat, fire, and flame were almost unbearable. His eyes were sunken and glazed from lack of sleep, and he had lost a lot of weight.

In a flash of what seemed to be divine guidance, he remembered what his brother-in-law had told him, and it occurred to him that he should try to meditate on the ida, the astral channel on the left of the spine, which is associated with cold, and see if he could neutralize the burning sensations. He lay on his bed and began to visualize a cooling force flowing up the centre of his spine. Suddenly, a miracle seemed to happen. In his autobiography he writes,

> There was a sound like a nerve thread snapping and in-
> stantaneously a silvery streak passed zigzag through the

spinal cord, exactly like the sinuous movement of a white serpent in rapid flight, pouring an effulgent, cascading shower of brilliant vital energy into my brain, filling my head with a blissful lustre in place of the flame that had been tormenting me.... I immediately fell asleep, bathed in light, and for the first time after weeks of anguish felt the sweet embrace of restful sleep.

On awakening, he found that his head was still filled with a glowing radiance and he was now in an expanded state of consciousness. He remembered what the yogic text had said about eating regularly and knew he must follow this advice. His wife fed him small meals of easily digestible food every two to three hours. Slowly, over the next few months, he regained his strength and mental tranquility. As time went on he learned the importance of following without fail the inner, divine guidance he received.

Although his condition had improved greatly, Gopi Krishna went through twelve difficult years of ongoing transformation. During this period he continued to study the yogic texts and have discussions with holy men. This eventually helped him to understand why his difficulties had occurred. Not only had he originally awakened kundalini through the wrong channel, he had also awakened it abruptly with his intensive practice of meditation and had activated the brahma randhra before his body was able to provide it with the necessary prana and ojas.

Over the next twelve years, while following a carefully balanced lifestyle he experienced a gradually increasing expansion of consciousness. He became aware of an increasingly brilliant silver luminosity that bathed his inner and outer vision, a silvery flame in his brain, and radiant currents of light that darted through his body and head. In addition, external objects seemed to be dusted with a whitish coating. Over time the luminescent circle in his head grew larger. He also noticed an inner sound, a buzzing in his ears that became louder with prolonged concentration.

During this time he often felt like a helpless observer. He watched his body and brain being remodelled, but he had no idea what the purpose or the end result of the transformation might be.

Throughout this period Gopi Krishna found that his system was more sensitive than before, especially to concentration and stress. He tired more easily, needed regular breaks from concentration at work, and had to sleep at least ten hours a night. He continued to eat several small meals at well-regulated intervals throughout the day. In addition, all of his five senses seemed to become keener and more refined. His intellect became more penetrating. His lost love for his family returned and increased. He also felt an increased love for his friends and for the world. Although his moods and emotions were far more stable than they had been during his period of extreme crisis, he was more sensitive than he had been before his experiences began.

During this twelve-year period of gradual transformation, Gopi Krishna did undergo one other serious crisis. He had begun to meditate again, gradually increasing his time to three hours a day. Then, hoping to speed up the process of transformation that was occurring within him, he meditated longer and longer, until he was sleeping only a few hours daily and beginning to meditate at midnight. At first, this very lengthy daily meditation practice propelled him to new heights, but after a few weeks the searing, burning sensations returned, the pleasant inner sound became a harsh tormenting noise, and his insomnia and loss of appetite returned. His suffering lasted for several weeks, but by decreasing his time spent in daily meditation, and forcing himself to eat small amounts of food frequently and regularly throughout the day, he was gradually able to rebuild his strength and regain his equilibrium over a few months.

Toward the end of this twelve-year period, he received his first indication that this transformation was leading to the development of new mental capacities and higher states of consciousness. One evening in 1949, he was strolling over a bridge with a friend. In the middle of their conversation, a deep absorption settled on him and he was no longer aware of the voice of his companion. He writes,

> Near me, in a blaze of brilliant light, I suddenly felt what seemed to be a mighty conscious presence sprung from nowhere encompassing me and overshadowing all the objects around, from which two lines of a beautiful verse in Kashmiri poured out to float before my vision, like

luminous writing in the air, disappearing as suddenly as they had come.

This spontaneous, inspired creativity grew and developed over the years. In addition to the many books he wrote in prose, he composed several books entirely in beautiful and moving verse. One, *The Shape of Events to Come*, was written in less than three weeks. Over the years, he also experienced revelations and prophecy. He eventually came to live in a state of perennial expanded consciousness while being able to function in the everyday world. In his autobiography, he described points of even deeper absorption:

> Language fails me when I attempt to describe the experience ... my lustrous conscious self is floating, with but an extremely dim idea of the corporeal frame in a vividly bright conscious plane, every fragment of which represents a boundless world of knowledge, embracing the present, past, and future, commanding all the sciences, philosophies, and arts ever known or that will be known in the ages to come, all concentrated and contained in a point existing here and everywhere, now and always, a formless, measureless ocean of wisdom from which, drop by drop, knowledge has filtered and will continue to filter into the human brain. On every visit to the supersensible realm I am so overwhelmed by the mystery and the wonder of it that everything conceived in this world ... above all even my own existence, life and death, appear to be trite and trivial before the indescribable glory, the unfathomable mystery, and the unimaginable extent of the marvelous ocean of life, of which I am at times permitted to approach the shore.

Eventually Gopi Krishna came to think that, during the twelve years of adjustment, his body and nervous system was being remodelled. This biologically based process had been necessary, he thought, in order to gradually transform his system so that it was able to produce and handle the increased flow of prana and ojas that were necessary for the brahma randhra to develop, mature, and stabilize. He thought that the basis for understanding this process lay in the yogic texts pertaining to kundalini, and that the ancient masters of yoga had fully understood how important it was for the body, mind, and spirit of the student of yoga to be completely prepared for the awakening of kundalini. He came to believe that the Eight Limbs of Yoga contained the disciplines that would sequentially prepare the student physically, psychologically, and spiritually for a healthy awakening of kundalini. Gopi Krishna was confident that the reality of spiritual transformation of consciousness would eventually be documented and verified through scientific investigation.

We Are Truly Spiritual Beings

If scientific research does in time confirm the yogic model of consciousness and the biological-psychological-spiritual model of kundalini to be true, there are a number of significant implications. First, the widely held belief that life is merely transient and totally physical is fundamentally wrong. The insights gained throughout history from profound mystical and paranormal experiences indicate that we are fundamentally spiritual beings, existing in a multidimensional universe. Further, the purpose of our physical existence on earth is to provide an opportunity for our Souls to learn spiritual lessons and grow, and to ultimately realize and experience our oneness with Spirit/the Higher Power.

The verification of the yogic model of consciousness and kundalini would also suggest that the world's great spiritual Masters were extraordinarily advanced, highly spiritually evolved individuals, who had an awakened kundalini mechanism, undergone complete spiritual transformation of their brains and consciousness, and achieved and sustained an expanded state of ongoing mystical communion, nirbikalpa samadhi. In this expanded state of cosmic consciousness, they were able to be clear vessels for the Divine, to bring divine inspiration and guidance to their respective cultures. The spiritual guidelines they taught represented divinely inspired insights into the morality, behaviour, and style of life that would increase the rate of spiritual growth and spiritual evolution.

Although the messages of the world's great spiritual Masters were by necessity influenced by their culture, their time, and what was then known about the universe, and were therefore slightly different, there were also many similarities. All the Masters taught that we are essentially spiritual beings and that certain ways of thinking and acting are necessary to realize a state of union with the Divine — whether it be called God, Allah, Brahman, Yahweh, or any other name.

If spiritual transformation of consciousness and mystical states are universal human phenomena, then all human beings, from all cultures and from all religious backgrounds, have the potential to manifest expanded states of consciousness. This concept could help unify all the world's races and great religions in pursuit of the same one goal — unitive mystical consciousness.

If the kundalini mechanism is validated scientifically, it will mean that there is a biological component to STEs. If this is established, further research might help us understand how to promote healthy transformation of the brain and consciousness. This would have tremendous implications for both medicine and religion. As a doctor, I can imagine a time in the future when promoting the balanced lifestyle factors needed for healthy spiritual transformation could be as important as preventative medicine is today.

A number of doctors and scientists are convinced that more research must be done. Many people are having Spiritually Transformative Experiences today, but the medical and scientific communities lack understanding of what STEs are or what they imply about the nature of consciousness. Investigating the biological-psychological-spiritual model of the kundalini mechanism offers a good opportunity for eliminating this lack and for eventually providing us with a workable model for understanding spiritual transformation of consciousness.

10

RESEARCHING STE EXPERIENCERS

WHEN THE DOCTORS, THERAPISTS, AND RESEARCHERS, including myself, met in the home of Dr. Bonnie Greenwell to form the Kundalini Research Network (KRN), in 1990, we decided to conduct a questionnaire project researching the relationship between kundalini awakening and other types of Spiritually Transformative Experiences of consciousness. After becoming chairperson for the KRN Questionnaire Project in 1991, I became the principal author of the KRN Questionnaire, and coordinated the questionnaire's development, reliability testing, pilot testing, and, finally, worldwide distribution.

Some result highlights from the Kundalini Research Network's Pilot Project were shared in my earlier books, *A Farther Shore* and *Farther Shores*. I am including some result highlights here again, because although the pilot study was relatively small, it showed some fascinating patterns. Fortunately, other researchers, notably in the USA and in Germany, have recently conducted other STE studies, confirming some aspects of the KRN pilot study findings. I hope my including these study highlights here will not only inform readers, but will also encourage other researchers to study larger populations of STE experiencers, to determine whether or not the patterns I found in this pilot study hold true in larger populations.

The KRN Questionnaire consisted of a series of standardized inventories to collect detailed case histories and information about the experiences of people undergoing kundalini awakenings and the other types of Spiritually Transformative Experiences. The eight inventories were: (1) Consciousness Experiences Inventory; (2) Medical History Inventory; (3) Lifestyles

Inventory; (4) Social History Inventory; (5) Family History Inventory; (6) Spiritual Practices History Inventory; (7) Detailed Consciousness Experiences Inventory; and (8) Kundalini Experiences Inventory.

Persons having any type of STEs and a small control group of non-experiencers were invited to complete a questionnaire. One purpose of the questionnaire was to collect detailed descriptions of both the physical and consciousness experiences of persons having any type of STE or STEP. Inventories 7 and 8 covered mystical experiences, Near-Death Experiences, psychic awakenings, inspired creativity and genius, and Kundalini Episodes as well as ongoing kundalini symptoms. Most experiencers reported having STEs in more than one category — and all were asked to fill out the section dealing with kundalini symptoms. Participants also rated their initial and most dramatic STEs, and the frequency of recurring STEs or STEPs.

A second purpose of the questionnaire was to discover whether there is any statistically valid evidence that all STE experiencers — regardless of their initial or most dramatic type of STE — might be undergoing kundalini activity. Among other purposes, the questionnaire was also designed to explore whether there are any statistically identifiable factors related to family history, medical history, lifestyle, social history, or spiritual practices that might predispose individuals to kundalini or other types of STEs.

More than six hundred completed questionnaires were collected from people around the world, including the United States, Canada, Switzerland, France, India, Australia, New Zealand, and Russia, who have undergone dramatic STEs.

Before the final version of the questionnaire was completed and distributed, a pilot project was carried out to iron out logistical problems and to check the reliability of the questions. Although the pilot study looked at a relatively small sample population, about thirty people, the preliminary results were so fascinating that I want to once again share them with you in this chapter. My clinical experience counselling STE experiencers also supports the patterns found in this study. These KRN Questionnaire pilot study results were first presented and published in the conference proceedings of the 1991 Annual Meeting of the Academy of Religion and Psychical Research as "Spiritual Emergence Syndrome and Kundalini Awakening: How Are They Related?" The principal investigators were me — Yvonne

Kason, M.D. — with contributions by Michael Bradford, B.Sc., Paul Pond, Ph.D., and Bonnie Greenwell, Ph.D. Later in the KRN research project Russell Park, Ph.D., Bruce Greyson, M.D., and Megan Nolan, Ph.D. also made contributions.

In the pilot study thirty questionnaires were completed. Of these, twenty-three were completed by high-level STEP experiencers and seven by controls (low-level STE experiencers). Potential control subjects were found by canvassing people who were interested in the types of experiences I call STEs but who had not had an STE. For the purposes of the study, however, they were identified and labelled as controls by their scores on the Consciousness Experiences Inventory rather than by their own perception of whether they were a control subject or an experiencer. Interestingly, some of the study participants who labelled themselves as non-experiencers actually were grouped as STE experiencers, based on their score on the Consciousness Experiences Inventory.

The age range of the STE experiencers was from twenty-one to fifty-three years, with the average age being forty-three. The control group's age range was similar, from thirty-four to fifty-four with an average age of forty-one. Of the experiencers, twenty-one were women and two were men. In the control group, two were women and five were men. The experiencers tended to be highly educated, with seventeen of the twenty-three holding university degrees; eight of these seventeen had completed doctoral degrees.

Frequency of Each STE Type in Experiencers

The Consciousness Experiences Inventory asked study participants to report which of the five categories of STEs they had ever experienced: mystical experiences; kundalini awakening; psychic experiences; Near-Death Experiences; and/or inspired creativity, as well a UFO encounter, or any psychotic episodes. Participants were also asked to indicate whether each type of STE occurred once only, or repeatedly. The overall results of the Consciousness Experiences Inventory are summarized in Table 1 (page 213).

Two of the most interesting findings from the study have to do with mystical experiences and psychic episodes. 100 percent of all STE experiencers in our study — regardless of the type of their initial or most dramatic STEs — reported having mystical experiences. In most cases, 87 percent, these mystical experiences occurred repeatedly and in almost all cases at least one of the mystical experiences was described as extremely dramatic. Three of the seven controls had also had mystical experiences, but each was reported as a single isolated episode that was not dramatic in intensity.

Among the STE experiencers, 91 percent also reported having ongoing or recurrent psychic experiences, while none of the control group did. In contrast, only two controls reported having ever had one single psychic episode, and one control reported having two isolated psychic episodes.

Although definite conclusions cannot be drawn with such small numbers of research participants, the pilot study findings in these two categories suggest that all types of STE experiencers have a mystical experience at some point, and that an extremely high percentage of STE experiencers have recurrent or ongoing psychic experiences.

Another fascinating finding was that 70 percent of the STE group experienced some type of inspired creativity. One had had outstanding creative abilities since childhood and was, in fact, considered a child prodigy. The other fifteen reported the spontaneous development of some degree of creative gifts in adulthood. None of the control group reported any inspired creativity at any point in their lives.

Other interesting findings were that only 13 percent of the STE experiencers reported having a Near-Death Experience, and that 30 percent reported having had a UFOE, a sense of communication or contact with beings whom they perceived as being from another planet or dimension. None of the controls reported having either an NDE or a perceived UFO experience. Finally, essentially the same percentage (13 percent vs. 14 percent) of both groups reported having had a psychotic episode.

These statistics certainly show that people having STEs tend to undergo more than one type of experience. More important, however, in relationship to the kundalini hypothesis we were examining, is the fact that a full 100 percent of the STE experiencers studied reported having repeated signs of ongoing kundalini activity with several symptoms ongoing or recurrent for many years.

Table 1*

CONSCIOUSNESS EXPERIENCES
INVENTORY RESULTS

	STE Experiencers (n=23)	Controls (n=7)
Mystical Experiences	100%	43%
repeated	87%	0
once only	13%	43%
Psychic Experiences	91%	43%
repeated	91%	0
once or twice	0	43%
Inspired Creativity	70%	0
Kundalini Experiences	100%	86%
repeated	100%	43%
once only	0	43%
Near-Death Experiences	13%	0
UFO (communication with a being from another dimension)	30%	0
Psychotic Episodes	13%	14%

Three of the seven controls also reported having kundalini-related symptoms on more than one occasion, and three other controls had one isolated transient experience of possible kundalini symptoms; however, for all of these controls, kundalini symptoms were described as being much less intense and occurring far less frequently than those reported by the STE experiencers. None of the controls had ongoing kundalini symptoms. Thus it seems that a fairly high percentage of controls may have had at least a minor, transient taste of kundalini activity. I would suspect that the reason for this might lie in how study participants were found. All potential participants were drawn from a body of people who were interested in STEs.

---

* The tables are all based on the KRN Questionnaire Project Pilot Study 1991.

It is my belief that there may be a direct correlation between having mild paranormal experiences and being interested in them. Since I also believe that the kundalini mechanism may underlie these experiences, it makes sense to me that people who are highly interested in STEs would also have had at least some minor experiences of the energy.

Future research might need to look at this issue more carefully. It might also be interesting to examine whether individuals who have absolutely no interest in or belief in STEs have ever had any brief tastes of kundalini/spiritual energy activity.

Kundalini Symptoms Experienced

Table 2 provides a breakdown of the five specific signs of kundalini activity that the study asked participants about.

It is fascinating that 100 percent of STE experiencers reported recurrent sensations of energy, light, or heat rising up the spine or body, the most classic kundalini symptom. None of the controls reported these recurrent energy rushes, although one control person reported an isolated episode of energy rising up their spine. The other kundalini/spiritual energy–related symptoms listed were all reported far more frequently by STE experiencers than by controls. These symptoms included bliss episodes, described as sensations of profound bliss, all-encompassing love, or overwhelming joy;

Table 2

FREQUENCY OF KUNDALINI SYMPTOMS

Kundalini Symptoms	STE Experiencers (n=23)	Controls (n=7)
Sensations of energy rising up the spine or the body	100%	14%
Bliss episodes, overwhelming love	87%	43%
Expansive episodes	83%	43%
Perception of unusual lights	74%	0
Perception of inner sounds	61%	14%

expansive episodes, described as a feeling of expansion of any or all of their consciousness, head, or body; perceptions of unusual light or sparks, pervasive luminosity, or enhancement of visual perceptions; and perceptions of inner sounds, described as similar to the buzzing of bees, the dull roar of distant waterfalls, the music of the spheres, etc.

First and Most Dramatic Type of STE

Table 3 lists the type of STE that the experiencers listed as their first and as their most dramatic. Mystical experiences were by far the most common first STE, 65 percent, and most dramatic STE, 39 percent. Kundalini Episodes and psychic awakenings were equally split as the next most common type of initial experience, 17 percent each. None of the experiencers listed inspired creativity, an NDE, UFO communication, or a psychotic episode as being their initial experience.

Close to 75 percent of the experiencers questioned listed either a mystical experience or a kundalini experience as their most dramatic type of STE. These two types of STEs were reported with almost the same frequency as being the most dramatic STE experienced. Psychic experiences,

Table 3

FREQUENCY OF SPIRITUALLY TRANSFORMATIVE EXPERIENCE TYPES

	First STE	Most Dramatic STE
Mystical Experiences	65%	39%
Kundalini Experiences	17%	35%
Psychic Experiences	17%	13%
Near-Death Experiences	0	9%
UFO Experiences	0	4%
Psychotic Episodes	0	0
Average age at the time	17.7 years	37.0 years
Age range at the time	3–42 years	20–48 years

NDEs, and UFO experiences were listed by a few people as their most dramatic STE. Once again, no experiencer listed either inspired creativity or psychotic episodes as their most dramatic STE. Table 3 also shows that the average age at the time of the first STE was 17.7 years; at the time of the most dramatic STE, it was 37 years. No information for controls is given on this chart since no controls had what could be classified as a dramatic STE or STEP.

Triggers for STEs

Another important piece of information gathered in our study was what types of activities or situations appeared to trigger STEs or STEPs. The findings from the pilot project, shown in Table 4 (page 217), are similar to what I found in my clinical work counselling STE experiencers. Meditation was listed as the most common trigger of STEs, followed closely by intense prayer. Triggers reported more than once were NDEs, breathwork, sex, and music.

What Helps and Doesn't Help Adjustment to STEs

Although much of the rest of the book deals in detail with ways of integrating STEs into daily life, it is interesting to look at what the KRN pilot study indicated in this regard.

When the experiencers were asked to rate the things they found most helpful to their adjustment and integration after an STE or STEP, they listed meditation, reading books about spiritual topics, talking with supportive friends, prayer, talking to others with similar experiences, nature walks, and a decrease in workload.

The items rated as least helpful were talking with family members, advice from medical doctors, advice from traditional religions, and the use of prescription medications. If this list is borne out by larger studies — and based on my clinical experience I believe it will be — it has some serious implications. It indicates that traditional medicine and traditional religion — the two most likely places for people to turn when faced with psychological or spiritual experiences they do not understand — are currently not very helpful to people undergoing these experiences. And family members, the people we most naturally look to for support, are providing as little, or even less, help.

Table 4

TRIGGERS FOR SPIRITUALLY
TRANSFORMATIVE EXPERIENCES

	First STE	Most Dramatic STE
Meditation	3	6
Prayer	3	4
NDE	0	3
Sleep	3	0
Breathwork	2	2
Sex	2	1
Music	2	0
Yoga	0	1
Vision quest	0	1
Contact with guru	0	1
Love	0	1
Church service	1	0
UFO	1	0
Concentration	1	0
Nature	1	0
Reading spiritual letter	1	0
Death of a relative	1	0
Don't know	2	3
TOTAL	23	23

Increasing Awareness of STEs by Health-Care Professionals

Fortunately, the situation seems to be improving slowly. A breakthrough occurred, when the American Psychiatric Association approved a new diagnostic code for inclusion in the *DSM-IV*, the 1994 edition of a handbook used by psychiatrists, doctors, and psychologists in diagnosing mental illness and defining psychotherapeutic foci. This diagnostic code, called "V62.89 Religious or Spiritual Problem," was proposed by a California psychologist, Dr. David Lukoff, and two California psychiatrists, Dr. Frances Lu and Dr. Robert Turner. The inclusion of this category in the *DSM-IV*, and now the *DSM-V*, means that the academic core of the American psychiatric community has officially recognized the occurrence of spiritual experiences, unrelated to any mental illness. It is my hope that this breakthrough, along with the transpersonal psychology movement's increasing vocalness on spiritual experiences and spiritual issues, indicates that Western health-care professionals are beginning to become more aware of, sensitive to, and supportive of Spiritually Transformative Experiences and spiritual transformation of consciousness.

Another breakthrough happened in 2000, when I co-founded the Spirituality in Health-Care Network (SHCN) together with Toronto psychiatrist Dr. John Thornton and a group of more than fifty founding members. The Spirituality in Health-Care Network was founded to promote multi-faith, intra-professional dialogue between diverse health-care practitioners, clergy, and spiritual support providers, relating to the emerging field of integrating spirituality and spiritual experiences with psychotherapy and healing. To my great delight the emerging specialty of spirituality in health care is now steadily growing in the West.

In 2009, ACISTE, the American Center for the Integration of Spiritually Transformative Experiences, was founded in the USA, as a community of STE experiencers and STE care providers, from diverse backgrounds and beliefs. ACISTE promotes STE research and offers education and training to mental health professionals, life coaches, and spiritual guidance counsellors relating to counselling STE experiencers. Pioneering groups and professional networks such as ACISTE, SHCN, and the Spiritual Emergence Network, as well as transpersonal psychology educational programs at progressive universities such as Sofia University (previously known as the Institute of Transpersonal Psychology) and the California Institute of Integral Studies will hopefully result in more STE experiencers finally being able to get the help and support they need from informed health-care professionals and clergy!

The results of the KRN Questionnaire pilot study clearly support the possibility that there is a relationship between kundalini/spiritual energy activity and the other types of STEs. Although very few experiencers in this study had a kundalini awakening as their first STE experience, all of them reported the development, over time, of the signs of either recurrent or ongoing kundalini activity. Notably, all of the STE experiencers reported repeatedly feeling rushes of energy up the spine — the classic sign of kundalini activity.

In addition, all of the STE experiencers had mystical experiences at some point, regardless of the type of their initial or most dramatic STE. Although for the purposes of this study mystical experiences and kundalini awakening have been put in separate categories, it is important to remember that, in the yogic tradition, the purpose of the awakening of the kundalini mechanism is to ultimately attain mystical states of consciousness. Thus, the fact that all the STE experiencers had both mystical experiences and signs of kundalini activity suggests that science might someday discover that kundalini activation is indeed the biological-psychological-spiritual mechanism underlying spiritual transformation of consciousness and STEs.

Unfortunately, the data analysis for the main KRN Questionnaire Project has not yet been completed. I am delighted that other researchers around the world are now studying STE experiencers, in larger, more current studies. Marie Grace Brook, Ph.D., recently conducted a much larger study of STE experiencers, collecting her subjects online via an internet survey. Among other things, her study confirmed the top items reported most helpful to STE experiencers in the adjustment and integration of their STEs. Many other researchers, such as Bruce Greyson, M.D., Pim van Lommel, M.D., Jan Holden, Ed.D., and Tony Benning, Ph.D., are studying individual STE subtypes, such as NDEs, After-Death Communications, or kundalini awakening, and publishing their findings in highly respected professional journals. I hope that my sharing the result highlights of the KRN pilot project study will encourage and stimulate others to do more STE research.

PART 3

LONG-TERM SPIRITUAL TRANSFORMATION: THE AFTER-EFFECTS OF STEs

| |

PATTERNS OF STEs AND THEIR AFTER-EFFECTS OVER TIME

A LONG-TERM PROCESS OF SPIRITUAL transformation of consciousness often begins in individuals after an initial Near-Death Experience, mystical experience, kundalini awakening, or other STE. This lifelong process is sometimes called "after-effects of STEs." Others view this as "kundalini process" or the "mystical path." It has definite physical, psychological, psychic, and spiritual symptoms, and is often punctuated with further STEs or STEPs. This long-term transformation and its symptoms have been alluded to in the mystical traditions of all major faiths, including in yoga, as mentioned in chapter 9, in Buddhism, as mentioned in chapter 2, and in Christianity. Evelyn Underhill wrote of the physical, psychological, and spiritual transformation process of Christian mystics as follows: "Living union with the One is arrived at by an arduous psychological and spiritual process ... the so-called Mystic Way ... entailing the complete remaking of the character ... It is an organic process."

When I speak of STE after-effects as "symptoms," I am not using the word as a sign of disease, but rather in the more general sense of a sign or indication that something is happening in the body — in this case, long-term spiritual transformation of consciousness. In my work I have found that all STE experiencers undergoing long-term spiritual transformation of consciousness tend to have a number of symptoms, or after-effects, from four broad categories: the physical, the psychological, the spiritual, and the psychic. This is true regardless of which type of STE or STEP the person had initially or most dramatically, or continues to have most frequently or most dramatically. This overlapping of associated after-effect symptoms provides even more support for the idea that a common biological-psychological-spiritual basis may underlie all types of STEs. What's more, the information we have about spiritual energy/kundalini — gained from the yogic model of consciousness and kundalini — can explain why a great many of these unusual symptoms occur in the body, mind, and spirit.

The STE after-effect symptoms tend to be ongoing or to reappear from time to time. They generally begin at about the same time as the first STE or STEP or shortly afterward, and tend to continue with varying intensity over time. In Multiple STE Experiencers, the symptoms also tend to be more marked around times of intense STE activity, and especially around the same time as STEPs.

I have found there to be seven different patterns that the occurrence of STEs and their associated symptoms/after-effects tend to follow over time.

Pattern 1: Slow, Gradual Increase in STEs Occurring Over Many Years

This pattern is frequently experienced by long-time meditators and practitioners of spiritual disciplines, and by intensely religious individuals. In this pattern the intensity and frequency of STEs and the associated symptoms increase slowly and gradually over time, with some fluctuating, short periods in which experiences and symptoms are somewhat more marked.

Frequently, people experiencing this type of pattern may, for many years, ignore, minimize, or simply not recognize their spiritual transformation symptoms as anything out of the ordinary. Eventually, however, the individual usually realizes that something unusual is happening. After that, they recognize that what is happening is part of a spiritual process occurring within them. Sandy, a thirty-eight-year-old public-school teacher, is an example.

When Sandy volunteered to complete a KRN pilot project questionnaire, she offered to be part of the "interested control group." She did not think she had had any mystical, spiritual, paranormal, or kundalini experiences. However, on the questionnaire Sandy reported having had numerous psychic experiences for at least ten years. She also reported having moderately intense, repeated symptoms associated with kundalini awakening, such as rushes of energy up the spine. These sensations had been going on for more than eight years. She also had a few mystical experiences and bliss episodes from time to time over the years while she was meditating.

When I informed Sandy that her score on the part of the questionnaire that identified people as either "controls" or "experiencers" had moved her into the experiencer category, she objected, saying that everybody had the types of experiences she was having. Suggesting that this wasn't necessarily so, I described the pattern of slow, gradual increase in experiences over a number of years and explained how this could be stimulated by regular, long-term meditation such as hers.

Sandy said she'd think about what I'd said. The next time I saw her, she admitted that, after much reflection, and after talking openly with some of her closest friends, she had finally concluded that she probably was having STEs and that they seemed to be following the pattern of slow, gradual increase over a period of years. For Sandy this was an amazing realization. She had previously believed that meditation-related spiritual and paranormal experiences were "normal" and that the types of experiences I call STEs included only earth-shattering experiences.

In terms of the yogic model of consciousness and kundalini as I interpret it, this type of pattern comes about when there is a slow, gradual increase in kundalini activity over the years. The resulting changes in the physical and astral bodies and in consciousness may be subtle and almost imperceptible, and are often not even noticed until the activation of the brain/astral brain centres progress to the point where repeated paranormal consciousness experiences begin to manifest.

Gopi Krishna contended that this type of slow, gradual transformation of consciousness was currently occurring to many highly intelligent or highly spiritually focused individuals without their being consciously aware of it. This pattern of transformation often seems to be the least fraught with difficulties, because it gives the physical, psychological, and spiritual aspects of the individual time to adapt slowly to the changes that are occurring.

Pattern 2: Episodes of Profound STEs Separated by Periods with Few or No STEs

People with this pattern have episodes of STEPs or marked STEs that vary in intensity. These profound or very marked experiences are then separated for varying lengths of time by periods of either low or no STE activity. These in-between periods are often characterized by normal levels of conscious functioning. However, some experiencers fall into periods of lassitude or depression.

The stormy lives of some creative geniuses such as Edgar Allan Poe and Dylan Thomas have been characterized by periods of amazing inspiration, insight, and productivity, alternating with periods of deep depression. Some mystics have exhibited similar patterns, notably St. John of the Cross, who described the bleak periods that sometimes followed his mystical experiences as "the dark night of the soul."

According to the yogic model of consciousness and kundalini, alternating peak and normal consciousness periods may simply be the result of periods of higher and lower levels of kundalini activity. During periods of positive, peak spiritual experiences the brahma randhra is functioning to some degree and the body is able to supply the necessary amounts of more potent prana/life-energy and ojas/spiritual energy. During the periods of normal conscious functioning, it seems likely that the activity level of the brahma randhra/astral brain centres has slowed down and, with it, the demands for prana and ojas. During the rebound periods of deep depression, it is possible that the evolving brahma randhra brain centres may stop functioning or continue to function at some level, but the body may be unable to supply consistently adequate amounts of prana and ojas, and this results in depression. Highly creative individuals who experience periods of depression and some people who have cyclothymic disorders may possibly be experiencing this type of pattern.

In cases where the discrepancy between the level of activity in the brahma randhra/astral brain centres and the need for prana/life-energy and ojas/sexual energy is less extreme, a person may simply experience periods of mental dullness, writer's block, or a temporary inability to draw on the source of creativity within. Future research will need to examine these possibilities.

A regular, balanced lifestyle and sexual moderation (discussed in detail in chapter 17) is essential to the process of spiritual transformation, as it can help minimize the degree of fluctuation in prana and ojas supply, and therefore fluctuation in moods.

Pattern 3: One STEP Followed by a Slow, Gradual Increase in STEs and After-Effects

In this pattern, after an initial STEP there is a return to normal conscious functioning. Then STE activity and the associated after-effect symptoms slowly begin to increase, gradually increasing over a number of months and years. The level of STE activity and number of associated after-effect symptoms may fluctuate. As in the first pattern, these changes may be so gradual that they are virtually imperceptible until a certain threshold is reached. Although this pattern can be experienced by anyone, I have found this pattern to be particularly common among people who have had a mystical Near-Death Experience.

This is the pattern that my own STEs and after-effects followed from 1976 to 1989. It was not until twelve years after my 1976 kundalini awakening and ten years after my 1979 NDE that I finally became absolutely convinced that some kind of ongoing spiritual transformation process was occurring in my body and consciousness.

As I mentioned in chapter 9, "The Yogic Model of Consciousness and Kundalini," according to the yogic tradition, the spiritual energy/kundalini mechanism can awaken and the spiritual energy rise rapidly up the spine to the brain/astral brain for a short period of time, in a number of different situations. This may occur through Divine grace, sincere spiritual practices, intense heartfelt prayer, intense meditation, selfless service, or during a Near-Death Experience. During an NDE, it seems probable that once the physical body is resuscitated, the spiritual energy/kundalini activity slows down almost to a stop and the person's consciousness returns to normal.

Since the brain/astral brain centres/brahma randhra have been activated once, and the spinal sushumna channel opened to some degree, a small amount of residual spiritual energy/kundalini flow up the spine may continue after the NDE. Over time this low-grade spiritual energy/ kundalini activity may gradually increase, and further stimulate the astral brain centres/brahma randhra, thus causing increasing after-effect symptoms and STE activity. Further, the once awakened kundalini may be more easily stimulated by meditation and other spiritual practices, so that people who begin or continue such practices after an initial STEP may begin to have noticeable STEs and STEPs sooner than those who do not, and may switch to Pattern 4 as I eventually did.

As more and more people are resuscitated from near-death situations, I suspect that there will be more reports of profound NDEs and, later, reports of these persons experiencing ongoing spiritual transformation and the development of multiple and different types of STEs.

Pattern 4: Recurring STEPs Separated by Periods with Gradually Increasing STEs

In this pattern STEPs or periods of intense STE activity recur, but are separated by varying lengths of time during which the level of STE after-effect symptoms gradually increases. In the early stages of this pattern the periods between STEPs and STEs may be characterized by no or extremely few after-effect symptoms. As time goes on however, the number of after-effect symptoms in the periods between the STEPs and STEs gradually increases, and may continue to increase until recurrent STEs — mystical, psychic, or inspired creative experiences — as well as after-effect symptoms suggestive of long-term kundalini activity, become ongoing in the experiencer's daily life.

According to the yogic model of consciousness and kundalini, this pattern is explained by gradually increasing but fluctuating spiritual energy/ kundalini mechanism activity. The first STEP indicates the first activation of the spiritual energy/kundalini mechanism and the first stimulation of the brain/astral brain's brahma randhra/brain centres. The activity of the spiritual energy/kundalini mechanism and the stimulation of the astral brain centres slows down between STEPs but does not stop completely. If further stimulated by meditation and other spiritual practices, the activating astral brain centres' range of consciousness perception expands to gradually include more and more realms perceived during STEs.

This is a common pattern for people who had a powerful STEP of a mystical experience, a Spiritual Energy/Kundalini Episode, or even a powerful mystical NDE, after which they further stimulated the spiritual energy/kundalini mechanism and their spiritual transformation process with intense prayer, intense meditation, depth psychotherapy, and/or in-depth psychological recovery work. This is the pattern my own spiritual transformation process has followed after my 1990 "calling" mystical experience, which I shared in chapter 3, "Mystical Experiences." This STEP seemed to definitely accelerate my spiritual transformation process, shifting me from Pattern 3 to Pattern 4.

Pattern 5: A STEP followed by Continuing High STE Activity

Continuing high STE activity and strong ongoing after-effects following an initial STEP is a rare STE pattern, and is usually the most dramatic and the most disruptive to an individual's life. This is especially true when it occurs to someone who is unprepared for a profound spiritual awakening and subsequent rapid spiritual transformation of consciousness.

According to the yogic model of consciousness and kundalini, this pattern occurs when the spiritual energy/kundalini mechanism suddenly leaps into activity and maintains a constantly high level of activity. This may be due to over-stimulation caused by extremely intense concentration and/or spiritual practices. The spiritual energy/kundalini mechanism continues to function at high levels after the STEP, causing a rapid, dramatic transformation of the brahma randhra/astral brain centres.

In my work I found that this type of spiritual awakening is the one most prone to difficulties. This type of awakening can result in sudden, intense, and long-lasting mystical or inspired creative states of consciousness. It also tends to produce pronounced physical discomfort and pain, and distressing, fluctuating mental states as the spiritual energy purifies the unconscious mind. The difficulties associated with this pattern can only disappear when the body is able to consistently provide the transforming astral brain/brahma randhra with enough psychic fuels prana and ojas, and when the necessary psycho-spiritual purification has progressed deeply. Unfortunately, this process of stabilization may take many years, as it did in Gopi Krishna's case (twelve years), and only rarely does it result in the stabilized, tremendously expanded consciousness that he eventually reached.

A man I know stimulated this type of pattern with the extreme concentration required in completing two doctoral degrees in succession. From the onset of his kundalini awakening, he experienced nine years of mental turmoil, during which he was often completely dysfunctional. After nine years, the pattern suddenly altered and the spiritual energy/ kundalini activity slowed dramatically. Only then was he able to resume a normal life. This illustrates once again just how unwise it can be to follow extremely intensive spiritual practices without the expert guidance of a highly realized guru or spiritual teacher, or to attempt to forcefully awaken kundalini.

Pattern 6: Ongoing High STE Activity from Birth

In the yogic tradition it is believed possible, in extremely rare cases, for an individual to have an awakened spiritual energy/kundalini mechanism from birth, manifesting STEs and STEPs from childhood. Depending on the degree of activity, these rare individuals may be child prodigies or, if born with fully transformed astral brain spiritual centres, a spiritual Master, who would have repeated or ongoing mystical experiences and profound spiritual insights from a very early age.

Guru Nanak, who is believed to have written profound spiritual poetry and dispensed spiritual wisdom long before school age, provides a classic example of this type of pattern. The same is probably true for other great world religious prophets. Even though traditional sources tell us little about Christ's early childhood, I believe he was born with a fully awakened kundalini mechanism and fully transformed astral brain centres, and therefore manifested a state of ongoing God-consciousness.

Sometimes an individual may have a partially active kundalini mechanism from birth, which spontaneously awakens to high activity later in life. These people are "born spiritual," and are drawn from early childhood to God and spiritual concepts. The yogis believe this happens to souls who were mystics or highly spiritual in their past lives.

Pattern 7: Prepared Shaktipat Awakening

According to the yogic tradition, the spiritual transformation process least fraught with difficulties is the spiritual energy/kundalini awakening stimulated by "shaktipat," spiritual energy transmission from a highly realized guru to a prepared disciple. Under a guru's supervision, the spiritual aspirant prepares himself in body, mind, and spirit, sometimes for years, by practising the disciplines of the Eight Limbs of Yoga. When the guru perceives that the aspirant has adequately prepared, the guru awakens (activates) the kundalini mechanism in the spiritual aspirant by energy transmission or shaktipat. This transmission may be done with a touch, with a glance, or by mental transference, and often results in a powerful STEP. In many yogic ashrams today, aspirants seek such a prepared shaktipat kundalini awakening.

Paramahansa Yogananda's Shaktipat Awakening

A dramatic and extremely beautiful example of a shaktipat-induced kundalini awakening and mystical STEP was described in detail by Paramahansa Yogananda in his classic book *Autobiography of a Yogi*. After many years of regular meditation, training, and preparation while living in his guru's ashram, Paramahansa Yogananda received a profound shaktipat-induced mystical experience of cosmic consciousness, with clear kundalini/spiritual energy symptoms, transmitted to him by the touch of his saintly guru, Swami Sri Yukteswar. Paramahansa Yogananda described his shaktipat experience as follows:

Sri Yukteswar ... struck gently on my chest above the heart.

My body became immovably rooted; breath was drawn out of my lungs as if by some huge magnet. Soul and mind instantly lost their physical bondage and streamed out like a fluid piercing light from my every pore. The flesh was as though dead; yet in my intense awareness I knew that never before had I been fully alive. My sense of identity was no longer narrowly confined to a body but embraced the circumambient atoms. People on distant streets seemed to be moving gently over my own remote periphery. The roots of plants and trees appeared through a dim transparency of the soil; I discerned the inward flow of their sap.

The whole vicinity lay bare before me. My ordinary frontal vision was now changed to a vast spherical sight, simultaneously all-perceptive. Through the back of my head I saw men strolling far down Rai Ghat Lane, and noticed also a white cow that was leisurely approaching. When she reached the open ashram gate, I observed her as though with my two physical eyes. After she had passed behind the brick wall of the courtyard, I saw her clearly still.

All objects within my panoramic gaze trembled and vibrated like quick motion pictures. My body, Master's, the pillared courtyard, the furniture and floor, the trees and sunshine, occasionally became violently agitated, until all melted into a luminescent sea; even as sugar crystals, thrown into a glass of water, dissolve after being shaken. The unifying light alternated with materializations of form, the metamorphoses revealing the law of cause and effect in creation.

An oceanic joy broke upon calm endless shores of my soul. The Spirit of God, I realized, is exhaustless Bliss; His body is countless tissues of light. A swelling glory within me began to envelop towns, continents, the earth, solar and stellar systems, tenuous nebulae and floating universes. The entire cosmos, gently luminous, like a city seen afar at night, glimmered within the infinitude of my being. The dazzling light beyond the sharply etched global outlines faded slightly at the farthest edges; there I saw a mellow radiance, ever undiminished. It was indescribably subtle; the planetary pictures were formed of a grosser light.

The divine dispersion of rays poured from an Eternal Source, blazing into galaxies, transfigured with ineffable auras. Again and again I saw the creative beams condense into constellations, then resolve into sheets of transparent flame. By rhythmic reversion, sextillion worlds passed into diaphanous luster, then fire became firmament.

I cognized the center of the empyrean as a point of intuitive perception in my heart. Irradiating splendor issued from my nucleus to every part of the universal structure. Blissful *amrita*, nectar of immortality, pulsated through me with a quicksilverlike fluidity. The creative voice of God I heard resounding as *Aum*, the vibration of the Cosmic Motor.

Suddenly the breath returned to my lungs. With a disappointment almost unbearable, I realized that my infinite immensity was lost. Once more I was limited to the humiliating cage of a body, not easily accommodative to the Spirit. Like a prodigal child, I had run away from my macrocosmic home and had imprisoned myself in a narrow microcosm.

My guru was standing motionless before me; I started to prostrate myself at his holy feet in gratitude for his having bestowed on me the experience in cosmic consciousness that I had long passionately sought. He held me upright and said quietly:

"You must not get overdrunk with ecstasy. Much work yet remains for you in the world. Come, let us sweep the balcony floor …"

Paramahansa Yogananda's eloquent and vivid description of the mystical state of consciousness he experienced after receiving shaktipat from his guru also gives clear reference to physical symptoms of a kundalini/ spiritual energy awakening, specifically spiritual energy flow, inner light, and inner sounds. Yogananda described the spiritual energy/kundalini flow as "amrita," which he said pulsated through his body with quicksilver-like fluidity. He described the inner light variously as unifying light, tissues of light, and luminescence. Finally, Yogananda described the inner sound as the vibration of the cosmic motor, or the "AUM" sound.

I think Paramahansa Yogananda, a yogic saint who was documented to be highly spiritual since his early childhood, was probably born with a partially active kundalini, similar to the case of Guru Nanak. I therefore think that the shaktipat transmission which Yogananda received in his twenties from his guru activated or stimulated the spiritual energy/kundalini to increase to a much higher degree of functioning. This could be compared to suddenly accelerating the motor of a racing car from low gear to an extremely high gear, which results in much higher speeds of travel. Thus, the prepared shaktipat awakening, at least in Paramahansa Yogananda's case, caused the sudden awakening of his kundalini mechanisms to a much higher level of functioning than before. This sudden high level of kundalini function enabled the profound expansion of consciousness to cosmic consciousness, which Yogananda described.

Almost all STE experiencers find that the spiritual transformation process continues to some degree for the rest of their life, unless blocked by something, such as strong drugs, alcohol, or major health problems. Regardless of which pattern a person's STEs follow, all STE experiencers share many of the same types of physical, psychological, and paranormal after-effect symptoms, which I will now describe in detail.

12

PHYSICAL STE
AFTER-EFFECT SYMPTOMS

THERE ARE SEVERAL PHYSICAL after-effect symptoms that I and other researchers have found reported frequently by STE experiencers who are undergoing long-term spiritual transformation of consciousness. It is important to remind STE experiencers, their friends, and their families that all unusual or marked new physical symptoms need to be investigated by a qualified medical doctor, even when the experiencer feels that the symptom is probably a side effect of the spiritual transformation process happening in the body. One can be experiencing spiritual energy/kundalini activity and also have other physical problems that need medical attention. People on the spiritual path are not immune to illness and disease. It could be a serious or even life-threatening mistake to assume, without a medical assessment, that any of the symptoms listed on the following pages do not have a medical cause. Please consult your medical doctor regarding any new and unusual physical symptoms before concluding that it is an STE after-effect symptom.

Common Physical After-Effect Symptoms

The physical after-effect symptoms often associated with STEs can be divided into eight broad categories: (1) sensations of pranic energy movement and kriyas; (2) undiagnosable body pains and chakra sensations; (3) metabolic changes; (4) changes in sleep patterns; (5) changes in sexual energy; (6) energy fluctuations; (7) increased sensitivities; and (8) yogic phenomena. The following section looks at each of these in detail, examines how they may be related to the awakening of the spiritual energy/kundalini, and considers a number of ways in which these symptoms can be minimized when people find them uncomfortable or distracting.

Sensations of Pranic Energy Movement and "Kriyas"

"Kriya" is a yogic term for "movement," which is sometimes used to refer to the spontaneous, involuntary jerking movements of muscles and limbs that can accompany the awakening of kundalini. Gwen, the young Canadian doctor discussed in chapter 4, described a classic experience of kriyas, spontaneous movements, when she said,

> My whole body started shaking uncontrollably. I felt rushes of energy coursing up my body to my head, and my whole body jerked with pulses of energy. My back, arms, and legs all jerked repeatedly ... My body was rocked and shaken by these energy pulses.

Although Gwen was beginning a STEP when this occurred, many people also experience kriyas/spontaneous muscle movements and sensations of pranic energy movement from time to time after having had an STE. They are often much milder than Gwen's, are generally not painful, and often last only a short period of time. Although the spontaneous or repeated jerking seen in some types of kriyas may resemble a seizure, there is no loss of consciousness or incontinence as there would be in a true seizure. Sensations of pranic energy movement and kriyas/spontaneous muscle movements generally occur most often and most intensely at times when STE activity is high. Here are some of the forms the episodes commonly take:

- Involuntary jerking of one or both arms or legs, sometimes associated with rapid rushes of energy.
- Abdominal contractions or spasms, or spontaneous pumping of the diaphragm, sometimes associated with energy rushes up the spine.
- An arching or jerking of the back, usually associated with energy rushes up the spine.

- An arching back of the head and neck, often accompanied by a rolling upwards of the eyes and a fluttering of the eyelids. May be associated with energy rushing up the spine and sometimes into the brain.
- A vibration or fine tremor in the arms or throughout the entire body, or a fluttering of the diaphragm.
- Sensations of energy rushing, trickling, pulsing, jumping, spiralling, or flowing — through parts of the body, through organs, up the arms and legs, through the entire body, or up the spine.
- Sensations like energy throbbing or radiating from the body, from the face, from the abdomen, at chakra points, or from the hands.

Along with a number of other doctors and therapists, I believe that the sensations of energy movement and kriyas/spontaneous body movements are probably the result of the increased flow of prana through the body and astral body that occurs after an STE associated with a spiritual energy/kundalini awakening. This seems logical, since experiencers often report that the involuntary jerking and movements of the body are accompanied by sensations of energy rushes. Some experiencers report they feel as if energy is flooding or "supercharging" their entire body, with or without spontaneous body movements.

In her book *The Energies of Transformation*, Bonnie Greenwell quotes a number of yogis, such as Swami Sivananda, who explain sensations of energy movement and kriyas/spontaneous muscle movements as the result of increased pranic activity. In addition to the types of kriyas I have seen in my practice, she adds such things as involuntary dancing, hopping, or spinning, and a sudden rigidity or freezing of muscles that may result in falling down. She also postulates that, in some cases, kriyas might be the result of the intensified energy affecting specific areas of the brain and stimulating involuntary muscle contractions.

The sensations of energy movement and kriyas/spontaneous muscle movements usually last for only a short period of time, often ranging from a few seconds to a few minutes. They are normally not painful and can often be tolerated until they stop of their own accord. For many experiencers, simply knowing that these are normal after-effects of STEs, and part of the long-term spiritual transformation process, reduces the anxiety sometimes felt when they occur and makes them much easier to tolerate. They can also be minimized by performing the grounding activities described in chapter 17, which help stabilize spiritual energy/kundalini activity and the flow of prana. Physical exercise such as walking, swimming, bicycling, or running sometimes temporarily stops the kriyas/body movements. Eating more regularly and moderating the amount of time spent in concentration and meditation can also help decrease them.

Undiagnosable Body Pains and Chakra Sensations

STE experiencers often report bodily sensations and transient pains that differ from those associated with physical illnesses. The sensations and pains often migrate to different locations and come and go without any obvious physical reason. Even when they are thoroughly investigated with extensive medical testing, no physical cause or abnormality can be found. Severe low back pain, for example, may appear and disappear at very irregular intervals, change location, and not be related to any type of disease, injury, physical exertion, or muscular back strain. Although these medically undiagnosable pains may occur in any part of the body, they are frequently located along the spine, in the central abdomen, and in the areas where the chakras are believed to be located. These transient pains seem to be felt to some degree by almost all people who have had STEs, especially those who had a kundalini awakening, but they are often more pronounced or persistent in people who have forcefully or unexpectedly awakened the spiritual energy/kundalini, who have never done any type of preparatory psychological housecleaning, or who practise some unusual meditation techniques. Common undiagnosable body pains or sensations associated with STEs and spiritual transformation include:

- Pressure or pulling sensations in the pelvic area. May be associated with the root chakra.
- Lower spine back pains or burning sensations. May be associated with the first two chakras, or with kundalini/spiritual energy rising up the sushumna, the central astral spine channel.

- Low back pain or burning sensations on one or both sides of the lower spine. May be associated with kundalini/spiritual energy rising up the pingala astral channel, which is located on the right, or the ida astral channel, which is located on the left, rather than through the sushumna or central spinal astral channel. Might also be associated with kundalini meeting a block in either channel.
- Sharp, piercing, sword-like pains pushing up the spine. May be associated with kundalini/spiritual energy rising up the sushumna.
- Abdominal pressure or pain, with or without nausea. May be central, or located off to one side. May be associated with the third, or solar plexus, chakra and surrounding nadis.
- Chest pains or pressure, sometimes mistakenly confused with a stomach disorder or even a heart attack. May be central or off to one side. May be associated with the fourth, or heart chakra.
- Mid-back pain or pressures. May be associated with the heart chakra.
- Tightening of the throat or esophagus, sometimes described as feeling as if there was a constricting band around the throat. May be associated with the fifth, or throat chakra.
- Pressure or pain between the eyebrows or on the forehead. May be associated with the "third eye" or the sixth chakra.
- Pressure or pain at the crown of the head, sometimes described as feeling as if the skull is too small or as if a force were trying to forcefully push up through the crown of the skull.
- Unusual headaches and sensations of pressure in the head, jaw, ears, or temperomandibular joint. May be associated with general kundalini activity.
- Marked, unusual sensations of energy, energy movements, or pressure in the centre of the brain. May be associated with activity of the brahma randhra/activating brain centres.

According to yogic theory of the astral body, these types of sensations and pains may be caused by or be related to "blocks" or "knots" in the astral channels/nadis or in the chakras. These blocks are often associated with "samskaras," unconscious psycho-spiritual issues unresolved from this lifetime or past lives, which hinder or interrupt the free flow and increased circulation of prana after the awakening of the spiritual energy/kundalini mechanism by STEs. This blockage results in sensations of discomfort or pain in the areas where the prana is unable to push through the astral block or knot. Some blocks may also be caused by physical factors such as impurities in the body, muscular tension or spasms, physical injuries, or misalignments of the spine. Abdominal discomforts may be worsened by the use of meditation techniques where the gaze and attention are focused on the abdomen rather than the forehead. It is believed in yoga that blocks can be cleared by ridding the body of impurities, through healthy diet, through physical activities such as hatha yoga and bodywork, through deep meditation with the gaze focused on the third-eye region of the forehead, and by resolving psychological issues by self-reflection and efforts at self-development. Doing personal recovery work or depth psychotherapy can also remove blocks, free up the flow of prana, and eliminate some of the physical sensations and pains.

The following story was told to me by a thirty-five-year-old police officer I will call Monty, who developed undiagnosable body pains after beginning intensive spiritual and martial arts practices.

I have been very active in the martial arts since I was sixteen. Over the years I have practised karate, kung fu, and kickboxing. About two years ago I was introduced to meditation and yoga. I started meditating and doing hatha yoga daily, and I now meditate for two hours per day.

One year ago I joined a Tai Chi club, and then learned the practice of Chi Kung. I have now added Chi Kung to my daily routine. About six months ago I started noticing sensations of energy circulating throughout my body during the Chi Kung. This was not painful or unpleasant. However, recently I have noticed that I get severe abdominal pain just to the left of my solar plexus, starting within a few minutes after I begin my Chi Kung practice. When I stop the Chi Kung, the pain slowly goes away. I went to my medical doctor for a checkup but my doctor says I am in excellent health. He could find no physical cause for the pains.

Monty was suffering from the typical undiagnosable body pains that can occur after a spiritual energy/kundalini awakening. When I questioned him closely, he recalled that around the time he started noticing energy currents moving through his body during Chi Kung, he also started noticing energy rushes going up his body and spine during meditation. Probably he was undergoing a gentle kundalini awakening, stimulated by the intensive meditation and yoga practices. Further, his system was probably "ripe" for a spiritual energy/kundalini awakening, because of his many years of practising the various martial arts, which also clear nadis. The pain in his abdomen was possibly due to a block to pranic energy flow that was now being pressed upon. He also told me that in the last six months he had started focusing his gaze on his abdomen during his meditations. I advised him to always keep his gaze focused upwards at the third-eye region during all his meditations, which would ease pressure on the abdominal block area, and to moderate the length of his meditations and yoga practices for a while, to decrease the stimulation to the spiritual energy/kundalini. I also suggested he consider psychotherapy, to help resolve any psychological issues that might be acting as an emotional block. When he did these things, the undiagnosable body pains during his Chi Kung practice stopped.

I have seen a number of cases, like Monty's, where unusual abdominal pains were related to practising a meditation technique where the gaze and attention were focused on the abdomen, rather than on the third-eye region of the forehead. Yogic tradition instructs that the gaze should always be uplifted during meditation, with the focus at the third-eye region of the forehead. This helps draw the actively circulating prana and ojas to flow upward toward the astral spine and brain.

Pains or pressures at the chakra points may sometimes be due to clairsentience, intuitively sensing the emotions of others as sensations in your body, which I discuss in chapter 14.

Of all the uncomfortable physical sensations associated with STEs, back pain is one of the most common. In my practice, I have found that doing yoga, Tai Chi, or deep muscle relaxation exercises sometimes helps provide pain relief. Avoiding slouching or poor posture and taking care to sit or stand with the spine erect and aligned can also help minimize the pains. Pains located to the right or left of the spine — and possibly related to energies flowing up the ida or pingala instead of the sushumna — can sometimes be relieved by sitting erect, meditating lightly with the gaze fixed at the third-eye region, and visualizing the energy shifting slowly to move up the central spinal channel.

Metabolic Changes

Many people experiencing STEs notice after-effects of episodic or sometimes long-term changes in their metabolism. During periods of frequent STEs and after STEPs, people often remark that they feel as if their bodily functions have sped up. The digestive and the cardiovascular systems seem to be most affected.

Commonly reported STE after-effect symptoms associated with metabolic changes include:

- Increase in appetite, from slight to very marked.
- Craving for specific foods, especially for high-protein foods, nuts, dairy products, fresh fruits, or vegetables.
- Aversion to specific foods, often to concentrated sugars, alcohol, red meat, caffeine, or fried foods.
- Development of new food sensitivities or food allergies.
- Perception of a need to eat more frequently or more regularly, for example every two to three hours.
- Desire to eat smaller portions of food at each sitting.
- Loss of appetite and/or development of nausea, a nervous stomach, or over-acidity of the stomach.
- Fluctuations in appetite.
- Increased frequency of bowel movements, for example increasing from an average of once a day to several per day during times of high STE activity.
- Increased bowel gas related to the increased bowel activity.
- Episodic racing of the pulse and pounding of the heart.
- Intolerance to heat or sensations of intense body heat, or night sweats — often described as "burning up," or hot flashes.
- Cold or chills.

According to the yogic model of spiritual energy/kundalini awakening with STEs, these metabolic changes would seem to be related to the way in which the body's various systems are stimulated into greater activity in order to provide the increased amounts of more potent prana and of ojas that are needed. In addition to being absorbed from universal prana, individual prana is believed to be extracted from the food we eat and the air we breathe, and produced by some of the body cells. If this is indeed the case, it logically follows that changes in metabolic processes would occur with the activation of the kundalini mechanism.

I have noticed several of the above metabolic changes related to my own spiritual transformation process. I usually eat three meals a day: breakfast at 7:00 a.m., lunch around 12:00 noon, and dinner at between 6:00 and 7:00 p.m. During times of high STE activity I often seem to require a small midmorning snack, or a midafternoon snack, and sometimes a small evening snack. During these high-energy times I also find that I intuitively feel the urge to eat smaller, lighter meals at each sitting. I develop an urge to eat simply prepared, protein-rich foods, fruits, and vegetables, and develop an aversion to starches, processed foods, sugar-laden sweets, and rich foods.

Many people undergoing STEs have found that the best technique for coping with these metabolic changes is to learn to listen to what their bodies are trying to tell them and to follow their intuitive urges. A craving for white meat or eggs during high STE activity, for example, may well be a signal that the body needs more protein in order to produce greater amounts of more potent prana. I have sometimes seen people resist an urge to eat more protein after awakening the spiritual energy/kundalini because they mistakenly believe that all yogis and mystics must be vegans or strict vegetarians, or that it is better or more spiritual to be a vegetarian. This is not so. Further, while it is essential to learn to respect your body's inner guidance, one needs to use common sense in interpreting these intuitive urges. In cases of extreme loss of appetite, for instance, common sense tells us that the body needs fuel and that every effort should be made to eat at least small amounts of highly nutritious food at regular intervals. In fact, many people find one of the keys to dealing with ongoing kundalini activity is to eat small, nutritious, well-balanced meals or snacks every two to three hours. People who are unsure about the appropriateness of their dietary urges should discuss them with a doctor or nutritionist. (See chapter 17 for more information on diet.)

Doctors should, of course, be consulted regarding metabolic changes that cause any concern, particularly where a history of medical illness is involved. For example, a racing pulse is a normal, temporary symptom that can be easily tolerated by most people. However, a person who has a medical heart condition should definitely consult with a doctor so that medication to slow down the heart can be prescribed if needed.

Several techniques can be used to moderate sensations of heat and cold. Often a simple change of clothing is all that is needed. Dressing in layers so that clothing can be taken off or added as needed is often helpful for people who are experiencing heat sensations and hot flashes and are away from home throughout the day. Extreme or persistent sensations of heat are sometimes relieved by remaining in a cool environment, putting cool compresses on the head or neck, drinking cool liquids, or taking cool baths or showers. Yogis sometimes recommend taking cold baths, eating cooling foods such as yogurt, and avoiding hot or extremely spicy foods.

Some yogic breathing techniques are also believed to have a cooling effect. One involves protruding the tongue slightly and forming it into "U," inhaling through the mouth, and swallowing the somewhat cooled saliva at the end of the inhalation.

Changes in Sleep Patterns

Many STE experiencers notice changes in their sleeping patterns as an after-effect of STEs, and particularly during periods of high STE activity. Although the reasons for changes in sleep patterns or biorhythms are unknown, I speculate that the increased need for more — and more regular — sleep and rest are probably related to the body's increased need to replenish itself during and after periods of intense spiritual transformation.

Common changes in sleep patterns include:

- Frequent middle-of-the-night wakening, often between 2:00 and 4:00 a.m.
- Frequent waking earlier in the morning, feeling fully refreshed — often between 4:00 and 6:00 a.m.

- Need for more sleep per night than previously. May include a desire to go to sleep earlier in the evening.
- Increased desire for naps in the middle of the day.
- Insomnia or difficulty falling asleep during periods of very high STE activity.
- Decreased requirement for sleep during periods of high-energy activity.
- Profound fatigue, especially just after periods of very high STE activity, or sometimes just before such periods.
- Interruption of sleep by night sweats and heat sensations.
- A feeling of being "hung over" or excessively groggy when sleep requirements are not met or the regular sleep schedule is disrupted.

Some yogic traditions contend that less sleep is needed after a kundalini awakening. This may be true during periods of high STE activity. However, my clinical experience is that most STE experiencers find they need the opposite — regular and increased amounts of sleep most of the time. The need for more sleep and rest in STE experiencers is probably due to the increased regenerative time needed for the transformation process happening in the body and astral body, just as a developing child needs more sleep than an average adult.

The best way to meet the body's need for sleep is to establish regular times for sleeping and waking and to stick with them even on weekends and holidays as much as possible. Current sleep research shows that a set wake-up time is the most important factor in helping the body restore healthy sleep cycles. If tired, go to bed earlier at night, rather than sleeping-in in mornings. Adequate amounts of sleep are also needed. For people undergoing STEs this is often as much as nine to ten hours a night. If brief daytime naps are needed, they should be taken.

In cases where excessive energy or sensations of pranic activity cause sleeplessness or insomnia, cutting out stimulants such as coffee, black or green tea, chocolate, and caffeine-containing carbonated beverages can help return sleep patterns to normal. Current studies on insomnia say that light reading is more likely to assist in falling asleep than exercising, watching exciting TV shows, or viewing a smartphone or computer screen. People who have difficulty falling asleep should also increase their grounding activities.

In general, increasing physical activity during the day, eating heavier, more protein-rich foods, and taking supplements of B vitamins, especially B-12, may all help. When insomnia persists, herbal sleeping preparations may help solve the problem. If necessary, a doctor should be consulted about getting a prescription for a mild sleeping pill. Taken for a few nights, a mild sleeping pill can break the cycle of sleeplessness and will do much less harm than many sleepless nights.

Over the years, I have experienced many of these changes in sleep patterns. The most noticeable change in my sleep pattern is the frequent middle-of-the-night waking. In fact, a great deal of my earlier book, *A Farther Shore*, was written between 2:00 and 4:00 a.m.! My body was often awake during this time period, my mind clear and alert, and the house quiet because my young son was asleep. So I used this time to work on the manuscript. Now I generally remain in bed during that time, pray, meditate, or read some spiritual material. When I talked to various groups about STEs and their after-effect symptoms, I often asked the audience how many of them suffered from middle-of-the-night waking. In a room full of people experiencing STEs, it was usually around 90 percent.

Changes in Sexual Energy

Sexual sensations and changes in sex drive are the physical symptoms that frequently cause the most distress in people having STEs and undergoing long-term spiritual transformation. Fortunately, the unusual sexual sensations seem to occur only periodically and the changes in sex drive are usually only temporary. In fact, the vast majority of STE experiencers who have consulted me regarding changes and fluctuations in their sex drive have found that the problems resolved themselves after a short period of time. For many, simply learning that these sexual sensations and changes in sex drive are a normal part of STE after-effects provides tremendous relief. Commonly reported sexual energy changes include:

- Periods of mildly to markedly decreased sex drive.
- Periods of markedly increased sex drive, sometimes to the point of distraction or discomfort.

- Periods of marked sexual tension similar to being pre-orgasmic but unrelated to sexual activity.
- Spontaneous erections in men at the time of kundalini energy activity.
- Unusual fluctuations in the level of sex drive.
- Temporary confusion about appropriateness of one's regular sexual partner.
- Temporary confusion about sexual orientation.
- Fluctuations in the size of the erect penis in men and episodes of swelling or engorgement of the labia in women. They may become larger during times of increased sex drive and smaller during times of decreased sex drive.
- Unusual increases or decreases in the amount of ejaculate produced by men or vaginal secretions by women.
- Unusual sensations in the pelvis and sexual organs described as: an internal, upward sucking sensation; pelvic pumping sensations; or sensations of energy movement in the sexual organs.
- Spontaneous orgasm related to meditation, prayer, or spiritual contemplation.
- Sexual orgasm centred in the spine or head (orgasms of this type may vary in intensity and are similar in sensation to genital orgasms; the orgasmic sensation is simply located in another part of the body).
- Sexual orgasm associated with an out-of-body experience, psychic experience, or mystical experience.

These sensations and changes in sexual functioning are logical when they are considered in terms of the activation of the spiritual energy/kundalini. The relationship between the sexual energy/ojas and kundalini is well recognized in yoga. The sexual organs have long been held to be the body's greatest reservoir of prana and ojas. If this is true, the sensations of activity in the genital area so often described by people undergoing STEs may well be simply that: a heightened activity that has been brought about by the transforming brain's increased need for the psychic fuels prana and ojas. The genital sucking sensations may be the result of prana and ojas being drawn out of the sexual organs and pulled upward toward the brain. These sensations are sometimes reported as being very strong and may be associated with a spontaneous erection in men, or occasionally with spontaneous orgasms.

I think it is important that STE experiencers and their counsellors realize that sexual symptoms including sexual arousal and erections can occur in some people as a normal STE after-effect symptom related to the activated spiritual energy/kundalini mechanism. I have met several STE experiencers over the years who were very troubled about the sexual arousal symptoms they experienced during their spiritual practices. This distress can be especially marked in a person who has chosen a life of celibacy, and who has no awareness that kundalini/spiritual energy activity can at times generate physical symptoms of sexual arousal. This was true of a man who I will call Sherman, whose kundalini awakening was associated with symptoms of sexual arousal.

> I had been practising yoga and meditating daily for about eight years when my kundalini awakening occurred at the age of thirty-four. I was a very dedicated yogi and meditator, and at the time of my first kundalini awakening I was regularly meditating for three and a half hours each day, and for five hours daily every weekend.
>
> My kundalini awakening happened while I was practising my usual morning meditation routine. I had begun my meditation period with a technique where I detachedly observed the flow of my breath. After a half hour or so of observation of breath meditation I felt a strange sensation develop at the base of my spine, close to my coccyx. Then, suddenly, I felt an inner hurricane of energy rise out of the base of my spine and swirl up my spine and entire body, reaching up to the level of my forehead third-eye region. I heard an inner roar as this energy poured upwards.
>
> At the same time as this powerful upward flow of energy, I also felt a strong sexual arousal. I spontaneously developed an erection of my penis. I was very disturbed by this sexual arousal. As a single man, I had been intentionally celibate for several years, as part of my yogic discipline.

I found the erection and feeling of sexual arousal distracting and disturbing to me, to the point that I came out of my meditation, and lost the inner kundalini awakening experience.

I was troubled by the fact that for several years following this kundalini awakening I experienced sexual arousal during my meditations. I was tremendously relieved when I finally read in one of Gopi Krishna's books that sexual arousal and, or, an erection could occur as a normal part of a kundalini awakening process.

Simply understanding that sexual arousal may sometimes be a normal, temporary physical symptom associated with STEs can be reassuring to many experiencers, like Sherman.

On the other hand, if the genital supplies of prana and ojas become low or depleted when strongly drawn upwards by the spiritual energy/kundalini mechanism, this could result in a decrease in the usual downward flow of the sexual energy that fuels the drive for procreation. In other words, the normal sex drive of an STE experiencer may decrease and in some cases disappear completely for a period of time. In my clinical experience, this tends to be a temporary decrease. The sex drive of STE experiencers tends to return to normal in time, probably once the body is able to provide and maintain an adequate supply of prana and ojas. However, many long-time meditators find that their sex drive gradually decreases over the years, probably as more and more ojas flows upwards to nourish the transforming brain.

In other cases, some STE experiencers notice periods of markedly increased sex drive. This may be due to production of more prana and ojas than is necessary for the brain/astral brain's needs, and the excessive amounts of these substances become stored in the sexual organs. This could lead to a buildup of energy that causes increased downward pressure, and a subsequent increase in sex drive. These changes in the activity of the sexual organs may also explain the episodic marked changes in the amount of ejaculate and vaginal secretions some STE experiencers report.

When understood as a normal part of spiritual transformation, the after-effects of fluctuations in sex drive and other unusual sexual symptoms are often coped with more easily. It also helps experiencers to know that these changes are a common sign of ongoing spiritual energy/kundalini activity.

However, since kundalini awakening and sexual energy are so closely related, this is an area that STE experiencers need to pay careful attention to. Common sense — as well as many spiritual traditions that recommend moderation and abstinence — would seem to indicate that unusual periods of decreased sex drive are the body's way of indicating that the sexual energy is needed elsewhere and that the frequency of sexual release needs to be decreased during those times.

When one is involved in an ongoing sexual relationship with another person this can, of course, cause difficulties that will need to be worked out with as much open, honest communication as is possible. Regardless, it is important that STE experiencers understand the reasons for their periods of diminished sex drive and that they avoid blaming their partner, blaming themselves, or feeling guilty about the situation. People undergoing STEs cannot simply force their sex drives to return to normal and, according to kundalini theory, they shouldn't try. In my practice I have heard many reports of negative consequences from people who engaged in sexual activity and had orgasms during periods of little or no sex drive. These included sensations described as "complete mental blackness," feelings of being "completely disgusted," and an experience like "falling down an unending, black well." Other experiencers have described feeling physically and/or emotionally drained, and some have even entered into states of despair. All of these experiences make sense when one considers the possibility that the highly activated brahma randhra/brain centres might be being deprived of much-needed prana and ojas when these substances are expended at the wrong time through sexual activity.

Although my advice is to follow the urges of the body when the sex drive is low, I am afraid my experience leads me to recommend the opposite when it comes to periods of increased sex drive. During these periods it is probably best to exercise self-control and maintain a moderate sex life, even when one gets strong urges for excessive indulgence, so that the much-needed supplies of prana and ojas do not become completely depleted. One can often reduce very strong sexual energy by vigorous physical exercise such as jogging or biking. Paramahansa Yogananda also recommended transmuting strong sexual energy into creative energy, by doing something intellectually or artistically creative while the sexual energy is high.

Spiritual teachers from many traditions recommend decreased sexual activity and even abstinence at certain times during the spiritual journey. Based on his own experience, Gopi Krishna recommended, for example, that people in an intimate relationship who are following the moderate spiritual path limit the frequency of sexual release to somewhere between twice a week and once every two weeks. Paramahansa Yogananda also recommended sexual moderation for married spiritual aspirants, and continence for single spiritual aspirants.

Some STE experiencers think that the need for sexual moderation can be circumvented by refraining from having orgasms while remaining sexually active. The advisability of having non-orgasmic sex — instead of being abstinent or moderate when needed — is, however, controversial. I do not recommend it. Some people promote the idea that the sexual energy stimulated in this way can then be sent back up the astral spine and into the brain. Some of these ideas may even be based on ancient Tantric practices. These practices, controversial in themselves, were developed in a culture and setting completely different from our own and were considered advanced esoteric practices. Further, I think that finding a spiritual teacher today who is knowledgeable enough to guide one safely through these practices would be difficult. Beyond this, some experts on kundalini, such as Gopi Krishna and Paramahansa Yogananda, said that during sexual arousal the sexual energy/ojas is transformed into a grosser form, and that this grosser form cannot be transformed back into the more subtle form of ojas that is needed to nourish the brain/astral brain.

In general, I think it is much safer to practise sexual moderation and abstinence when it is required, than to indulge in non-orgasmic sex. It will undoubtedly be a long time before we understand this process completely, and it is far better to err on the side of safety.

Energy Fluctuations

Among people experiencing STEs and long-term spiritual transformation, fluctuations in energy levels and moods are fairly common. All of the experiencers I have worked with have reported at least some fluctuations in their energy levels that were not brought about by any of the usual physical causes, such as illness or lack of sleep. In different cases — and at different times — these fluctuations range from what is often described as feeling low in energy or not having enough energy to carry out daily tasks, to periods of markedly increased physical or mental energy. Many experiencers also report periods of increased emotional lability that either are not related to events in their lives or are intensified by events far more than normal.

Common fluctuations associated with energy and mood that STE experiencers report as after-effects include:

- Unexplainable fluctuations in physical energy, from highly energetic to lethargic.
- Unexplainable periods of fatigue or increased susceptibility to illness.
- Periods of exceptionally high physical energy that may include strong urges to exercise strenuously or run for long distances.
- Episodes that are sometimes described as feeling "speedy" or "revved up"; sometimes accompanied by dizziness or light-headedness.
- Periods of exceptionally high mental energy and mental clarity.
- Periods of low mental energy or mental states sometimes described as "mental dullness," often characterized by an inability to think as quickly, efficiently, or clearly as normal.
- Unexplained fluctuations between extremely high and low mental energy.
- Periods of increased irritability or an increase in moodiness or mood swings.

In terms of the yogic model of consciousness and kundalini, these unexplainable energy fluctuations and mood swings in STE experiencers are related to the body's fluctuating ability to meet the nervous system and the brain/astral brain's need for prana and ojas. When the supply of prana is being consumed more rapidly than it can be replenished, the body feels low in energy. The various levels of fatigue may well be directly proportional to the level of depletion of prana. When the body is meeting demands adequately, energy levels are normal or higher than normal.

Moods may be affected in the same way. When adequate supplies of prana and ojas are reaching the brain, moods are normal or good. When the supplies are inadequate, moods are proportionally lower. Both high physical energy and elevated moods could be explained by the body's producing very large amounts of prana.

In my work, I have found — as Gopi Krishna did from his research and from his correspondence with hundreds of people around the world — that these fluctuations in energy and swings in mood are often more pronounced in STE experiencers who have immoderate, irregular, or stressful lives; who disregard the importance of regular, well-balanced meals; or who indulge in smoking, excessive drinking, drugs, or excessive sexual activity.

Some STE experiencers seem to be more prone to fluctuations in energy and moods than others. Although a certain amount of energy fluctuation is probably unavoidable during the process of spiritual transformation, doing the psycho-spiritual housecleaning described in chapter 18, living the well-balanced, regulated lifestyle described in chapter 17, and adopting a daily practice of prayer and meditation may be the most effective ways to moderate energy and mood swings. Further research may also show that some individuals may be genetically predisposed to have mood swings after beginning to have STEs. We know that a genetic predisposition exists for the more extreme type of mood swings, bipolar or manic-depressive disorder.

Increased Sensitivities

Many STE experiencers find themselves developing new increased sensitivities following their STE. This may include new food sensitivities or food allergies, as previously mentioned. Some STE experiencers also find they develop a new or increased sensitivity to energy fields, electromagnetic fields, bright lights, food additives, scents, and/or noises and sounds.

"Electromagnetic sensitivity" is an interesting STE after-effect that has been quite well documented in NDE experiencers. People with electromagnetic sensitivity may find that they are sensitive to electromagnetic fields around them, and feel physical discomfort when close to a strong electromagnetic field. Some STE experiencers discover that their own energy field now seems to somehow affect electronic equipment around them. They may notice that their presence tends to make microphones, computers, and other electronic equipment malfunction. Their wristwatches may repeatedly stop working. Coins held in their pockets may inexplicably not function in vending machines. Some find their presence tends to make light bulbs flicker or pop out. Two STE experiencers have told me that while walking down a street at night they seemed to cause several street lights to flicker and then pop and go dark in succession as they walked by.

It also seems that people undergoing STEs may react differently to drugs and medical treatments than the general population does. Many STE experiencers seem to require a lower dosage of medications, or become more prone to side effects from drugs, more sensitive to anaesthetics, and more likely to notice subtle or even sometimes pronounced after-effects from anaesthesia. These anaesthesia after-effects may include temporary depressed mood, fatigue, and suppression of the creative impulse. One STE experiencer who is a writer told me that his writing ability and inspired creativity disappeared for almost two years after he was under anaesthesia for eighteen hours during a complex operation.

Why many STE experiencers find their bodies much more sensitive to diverse physical and environmental factors following their STEs is not known. From the yogic perspective, I speculate that this increased sensitivity may be due to the body and astral body's new and increased need for a more pure form of prana, as well as the increased flow of prana throughout the body and astral body. Electromagnetic sensitivity may be related to the increased pranic flow and chakra openings occurring in the astral body. Additionally, I suspect that the purity of an individual's prana may be adversely affected by drugs, surgery, and especially by powerful anaesthetics. Certainly the physical body and the brain are strongly affected by these things. More research will be needed to help determine the cause of these increased sensitivities in STE experiencers.

Yogic Phenomena

A number of professionals, including myself, who have been working with people undergoing STEs and long-term spiritual transformation of consciousness, have noted physical after-effect symptoms that can be loosely characterized as yogic phenomena. These include a variety of movements and postures that the experiencer either does spontaneously and without volition or feels an overpowering inner urge to do. Many of these movements are hatha yoga postures or mudras — certain hand movements used in some spiritual rituals, postures, and meditation practices. Other experiencers may spontaneously or involuntarily do yogic breathing techniques. One of the most fascinating things about these phenomena is that people who have no training in or knowledge of yoga often report doing these yogic activities spontaneously. Some even report spontaneously uttering words or mantras that they believe to be — and, in some cases, are verified to be — Sanskrit, the ancient and sacred language of India.

Although the yogic model of consciousness and kundalini does not offer a specific explanation for these unusual occurrences, they may be the result of a kind of "wisdom of the body" that intuitively urges the experiencers into positions that facilitate the flow of prana throughout the body during periods of spiritual energy/kundalini activity. Perhaps some of the many yogic postures and hand movements were originally developed by yogis who spontaneously did them after awakening kundalini and then, because they were beneficial, continued to do them until they eventually became systematized as part of the yoga teachings.

In *Energies of Transformation*, Dr. Bonnie Greenwell postulates that the postures might occur "because of an unconscious force that knows exactly what the body needs to release a block." About the yogic breathing patterns that sometimes occur, often during intense meditation, she writes that perhaps they are "stimulated by physiological needs, or connections with memories in the collective unconscious, or triggered for specific healing purposes unknown to the conscious mind."

Although these yogic phenomena are generally not painful — and, in fact, are often quite pleasant — their sudden appearance after an STE can be distressing, especially to people who know nothing about yoga, and who do not understand the beneficial effect postures, hand movements, chants, and breathing techniques may have on spiritual energy flow. These yogic phenomena can also be socially inappropriate and embarrassing if they happen spontaneously in a public place. Fortunately, they usually occur only when the experiencer is meditating or involved in some other spiritual practice. When this happens, it is beneficial to follow the inner urge, relax, and allow the body to move, slowly and gently, into the position, movement, or pattern of breathing it desires. In the same way, spontaneous chants and sounds can be allowed to flow freely rather than be struggled against.

When the urge to begin one of these yogic phenomena occurs in a public place, it can generally be suppressed for a short time until a private or socially appropriate place for flowing with the inner urge can be found.

Distinguishing Physical Illnesses from STE After-Effect Symptoms

The unusual physical symptoms that appear as STE after-effects and part of the spiritual transformation process often cause a great deal of confusion, and leave STE experiencers wondering whether a particular sensation or symptom is related to their spiritual process or to some unknown physical illness. I cannot emphasize enough how important it is that unusual physical symptoms be investigated by a qualified medical doctor.

Unfortunately, some people have gotten the idea that true spirituality brings with it an immunity to normal physical illness or some sort of paranormal ability for self-healing. In reality, there are countless examples of highly spiritual people who have died from disease. Sri Ramakrishna died of cancer, Krishnamurti of pancreatic cancer, and Gopi Krishna of complications arising from pneumonia. How, then, can those of us who are simply moving at our own pace along the spiritual path expect to have physical invincibility? People who have STEs can develop cancer, diabetes, pneumonia, heart attacks, AIDS, and other physical illnesses just like the rest of the human population.

In fact, in my practice I have found that certain physical illnesses actually seem to occur more frequently in people undergoing STEs than in the general population. These include respiratory allergies, skin contact allergies, food allergies, hypoglycemia, diabetes mellitus, and thyroid disorders.

One thing is certain: it is a mistake to presume that intensive spiritual practices, meditation, positive thinking, or repeated affirmations make one immune to the biological laws of nature. I have also seen a number of individuals in my practice who tried to deny the reality of a physical illnesses they had because they believed that acknowledging the illness would somehow "give it power" and make it worse. This prolonged denial led to unnecessary delay in obtaining much-needed medical treatment.

Although I certainly believe that positive thinking, positive visualization, affirmations, prayer, and meditation — along with a healthy lifestyle — can optimize the body's ability to fight off disease and heal itself, I also believe that God works through people to bring about better conditions for humanity — including through herbalists, medical researchers, scientists, and doctors.

Like everyone else, people undergoing STEs should find a medical doctor with whom they have good rapport, and go for a thorough physical examination about once a year. STE experiencers should also inform their doctor of any unusual or distressing physical symptoms so that the doctor can investigate these symptoms thoroughly. Only after all the tests and investigations are completed and the doctor feels certain that there is no underlying medical cause can an STE experiencer assume that the unusual physical symptoms are a normal part of the spiritual transformation process.

13

PSYCHOLOGICAL STE
AFTER-EFFECT
SYMPTOMS

PEOPLE HAVING STES and undergoing long-term spiritual transformation of consciousness experience many psychological changes as well as the physical ones. These STE after-effects are evidence that something else is going on, and thus they can be thought of as "symptoms," just as the physical symptoms and changes can.

The immediate emotional and psychological impact of STEs varies tremendously from individual to individual, depending on such factors as personality, the amount of stress in the person's life, and whether they are in a supportive environment in which their STEs are treated as valid and positive. Most STE experiencers also notice episodic or long-term psychological symptoms or after-effects. It seems as if the STE started or accelerated a psychological transformation process that propels them at some point into intense self-reflection, emotional recovery work, inner healing work, and/or depth psychotherapy. It seems like the personality is being purified, morally developed, healed, and polished by a Higher Power. Christian mystics refer to this process as "purification" and "purgation." I call it spontaneous psychospiritual housecleaning, and will discuss it in more depth in chapter 18.

Some of the psychological after-effects and reactions to STEs are positive and demonstrate inner growth or healing. Others are challenging or distressing and indicate that more inner work needs to be done. Almost everyone undergoing STEs has both kinds of reactions. Fortunately, in my work, I have found that, in the long run, for most people the positive psychological reactions to STEs far outweigh the challenging or distressful ones. Further, when negative psychological reactions are treated as challenges and growth opportunities, they can often be worked through, healed, and turned into opportunities for personal growth. Although I have characterized these reactions generally as "psychological," many of them have to do with our attitudes and spiritual values.

Positive Psychological Symptoms and Reactions

STE experiencers report many positive psychological changes that are wide-ranging, and relate to personality, emotions, attitudes, outlook, and values. Some of these changes may occur suddenly; others may develop gradually over time. Many STE experiencers have several of these positive symptoms and reactions; others have only a few, and the experiences themselves do not necessarily manifest in exactly the way I describe them. Here are some of the positive psychological symptoms and reactions that can be after-effects to STEs and accompany the spiritual transformation process:

1. *Maturation of the personality.* Experiencers may abandon irresponsible and immature behaviours and exhibit new independence, clarity of thought, personal strength, and social responsibility.
2. *Spontaneous abandonment of self-destructive habits.* Experiencers may develop a strong inner urge for a healthier lifestyle and suddenly give up smoking, excessive alcohol use, use of recreational drugs, or a sedentary lifestyle.
3. *Re-evaluation of jobs.* Experiencers may decide to modify or leave work situations that are unsatisfactory, stress-producing, or emotionally unfulfilling.
4. *Re-evaluation of relationships.* Experiencers may examine relationships with family, friends, and partners and attempt to improve communication and understanding, and to resolve conflicts that have been simmering for years. When all else fails, they may finally find the clarity and inner strength to break off dysfunctional or unhealthy relationships.

5. *Resolution of psychological blocks.* Repressed memories of unresolved psychological issues and conflicts, including forgotten childhood memories, may spontaneously surface in the experiencer's conscious mind, become clear, and eventually be resolved. This resolution may take some time and require professional help, but sometimes resolution occurs much more rapidly than normal.

6. *Setting healthier interpersonal boundaries.* Experiencers may find themselves increasingly self-aware and self-reflective, recognizing their own codependent relationship patterns or abusive tendencies, and their previous denial or minimization of abusive relationships. They may begin to set clearer, healthier boundaries in their relationships, reduce or stop abusive behaviours, and break away from "victim" and "rescuer" roles.

7. *Absolute belief in the existence of a Higher Power.* Experiencers may develop an unshakable conviction concerning the reality of the existence of the Creator, God, Allah, Brahman, or some type of omnipotent, omnipresent, omniscient, and loving Higher Power behind the universe, or an existing belief may become much stronger.

8. *Loss of the fear of death.* Experiencers may no longer perceive death as the end of life but as a transition from physical to spiritual form, or perhaps as a "coming home." They may come to believe in reincarnation, and thus view death as a positive transformation, but suicide as unacceptable.

9. *Being inspired by the memory.* Experiencers may feel uplifted by the memory of STEPs or profound STEs; these memories seem to act as beacons in times of darkness or as guideposts in the continuing attempt to become a better human being.

10. *Increased humanitarianism, love, and empathy.* Experiencers may develop or strengthen any or all of the following: a belief in the oneness of all humankind; a greater capacity to feel unconditional love for friends, family, and humanity in general; a greater love for all living creatures; a greater capacity for forgiveness; deeper understanding; greater sensitivity to and awareness of others' suffering;

less rigid or intolerant thinking; and greater compassion. This often leads to an increase in humanitarian attitudes and actions.

11. *Increased altruism.* Experiencers may develop a more selfless nature and a greater desire to be of service to others.

12. *Increased morality.* Experiencers may be conscious of a desire to be more honest, truthful, and fair and have an increased desire to follow spiritual ideals and live by a moral or ethical code.

13. *Decreased materialism.* Experiencers' desire for material possessions, financial success, and fame may lessen. Achievements in business and finance may become less important.

14. *Increased spiritual focus and deeper spiritual insights.* Experiencers place more importance, and spend more time, in prayer, meditation, reading about spiritual subjects, or participating in spiritual practices. They may desire more and more to live in accordance with the world's great spiritual teachings. When they read or discuss the scriptures of the world's great religions or other spiritual writings, they may have new spiritual insights and far deeper levels of understanding.

15. *Increased religious tolerance.* Experiencers often develop broader and more tolerant religious views, and become less fundamentalist in their spiritual beliefs. They often become more respectful and appreciative of the value and importance of all the world's major religions, as well as the diversity and wisdom of the world's great prophets.

16. *Increased intuitiveness.* Experiencers may develop or increase the ability to hear an "inner voice," learn from higher, inner guidance, and be intuitive in all aspects of life.

17. *Increased creativity.* Experiencers may feel a stronger urge to express the self through writing, the media, music, or art; in some cases, their ability to do so also develops or increases.

18. *A belief in the reality of one's spiritual experiences.* Experiencers may be strongly, even unshakably, convinced of the reality of their STEs, and especially their STEPs. This conviction remains firm in the face of opposition and is often a source of inner strength.

The following story was told to me by a forty-eight-year-old woman, Pam. Her kundalini awakening, which was stimulated by five years of intensive psychotherapy, dream analysis, and regular meditation practice, was marked by dramatic rushes of energy up her body, strong sensations of light, and overwhelming feelings of love and bliss. This STE led to tremendous positive psychological changes.

> I'm not too proud of the person I used to be. I suppose it was all part of my growing-up process. Before my spiritual awakening, I was a pretty mixed-up person. I used marijuana and hashish regularly. I drank alcohol to excess almost every weekend. But I was most unhappy with my personal relationships. I felt powerless and needy of love, so I put up with a lot of emotional abuse.
>
> After my kundalini awakening I found it very easy to quit drinking alcohol, using drugs, and smoking. I suddenly became aware that the physical and sexual abuse I had experienced in my childhood was affecting my behaviour today. I started working with my psychotherapist with renewed vigour, to try to work through my childhood traumas and sexual abuse that had helped make me act this unhealthy way.
>
> Now, five years after my kundalini awakening, I feel that I am a different person. I have completely changed my circle of friends. I am happy in a long-term monogamous gay relationship that is tender and caring. I have been drug-free for years. I volunteer regularly for a small community-service organization that helps sexual-abuse survivors. I strive to be as loving and open as possible in all my relationships. My spiritual growth has become the most important thing in my life.

In some people, the most noticeable positive psychological impact of STEs is decreased materialism combined with increased humanitarianism. This was true of Gerald, a successful sixty-year-old businessman.

Prior to my mystical experience, my business was the most important thing in my life. I was the president of a medium-sized publishing house, and I aspired to be a multi-millionaire. I worked hundred-hour weeks, and I had time for little else than my work.

In 1975, while at a conference in the Rocky Mountains, I had a profound mystical vision, which changed my life. I saw the face of the man who was to be my future spiritual teacher. With the image of the face came a feeling of profound love, overwhelming compassion, and understanding. I wept. I suddenly felt ashamed of my life, which was so materialistic and devoid of love.

When I returned home, my wife hardly recognized me. She said that my face was beaming with light. She was amazed and delighted when I told her that I was cutting down my work hours and beginning to practise a spiritual discipline. I sought out the teacher who had appeared in my vision. When I found him, I began to study with him, learning yoga and meditation. I began donating at least 10 percent of my income to spiritual causes, and still do so to this day.

My spiritual quest is the most important thing in my life now. I have toned down my work. Money is not important to me anymore — I give away more of it than I keep.

Challenging or Distressing Psychological Symptoms

I have found that many of the psychological reactions to STEs that might be considered distressing or difficult to deal with are caused, at least in part, by a lack of an appropriate framework for STEs, and a lack of information or incorrect information about spiritual transformation of consciousness and kundalini. Significant unresolved psychological issues can also intensify or increase the difficult reactions. Although most of the following reactions can be thought of as negative, I prefer to regard them as challenging personal growth opportunities. This underscores the idea that they usually can be dealt with, worked through, or resolved in a variety of ways. Most people undergoing STEs have some temporary challenging reactions and after-effects from time to time. And all of the following reactions can be experienced in different ways and degrees:

1. *Anxiety.* A sense of anxiety or general emotional distress may occur, often because of uncertainty about the nature of STE experiences and spiritual energy after-effect symptoms, what they mean, and why they happened. Anxiety is often intensified by not having anyone to talk to who can understand or interpret the experiences in a positive way.

2. *Confusion.* A sense of confusion may result from not understanding the nature or meaning of an STE or why it occurred. There may be confusion about the nature of reality itself, especially when "reality" as it was perceived during the STE does not fit with previously held beliefs and assumptions about the universe.

3. *Isolation.* Experiencers sometimes feel very isolated after an STE because they feel unsafe to talk to anyone — friends or professionals — feeling that nobody would understand or interpret their STE and after-effects in a positive way.

4. *Mental dulling.* Difficulty concentrating may occur, with a feeling that the brain is "overloaded"; feeling incapable of coping with normal mental tasks or emotional stresses. This occurs most frequently immediately after STEPs or intense STEs.

5. *Fixation with experiences.* Some experiencers may think about or focus on the STEs or STEPs to the exclusion of all else, so that it interferes with daily functioning and performance.

6. *Despair that a STEP has ended.* Despair or deep sadness may develop, that a STEP or profound STE has ended and cannot be re-created or reexperienced at will.

7. *Rebound depression and lassitude.* Temporary mental exhaustion, lassitude, or depression may occur immediately after a STEP or intense STE. It usually disappears within a few days or weeks.

This reaction may be due to a depletion of the stores of prana or ojas.

8. *Decreased capacity to love.* Feelings of emotional depletion may occur, including being incapable of feeling affection or love for one's spouse, family members, and friends. This rebound reaction tends to be most common after the emotional high of an intense STEP, or periods of high STE activity. This reaction may also be related to a depletion of prana or ojas. The capacity to feel love usually returns in a matter of days or weeks.

9. *Fear of losing control.* A sense may develop that one is no longer in control of one's life and actions, and subsequently an experiencer may attempt to suppress their STEs and after-effect symptoms. This fear is often aggravated by the fact that, in truth, no one can completely control the spiritual transformation process.

10. *Fear that one is dying.* A fear may develop that a STEP or profound STE is a signal that one is going to die soon.

11. *Fear of being labelled mentally ill.* Many STE experiencers fear that others, especially health-care providers, will incorrectly label them as mentally ill if they disclose details of the STE or STEP to them.

12. *Fear of going insane.* A fear may occur that one is going insane or is already insane without having realized it. This reaction is more common when the realms glimpsed in STEs conflict with one's previous view of reality or are completely outside the range of one's life experience.

13. *Fear of possession.* A fear may arise that one is being taken over or controlled by evil spirits or entities. This reaction is more common in people who believe strongly in such evil entities, who attempt to "play" with channelling or with the dark forces, or who have little or no information about kundalini or the process of spiritual transformation of consciousness.

14. *Fear of the devil.* A fear may occur that STEs are the "work of the devil." This is more frequent in individuals who belong to rigid, fundamentalist religious groups and/or are told by the leaders of those groups that the phenomena associated with STEs are evil and caused by the devil.

15. *Inexplicable mood swings.* Unexplainable and sudden temporary changes in mood may arise; waves of anger, guilt, anxiety, or depression that may resolve as suddenly as they appear; uncharacteristic emotional lability or irritability, characterized by bursting into tears, getting upset, or becoming very angry quickly and easily over small things. This can be more marked immediately after STEPs or strong STEs.

16. *Cyclothymia.* Recurrent cycles of mild depression or lassitude that alternate with cycles of normal or high-level functioning may occur.

17. *Intensification of unresolved psychological issues.* Awareness of unresolved psychological issues may arise spontaneously after STEs, and cause the associated emotional conflicts to become more intense. Repressed memories of traumatic events may surface, and cause relationships with people responsible for childhood trauma or other emotional conflicts to become increasingly dysfunctional. Anger, guilt, fear, depression, or anxiety concerning these issues may intensify.

18. *Emotional distress.* The surfacing of memories and unresolved issues, or discomfort with the nature of an STE, may cause generalized psychological distress, and an inability or unwillingness to deal with these issues may aggravate the distress. Sometimes this reaction is described as feeling "less centred," or "less together." This reaction is most common after some types of psychic experiences.

19. *Sexuality crisis.* Uncertainty over sexual orientation and/or gender identity sometimes develops, particularly when the experiencer is undergoing the physiological symptom of greatly intensified sexual urges. This reaction is usually temporary and generally resolves itself when the experiencer's sexual drives return to their equilibrium.

20. *Poor ability to control increased sexual urges.* An inability to cope with or poor self-control with the physiological symptom of intensified sexual drives may occur, resulting in a period of inappropriate or uncharacteristic promiscuous sexual behaviour.

This reaction is sometimes reported as strong feelings of sexual attraction to all persons of the gender(s) the experiencer is usually attracted to, and sometimes other genders. This condition is usually temporary and resolves itself when sexual drives return to normal.

In some cases, challenging psychological symptoms and reactions can intensify and develop into the types of crises, spiritual emergencies, or psychoses discussed in chapter 15. One of the signs that this might occur is the experiencer's beginning to have trouble discriminating between inner and outer realities. An experiencer may begin to think that his or her paranormal and spiritual experiences are being shared by everyone.

Delusions are another sign that negative psychological reactions may worsen. STE experiencers with delusions of grandeur may assume that their experiences have far greater significance than they actually do, or that they are special divine messengers meant to save the planet. Paranoid delusions are another sign of potential trouble — when experiencers begin to think that others are using special mental powers to control their behaviour or to cause the unusual or paranormal phenomena they are experiencing.

Tensions and Conflicts in Relationships

In my clinical work, I have sometimes seen STE experiencers become uncertain about their relationships after a STEP or in the course of the long-term spiritual transformation process. In cases where incompatibilities already existed, they often become magnified — and conflicts and disagreements tend to increase.

Another very common area of difficulty relates to changes in the experiencer's sex drive. A dramatic increase or decrease in one partner's desire for sex can throw any relationship into turmoil. An STE experiencer's decrease in sex drive may be poorly understood by the partner, and may be misinterpreted as a lack of love or a lack of commitment to the relationship. An increase in sex drive may also confuse the partner, or make them feel pressured into having more frequent sex than they desire. Matters are complicated even further when the increase in sex drive is so great that the

STE experiencer has difficulty with their self-control, and begins to desire other sexual partners.

Relationships may also be challenged by the love/bliss after-effects of some STEs. I have seen several cases where the experience of overflowing love associated with a powerful bliss-type mystical experience, or heart-chakra opening, was mistaken for "falling in love" with someone, possibly outside the marital relationship. Similarly, others may misinterpret an STE experiencer's outpouring of spiritual love following a bliss-filled STE, and mistake this for an indication of romantic interest. Alternatively, dealing with the opposite, the temporary loss of the ability to feel love and affection that sometimes follows intense STEs, can also be very hard on both partners.

Spiritual pride can cause serious relationship problems, too, especially when it leads an experiencer to become dissatisfied with a partner who does not have the same spiritual ideas or focus.

Other types of relationship problems may arise, depending on the partner's reaction to what the STE experiencer is going through. A partner's disbelief in or ridicule of an STE, for instance, can be very difficult for the experiencer to handle. I have also seen partners who were aware of STEs and became jealous because their own experiences were not as profound or dramatic.

In other cases, I have seen partners who were unable to adjust to the STE experiencer's changing interests, values, and increasingly spiritual focus. Some partners are also unable to accept the experiencer's desire to make lifestyle changes or to deal with the changes in personality that accompany long-term spiritual transformation. It can also be difficult for a partner to cope with the challenging psychological after-effects STE experiencers sometimes go through.

Risa, one of my patients, experienced several of these typical difficulties in her relationship with her husband once her STE experiences began, and she unfortunately responded negatively.

> I noticed a tremendous variability in my sex drive after my intense kundalini awakening experience. I also felt a strong desire to spend large amounts of time each day in

meditation, writing in my journal, or practising yoga. My husband did not support these changes and started to ridicule me about my increasing spiritual focus. My husband also did not understand how my sexual drive could swing from very intense to virtually nonexistent. He was uncomfortable with and resistant to my new sexual exploration during periods of high sex drive. I in turn found myself wanting to have sexual relations outside the marriage, and I began to feel that my husband was not an appropriate partner for me. I eventually started a sexual affair outside the marriage, an action I now regret.

Fortunately, Risa and her husband were able to heal the marriage by going for marriage counselling and by their consultation with me, which helped them both understand how the kundalini awakening had affected the variability in Risa's sex drive, and had also enhanced her urge to do daily spiritual practices.

Coping with Challenging Psychological Reactions

A great deal can be done to heal and resolve some of the challenging psychological after-effects and reactions associated with STEs and spiritual transformation of consciousness. In many cases, these are the same measures that help one resolve and cope with various degrees of spiritual crises and spiritual emergencies. One of the best is to find a qualified doctor, psychotherapist, or spiritual counsellor to help you through the process. Ideally, this person would be familiar with and have an open, positive attitude about spiritual and paranormal experiences. If such a person is not available in your area, an alternative is to find a sensitive, supportive, open-minded doctor or psychotherapist who is willing to accept your reports of your STEs at face value and seems willing to learn more about the whole process of spiritual transformation.

Although a number of strategies for dealing with challenging psychological reactions and other difficulties sometimes associated with STEs are discussed in detail in chapters 17, 18, and 20 (on "Strategies for Living with

Spiritual Transformation," "Psycho-Spiritual Housecleaning," and "Finding Our Way Home"), I will summarize the main ones here for quick reference:

1. Realize that these challenging psychological reactions are experienced by others on the spiritual path and that many of them have been recorded in the yogic literature and in other mystical traditions. This realization can help "normalize" the reactions, make them less frightening, and help put them in better perspective.

2. Remember that these reactions are, in most cases, temporary — even though they might recur from time to time. Knowing that STEs and after-effect symptoms are temporary is reassuring and helps experiencers cope with them while they are occurring.

3. Focus on the positive aspects of STEs and be grateful for them rather than thinking too much about the negative reactions. This helps develop a sense of positive perspective and prevent the negative cycle in which the experiencer spends more and more time focusing on the negative.

4. Pray, meditate, read spiritual material, and/or repeat positive affirmations for moderate amounts of time each day. Turn your problems over to the Divine. Ask for his or her help in your healing, learning, and growth. This can be a tremendous source of strength.

5. Develop a more moderate, healthy, and balanced lifestyle. This can improve the body's general health, contribute to better mental health, and help regulate and moderate the flow of the spiritually transformative energies within the body.

6. Temporarily relocate to a tranquil, supportive environment — for example, a spiritual retreat or even a cottage — to get away from daily stresses and to work psychological issues through. Perhaps go on pilgrimage to a holy site.

7. Talk to a supportive person — a friend, doctor, spiritual teacher, or counsellor.

8. Associate with like-minded spiritual persons. Decrease contact with persons who are opposed to and critical of your new spiritual outlook.

The following story shows how one of my STE patients, Arlene, used these strategies to cope with the emotional challenges she faced after her psychic opening, in which she started to unblock past-life memories:

> Two years ago, about five years after my NDE, I started having bad relationship problems. My long-time common-law boyfriend, Bill, was starting to become rude and verbally abusive. I started suspecting that he was having an affair. This was a phase in my life when I had been meditating for one hour a day. I had been praying for guidance to God, to help me understand what was going wrong with my relationship.
>
> Suddenly one day during my meditation, I got a clear visual memory of a past life in which I had seemed to be married to Bill. I was the man in that life, and Bill was a woman, my wife. In the past-life memory, I had caught my wife having an affair with another man. I saw myself kill my wife (Bill) in the heat of an argument.
>
> This past-life memory had a devastating impact on me. I suddenly felt very guilty, responsible in some way for the problems I was now having with Bill. Further, I had nobody to talk to. I had no friends who believed in past lives, and I certainly couldn't talk to Bill. Our relationship became even more strained than before.
>
> A few weeks later another past-life memory came to me during meditation. In this one, I was a woman and Bill was my husband. This time he was very abusive. He was unfaithful, having numerous affairs. I could see a real parallel in how Bill was beginning to be abusive toward me in this life.
>
> I felt overwhelmed and confused by these two past-life memories. I had no idea how to integrate them into my life. I started worrying that they were hallucinations and that I might be going crazy. I was totally preoccupied with them and found it difficult to concentrate on my work. I heard about Dr. Kason, so I went to see her for help.

She reassured me that what seem to be past-life memories commonly surface as after-effects of STEs, and were not a sign that I was going crazy. She helped me see them as something positive, a gift from the unconscious mind to help me understand my problems with Bill. I read a book she recommended about other people who had past-life memories. I took Dr. Kason's advice and adopted a more regular lifestyle, with more sleep and more exercise. I started going for weekly psychotherapy sessions with a psychologist in my area. Within a few weeks I felt much calmer. Several months later, with the help of psychotherapy, I had the inner strength to stop what seemed to be a many-lifetime cycle of abuse, and end my unhealthy abusive relationship with Bill.

The self-help strategies listed above, along with the ones discussed throughout the rest of this book, should reassure any STE experiencer who is experiencing negative or challenging psychological after-effects. Even though these reactions can be painful while they are occurring, they are usually temporary, and much can be done to help resolve them. Finally, STE experiencers can take comfort in the knowledge that the often challenging psycho-spiritual housecleaning has been recognized for centuries by yogic and other mystical traditions as an essential part of the long-term spiritual transformation process.

SPIRITUAL AND PARANORMAL STE AFTER-EFFECT SYMPTOMS

PEOPLE UNDERGOING LONG-TERM spiritual transformation of consciousness develop a similar range of spiritual and paranormal after-effect symptoms, after or between STE experiences, no matter which type of STE they have had. Many of these symptoms have been touched upon in chapters 3 and 7, which dealt with mystical and psychic STEPs.

In the beginning, spiritual and paranormal symptoms may simply be very subtle shifts in consciousness. They do vary in intensity, however, and over time they tend to increase in strength and frequency until often they become a permanent feature of the experiencer's consciousness. In general, the gradual increase in these symptoms can be thought of as a slow expansion of the experiencer's "baseline" range of consciousness to include spiritual and paranormal dimensions. These spiritual and paranormal symptoms can be thought of as part of the vast continuum of experiences that characterize the process of long-term spiritual transformation of consciousness.

Sometimes, when I am giving a presentation, I draw an analogy with the development of colour vision to illustrate this long-term process. A person having a profound STEP would be like a person living in a colour-blind society who, like everyone else, can see in only black and white — until suddenly he or she has an intense experience of full-spectrum colour vision. This would radically alter the person's world view and have a definite transformational impact. People who have ongoing or recurrent STE activity can be compared to people with black-and-white vision having episodes in which they perceive one or two colours — perhaps primary colours like red or blue. This would enrich their lives and change their world view, but would have less transformational impact than a sudden change to full-colour vision would have.

The changes in consciousness associated with paranormal symptoms are even more subtle and gradual. This gradual change in baseline consciousness and range of perceptions would not radically alter a person's world view or have any significant transformational impact, but would enrich their normal consciousness.

Most paranormal and spiritual after-effect symptoms seem to add to the experiencer's normal conscious functioning. Eventually they may become a permanent feature — and indication — of the transformation that has occurred in consciousness. For example, a woman who has had a profound mystical experience may notice that she is becoming more intuitive, and eventually she may begin to have premonitions or other types of psychic experiences. These experiences may become more frequent until they are an accepted part of her everyday inner life.

While many of these spiritual and paranormal after-effect symptoms are nondisruptive or even mildly positive or pleasurable, some may be disturbing or disconcerting. Others are disturbing to certain experiencers simply because they represent an unknown, or are quite different, unusual, or even bizarre compared to the type of STE experience that the person has become accustomed to. For example, a deeply religious man may have experienced meditation-related mystical STEs of bliss and love so often in his life that he thinks of them as a beautiful part of existence. He may, however, be puzzled or distressed if he suddenly begins to have recurrent psychic experiences that he does not consider compatible with his religion.

The following list of spiritual and paranormal STE after-effect symptoms can reassure STE experiencers and let them know that it is perfectly normal to be having a wide range of after-effects and symptoms of varying intensity. In addition, the list contains strategies that I have found helpful to STE experiencers in dealing with symptoms that are distressful.

I have organized these spiritual and paranormal symptoms into five broad categories: (1) the mystical and spiritual, (2) spiritual energy/kundalini, (3) the psychic and paranormal, (4) changes in dream life, and

(5) changes in visual perception. Experiencers may have symptoms from any or all of the categories.

Spiritual and paranormal symptoms tend to develop in the same way that other after-effect symptoms do: Most frequently, they first occur when the experiencer is actually taking part in a spiritual practice such as meditating, praying, doing yoga, or reading spiritual works. They tend to occur more frequently when the experiencer is spending a lot of time in spiritual practice. The symptoms also tend to be more marked just after STEPs or during periods of high STE activity. Later, the symptoms may begin to occur at any time and, eventually, become part of normal conscious functioning. The symptoms come to represent a richer state of consciousness than the one the STE experiencer had before the spiritual transformation process began.

Positive Symptoms Associated with the Mystical and Spiritual

Symptoms associated with the mystical and spiritual may include subtle or minor experiences of any type of STEs listed in chapter 3, "Mystical Experiences." The following, however, are the ones that tend to cross STE boundaries and become ongoing, recurrent symptoms of the process of spiritual transformation.

Prayer or meditation-related mystical visions. Visions of gurus, saints, or religious figures may appear intermittently during meditation, intense prayer, or spiritual contemplation. This symptom is often reported by long-time meditators who eventually begin to have repeated visions of their guru or of other spiritual figures during deep meditation. These visions can also occur spontaneously and at any time but are more usual during different types of spiritual contemplation. The experience is uplifting and inspiring, but not as transformational in impact as an STE.

Bliss. Recurrent feelings of deep inner happiness or waves of bliss and peace may occur, sometimes experienced as an inexplicable urge to laugh or smile radiantly. Bliss may become a frequent occurrence during meditation, and may last from hours to days afterward.

Union. Recurrently feeling the unity of all things may occur; feelings of oneness or connectedness with the Source/God/Brahman/Allah/the

Creator and/or with all creation. An inner certainty may develop that all is right in the universe. Recurrent sensations of merging or union may happen, merging with a person, a thing such as a tree, or the entire universe. While unitive mystical experiences are STEPs in themselves, the milder symptom of union is much less intense, and may occur, recur, or last for fairly long periods of time — often after a STEP. Feelings of union may also manifest as a mild blurring of personal boundaries, a feeling of melding with nature or others.

Higher guidance. STE experiencers often report occasional, recurrent, or ongoing impressions of being able to ask your higher self or the Higher Power for guidance, or being able to tap into the divine cosmic intelligence to ask for and receive guidance. The guidance coming from the higher self or divine source may appear in a variety of ways. For instance, it may be experienced in dreams, felt in terms of a sudden inner urge, heard as a voice inside the head, seen as words flashing across the mind, seen as a clear visual image, or appear as a symbolic visual image in the mind's eye (e.g., seeing a red light that means "no" or a green light that means "yes"). Some people feel surges or rushes of energy through the body; a certain type of sensation, for example, might indicate for a particular person that a decision is correct or that something they have just heard is particularly important.

Divine inspiration. STE experiencers may have occasional, ongoing, or recurrent feelings that a higher spiritual source is inspiring them, guiding them and encouraging them, often to work in service to humanity, for the betterment of humankind, or for humanitarian goals. This divine inspiration may take such forms as innovative ideas for public-service projects; creative compassionate solutions to complex life-problems; ideas for inspirational presentations, workshops, or talks; ideas for socially minded or inspirational articles or books; or the strong urge to humbly serve others, perhaps in an anonymous manner.

Expansions of consciousness. Occasional, recurrent, or ongoing sensations of consciousness being expanded beyond the size of the head may occur. This may last for minutes, hours, or even weeks.

Dharshan/spiritual blessings. Increased sensitivity to, and experiencing a spiritual blessing by: (1) viewing a holy image; (2) viewing or being in the presence of a saint or holy person; or (3) going on pilgrimage, and physically being at a holy site where a saint or spiritual Master previously lived and communed with God.

Higher Guidance

Of the above, higher guidance is probably the most common spiritual symptom reported by STE experiencers. I have received higher guidance many times, most notably during the airplane crash in which I had my 1979 NDE. As I described in chapter 1, a voice inside my head repeatedly urged me, "Swim to shore!" Swimming to shore undoubtedly helped save my life.

A similar episode of clear higher guidance happened to me a few years later.

> I had been diagnosed by my gynecologist as having an ovarian cyst. I chose to not have surgery, hoping that the cyst would slowly resolve on its own. One morning, while I was in the kitchen making a cup of coffee, I was suddenly stabbed with searing lower abdominal pain. I doubled over and grabbed the edge of the counter, close to fainting from the pain. My husband had already left for work, and I was alone in the house with my infant son, who was sleeping upstairs in his crib. Overwhelmed by the pain, I collapsed to the floor. I prayed to God for help.
>
> Suddenly a voice in my head said, "Lie on your back!" I could barely find the strength, but somehow I forced myself to roll over. Within seconds the pain began to fade. I remained on my back for several minutes, until the pain went away completely. I realized that the ovarian cyst must have ruptured, and the excruciating pain was due to internal bleeding. Somehow, lying on my back had made the pain and bleeding stop. When I rose a few minutes later to tend to my son, I felt weak but pain-free. Later tests confirmed that my cyst had ruptured.

I can only attribute the inner voice that aided me in both situations to some higher wisdom — inner higher guidance.

Dharshan — Spiritual Blessings

A heightened sensitivity to dharshan, experiencing a spiritual blessing, is another spiritual symptom that many STE experiencers report. Many STE experiencers have reported an upliftment in consciousness, or a healing experience, precipitated by dharshan/blessing caused by: (1) viewing a holy image, icon, or photo of a saint; (2) viewing, touching, or being in the presence of a saint or holy person; or (3) going on pilgrimage to holy sites, physically being in the place where saints or spiritual Masters once lived and communed with God.

George Harrison, former member of the Beatles, shared, in the 2015 film *Awake: The Life of Yogananda*, that he received a strong dharshan spiritual experience when he first looked at a photo of Paramahansa Yogananda. George Harrison stated:

> While I was in India, I was with Ravi Shankar. He gave me *Autobiography of a Yogi*. I just looked at the cover [a photo of Paramahansa Yogananda], and he just zapped me with his eyes. I mean, I can't imagine — if I hadn't read that.... It just gave meaning to life.

Other STE experiencers have reported healings, or profound spiritual experiences, brought on by being in the presence of a saint, or by being touched by the saint. Famous stories of this phenomenon of healing dharshan/blessing by touch are found in the New Testament of the Bible. In addition to the numerous accounts of Jesus actively healing many persons, it is said that many people were healed by merely touching the hem of Jesus's robe (Matthew 9:20–22; Mark 5:25–34; Matthew 14:34–36). STE experiencers have told me of similar, if less dramatic, dharshan blessing experiences brought on by the touch of a saint or Master.

Sherman, whose kundalini awakening story I shared in chapter 12, had a powerful dharshan/blessing experience brought on by the gaze of a contemporary saint. This happened ten years after Sherman's first kundalini awakening, when he was about forty-five years old. Here is the story of Sherman's powerful dharshan experience by a saint's gaze:

I felt inwardly very drawn to meet Swami Muktananda in 1979 while he was visiting the USA. By this time I had been meditating regularly for almost twenty years, and I felt the strong desire to meet a living saint, a living yogi who was in an expanded state of spiritual consciousness. I felt intuitively that Swami Muktananda was indeed such a highly realized yogi.

On the day that I first saw Swami Muktananda, I sat in a large auditorium hall in Miami with a couple hundred other people who were waiting to hear his presentation. I sat in my seat silently meditating, to try to make myself receptive to the Swami's high vibration. As soon as Swami Muktananda entered the back of the room, I immediately noticed a shift in my consciousness. My inner vision in my meditation shifted into an intense deep-blue colour. This blue colour deepened and intensified as the swami walked past me down the aisle, toward the auditorium stage.

Slowly Swami Muktananda began his presentation. I opened my eyes to look at him. He moved his gaze slowly around the audience in the room as he spoke. I was seated at least fifty feet away from him, amidst the crowd in the audience. After several minutes of his inspiring presentation he turned his head to look my direction, and then he briefly looked directly into my eyes.

The instant our eyes met I felt a burst of energy rise out of the base of my spine. It was the kundalini energy, like I had felt awakening many years earlier. Stimulated, it seemed, by Swami Muktananda's gaze, the kundalini energy now rose up from the base of my spine, churned through my belly, and flowed up to my head, exploding inside my head. My head was physically thrown back and I inadvertently uttered "uh" out loud, from the force of the sudden upwards explosion of energy.

Tears began to pour down my cheeks as the upwards flow of energy through my body and spine continued and continued. I began to quietly sob. My entire body was flooded with continuous pulses of energy, coursing upwards. I felt releases occurring throughout many parts of my body, releases of stresses, pains, and anxieties. I felt that I was undergoing a deep purification process, a deep healing. I was being freed from all my tensions.

After a period of tears, sobbing, and releasing of tensions, my consciousness shifted into an expanded, glorious state. I felt like the crown of my head had blown wide open. My diaphragm was thrown up, and the air was thrown out of my lungs. I entered a profoundly beautiful expansive mystical state of consciousness, a state of consciousness where I felt free of all the nonsense and worries of the world. I felt totally stress-free, safe, and content, for the first time in my life.

I stayed in this expanded state of mystical consciousness for an entire week following my first dharshan/blessing experience with Swami Muktananda. My body was unusually healthy and strong during that extraordinary week of ongoing mystical communion. My usual digestive problems seemed to disappear, and my regular physical body pains seemed to have vanished.

Sherman went on to have repeated experiences of dharshan/spiritual blessings whenever he caught the gaze of Swami Muktananda over the next several weeks. Sherman humbly confided to me that ultimately the receipt of this repeated dharshan over a several-week period enabled him, as a long-time meditator and devoted yogi, to slip into an ongoing state of mystical communion that lasted for almost twenty years. He has been striving to reattain that mystical communion ever since it disappeared.

Pilgrimage to holy sites can also have a much stronger dharshan/ spiritual blessing impact on STE experiencers as compared to the average person. Many religious traditions advocate the benefit to all persons of pilgrimage to holy sites, the physical locations where great saints or spiritual Masters once lived, walked, prayed, and communed with God. According to the yogic tradition, the physical sites where spiritual Masters lived and communed with God become impregnated with the high spiritual vibrations of the Master. Paramahansa Yogananda, for one, stated that this elevating spiritual imprint left by the great spiritual Masters will remain at the holy site to perpetuity. Yogananda went on to say that all persons will spiritually benefit by pilgrimage to holy sites, the depth of the benefit being in accordance to their spiritual receptivity.

A powerful pilgrimage dharshan experience happened to me unexpectedly in 2000, when I travelled to Israel with a group of doctors for a medical conference. Here is my pilgrimage dharshan/blessing story:

> I was on a short outing in Israel, vising some of the Christian and Jewish holy sites. I had an intellectual curiosity about the sites, but I was skeptical about the locations' historical accuracy. This day a tour leader took a group of us close to the Sea of Galilea, to a site where some claimed Jesus Christ delivered his first and very profound sermon, the "Sermon on the Mount."
>
> The tour leader walked us around the site and then began to read excerpts from the "Sermon on the Mount" out loud. "Blessed are the poor in spirit; for theirs is the kingdom of heaven. Blessed are they that mourn; for they shall be comforted.... Blessed are the merciful; for they shall obtain mercy.... Blessed are the peacemakers; for they shall be called the children of God ..." (Matthew 5: 2–7)
>
> To my great surprise, as he read these sacred words, I began to tremble inside. I found myself starting to silently weep. When the tour leader finished talking, I moved away from the group to reflect in the serene garden. As I gazed

at the Sea of Galilea I felt a powerful PRESENCE pour down upon me and permeate me. I knew intuitively that this was the holy vibration of Jesus the Christ. I started to sob openly. I felt like a fountain of love was cleansing my soul. Although I heard no words, I intuited the higher guidance to "be more loving" and "be more forgiving" relating to relationship difficulties I was having at that time. I felt like the holy and powerful spiritual vibration at the site had healed something in me, as if a dark fleck or knot had been cleansed from my heart, allowing my heart to open wider, thus enabling me to be more loving and more forgiving.

I left the site with the tour group several minutes later. The powerful healing energy dissipated as I left. I knew with inward certainty that this was indeed the correct site. This was definitely where Jesus Christ had walked and talked, and His sacred vibration remains at the site.

This was my first experience of dharshan, spiritual blessing, from a holy site. I have heard many other stories from STE experiencers about having strong healing or spiritually elevating experiences at holy sites of diverse spiritual traditions. Many average persons, in addition to STE experiencers, have attested to healings and deep spiritual experiences at holy sites such as Assisi and Lourdes. Based on my strong dharshan, spiritual blessing, experiences at holy sites in Israel, I began to realize the sacred importance and benefit of pilgrimage to holy sites. It is a sacred opportunity to receive the blessing of the saint's spiritual vibration, which is still permeating the site. Since that time I have striven to go on pilgrimage to holy sites regularly, to pray and meditate there as part of my long-term spiritual practice.

Distressing Spiritual Symptoms

The idea that dark forces, demons, and/or the devil might actually exist is a frightening one. And, although it is beyond the scope of this book to discuss concepts of evil, it must be recognized that some people undergoing STEs believe absolutely that they have had experiences that involve evil or dark forces. This is supported by the fact that most spiritual traditions also allude to the existence of evil and evil beings or entities. A number of highly credible STE experiencers have told me they have had encounters with an "evil presence," or alternatively, "negative visions."

Negative visions. Some STE experiencers report occasional or sometimes recurring visions of such negative, frightening things as Satan, the Antichrist, devils, demons, evil spirits, or horrible scenarios that feature such personifications of evil. These negative visions usually appear on what is sometimes called the "screen of the mind" or simply flash in front of the mind's eye, or they may appear in dreams.

Evil presence. Some STE experiencers report occasional or recurring experiences when they feel that they are in the presence of an evil force, an evil entity, the devil, or the forces of darkness. In some rare cases the experiencer even feels temporarily taken over or possessed by these dark forces or entities. Sometimes it seems as if for a short period of time the STE experiencer's thoughts and feelings are being affected by the evil presence, which seems to be implanting negative, fearful, or paranoid thoughts into the person's mind — thoughts such as that God cannot be trusted.

A dramatic story of a distressing spiritual symptom, an encounter with an evil presence, was told to me by a forty-eight-year-old man, whom I will call Jacob. Jacob was a long-time meditator, who had already had several very positive and beautiful STEs at the time of his experience of an evil presence.

> My fiancée and I had a very strange fight the day this happened. Her behaviour had been very uncharacteristic of her, and strange, compared to the previous nine months of our positive and very beautiful relationship. I felt as if my fiancée's personality had changed abruptly that day, in a negative way, as if some external influence had caused her to suddenly, and for no apparent reason, to become hostile toward me and highly suspicious. She abruptly broke off our engagement.

I was contemplating our suddenly disintegrating relationship while I was watering my front lawn with the garden hose later that day. Abruptly, I had a sickening and alarming inner sensation, as if a negative and hostile invisible entity was nearby. Simultaneously I had a strong intuitive flash — perhaps my fiancée was being influenced by a dark force or evil entity. This was an extremely unusual thing for me to think, although I had heard of others who believed in evil entities, I was not convinced of their reality, and certainly I had never previously thought about evil entities relating to myself or anyone I knew.

A moment after the thought of an evil entity crossed my mind, a swarm of angry hornets appeared from nowhere in my garden. The hornets swarmed and started to repeatedly attack me, trying to sting me. Instinctively I started defending myself, aggressively spraying at the hornets with the garden hose. Like a reflex, my mind cried out "Satan be gone!" and "In the name of Jesus Christ be gone!" I repeated this over and over as I fought off the hornets with the hose. I had never said these words before in my life, but at that instant they came out of my mouth and mind like a reflex of protection. After about ten minutes of vigorous hosing and intense verbal "casting out," the hornets finally dispersed and disappeared. With them, the strong nauseating feeling of negative energy also finally went away.

I am convinced that some sort of dark or demonic entity or force was attacking me that day, and possibly also contributed to my fiancée's sudden dark and hostile mood.

Two other cases of distressing spiritual symptoms that were reported to me were very similar to each other, and seemed to follow a pattern that many distressing spiritual episodes take. In both cases, the STE experiencers were women who suddenly sensed an evil presence in their bedroom with them at night. The sensation was quite strong to both, and they both instinctively felt a need to turn on the lights. They then forcefully told the presence to leave. The women both felt that the evil presence still remained there in their bedrooms, however, and in both cases typical poltergeist phenomena, such as objects suddenly falling from shelves and walls, occurred throughout the night. They also heard footsteps in their rooms and felt movements across their beds. Both women had the inner urge to repeat the Lord's Prayer over and over, and continued to stay awake and pray throughout the night. One woman held her Bible as she prayed. In both cases, the negative presence seemed to vanish near dawn, and both women were then finally able to fall into a peaceful sleep.

Coping with Distressing Spiritual Symptoms

From the above cases and others that I have heard of, it seems clear to me that both dark or demonic visions and the sensations of evil presences are best coped with through focusing on the Divine. Here are some strategies that may be helpful to cope with distressing spiritual symptoms.

Focus on God. Focus on God and strongly affirm that God's divine light and love is protecting you. Make mental or verbal affirmations of the presence of divinity in yourself, in humanity, in the world, and in the universe. Or, repeat simple affirmations such as "God is with me," "God is love," "God is protecting me," or simply "God, God, God!" Tell the presence to go to the light, to God.

Visualize your spiritual Master or God. Look at a photo or image of your spiritual Master. Visualize an image of Divine white light, or of your beloved spiritual Master in your mind.

Hold a holy scripture or a holy item. Hold a Bible or other holy scripture in your hands. If you have a holy icon or blessed item, hold it in your hands.

Pray. Pray to God/Brahman/Allah/Buddha/the Creator to protect you. Repeat your spiritual Master's name, and pray for his or her protection. Say The Lord's Prayer, or other sacred prayer repeatedly. If you feel an inclination to repeat certain prayers or verses from the Bible or other holy books, do so.

Read from a holy scripture. Read the Bible or other holy books, mentally, or out loud.

Command the dark entity to leave. In a strong, forceful voice, command the dark entity to leave. Tell the demonic vision or presence to be gone, that you are God's child, that evil has no hold on you. Cast out the dark entity directly with commands like, "In the name of Jesus Christ be gone," or "Satan, be gone."

Go to a different location, ideally to a holy site or sacred location. Leave the physical location where you are experiencing the distressing spiritual symptom, and if possible go to a holy site, such as a church, a chapel, or a temple. Entering a place where many people have prayed and meditated sometimes seems to cleanse lower astral energies, and may help you to uplift your consciousness to a higher realm of spiritual awareness.

Do the Divine Light Invocation. Visualize God's divine light pouring down upon you, filling your entire being, and surrounding you in a protective bubble of divine energy and light. Repeat the "Divine Light Invocation" that is found in Paramahansa Yogananda's *Scientific Healing Affirmations*:

> ### Divine Light Invocation
> *I am submerged in eternal light;*
> *It permeates every particle of my being.*
> *I am living in that light.*
> *The Divine Spirit fills me within and without.*

Light incense or smudge with sage. Light some incense beside you or smudge the perimeter of your room with sage smoke. Many spiritual traditions use incense or burning sage to help cleanse an area of dark energies.

If you do ever have a type of negative spiritual symptom, keep in mind the often-taught spiritual concept that negativity can have no hold on you as long as you focus on God, love, and light. Darkness cannot exist in the presence of the Light.

Of course, if you have found that a particular meditation technique, psychic exercise, or any other factor triggers negative spiritual symptoms, stop doing it. If the episodes seem to be triggered by meditating in a certain place, try meditating elsewhere. If this is impossible, spend some time before you meditate visualizing the place cleansed and filled by all-loving, all-powerful, divine white light.

Like many scientists, I approach the question of whether dark forces and evil entities exist with a healthy skepticism, but I have heard so many reports from credible people about these types of experiences that I have given the matter a great deal of thought. There are many possible interpretations of these experiences. One tentative hypothesis is that experiences of demonic entities or presences may be related to the multidimensional nature of our universe. As mentioned in chapter 7, "Psychic Experiences," highly credible mystics and seers have reported "seeing" vast numbers of dimensions beyond ours populated with disembodied spirits and diverse life forms. Even physicists are now postulating that there are far more than four dimensions. If the life forms and disembodied spirits in other dimensions do indeed exist, they likely vary in their levels of spiritual and moral development just as human beings vary in theirs. The yogic and Buddhist traditions describe the etheric or "astral plane" as having levels, with less spiritually developed entities and souls living on lower astral planes, and more highly spiritually advanced entities and souls living on higher astral planes.

As the channels of perception in people who are undergoing spiritual transformation become more open, other types of entities may sometimes try to make contact. Less spiritually developed entities or those from lower astral planes may then be perceived as evil or demonic presences. Alternatively, sometimes our own unconscious fears may also manifest as dark experiences. STE experiencers may also sometimes perceive the dark or evil thought vibrations of another person.

Of course, until far more research is done and our understanding of these matters is greatly increased, we have no objective way of knowing exactly what is going on when these types of negative experiences occur. Still, people should never, under any circumstances, attempt to experiment or "play" with dark forces in any way. We should always strive to align ourselves with the love, light, and protection of the Divine Higher Power.

Symptoms Associated with Spiritual Energy/Kundalini

Ongoing, low-grade spiritual energy/kundalini-type symptoms commonly occur in STE experiencers having long-term spiritual transformation of consciousness. Although these after-effect symptoms may take the mild form of any of the characteristics of Spiritual Energy/Kundalini Episodes, the following seem to be the most common.

Cranial pressures. Many STE experiencers report sensations of energy pushing outward and upward through the top of the head. This is sometimes described as feeling as if a cone of energy was pushing up through the crown, or sitting on top of the head, or sometimes a feeling as if the top of the skull was open. In some cases, these cranial sensations may involve an expansion of consciousness like the one associated with mystical states. Like other symptoms, they can last for varying lengths of time. One experiencer reported that she had these types of cranial sensations last for hours, even when doing mundane chores like driving to the cottage or cleaning the house. Following a STEP, varying degrees of cranial pressure or sensations of expansion sometimes remain for months.

Inner sounds. These are recurrent or continuous inner sounds that do not come from external stimuli. They are commonly and variously reported as sounding like the humming sound of bees, the musical murmur of a distant brook, the chirping of crickets, the low-pitched rumbling of a distant motor, the roaring of a distant waterfall, the rushing sound of wind or large wings beating, the sound of a gong ringing, the fine tinkling of distant bells or wind chimes, the music of the spheres, or the ringing of church bells. As mentioned previously, in the yogic tradition, these inner sounds are thought to be the astral sounds of the chakras and nadis.

Like all the paranormal symptoms listed in this section, the inner sounds are more common at first during spiritual practices. In addition, inner sounds are often more marked in the middle of the night. Many people report hearing inner sounds constantly for many years following an initial STEP. Further, the types of sounds heard tend to change over time, and sometimes one type of sound is superimposed on another. For example, I now hear the fine tinkling of distant bells almost constantly, sometimes superimposed on a sound similar to the low-pitched roar of a distant waterfall. Earlier on in my spiritual process I also episodically heard inner sounds like the chirping of crickets, the ringing of a gong, or other times like the rumbling of a motor.

Energies up the spine. Many STE experiencers report recurrent or ongoing sensations of energy rushing up the spine, vibrating or tickling sensations in the lower back, gentle sensations like a liquid moving up the spine, and/or the feeling that heat is moving up the spine toward the brain. These symptoms can occur at any time, but seem to be more frequent when one has a deep psychological or spiritual insight, when admiring a scene of natural beauty, when performing an act of selfless service, or when praying or meditating.

A fifty-five-year-old businessman from California whom I'll call Richard provides a more general example of how the symptoms related to kundalini can occur or develop over a period of time. Richard had his first STEP when he was forty; it was a profound mystical experience that changed him from a materialistic businessman to a person devoted to spiritual growth and to working for world peace. His spiritual energy/kundalini symptoms developed afterward.

> After my mystical experience, I had the strong inner urge to begin a regular daily practice of meditation and deep prayer. I soon found a yoga path that taught me a series of progressive meditation techniques. Over the years I had several mystical visions during meditation and occasional episodes of inspired spiritual insights.
>
> I also developed two ongoing spiritual energy/kundalini symptoms that were not strong enough for me to think of as STEs, but were still strong indicators to me that I was undergoing some degree of long-term spiritual transformation. One is recurrent, but sporadic rushes of energy up my spine. The other is constant inner sounds for many years now. My experience of inner sound varies from the roar of a distant waterfall, to the buzzing of bees, to the tinkling of bells. The experience of inner sound is always with me, and, over time, has become part of the background noise in my normal conscious functioning.
>
> I recognize the energy rushes up my spine and the inner sounds as part of my personal spiritual process, and I feel reassured and comfortable with them.

Positive Symptoms Associated with the Psychic and Paranormal

Psychic and paranormal after-effect symptoms tend to be some of those most commonly experienced by STE experiencers in long-term transformation. In the KRN Questionnaire pilot project, 90 percent of mystical and kundalini STE experiencers reported that they eventually began to have recurrent psychic or paranormal experiences. Often experiencers don't know what to call these unusual, subtle experiences and, at first, do not think of them as being "psychic" in nature. They may label these psychic after-effects simply as "increased sensitivity."

When these symptoms occur, they sometimes seem to impart information that the experiencer can use in a positive or helpful way. At other times the psychic symptoms seem to reflect the increased sensitivity of the experiencer to the thoughts and feelings of others. Over time many experiencers go through a kind of trial-and-error learning process in which they gradually learn to interpret with increasing accuracy the meaning of symbolic images or particular sensations and to develop an appropriate perspective concerning the validity of the paranormal/intuitive messages they are receiving.

Enhanced intuition and psychic messages. Most STE experiencers notice that their intuition seems to become more enhanced and pronounced over time. Intuitive flashes may become so clear that they appear to the experiencer as messages. These messages may be sensed or felt in any way. They are often perceived with the inner eye or ear as words, sounds, or visual symbols, or they may be felt as strong impulses. They may even become so pronounced that they seem to be physically seen, heard, or felt. For example, many people report that they felt a sudden strong inclination to open a spiritual book, did so, and discovered a passage that had deep significance for them at the time.

This type of experience may also take the form of a direct message. A friend of mine had been wondering about the answer to a specific question when, out of the blue, his inner ear heard the words "Go to the library" and an image of the library flashed in his mind. He felt compelled to go. At the library, he received another message which told him to go to the rear bookshelf. There, he had an urge to grab a certain book off the shelf. He skimmed through the book and suddenly found the answer to the question that had been plaguing him.

Psychic messages may also appear in the form of symbols like a red or green light or the words "yes" or "no" flashing across the screen of the mind. Like other spiritual and paranormal symptoms, increased intuition and psychic messages often initially occur more frequently during activities such as prayer or meditation.

Clairsentience. The ability to feel the emotion or pain that another is feeling seems to be the most common psychic symptom developed by people undergoing STEs. It includes the ability to sense or locate pain in another's body by experiencing it — or perceiving it in some way — in one's own body. For instance, when a woman who is developing clairsentience is near an individual who is in mental turmoil, she might feel a pressure sensation in the third-eye region. When near a person who is very sad, she might feel a pressure in the region of her own heart chakra. When near a person who is in physical pain, she might feel physical pain exactly where the other person is experiencing it. These clairsentient perceptions usually occur spontaneously. Most people developing this symptom do not, at first, understand what it is. Later, they begin to understand that they are becoming increasingly sensitive to the emotions and mental states of others.

Premonitions. Premonitions were mentioned in chapter 7, "Psychic Experiences," as being a form of precognition and, of course, they are. However, precognition is a more powerful experience than are premonitions when they first begin to appear as symptoms. At this time, they are often simply strong hunches or quick intuitive flashes that give a hint that something is going to happen. For instance, a woman might, when asked on a date, have a feeling that she shouldn't go, even though the man who has asked her seems to be very nice. But because she has never had a premonition before and was never particularly intuitive before her STEs began, she — using her rational mind — decides to ignore her hunch. When she does go out with the man, he makes an unsolicited pass at her and, although she isn't harmed, she has a very unpleasant evening. After experiences like this, in which premonitions are proven to be correct, most experiencers learn to pay more attention to them. As time goes on they also learn how to better interpret their premonitions and understand more clearly what they mean. Like other symptoms, premonitions may increase in frequency, clarity, and intensity over time and develop into clear-cut premonitions or powerful instances of psychic precognition. Most people undergoing STEs find that, over time, they begin to repeatedly have premonitions concerning significant life events. These often appear in dreams.

Over the years I have often been given premonitions in my dreams regarding major events in my life. A dramatic instance related to my dear, and now deceased, grandfather:

> Several years ago, I was scheduled to make a presentation at a medical conference in Oxford, England. My life was very busy, so I had planned to fly to England the day before the conference and return to Canada the day after. About two weeks before the conference, I had a dream that told me to visit my grandfather (who lived in Switzerland) after the conference. I was told it would be my final visit with him.
>
> At first I tried to put the dream out of my head, but somehow it kept haunting me. Finally, late that same day, I phoned my travel agent and asked if she could book me a two-day side trip from England to Switzerland. (My schedule was very tight and the side trip could not be for more than two days.). I then went to the conference in England, and proceeded on to Switzerland for two days afterward. I had a wonderful visit with my grandfather. We discussed my Near-Death Experience and other STEs in great detail, and he told me about some of his spiritual experience. When I flew back to Canada I felt a very strong, close bond with my grandfather.
>
> My grandfather died suddenly, and unexpectedly, about two months later. My two-day visit was indeed my final visit with him, and I am deeply grateful to Spirit for the strong premonition which alerted me and enabled me to see my grandfather that one last time.

Frequent synchronicities. The concept of synchronicity was developed largely by Dr. Carl Jung. Synchronistic events are often defined simply as meaningful coincidences. Synchronicities take infinite forms and can have many types and levels of meaning; however, they all seem to suggest to the experiencer that some Higher Power or higher intelligence is guiding them or validating their insights. An Indigenous spiritual elder undergoing spiritual transformation for many years told me a beautiful example of synchronicity.

> I had been invited to speak at a small First Nations community in Nova Scotia. I had been asked as an elder to reintroduce a number of Aboriginal spiritual concepts to the adults in the community, since they had all been sent to Roman Catholic residential boarding schools as children, and had received only that religious training.
>
> We were all gathered together outdoors to begin the lesson circle. I began by telling the gathering that I had come to teach the traditional way of contact with the Creator, through nature. To my amazement, just as I said these words, four eagles flew directly overhead and began to circle lower and lower until they were circling right above the crowd.
>
> As we watched the eagles above us with awe, I told those present what many of them already knew. In the Native spiritual tradition, the eagle is the totem or symbol for connecting with the Great Spirit, the Creator. Many people present that day were very deeply moved by this synchronicity — a visible response to us from the Creator, it seemed.

A great many STE experiencers notice synchronicities for the first time after their STEs begin — or notice that this type of event begins to occur much more frequently than before. When it does occur, synchronicity is often delightful and, frequently, deeply enriching. For many people, it is yet another sign that a divine, loving, and unimaginably vast intelligence is running the universe.

Past-life memories. Many people having STEs and long-term spiritual transformation of consciousness find that at some point they begin to experience the spontaneous memory of relationships or events that seem to be from past lives. Often these memories may mirror present-life situations and/or help experiencers understand current relationships, reaction patterns, or life problems. These past-life memories may come in dreams or meditations, or be triggered by a location, person, or event. I will discuss this in more depth in chapter 18, "Psycho-Spiritual Housecleaning." A number of other psychic and paranormal experiences listed in chapter 7 can also occur in milder form as STE after-effects.

It is important to realize that even subtle paranormal symptoms can be disconcerting — especially when the experiencer doesn't understand what they are. Labelling the symptom is helpful because it defines it, puts it within certain parameters, and helps the experiencer realize it is something he or she can adjust to or deal with.

Distressing Psychic Symptoms and Psychic Disorders

The idea that distressing psychic symptoms and psychic disorders might occur to some people undergoing the process of spiritual transformation of consciousness is disconcerting at best and frightening at worst. It is important for STE experiencers to realize that psychic disorders do not occur to the vast majority of people involved in the process of spiritual transformation, and that, if they do occur, there are a number of effective strategies for dealing with them.

Many thoughtful people have difficulty in accepting the idea of psychic disorders — even those who accept the majority of concepts associated with spiritual transformation. This is particularly true in the case of the symptoms labelled here as channelling disorders, psychic assault, and possession. And, while these concepts are difficult for some spiritually open thinkers to accept, they are completely unacceptable to traditionally oriented thinkers. Nevertheless, the people who experience them perceive them as real — and I have found that many of these people are credible and mentally healthy.

Further, anyone who experiences any of these symptoms is in pain and needs help.

Some STE experiencers have reported the following distressing psychic symptoms.

Painful clairsentience. This symptom can manifest in any of the ways that regular clairsentience does, but much more strongly. It is not unusual for a person who is clairsentient to feel some pain or uncomfortable pressure when perceiving another's distress or pain. In painful clairsentience, however, experiencers feel severe pain or pressure and often find it difficult to function when these sensations are occurring. Painful clairsentience often takes the form of an excruciating headache. This was true in the case of Jeneane, the businesswoman whose painful clairsentience I described in chapter 7, "Psychic Experiences." When she was with people experiencing anger or mental turmoil, she developed a severe pain in her mid-forehead. When she was with persons experiencing great sadness, she felt central chest pain.

People with painful clairsentience may become extremely and painfully sensitive to negative emotions of others, and therefore have difficulty going into crowded places. These persons report feeling bombarded by negative emotions in crowded public places, especially ones that are closed in and do not allow them to get out at will, such as subway cars and transit buses. They also frequently report feeling tremendous discomfort or pain when they are in the presence of people with severe emotional or psychiatric difficulties.

Excessive clairvoyance. This symptom, too, differs in degree from its regular counterpart. The experiencer clairvoyantly receives too much information and is unable to stop or block the input. Some experiencers report being bombarded by visual images or symbols of such things as another person's actions, spiritual conflicts, physical problems, or past-life issues. Such constant bombardment can put a great strain on everything from interpersonal relationships to casual conversations.

Intrusive past-life memories. In this disorder, one's own past-life memories surface too rapidly, too intensely, or too frequently. They may be so distracting that the experiencer has difficulty functioning in daily life. Some experiencers also become confused about how psychological issues from past lives overlap with those from current life situations. When past-life memories become too overwhelming or when the psychological issues they represent cannot be dealt with, they can precipitate crises or spiritual emergencies (as explained in chapter 16).

Horrific visions. The visions common to this disorder are recurrent, persistent, and horrific, and cause tremendous mental distress. They can be almost unbearable and even, at times, as mentioned in chapter 15, be associated with a temporary psychosis. These visions often include scenes of atrocities humans have committed against other humans, such as torture, mutilation, or nuclear war; or gruesome or evil figures suddenly appearing in buildings, windows, shadows, or trees. Without warning, a lovely visual image may turn into a horrifying one. Sometimes horrific visions can become personal and feature the self or loved ones being tortured, mutilated, or terrorized.

Channelling disorders. This disorder is characterized by the experiencer's inability to take voluntary, conscious control of a channelling experience. These disorders take several forms:

1. The channelled "entities" may seem to be able to force the experiencer to lapse into trances so that channelling can proceed, even when the experiencer has no desire to channel at that time.

2. More than one entity may appear to be attempting to channel through the experiencer at the same time. The experiencer may hear the different entities and feel the tension and conflict as they vie for the controlling or dominant position.

3. Negative entities may appear to be attempting to channel through the experiencer. These entities are often described as using foul language, being harsh and critical, and communicating concepts that are tormenting to the experiencer.

4. Negative or morally questionable entities appear to masquerade as gurus, angels, divine guardians, beings from "higher dimensions," or even God. Rather than being humbling and uplifting like true contact with the Divine, these experiences inflate the ego, make the experiencer feel special, and may even trick him or her into acting inappropriately.

Since channelling disorders may sometimes be confused with and closely mimic schizophrenia or mania, anyone who seems to be suffering from them should seek counselling so that the true source of the problem can be determined.

Psychic assault or telepathic invasion. In this disorder, it seems that the experiencer is not able to block invasive techniques being used by an unscrupulous or immoral person with strong psychic abilities. Reported experiences of this type include thoughts, visual images, messages, or even physical sensations that intrude on the experiencer's mind or being and clearly seem to come from a specific outside source. Often the experiencer has a very clear sense of the identity of the invader.

Some contemporary spiritual teachers believe that psychic powers cannot, in reality, be used for such evil purposes; others believe that they can. Future research will show which view is correct. In the meantime, however, the fact remains that credible people report having these experiences. One was a highly educated, articulate nurse I'll call Rachel. Rachel's life was dramatically disrupted after a sudden psychic awakening that occurred when she was thirty-one.

> I met Karl through some associates at the office. When he asked me out for a date, I decided to go, since I thought there could be no harm in one dinner date. During the date, Karl told me that he was a practising "wicken" or warlock. I didn't know what to think of this, as he went on to describe his somewhat unbelievable psychic abilities. It seemed to me that he liked to play psychic games.
>
> I was very surprised to find myself very strongly physically attracted to him by the end of the evening. When he kissed me goodnight, I felt what seemed like an electric current run through my body. From that moment onward I started receiving telepathic messages from him. I found this interesting, because I had never previously had any psychic experiences.
>
> Karl had to leave town for business reasons, and I did not see him again for six weeks. Two weeks after he left,

however, I had an extremely strange experience that I can only describe as feeling as if I was being psychically sexually assaulted by him. I was lying in bed, about to go to sleep, when I got the sensation that my body was being sexually stimulated. I knew telepathically that it was Karl. I felt my genitals become moist and excited, my abdomen was heaving, as if being stroked. I felt my back arch repeatedly, and I had the sensation of sexual intercourse. The experience was so vivid that I could actually smell the odor of semen. Initially I found the whole experience intensely pleasurable. Then, I suddenly became overwhelmed with a sense of guilt, anger, and shame. I barely knew Karl, and our relationship was not at a stage where I would consider being sexually intimate. I felt as though I had been raped remotely, by his psychic powers.

I continued receiving strong telepathic communications from Karl, but was determined to resist them from this point on. However, I continued to feel so attracted to him that I went out with him again about a month after my psychic encounter with him. I felt very uncomfortable, as if we had actually already had sex together. It seemed natural that the next logical step was to physically have sex, so we did. When I had my climax from our lovemaking, I felt my consciousness slip out of my body. I was floating above our two bodies, looking down at us below. After a few moments, my spirit reentered my body.

From that instant onward, I had repeated and increasingly dramatic psychic experiences. These experiences were uncontrollable. I would look at a person and know things about them. I would accurately locate pain in other people's bodies by feeling it in my own. I had accurate premonitions about friends and relatives, as well as about world events. I could clearly see auras and people's chakra activity.

I could not seem to turn off the psychic input. Finally I had to take a leave of absence from work until these psychic energies slowed down. I cut off all contact with Karl. I was angry that he had admittedly deliberately tried to stimulate my psychic energies without my consent, and had psychically invaded me sexually that evening against my will.

Rachel found a number of things that helped her get her feet back on the ground after her tumultuous psychic awakening, psychic assault, and the period that followed. She took a four-month leave of absence from work. During this period she focused on "grounding" herself, started psychotherapy, and worked on resolving the psychological and spiritual issues that began to surface as part of her process. Although Rachel's psychic gifts have continued to develop, the pace has slowed and she has learned to filter and integrate the input so that it does not interfere with her day-to-day functioning.

I should stress that reports of psychic assault, especially in this degree, are rare. I also believe there are ways we can help prevent psychic disorders of all types.

Possession. Although little is known scientifically about possession, and the phenomenon is not yet widely recognized, many respected scholars have documented it. I have hypothesized that it may be related to multidimensional phenomena such as UFOs and "evil presences" or lower-astral disembodied entities. Some similar ideas have been put forward by Dr. M. Scott Peck in *People of the Lie* and by Dr. Adam Crabtree in *Multiple Man: Explorations in Possession and Multiple Personality* — two informative, if controversial, books. The possibility of possession or a "walk-in" by disembodied astral entities (described next) is known within the yogic tradition.

In a possession psychic disorder, a spirit entity appears to have entered the experiencer's body against his or her will. The intruding entity seems to struggle to control the experiencer's actions or thoughts. In some cases, a split may occur, with the experiencer's personality and the entity personality surfacing and controlling at different times. According to Crabtree, the experiencer may be unaware of the invasion, and the condition may be confused with multiple personality disorder.

People who believe they are experiencing possession need to seek help from either a spiritual counsellor or a psychotherapist, or perhaps even both. Fortunately, this disorder can often be dealt with on a number of psychological and spiritual levels.

Walk-In. Another poorly understood psychic disorder is that of the walk-in (sometimes called a step-in), in which it appears that the spirit of a disembodied entity has taken over the body of an individual at their moment of death. Thus the entity's spirit then inhabits and lives in the deceased person's physical body, keeping it alive. This phenomenon has been depicted in Hollywood films such as *Ghost Whisperer, The Astronaut's Wife,* and *Heaven Can Wait.* The walk-in phenomena is described in yoga and in some literature on psychic phenomena. A few authors think that walk-in souls may sometimes be a generally more advanced soul. Although I am not an expert in this rare phenomenon, in my clinical experience the cases of apparent walk-in that have come to my attention did not seem to be "advanced souls," but rather entities that caused great disruption to the departed person's loved ones and family members, because of their marked difference and often negative personality as compared to the departed soul's.

Here is the story of a woman I will call Dorothy, who became convinced that her partner "Bill" had been replaced by a walk-in soul, after Bill died several times during heart surgery and was repeatedly resuscitated. Dorothy was a high-functioning, highly educated professional woman, and a long-time meditator. Her very disturbing, but highly believable account of a walk-in attaching to her partner was as follows:

> Bill and I were childhood sweethearts who went different directions after high school. We met again when we were both in our sixties and single, a widow and a widower, respectively. Our teenage attraction rekindled quickly and we started dating. We fell in love rapidly and intensely.
>
> Our relationship was very close. We spoke on the phone at least twice each day. Bill sent me "love letters" by email every evening and text messages several times a day. We were real communicators, talking with each other openly and at length about anything and everything. We also shared a deep spiritual bond. We both had strong faith, read the Bible, prayed, and meditated daily.

After about nine months of a powerful romance we became engaged to be married. Bill felt strongly that we were soulmates. Together we planned our wedding and honeymoon.

Unfortunately, being in his sixties, Bill had some medical problems, including a serious heart condition. A couple months before our planned wedding Bill had a major heart attack. His cardiologist recommended heart surgery, a somewhat risky procedure due to Bill's age and weak heart. Bill decided to take the risk, in hopes of stabilizing his heart condition.

The morning of the surgery Bill and I prayed and meditated together. We tenderly held hands as I accompanied Bill to the operating room doorway. We gave each other a long hug and final kiss before he went in. Then he was gone.

The operation lasted almost the entire day. Finally the surgeon emerged from the operating room and explained to me that there had been complications during Bill's surgery. Bill's heart had stopped four times during the surgery, but fortunately the doctors had been able to resuscitate him.

I was ushered into the recovery room after Bill woke up. Oddly, at first I didn't recognize him as he lay groggy on his stretcher. He seemed to look different somehow. I sat by his bedside and gently reached out to take his hand. I bent over him and gently whispered to him "Bill honey, it's me. The surgery is over. You came through fine!"

Post-op Bill flinched and pulled his hand away from mine. "Don't touch me" he growled. I thought perhaps this grumpiness was because of pain or due to the powerful drugs he had been given, so I quietly pulled my hand away. His entire time in the recovery room, post-op Bill repeatedly pulled his hand away each time I tried to touch him. *How odd*, I thought. This was very unlike his usual self, who wanted to hold my hand constantly.

Post-op Bill lay silently on the stretcher, ignoring me, and constantly looking away from me. Whenever I tried to speak to him he said "Be quiet!" *How unlike Bill*, I thought. Bill was usually very eager to hear the sound of my voice, and had been comforted by my presence before.

The next morning when I returned to the hospital, post-op Bill was still not his old self. He was not making eye contact with me and still did not want me to touch him or hold his hand. He turned his face away when I tried to kiss him. When I said "I love you" he did not say it back, as he normally would. When he was discharged from hospital later that day, he openly flirted with his young nurse in front of me before he left the ward — very rude and uncharacteristic behaviour for my fiancé Bill. Again, I thought that perhaps this marked change in behaviour might be due to the lingering effects of anaesthetic drugs still in his system. I took him to my home for his convalescence, as we had previously planned.

Post-op Bill did not behave at all like my beloved Bill of the previous nine months, a man who had loved me intensely and expressed his affection openly. He was cold and distant, behaving like a complete stranger. I did not recognize the post-op Bill. Post-op Bill also did not want to read from the Bible in the morning, and did not want to pray or meditate with me, as had been our solid routine for many months. Post-op Bill did not even love his morning coffee the way my fiancé Bill always did. All in all ... he seemed like a different person ... totally.

On his third post-operative day, suddenly post-op Bill announced that our relationship was over, and he was breaking up with me. No reason given. He "just changed his mind," he said. When I asked post-op Bill "What about the fact that we are engaged to be married soon? ... and that you told me you thought God had brought us together, that we are soulmates? ... that we are meant to be together?" Post-op Bill sharply retorted "I do not want to do what God wants me to do. I want to do what I want to do." I was stunned. That statement went 100 percent against my fiancé Bill's spiritual values.

With that, post-op Bill stormed away, stating that he did not want to talk to me about this matter. He left my house immediately and told me not to try to contact him any further.

At first I was in shock. How could he not want to talk about something so major, when we openly talked about everything in our relationship? I thought perhaps the anaesthetic drugs had affected his thinking, and that in a few days Bill would phone me and apologize profusely. But no phone call, email, text message, apology, or explanation ever arrived.

I was heartbroken. This made no sense to me. I couldn't believe this had happened. How could Bill have changed so much — 100 percent — over the course of his heart surgery?

I grieved for several months. It felt to me like my beloved fiancé Bill had died on the operating room table. I did not recognize the cold, uncommunicative person in post-op Bill's body. I even wore black for two weeks to mark my period of mourning.

Several months later, I was discussing this break-up and Bill's sudden change in personality with a medical intuitive. The intuitive emphatically told me, with great certainty, "Bill died completely on that operating room table when his heart stopped. His soul went up into the light of Heaven. The soul now living in Bill's former body is not Bill, it is a 'walk-in,' another soul, an entity that stepped into Bill's dead body when it was resuscitated."

At first I was shocked by this idea, but somehow this explanation rang true for me. It felt right. This explanation finally made things make sense somehow. I had heard of walk-ins, and I had seen some shows on TV about this sometimes happening when somebody dies and then is re-suscitated. I also remembered an incident that happened a week or so before the heart surgery, when Bill told me that while he was meditating it felt like an entity was trying to get into his body. He had pushed it away. It seemed to me like an entity did eventually enter Bill's body, when he died during surgery.

As unusual as this "walk-in" explanation was — it was a huge relief to me. Bill's complete change in personality made sense to me now. It had always felt to me as if my beloved Bill had died on the operating room table, and the man in his post-op body now was not him.

My realization about my fiancé Bill's actual death was confirmed about a week after I spoke with the medical intuitive. It happened while I was on an airplane flight. I was looking out the plane window when we were high above the clouds. *Close to Heaven*, I thought, and then suddenly I felt Bill's presence with me. I could feel his loving energy, as if his spirit was giving me an energetic hug, I heard his voice inside my mind, and I could actually smell the scent of his aftershave. *I love you*, he said, as I felt a burst of love permeate me. *I will always love you*. I basked in this feeling of being loved by my fiancé Bill for about ten minutes, before it began to fade. With this experience I knew for certain that my beloved Bill had died during the surgery. His spirit had come to me now, to say goodbye, and to remind me that he truly loved me.

Dorothy went on to have more experiences that confirmed for her that Bill had died during the operation, and that this entity living in Bill's body was another soul. The incident in the airplane when Bill's departed spirit communicated with Dorothy is an After-Death Communication (ADC), as I described in chapter 6. ADCs happen quite frequently after the death of a beloved spouse or partner.

Post-op Bill died a few months later. The realization of the post-op "walk-in" soul helped Dorothy greatly in making peace with her fiancé Bill's memory.

Several other highly reputable persons have told me of similar stories. This phenomenon of a "walk-in" may account for some other reports of dramatic and negative personality changes that can sometimes occur after individuals have been resuscitated after being clinically dead. Although some persons may question the validity of such a phenomenon, there are definitely some individuals, like Dorothy, who are convinced that a "walk-in" can and does sometimes occur.

Causes of Distressing Psychic Symptoms and Psychic Disorders

Distressing psychic symptoms and psychic disorders can be very challenging and disruptive to a person's daily functioning. However, I and other psychotherapists working in this field have found that a great deal can be done to alleviate these symptoms.

In my clinical experience I have found a relationship between distressing psychic symptoms and psychic disorders, and overly excessive, or inappropriate, types of meditation. For example, painful clairsentience, excessive clairvoyance, and intrusive past-life memories are experienced most commonly, although not exclusively, by people who were meditating excessively, people who suddenly began to meditate for long periods daily without any spiritual guidance or supervision. In terms of the yogic model of consciousness and kundalini, this sudden practice of long meditation in an unprepared individual could activate paranormal channels of perception prematurely, too rapidly, too intensively, or in an unbalanced manner. Possibly the brahma randhra in the transforming brain/astral brain may become overstimulated, with the unprepared body being unable to provide adequate supplies of prana and ojas, or the prana supplied may have impurities.

When this happens in relation to psychic disorders, an analogy can be drawn between the activation of these paranormal channels of perception and a radio receiver. In the case of painful clairsentience, excessive clairvoyance, and intrusive past-life memories, and perhaps some cases of horrific visions, the radio receiver can be thought of as having a broken volume control. The psychic input comes blaring in so loudly and powerfully that it disrupts the experiencer's normal thought processes or detracts from his or her ability to function in the world.

Channelling disorders and other types of disorders that feature some type of invading or intrusive entity or force such as possession and walk-ins may sometimes be related to inappropriate meditation practices, in particular ones that leave the inner self and mind open to input from anyone or anything in the cosmos. These inappropriate techniques may include such dangerously open affirmations as "I open myself to the universe," or a deliberate attempt to channel a disembodied spirit, when, in fact, one should not open oneself to anything but the Divine!

In intrusive channelling disorders, the altered perception might be likened to a radio receiver with a broken fine-tuning control that allows hundreds of different radio signals to pour in without any means of filtering out the undesirable ones, or to the meditator's naively tuning their receiver to inappropriately low-quality signals.

Paramahansa Yogananda warned about the risk of making oneself open to both possession states and walk-ins by using inappropriately open meditation techniques. In *The Divine Romance,* Paramahansa Yogananda stated:

> You must never be negative — that is, never sit quietly and make your mind blank in order to become "open" to messages from the other world. This practice makes one receptive to tramp souls that are roaming in the ether, seeking human vehicles for expression and experience in the physical world. These souls are of low type, with strong attachment to this world, which prevents them from natural adjustment to the better life in the astral world. Instead of remaining in the astral world, they hover between the astral and physical planes and are occasionally successful in possessing someone.

From my clinical experience I have come to the conclusion that psychic disorders are real and, consequently, that "playing games" with psychic energies, deliberately opening yourself indiscriminately to other dimensions, or dabbling with occult powers can be very dangerous. This may well be why the religious traditions that have recognized the development of psychic gifts, such as the yogic tradition, have also emphasized that psychic phenomena are simply a byproduct of spiritual development and that they should not be focused upon excessively or striven after.

The yogic tradition also emphasizes that a spiritual seeker should live a balanced lifestyle in accordance with the Eight Limbs of Yoga, and follow a spiritual teacher or guru's guidance for their meditation practice, in regards to specific techniques of meditation, and also regarding the length of time spent in daily meditation. As I will discuss further in chapter 19, the length of a beginner's meditations should be short at first, maximum one half hour or so, and gradually increased with time.

Coping with Psychic Disorders

The following are some of the strategies I have found effective in dealing with psychic disorders. Although they overlap to some extent with other helpful strategies mentioned throughout the book and detailed in the final four chapters, they are summarized here for easy reference.

Adopt a more grounding lifestyle. Grounding activities are particularly helpful in slowing down the paranormal perceptions. As detailed in chapter 17, they include reducing and moderating the amount of time spent in all forms of meditation, cutting back on concentration, eating more regularly, decreasing time spent in spiritual exercises such as yoga or Tai Chi, participating in aerobic physical exercise, and taking a holiday from your work and daily stresses.

Visualize a protective bubble. Begin every day with a short visualization that affirms the presence of the divine light within you, like the Divine Light Invocation. Then visualize this divine white light expanding outward and forming a protective bubble or egg around you. (Some people find it more effective to visualize a crystal bell or a thick protective wall.) Affirm that the barrier acts like a one-way mirror, allowing your positive energies and love to shine out, but not allowing external negative energies to penetrate. Affirm that the divine light is protecting you.

Prepare yourself for situations you think might be difficult by using this strategy, and repeat it if distressing psychic input begins.

Keep your focus on the third eye and the Divine during meditation. When meditating, be sure your attention is focused on your third-eye region, between the eyebrows, and focus your thoughts on the Divine. Yogananda says this will minimize your susceptibility to low astral perceptions.

Cleanse negative energy. When you feel negative energy around you or being projected at you, take a moment to visualize the negative energy in your mind's eye, perhaps as a grey cloud. See this cloud being cleansed from your aura. Some people like to imagine something like a giant sponge that washes over them and removes the negative cloud. Others like to perform something like the yoga "ha" breath that is believed to cleanse the astral body. Still others like to visualize the grey cloud and see it coalescing into a small ball that can easily be thrown into a flame of love and divine light that destroys it. Some people send the energy back where it came from with wishes of love and light.

Remove yourself from negative environments. If you find that a particular situation, for example a room filled with extremely tense, angry, or hostile people, is causing negative psychic input, remove yourself. If you can't leave for good, go to the washroom, or go for a walk in the building, or even better, outdoors for several minutes. While you're out, visualize your protective bubble, affirm the divine presence, and visualize your chakras closing. In future, avoid entering similar settings whenever possible.

Mitigate horrific visions. When horrific visions occur, turn your thoughts inward and focus on God or spiritual concepts and affirm the Divine. Some experiencers find the visions can be turned around and used in a positive way as an impetus to work toward improving the world situation. In most cases, horrific visions stop on their own after a period of time. If they do not, they can often be helped by many of the strategies used in dealing with crises and spiritual emergencies.

Attune yourself to God only. No matter what images you see, what sensations you feel, or what other psychic input you receive, focus yourself totally and only on the Divine. Say familiar prayers, read Holy Scriptures, focus on uplifting spiritual passages or concepts, and pray that God's divine light will shine on you and cast out the darkness. Affirm that God's voice is the only voice you will hear or listen to. Affirm that God is present in you at all times. Pray for God's direction, guidance, and grace to rid you of all negative psychic input. If you are experiencing intrusive energies, tell them that you are God's child, protected by God, and that they have no hold on you.

Pray for protection. Pray to the Divine to protect you and shield you from negative psychic influences. Repeat your prayers as often as you feel the need during the day. Many people have learned that such simple prayers can be the most powerful of strategies.

Changes in Dream Life

Most STE experiencers notice a gradual and increasing change in their dream life after their STEs begin: that is yet another symptom of the transformation of consciousness. The content of the dreams may change in a number of ways. Experiencers' dreams often contain more premonitions than those of people not undergoing STEs. Common premonitions include warnings that loved ones need medical attention or may soon die, or that something negative — and sometimes preventable — is going to happen. For example, a woman may dream repeatedly that a particular man at work is trying to discredit her in order to make himself look better. When the woman discovers this is, in fact, true she can then begin to take precautions to protect herself and her job. STE experiencers' dreams also often seem to contain more messages about major life issues than they did before the STEs began, and/or they may dream about major world events or world disasters at the time the event occurs. Although it is thought that everyone's dreams may sometimes contain this type of information, the dreams of STE experiencers often seem to be more clear, dramatic, or easily interpreted than they were before the experiences.

Dream content may also become increasingly complex, with intricate, detailed plots and complete story lines. Experiencers sometimes report feeling as if they are living in a movie or a short novel during their dreams. Some experiencers report spontaneously developing lucid dreams — the ability to be consciously aware of the dream while it is going on and to alter or influence the path the dream is taking. Lucid dreaming frequently occurs during twilight sleep, the period just prior to actual sleep, or just before waking.

Also during twilight sleep, some STE experiencers find unusual visual images may flash rapidly across the screen of the mind. The images are frequently of scenes and faces that are unfamiliar to the experiencer. Although they begin spontaneously and seem to flash uncontrollably, they usually stop on their own after a few minutes.

Dreams that deal with spiritual themes often become more frequent. Some of these are inspirational and guide the STE experiencers into ways of expressing themselves in more spiritual or humanitarian ways. Others receive creative guidance in their dreams. For instance, Ellen, the artist mentioned in chapter 8, received all the subject matter for her paintings in her dreams. Synchronicity in dreams often increases. It also becomes more common for experiencers to receive answers or solutions to problems that have been plaguing them. These solutions may come either in a dream or immediately on waking.

The dreams themselves — not just their content — also often begin to change. One of the most common changes is an increase or change in colour perception. People who dreamed in black and white before their STEs often begin to dream in colour after them. Sometimes people realize that they once normally dreamed in black and white only after they begin to dream in colour. In time, the colour in their dreams may become far more intense, vivid, or brilliant. For some, it may even become luminescent. People may also begin to remember more of their dreams.

Many people find it helpful to their personal development and their process of spiritual transformation to begin to pay more attention to their dreams and also begin to remember them more frequently. Keeping a dream journal has long been recognized as an effective tool. Dreams should be recorded in the journal in as much detail as possible immediately on awakening. Once the dreams are written down, they should be reflected upon and possible significance, meanings, and interpretations noted. Sometimes the symbolic meaning of dreams becomes clear only hours or days afterward. During the process of keeping a dream journal, many people begin to remember far more dreams than they ever did before. They also notice that their dreams seem to contain more guidance and more information that helps them in their growth and spiritual development. The analysis of dreams may be a useful tool in the psycho-spiritual housecleaning that is so much a part of the process of spiritual transformation, and is, in fact, recommended for spiritual seekers in Patanjali's *Yoga Sutras*.

Changes in Visual Perception

STE experiencers often report repeated episodes when their visual perceptions seemed to be temporarily altered in a paranormal way. The following are some changes in visual perception that have been frequently reported to me.

Increased perception of beauty. Many STE experiencers have described episodes where they have an increased capacity to perceive beauty, and intricacy of detail, particularly in nature. Simple things, such as a flower, an insect, or the ripples on a pond may appear more beautiful than ever before. Such images — or larger ones such as sunsets or mountain vistas — may cause entrancement, awe, rapture, or overwhelming devotion to the Divine.

Luminescence. Some STE experiencers report that at times objects in the physical world seem far more vivid than normal, or even seem to glow with an inner light. They report that objects or living things such as plants were radiating light and had become luminescent. For some the entire outer world appears luminescent. Things in the visual field may also seem more whitish in colour than before — almost as if they had been dusted with a white or silvery powder. Some STE experiencers have reported that outside observers told them that their face seemed to glow, or radiate with an inner light. This facial glow or luminescence is reported most frequently when the STE experiencer is meditating deeply, or during one of their STEPs.

Perceiving air or prana/cosmic energy. Some STE experiencers episodically perceive what appears to be a fine cosmic energy everywhere around them. Experiencers sometimes say they feel as if they are "seeing air" or perceiving prana. One experiencer characterized it as seeing an "energy snow." For some, microscopically tiny energy particles seem to vibrate or flow everywhere in the field of vision, while others perceive patterns in this cosmic energy that are specific to different plants, animals, or even other people's emotional states.

Light experiences. STE experiencers often report recurrent or ongoing sensations that one's consciousness is filled with light. Sometimes they report the perception that normal external light seems much brighter than it actually is. Others may perceive episodic flashes of light or inner light during deep meditations.

These changes in visual perception can be disconcerting, and the experiencer should be given a thorough examination to make sure no medical problems exist. However, once a person adjusts to having these new paranormal visual perceptions, they are generally found to be tremendously enriching, serving as a constant reminder of the infinite beauty in the world and the ultimate oneness of all things.

An eighty-two-year-old patient of mine whom I'll call Ivy provides a good example of how changes in visual perception can manifest. When Ivy was seventy-eight, during a cataract operation she had an NDE that was a profound STEP, and her perception of light experiences began afterward. Here is her story:

> Unfortunately, my eye surgery was not successful, and I was declared legally blind afterward. In the weeks and months after my white-light Near-Death Experience in the operating room, it seems God blessed me with two beautiful gifts. First, I began to have repeated episodes of bliss and mystical insight. It seems that after the NDE I had now developed a new and deeper understanding of the meaning of the Holy Scriptures.
>
> Second, although my eyes were now blind, I started to see light. Although my very limited physical vision only allows me to see vague shadows and shades of grey with my physical eyes, I have now begun to have repeated experiences of light. At times, the room I am in suddenly seems to be flooded with light. My mind's eye becomes aglow with light, even though the room I am in is actually dark, and I am physically unable to see external lights.

These light episodes happen again and again, and can happen at any time of the day or night — even when I and the house are in total darkness.

In general, I think the commonality in types of STE after-effect symptoms in long-term spiritual transformation of consciousness that we have seen throughout the last three chapters — no matter what type of STE or STEP a person has had predominantly — supports the idea that all STEs have a common biological-psychological-spiritual base.

STEs, SPIRITUAL EMERGENCIES, AND PSYCHOSES

STEs, STEPs, AND THEIR POWERFUL after-effects — despite all their bliss, joy, and wonder — may sometimes be very challenging for experiencers. The process of spiritual transformation of consciousness can sometimes lead to emotional and mental turmoil that is extremely hard to deal with. For some people, the intensity and/or the content of their experiences becomes so overwhelming that they have great difficulty in coping. This STE-related crisis situation is sometimes called a "spiritual emergency." If the difficulties move beyond this level of intensity and a person becomes so disturbed that they lose their ability to function in society or lose their contact with reality, the person becomes, by definition, psychotic.

Fortunately, in many cases the difficulties are only temporary. Still, they involve periods of tremendous turmoil and suffering. For this reason, much of the rest of this book is dedicated to information that can help people adjust to STEs and STEPs, and work harmoniously with the process of spiritual transformation of consciousness, so that crises and spiritual emergencies are minimized or avoided. Let me start by looking in detail at how some of these crises and difficulties manifest themselves and what some of their causes might be.

Spiritual Emergence and Spiritual Emergency

The terms "spiritual emergence," "spiritual emergency," and "Spiritual Emergence Syndrome" were coined by California psychiatrist Dr. Stanislav

Grof and his wife, Christina Grof, two pioneers in bringing awareness of STEs to the mental health community. According to the Grofs, spiritual emergence is the process of spiritual transformation and personal growth, whereas spiritual emergencies are "dramatic experiences and unusual states of mind that traditional psychiatry diagnoses and treats as mental illness that are actually crises of personal transformation." By their definition, Spiritual Emergence Syndrome includes all the types of STEs that I discuss, as well as two psychological phenomena: psychological renewal through return to centre, and shamanic crisis.

Spiritual emergencies have also been written about by several other prominent California psychologists. Dr. Emma Bragdon has written several books on spiritual emergency, sharing the approaches that she and other therapists at the Spiritual Emergence Network have found most successful in helping people undergoing these spiritual crises. Dr. David Lukoff has done groundbreaking research on what he calls "Transient Psychosis with Mystical Features." One of his main goals is to help the psychiatric community recognize that mystical experiences are peak and normal expression of human consciousness, which can in some rare cases be associated with transient psychotic features.

A Spectrum of Difficulties

It is helpful to view the range of difficulties that can occur after STEPs and throughout the spiritual transformation of consciousness process as a spectrum. At one end we have the difficult periods that occur from time to time in every long-term process of spiritual transformation. Then, along the spectrum are various types and degrees of crises, spiritual emergencies, and at the far end, psychoses. Like spiritual crises and emergencies, the different types of psychotic episodes last for varying lengths of time and may be recurrent.

Although almost everyone meets with some challenges on their spiritual journey, not everyone undergoing STEs and spiritual transformation of consciousness will experience a spiritual emergency or psychotic episode. Spiritual emergencies can be a perfectly natural part of the spiritual process. I like to think of them as a "healing crisis." People who experience these phenomena do not have anything "wrong" with them; they are in no way less "normal" than those who don't, and they certainly are no less spiritual. In *The Call of Spiritual Emergency*, Emma Bragdon refers to the extremely difficult periods that Gopi Krishna endured as an example of serious spiritual emergency. He was sometimes unable to either work or attend to the business of daily life — and yet he went on to do groundbreaking kundalini research, write eighteen books, have them translated into many languages, speak at scores of international conferences, and make a tremendous positive impact on the spiritual lives of thousands of people.

In my work, I have met many people undergoing STEs and spiritual transformation of consciousness who have had extreme spiritual emergencies and who worked through their difficulties to become more spiritually connected and emotionally adjusted than they were before.

Distinguishing Spiritual Transformation from Spiritual Emergency

STE experiencers sometimes ask me how to distinguish between a challenging period in the process of spiritual transformation and a true spiritual emergency. The distinction depends primarily upon the overall state of mind and the degree of distress of the person going through the challenging period. Every person's spiritual journey is unique, but the majority of STE experiencers have a relatively smooth and balanced process of spiritual transformation, punctuated at times with more challenging periods. In general they feel enriched by their STE experiences and after-effect symptoms, and are aware, at some level, of being on a path of spiritual transformation and inner growth. For the most part, dramatic STEs and STEPs are cherished and seen as uplifting, inspiring events. These people function well in society and often hold responsible jobs and positions. They have a firm mental grasp of reality, understand clearly how others view reality, and are aware that their own personal STEs might be considered odd or even "crazy" by some other persons.

Since these STE experiencers maintain an accurate perspective, they do not develop inflated or grandiose ideas about themselves or their STE experiences. Their intellectual functioning is generally clear — or even enhanced — and they make logical decisions. Discriminating between their inner and outer realities does not pose a problem. Their emotional responses are appropriate, and they have strong, healthy interpersonal relationships. Those people who are experiencing the traditional signs of spiritual energy/kundalini activity find them pleasant or tolerable, or at least not disruptive to their ability to function in their daily lives. As part of the positive process of spiritual transformation of consciousness, they are embracing their psycho-spiritual housecleaning and they tend to develop even stronger ethical values, humanitarian concerns, and convictions about the spiritual unity of all humanity.

Within this overall positive framework, difficult or crisis periods occur to almost everyone on the spiritual journey. A crisis — even a severe one — is almost always relatively short-lived and does not significantly disrupt the person's ability to function in his or her daily life.

Spiritual emergencies, in contrast, can be extremely disruptive. People who are undergoing spiritual emergencies may find their STEs and paranormal experiences severely challenging rather than uplifting. As long as the spiritual emergency continues, they generally do not welcome STEs and STEPs, for the intensity of these experiences is distracting, disturbing, and/or disorienting to them.

During a spiritual emergency people find it difficult or impossible to perform their daily duties. At best, they feel emotionally or spiritually off-balance. At worst, they are prone to periods of depression, anxiety, or mood swings. Although people going through spiritual emergencies generally have appropriate emotional responses, they may become extremely sensitive and sometimes have exaggerated emotional responses. From time to time they may have difficulty judging whether their reactions and behaviour are appropriate.

Even though their thought processes are still basically clear, people undergoing a spiritual emergency often have great difficulty integrating their paranormal experiences into their view of reality. They may also develop inflated, grandiose attitudes about themselves. A person might, for example, begin to think he is a prophet or to believe he has reached a rare, extraordinarily high level of spiritual attainment, when in truth he has not. In some cases, paranoid tendencies may appear, causing the person to believe, for example, that an STE has been caused by a malevolent person or dark force. Inflated ideas and paranoid thoughts are, however, temporary in spiritual emergencies. The person is able to come to grips with them and eventually to dismiss them by using logic and rational thinking.

At times people who are going through spiritual emergency may also feel they are close to losing control, live in fear that they are going "crazy," or have difficulty distinguishing between inner and outer realities. Some people in spiritual emergency may also see horrific visions or hear outbursts of tormenting inner voices. They usually realize that all these experiences are temporary and not based on physical reality. They are thus able to struggle to tolerate them until they pass.

However, people in a spiritual emergency episode may have difficulties communicating clearly with others and maintaining their interpersonal relationships. They are often preoccupied with their inner experiences, and other people may see them as "spaced out." Individuals in spiritual emergency having the classical signs of spiritual energy/kundalini activity sometimes experience them as intense, disruptive, and even painful.

In spite of these difficulties, people in spiritual emergency generally maintain their ethical and moral values.

Distinguishing Spiritual Emergency from Psychosis

Psychotic episodes are the far end of the spectrum of difficulties had by some STE and STEP experiencers. A number of differences in thought processes, emotional reactions, and behaviour distinguish a person who is in a spiritual emergency from one who is psychotic. Table 5 (page 320) points out some of the main differences. People who are having intense or frequent STEs often ask me if they are "going crazy." Although no one but a qualified mental health–care professional can make an individual's diagnosis involving mental illness, the following rule of thumb is often helpful: If a person can distinguish between inner and outer experiences, is clearly aware of which inner experiences do not fit into the prevailing world view of reality, is able to function in the world, is able to make sound discerning judgments, and has appropriate control of his or her emotions, he or she is, by definition, not psychotic. This is true no matter how unusual or bizarre the inner experiences may seem.

I wish to emphasize here that there are clear diagnostic distinctions between mental illnesses — thought disorders and mood disorders — and STEs. However, a person with a mental illness can, like anyone else, have an STE, like my patient June with an intellectual disability and chronic schizophrenia, who had a white-light mystical NDE during a suicide attempt, described in chapter 5 on NDEs. I know several other persons, suffering with bipolar or schizophrenic illness, who were blessed with an STE at some point in their life, unrelated to and independent of their mental illness. Alternatively, a person who has had an STE might subsequently develop a psychotic disorder later in their lifetime, as can any person. To be clear, mystical experiences and other STEs are peak human experiences, exceptional human experiences. STEs are not delusions or hallucinations related to mental illness.

Of course, anyone having paranormal experiences who is at all concerned about their mental health should see a mental health–care professional — ideally one who has some familiarity with and an accepting attitude toward STEs.

In Table 5 (page 320), I have briefly outlined the features of spiritual emergencies compared to those of a psychosis. The chart is only a simplistic look at an extremely complex subject. Like spiritual emergencies, psychotic illnesses manifest in a wide variety of ways in different individuals.

It is not the purpose of this book to examine the many different types of psychotic illnesses, or to look at the ways they are distinguished from each other. However, I would like to add a few interesting observations I have made over the years. The vast majority of STE experiencers I have seen who slipped from a very difficult spiritual emergency into a psychosis developed the symptoms of acute mania. Over the years I have seen at least twenty such cases.

In persons suffering from STEPs mixed with acute mania, the traditional mood-stabilizing drugs prescribed for mania, such as lithium and clonazepam, were effective and helpful. The few patients with powerful STEPs mixed with psychosis diagnosed as schizophrenia or schizoaffective disorder were helped by the major tranquilizers commonly prescribed for these conditions. All the mixed STEP-psychoses experiencers were also helped by grounding techniques that I discuss in detail in chapter 17, and by counselling that focused on distinguishing more clearly between inner and outer realities. Because I have seen such a high percentage of people with STEP-related psychosis developing acute mania, I have included in Table 6 (page 321) the major criteria for the diagnosis of manic episodes.

Table 5

Spiritual Emergency	Psychosis
Challenged by experiences	Overwhelmed by experiences
Great difficulty functioning	Unable to function
Thought processes clear	Thought processes incoherent or contain loose associations
Transient grandiose ideas	Delusions of grandeur
Difficulty separating inner and outer realities	Unable to distinguish inner and outer realities
Aware at some level that experiences are part of an inner process	Has paranoid delusions and projects cause of experiences onto others
Fears losing control	Is out of control
Exhibits mildly unusual behaviours	Exhibits inappropriate behaviours including outwardly destructive acts, self-destructive acts, disorganized behaviours, fixed obsessions
Able to tolerate negative visions	Overwhelmed by horrific visions
Can ignore voices heard	Overwhelmed by voices heard
Fairly appropriate emotional responses	Inappropriate emotional responses
Difficulty making discerning judgments	Unable to make discerning judgments
Moral and ethical values remain intact	Moral and ethical values may be lost

Table 6

Main Diagnostic Criteria for a Manic Episode

For a diagnosis of a manic episode, criteria A, B, C, and D all need to be present.

A. A distinct period of abnormally and persistently elevated, expansive, or irritable mood, and abnormally and persistently increased goal-directed activity or energy, lasting at least one week and present most of the day, nearly every day.

B. During the period of mood disturbance and increased energy or activity, three (or more) of the following symptoms (four if the mood is irritable) are present to a significant degree and represent a noticeable change from usual behaviour:

1. Inflated self-esteem or grandiosity.

2. Decreased need for sleep (e.g., feels rested after only three hours of sleep).

3. More talkative than usual or pressure to keep talking.

4. Flight of ideas or subjective experience that thoughts are racing.

5. Distractibility (i.e., attention too easily drawn to unimportant or irrelevant external stimuli), as reported or observed.

6. Increase in goal-directed activity (either socially, at work or school, or sexually) or psychomotor agitation (purposeless non-goal-directed activity).

7. Excessive involvement in activities which have a high potential for painful consequences (e.g., engaging in unrestrained buying sprees, sexual indiscretions, or foolish business investments).

C. The mood disturbance is sufficiently severe to cause marked impairment in social or occupational functioning or to necessitate hospitalization to prevent harm to self or others, or there are psychotic features.

D. The episode is not attributable to the physiological effects of a substance — e.g., a drug of abuse, a medication, other treatment — or to another medical condition.

The information in Table 6 is taken from the *DSM-V*, the American Psychiatric Association 2013 handbook that contains the criteria for the diagnosis of psychiatric disorders.

STEP Mixed with Acute Mania

One of the STE experiencers I have seen slip from spiritual emergency into acute mania was a man I'll call Jurgen.

> Jurgen was a very successful businessman in his midthirties. He was the president of a large corporation that he had founded, and he had accumulated assets worth well over two million dollars.
>
> While reading late one night, Jurgen suddenly began to receive channelled material. He began to write down the material, which he perceived as being "dictated" to him inside his head. Over a three-month period, Jurgen meticulously recorded three entire books. These books described the spiritual shortcomings of humanity and the need for humanity to rediscover its true spiritual nature.
>
> After these books were completed, Jurgen began to develop some inappropriate and inflated ideas about himself and what had happened to him. He believed he had received these works directly from God and thought that these channelled books were proof that he was God's special messenger. Eventually Jurgen's wife became concerned about these delusions and brought him to my office.
>
> When I talked to Jurgen, I found he was unable to put his channelling experience into any balanced perspective. He saw his experience as special, even unique. Convinced he was God's special messenger, he believed his message was of utmost importance for the world. Despite these inflated ideas about himself, somehow Jurgen continued to function very well at his workplace for a few months.

Then, however, he started to again channel more books but this time he lost the ability to judge when and where it was appropriate to discuss his channelled materials. He began to speak about them, and his belief that he was receiving direct communications from God, at business meetings, with business associates, legal advisers, his secretary, cab drivers, and finally with almost everyone he met.

As the same time, Jurgen began to exhibit the classic signs of mania: he became very excited and agitated, he developed rapid-fire speech, his appetite dwindled completely, and he spent his nights writing, channelling, and walking rather than sleeping. Soon he became so preoccupied with his inner experiences that he was no longer able to function at work. Jurgen had clearly slipped from spiritual emergency into psychosis. He was admitted to a psychiatric hospital and diagnosed as suffering from a manic psychosis.

Analyzing Jurgen's case in terms of spiritual experiences, spiritual emergency, and psychosis, we can see that he had a powerful STEP, a spontaneous psychic opening — such as countless people have had — but perhaps due to the intensity of the experience, was unable to put it into a balanced perspective and instead developed grandiose delusions and inflated ideas about himself and his new psychic ability. Eventually, he was no longer able to function in his day-to-day life. Jurgen then met the *DSM-V* diagnostic criteria for mania, as his expansive mood lasted for many weeks, incapacitating him from working, and he demonstrated grandiosity, a decreased need for sleep, more talkativeness than usual, and flight of ideas.

Following his discharge from hospital, Jurgen continued to take the mood-stabilizing medication that had resolved his manic episode. I also worked with Jurgen to help him develop a far more balanced perspective on his psychic experiences. Throughout the process Jurgen remained convinced that the psychic experiences themselves were real. I did not challenge the reality of his experiences — only the way in which he interpreted them.

In the course of counselling, I helped Jurgen to see that a great many people had received channelled material and produced channelled books. As he familiarized himself with some of these books, he began to realize that his experiences were not at all unique. With my urging, Jurgen also re-examined his assumption that the channelled material came directly from God. One technique he finally decided to try was to ask the channelled voice to identify itself. It did — as the spirit of a long-deceased person. Jurgen was then able to admit, rather sheepishly, that he was mistaken in thinking he had been channelling God.

Although Jurgen's journey to maintain complete mental health continues, with the help of medication and his growing ability to keep his experiences in perspective and to let go of his grandiose ideas, he has been able to remain nondelusional and to function fully in the working world again.

Aberrant Kundalini Awakening and Mental Illness

Gopi Krishna thought problems or imbalances that can occur with a spiritual energy/kundalini awakening might sometimes cause some forms of mental illness. He often referred to this as an aberrant or malignant awakening of kundalini. The risk of mental disorder as the result of a faulty awakening of kundalini is mentioned repeatedly in various yogic traditions.

Based both on his years of study and on his own experiences, Gopi Krishna described a number of problems that could occur during a kundalini awakening that could cause mental imbalances. These include: the spiritual energy/kundalini could rise, as it did in his own case, through the incorrect nadi — up the ida or pingala rather than up the central astral sushumna spinal channel; the body might be unable to supply the brain with either great enough quantities of or pure enough prana after a kundalini awakening; the body might not be able to supply the brain with enough ojas after the kundalini awakening; and genetic factors, psychological imbalances, or physical imbalances in the body or brain might adversely affect the kundalini mechanism and/or the transforming brain.

Some people may run into difficulty because they are activating the spiritual energy/kundalini long before their body and consciousness are ready. This may result from improper, unbalanced yoga and/or meditation practices. They may not have the physical strength or mental discipline necessary to handle the awakened spiritual energy/kundalini, and they may not have developed the sexual discipline needed to ensure that the essential ojas is not squandered externally. Paramahansa Yogananda warned, "To attempt to raise the life current [kundalini] through the chakras by unscientific methods taught by unenlightened teachers can cause bodily harm. An advanced yoga technique such as Kriya [a form of pranayama] should be practised under the blessing of a true Guru's instruction ... Kriya instruction given by the Guru and blessed by his inner guidance bestows the highest benefits, regardless of one's age and health."

We can better understand how these and other difficulties with spiritual energy/kundalini awakening might occur by reflecting on the Eight Limbs of Yoga, discussed in chapter 9, "The Yogic Model of Consciousness and Kundalini." One can see how by spending years carefully following the prescribed disciplines, spiritual aspirants would be prepared physically, psychologically, mentally, and spiritually for the activation of the spiritual energy/kundalini mechanism, and for the gradual attainment of expanded higher states of consciousness.

Unfortunately, a great many people are intensely practising some aspects and certain types of yoga or meditation and ignoring the system as a whole. In North America, a vast number of people are rigorously doing the physical postures, the breathing exercises, and/or intensive meditation techniques, but few are making any attempt at doing the groundwork involved in the moral and psychological discipline of the dos and don'ts of yama and niyama. Further, many people are unwittingly mimicking the limb known as dharana (concentration) through the intense levels of concentration that are required for long periods of time in so many of our jobs and activities today.

Based on my clinical work, I have come to the conclusion that improper and unbalanced yoga and/or meditation practice may sometimes indeed result in, or contribute to, unhealthy awakening of the kundalini/spiritual energy, and contribute to some forms of spiritual emergencies or even mental illness. The relationship between an imbalanced or aberrant kundalini awakening and psychiatric illness is an area that definitely needs future research.

Better Treatment in the Future

As a medical doctor and transpersonal psychotherapist, one of my main reasons for researching kundalini, STEs, and spiritual transformation of consciousness has been the hope that greater understanding will aid the medical and psychological communities in their efforts to help people who are having difficulties associated with these types of experiences.

Distinguishing among crises that are part of the spiritual journey, spiritual emergencies, and psychoses is sometimes difficult even for doctors and psychotherapists who are familiar with all of them. Imagine, then, the difficulties that can arise when the professionals treating people having STEs are unaware of or don't accept the reality of such things as STEs, spiritual emergence, and spiritual emergency.

Dr. David Lukoff is one of the people working to heighten people's awareness. As mentioned in chapter 10, he was one of the doctors who suggested the new classification of religious or spiritual problem for the *DSM-IV*. He has also put forward the idea that some people have a transient psychosis associated with a powerful mystical experience/STEP, and that these experiences are quite different from other types of psychoses. Dr. Lukoff has observed that they are relatively short-lived psychoses, and tend to eventually resolve themselves spontaneously as long as the person is simply cared for supportively, rather than being hospitalized in a psychiatric ward, labelled as delusional, and automatically medicated with the major tranquilizers used in these settings.

Use of Psychiatric Medications in STE Experiencers — FAQ

STE experiencers and their loved ones often ask me questions relating to the use of psychiatric medications by STE or STEP experiencers who develop a psychosis. Most are concerned that the powerful drugs used in Western medicine today to help manage psychoses might permanently block or harm their spiritual transformation process. Others think that they can move forward in their spiritual deepening only if they take themselves off psychiatric medications that their physician or psychologist recommends that they continue. Still others question the accuracy of the diagnosis of a psychotic episode that was mixed with their STEP, rather than embracing that they could have had a mixture of both — a STEP plus a psychotic episode at the same time, or a transient psychosis with mystical features. These are complex questions, which need individualized consideration. But, since I am asked them so often, I will share my general professional opinion about these frequently asked questions:

Will taking anti-psychotic psychiatric medications permanently harm or stop the spiritual transformation process?

No. This is the most common question I have been asked by STE experiencers and their family members after the experiencer was hospitalized with a psychotic episode and put on mood stabilizers or antipsychotic medication for a period of time. My clinical impression is no. I do not think that taking a major tranquilizer antipsychotic or a mood-stabilizing drug for a period of time will permanently stop the spiritual transformation process. These drugs will slow down the transformation process while they are being taken, especially when taken at high doses.

During an acute psychotic episode, whether related to a STEP and spiritual emergency or not, I think it very important that individuals get the medical help and care they need, to protect their safety and others' safety while they are cognitively impaired because of their psychosis. If this means taking strong psychiatric medications for a period of time to control the psychosis, so be it.

I have seen a few STE experiencers who went psychotic after a powerful STEP, who were treated with Western psychiatric medication for a period of time, then were able to later stop their medication under medical supervision. These individuals went on to have continued long-term spiritual transformation with repeated, albeit less dramatic, STEs. On the other hand, some STE experiencers who develop a psychotic disorder have found they need to stay on their medications long-term, to control the psychotic disorder and be able to function in the world. They too may continue in their spiritual transformation process, but more slowly and gently.

Do I need to come off my prescribed mood-stabilizing drugs for bipolar disorder if I want to progress in my spiritual transformation process?

No. Some STE experiencers who develop bipolar disorder mixed with a STEP find they are not able to come off their psychiatric medications without having a relapse of their mania. They can be reassured that in my clinical experience mood-stabilizing medications do not seem to stop the spiritual transformation process, although they likely slow it down somewhat. I recommend continuing with your prescribed psychiatric medication while adopting a balanced lifestyle and regular daily practice of meditation, in accordance with the Eight Limbs of Yoga, and the strategies I will be discussing later in this book.

I have seen several tragic incidents that occurred when a person who had a psychosis mixed with STEs took themselves off their prescribed psychiatric medication against medical advice and subsequently did great harm to themselves during a relapse of their psychosis. One fellow jumped off a high bridge, delusionally thinking he could fly, and became permanently disabled as a quadriplegic from his injuries. Another fellow took himself off his medications and later committed suicide, leaving a suicide note stating that he thought God had instructed him to kill himself. These tragic misfortunes have highlighted to me the importance for STE experiencers with psychotic disorders to stay on the medications prescribed by their doctors to control their mental illness, as long as the doctor thinks the medication is truly needed. If in doubt, get a second opinion from a licensed psychologist or psychiatrist who is knowledgeable about STEs and spiritual emergencies.

It is my hope that the raising of awareness of STEs, spiritual transformation of consciousness, and spiritual energy/kundalini will help healthcare providers and society as a whole recognize that STEs and STEPs are not mental illness, and help stimulate correct diagnosis of STEs. I also hope this increased awareness will promote more supportive care for people undergoing STE-related spiritual crises, spiritual emergencies, and psychoses mixed with STEPs.

In the next chapter we'll consider some of the factors that seem to precipitate severe difficulties with STE after-effects and the spiritual transformation process, examine how many of them relate to the failure to follow the Eightfold Path of Yoga, and look at a number of case histories of spiritual emergency and psychosis.

16

WHO HAS SPIRITUAL EMERGENCIES AND WHY?

IN MY CLINICAL WORK COUNSELLING STE experiencers, I found a number of specific factors that seem to predispose people undergoing STEs to slip into spiritual emergency or even into psychosis. A number of them relate directly to disregarding or contradicting the teachings of the ancient yogis regarding the physical and psychological preparation that is necessary before one begins the more intensive meditation practices that can lead to expanded states of consciousness. I have noticed that the greater the number of contributing factors present, the greater the likelihood that the person will develop a spiritual emergency or — as the number increases even more — possibly even a psychosis. As well, the greater the intensity of the factors, the greater the problem.

Spiritual Emergency and Psychosis — Possible Predisposing Factors

Although I have found at least twelve possible predisposing factors, the two most common are an out-of-balance lifestyle and excessive spiritual practices. These two factors have a more wide-ranging effect than the others:

1. *Out-of-balance lifestyle.* An out-of-balance lifestyle exacerbates any of the other difficulties that may arise. It includes irregular or skipped meals; an unbalanced, low-nutrition diet; insufficient sleep; excessive indulgence in sex; alcohol or drug abuse;

smoking tobacco; a stressful and hectic irregular schedule; lack of physical exercise, outdoor activity, and recreation; and lack of time for reflection or quiet contemplation.

Although this unbalanced lifestyle is unfortunately quite common in the West today, it is very different from the one that aspirants on the yogic path led centuries ago. They were taught moderation in all things. Their lives were peaceful rather than stressful and hectic, they were moderate in their sexual practices or completely abstinent, and life in an ashram tended to be orderly and regulated. Diet was also considered important. One hatha yoga manual says that mita-ahara (moderate diet) was one of the essential prerequisites to beginning pranayama.

The adverse effect of an out-of-balance lifestyle relates to the yogic model of consciousness and kundalini in a number of ways. In order to manufacture and supply adequate amounts of life-energy/prana, the body's organs and nervous system need to be strong and in good condition. This cannot occur without an adequate, balanced diet and exercise. Sufficient sleep is very important because it is during sleep that the body regenerates and builds up energy. Drug and alcohol abuse, and smoking tobacco, may also affect the purity of the prana. It has long been believed in the yogic tradition that excessive sexual release leads to the depletion of vitally necessary sexual energy/ojas. (See chapter 17, "Strategies for Living with Spiritual Transformation," for a more thorough discussion of a balanced lifestyle.)

2. *Extremely intensive spiritual practices.* Although such practices as hatha yoga, meditation, prayer, contemplation, and Tai Chi are generally positive when practised in moderation, sudden intensive practice of any spiritual technique by a beginner, unsupervised practice of multiple spiritual techniques, or excessive practice of spiritual techniques for very long periods of time may overstimulate the kundalini mechanism and cause it to awaken before the individual is psychologically and/or physically prepared. This is particularly true with the intense practice

of those spiritual techniques that have been designed specifically to awaken the kundalini/spiritual energy mechanism.

This is probably one important reason why many of the ancient yogis — like teachers from many traditions — taught aspirants to proceed gradually along the spiritual path and recommended that they have a guru or experienced spiritual teacher who could monitor their practices and tell them when they were ready to proceed to the next stage.

When the spiritual energy/kundalini mechanism is activated too rapidly or aggressively in an unprepared spiritual seeker, the strain on the body, the physiological symptoms, and the massively altered states of consciousness may be too much for the experiencer to bear. Similarly, when the kundalini mechanism is activated forcefully or suddenly in an unprepared person, the body's organs and nervous system may not be able to the produce the greater quantities of pure, potent prana required. The much-needed supply of ojas/sexual energy may also be missing or inadequate. The problems arising may be particularly severe if the kundalini mechanism is activated so forcefully that it reaches the crown chakra on its initial awakening, and over-activates the brahma randhra region of the brain/astral brain.

Continuing to practise intensively, or for long periods of time, the spiritual techniques that have awakened kundalini prematurely makes the problems even more severe.

3. *Extremely intensive concentration.* The long, intense periods of concentration demanded by so many of today's activities, particularly work and study, can have a similar effect on the brain as the forms of concentration so assiduously developed by the yogis. The sixth limb of yoga is dharana, or concentration. When carried to extremes, scholarly concentration may have a similar stimulatory effect on the spiritual process as intense or excessive spiritual practices.

In my practice I have seen several people (for example, Gwen, the young medical student whose story I shared in chapter 4, "Spiritual Energy/Kundalini Episodes") who awakened the kundalini/spiritual energy when they were studying and reading large amounts of material during difficult, advanced academic programs.

4. *Inadequate psychological "housecleaning."* When spiritual energy/kundalini awakens and the spiritual transformation of consciousness moves into high gear, unresolved psychological conflicts that are held repressed in the unconscious — often those left over from childhood or early adulthood — frequently begin to surface to conscious awareness. This process is very different from the one that occurs during psychotherapy with a competent therapist in which previously repressed memories are encouraged to gradually resurface in a supportive environment. With the sudden awakening of the transformative energy, these repressed memories seem to shoot into the conscious mind with great clarity and intensity and without any prior warning. Sometimes several memories resurface in rapid-fire succession. Since these memories were originally repressed because the conscious mind was not able to deal with them, their rapid resurfacing can be so psychologically overwhelming that it may cause the STE experiencer to slip into spiritual emergency or psychosis. This is especially true when the memories are of traumatic childhood events such as sexual abuse or incest. Such horrible memories are difficult to deal with even in carefully moderated, supportive psychotherapy. When they surface without warning, they can be devastating.

The prepared spiritual seeker who has worked gradually over the years on their psychological housecleaning will already have come to terms with many difficult or traumatic memories. And, in the event that other memories do become unblocked, the person who has already done a great deal of psychological work is already familiar with how painful this process can be and has probably developed a number of strategies, supports, and skills for facing and resolving the surfacing issues.

5. *Unblocking unresolved psychological issues from perceived past lives.* The activity of the transformative energy seems not only to

unblock psychological issues from this life but also from what appear to be past lives. I, along with many other psychotherapists, have observed this to be a common and normal part of spiritual transformation. In the yogic tradition, reincarnation and past-life memories are accepted as reality. In fact, Patanjali states that yogis will, at some point in their development, begin to experience past-life memories. In Western culture, however, reincarnation is not widely accepted, and some Western psychologists interpret past-life memories as meaningful symbolic metaphors, created by the subconscious mind. Whatever the actual origin, when past-life memories occur, they often generate strong emotional reactions. This suggests that some type of residual, unresolved psychological conflict exists and is associated with (or symbolized by) the remembered incident. These conflicts often seem to relate to people with whom the experiencer is currently having difficulties. The memories, and the associated guilt, pain, or anger, may sometimes be so intense and overwhelming, and seem so difficult to resolve, that they trigger a spiritual emergency.

Perceived past-life memories are even more likely to trigger crises if the experiencer does not believe in reincarnation or cannot find supportive persons to talk to about the past-life memory. In these cases, the person who has already done some psycho-spiritual housecleaning is often far better able to deal with these memories and to distinguish and integrate what psychological and spiritual lessons can be learned into his or her daily life. Perceived past-life memories are discussed in more detail in chapter 18, "Psycho-Spiritual Housecleaning."

Concepts that relate to both psycho-spiritual housecleaning and past-life memories can be found in the ancient yogic teachings. In them, "samskaras" are described as the imprints left on our astral body by our past actions, both in this lifetime and in past lives. Western psychologists might conceptualize samskaras as traumatic memories repressed into our unconscious mind. More information about yogic views on samskaras can be found in Mircea Eliade's *Yoga: Immortality and Freedom,* and

Paramahansa Yogananda's *God Talks with Arjuna: The Bhagavad Gita*. Parallels can be found between the process of self-examination required in psychotherapy and the first two limbs of the eightfold path, yama (the don'ts) and niyama (disciplines — the dos), which were designed to purify the personality. (I discuss samskaras in more detail in chapter 18.)

6. *Excessive greed and desire for wealth.* In my work I have seen a number of people on the spiritual path experience tremendous conflict when they have strong, unresolved desires for wealth and possessions. They almost invariably come to a point in their spiritual journey where they must choose between their materialistic desires and their spiritual goals. When most of a person's time and energy has been tied up with the pursuit of money and possessions, the shift in focus required when one begins the process of spiritual transformation can be so disconcerting — and require so many lifestyle changes — that the person can be thrown into crisis or even spiritual emergency.

   I have also seen a few people whose lust for wealth corrupts their spiritual process and causes them to try to use some aspect of their spiritual or paranormal gifts unscrupulously to amass vast personal wealth.

   These types of crises are less likely to occur to aspirants following the sequential stages of the Eight Limbs of Yoga, for they would begin striving to overcome greed and detach themselves from material possessions at the very beginning of their spiritual journey.

7. *Excessive ambition and lust for power.* The same type of conflict arises when people cling to the desire for power, status, and position when they have awakened the transformative energy.

   Some people I have met have had STEs but have never gotten their lust for power under control. Some of these people eventually got involved in "psychic games" and tried, for example, to influence or control other people's behaviour with their "psychic abilities." People who try such things are certain to experience intense inner conflicts and are likely to experience a difficult spiritual transformation. They may even become delusional.

The Eightfold Path of Yoga helps prevent these types of situations by developing such characteristics as "greedlessness," "truthfulness," and "nonattachment." Further, many spiritual masters have repeatedly warned aspirants about the dangers inherent in paying too much attention to psychic gifts that undoubtedly develop as one successfully undergoes spiritual transformation.

8. *Fixation on psychic gifts.* In my work I have seen a number of people who have become fixated on their newly developing psychic gifts, to the exclusion of their spiritual and psychological development. In previous chapters there have been examples of people, like Jurgen, whose belief in the uniqueness of their gifts contributed to their severe ultimate state of delusion.

One of the reasons the yogic and other spiritual texts warn against the fixation with siddhis, or psychic gifts, is that individuals may begin to focus their energies on striving for greater psychic gifts rather than on attaining deeper spiritual states of consciousness. As their focus on the psychic increases, such individuals are in danger of being led even further off the path by the temptations that come with the increased attention, fame, and adulation they may receive, and with the impression that they are gaining power over others.

It is my experience that this often leads to ego inflation, grandiosity, an increasing loss of perspective, or even loss of contact with reality, that can in turn lead to spiritual emergencies or psychoses.

9. *Unresolved conflicts with the God concept.* I have come across a number of people who had difficulties when they began to undergo the process of spiritual transformation while they still had deep-seated inner conflicts concerning the divine power behind the universe. In some instances, these people harbour a tremendous anger toward God. In many cases, the person originally believed deeply in the concept of God they were taught during childhood and then felt let down or abandoned when they believed God allowed some terrible event to happen or did not answer their prayers. In my

practice, I have seen people who had this reaction to such events as the death of a child, the suicide of a brother, or the torture or death of their relatives in a concentration camp. Similar conflicts can also arise in people who have turned away from God because they cannot accept the fact that a divine power could exist and yet do nothing to prevent the tremendous suffering they see in the world around them. Others are conflicted because they turned away from God because they were repulsed by the judgmental and punishing nature of God they had been taught, or repulsed by some rigid dogmas in the church of their childhood.

When people begin to undergo the process of spiritual transformation while harbouring these unresolved conflicts about their God concept, they may experience intense inner turmoil, spiritual crises, and spiritual emergencies. People who are angry with God, or who have turned away from a God they once loved, need to resolve these feelings if they want to minimize the difficulties in their spiritual process.

10. *Turning to the dark side.* Whether one believes in the existence of such things as the dark side, the devil, or Satan, it cannot be denied that many people do believe in this negative concept, and in some cases consciously embrace it. I have spoken with several patients who were severely psychologically traumatized or even physically or sexually abused by persons who claimed to be working with the dark forces.

Leaders of Satanic cults would fall into this category. They may even be striving to awaken the spiritual energy/kundalini mechanism forcefully because they believe it will bring them power that they can use for their own selfish or evil purposes. In the rare event that such a person did activate kundalini, I believe their negativity, ego-involvement, and grandiose ideas would eventually lead to spiritual emergency or psychosis. In extreme cases, the person's efforts might end in madness or self-destruction.

11. *Unresolved spiritual guilt.* Like repressed memories of traumatic events, the memories of events we feel guilty about often resurface during the spiritual process and sometimes become more

intense. The feelings themselves can become so strong that the experiencer is pushed into crisis or emergency. In some cases, people who feel they have done something "bad" in the past may suffer from severe conflict when they begin to have positive spiritual experiences, because they feel they don't deserve them. For example, I have seen this intense unresolved spiritual guilt in some women experiencers who had an abortion earlier in their life.

As you'll see later in this chapter in Minnie's story about abortion and unresolved guilt, examining our feelings about past actions and life-events is an essential part of the spiritual journey, and refusing to forgive ourselves for them can be extremely detrimental.

12. *Terminal illness.* Although terminal illnesses are very different from the other types of factors that have been discussed here, they can precipitate spiritual crises and emergencies in a number of ways. Facing a terminal illness often forces people to examine large spiritual questions and look at specific spiritual issues that they have avoided facing for years. Sometimes a feeling of urgency makes the person try to deal with too much, too fast.

In some cases, people facing terminal illness begin intense spiritual practices or long periods of highly focused prayer. When these practices inadvertently stimulate the transformative energy, the person's weakened body may have difficulty handling it. Further, if the person is still psychologically troubled about impending death, the other processes often triggered by the energy, such as the unblocking of past memories, can be very difficult to deal with.

13. *Hereditary factors.* The fact that heredity plays a role in some types of mental illness is no longer disputed. I feel it also plays a role in predisposing some people to having spiritual emergencies or psychoses — especially when they are undergoing a very rapid spiritual awakening.

Unfortunately, medical science is only beginning to understand the role of genetics in mental illness, and a great deal of research will be needed to determine how it relates to spiritual emergencies. In my practice I have noticed that individuals with family histories that include psychiatric disorders, particularly manic-depressive illness or schizophrenia, have difficulties with their spiritual process far more frequently than those who have no family history of mental illness. This is one more reason why I feel the research on spiritual energy/kundalini and its relationship to mental illness is so important.

Excessive Spiritual Practices

In my clinical work, I have seen several people who, in their over-eagerness to have spiritual experiences, did themselves great harm. One was a man I met at a conference years ago, whom I'll call Jerrit. Jerrit's story is a stark reminder that an out-of-balance lifestyle combined with excessive, unsupervised, intense spiritual practices is an unhealthy mix, and can induce a spiritual emergency.

I was a university professor in a town in the midwestern United States. When I was in my thirties I had a profound mystical experience and decided I would do anything to have a mystical experience again.

Both the university I taught in and the community I lived in were very conservative in their approach. At the time when I had my mystical experience, topics such as Eastern religion and meditation were considered strange. Even the practice of hatha yoga was looked at askance. After my mystical experience, however, I did find someone who recommended Gopi Krishna's books on kundalini. I managed to obtain them and pored over them, absorbing as much as I could. I noticed that Gopi Krishna repeatedly urged moderation and balance and warned against the dangers of excessive spiritual practices. However, in my intense desire to stimulate the kundalini to have another spiritual experience, I decided not to follow this advice, and I went so far as to find everything that I could that might stimulate kundalini and then begin to practise them all at once. I threw myself into intensive hatha yoga, meditation, and Tantric practices. Although I was a beginner at meditation, in my overzealousness, I forced myself to meditate five or six hours per day and sometimes longer, using several advanced kundalini meditation techniques. And I did eventually stimulate the awakening of the spiritual energy/kundalini.

My body and mind were totally unprepared for the tremendous shock to my system. I was thrown into spiritual emergency, and then psychosis. Unable to function, I lost my job. I felt as if I were on fire or burning alive, and I endured sensations of light so bright that they were excruciatingly painful. I suffered through horrific visions, nightmares, and the blackest pits of despair and depression. Unfortunately, I was forced to endure this suffering alone for almost three years, because I couldn't find anyone who understood what I was going through.

Finally, I found a sympathetic therapist in a nearby city through the Spiritual Emergence Network. She guided me to begin to practise grounding techniques and to follow the moderate approach to life and spirituality I had first read about in Gopi Krishna's books. I began my self-reflection and emotional healing work. But even then I continued to suffer from spells of severe depression for some time. I later found it necessary to go to a men's healing retreat in Arizona for a year, to further ground and heal myself. Finally, after years of effort, I have come close to full recovery.

Jerrit's story serves as a powerful warning, as do the case histories of others who have inadvertently brought on spiritual emergency by unsupervised and out-of-balance intensive, excessive spiritual practices. At the conference where we met, Jerrit spoke openly about his experiences and his suffering and literally begged people not to do multiple, excessive practices, as he had done.

Inadequate Psycho-Spiritual Housecleaning

When the transformative energy awakens, it is like a bright light that shines in the inner "house" that is our consciousness. The brilliant light illuminates the cobwebs and debris that need to be cleaned away — our unresolved psychological issues and wounding. In general, the less psychological housecleaning a person has done, the greater the number of inner issues and wounds they may discover and the less their supports and coping skills to deal with these will likely be. Therefore, the more distressed they may be to discover that the cobwebs and debris exist at all.

This was true of a medical technologist I'll call Beth who came to see me in my office for the first time when she was in her late forties. Beth told me that she was afraid she was losing her mind. Memories from her childhood kept flooding, unwanted and unbidden, into her conscious mind, and she desperately wanted help in finding a way to stop them. At that time in her life, she felt she simply couldn't bear the distress they were causing.

> I always thought of myself as a very anxious person. When I was in my late twenties, I became interested in meditation and began to hope that it might cure my constant anxiety. I even joined a Buddhist temple and was involved there for several years. Unfortunately, I discovered that my anxiety increased the longer I meditated.
>
> Frustrated, I finally left the temple thinking that I had inherited some type of imbalance in my brain chemistry from my parents and that I was doomed to suffer forever from chronic anxiety. Matters became worse when I lost my hospital job because of local budget cuts. About the same time, my common-law husband of several years announced that he had found a new girlfriend and was leaving me. Realizing that I could not afford my apartment any longer, I was forced to move in with my parents until I could reestablish myself. Although I was on speaking terms with them, I did not particularly like either of my parents.

I found living at home as an adult very anxiety-provoking and uncomfortable.

During this extremely stressful time, one of my friends convinced me it would be a lot of "fun" to participate in an intense, two-day seminar on "breathwork."

Eager and excited, I signed up for the seminar with my friend, expecting to have a fun and relaxing weekend that would provide a much-needed escape from my mental turmoil and anxiety. My experience at the seminar proved to be dramatically different from my expectations. After doing about two hours of the breathing techniques I had been taught, I suddenly began to experience powerful rushes of energy up my body and spine. Then, quite without warning, I began to unblock a number of horrific memories from my childhood that had been completely repressed. As the first of these memories arose, I began to experience clear, vivid flashbacks of being raped by my uncle in the barn on my grandparents' farm when I was fifteen years old. I then began to unblock memories of being sexually abused by my father for several years during my early childhood. Terrified, overwhelmed, and horrified, I received no help from the seminar instructors when I explained what was happening. Finally, I bolted from the seminar.

At this point in my life, I felt I was incapable of dealing with such memories. I desperately hoped they were not true and was unable to face the fact that they might be. After leaving the seminar, I went into a state of extreme anxiety and agitation.

I had been under a great deal of stress when I began to experience the energy rushes and was poorly equipped to deal with the unblocked memories. The situation grew worse when I tried to return home and live in the same house with my father, whom I now suspected might have abused me, and the mother who might not have protected me.

By the time Beth came to my office for help she could barely function in her parents' home and was in a severe state of spiritual emergency. She had experienced an intense spiritual energy/kundalini awakening during the intense breathwork session, after many years of meditation practice. She unblocked very traumatic repressed memories for which she was totally unprepared, as she had never done any prior psychological housecleaning. Thankfully, continued therapy is now helping her sort through and come to terms with her traumatic childhood memories. Also, a number of the techniques discussed in chapters 17 to 20 have helped her moderate her energy experiences.

It is my opinion that Beth's system was ripe for a kundalini awakening because of her several years' intense meditation practice in the Buddhist temple. The breathwork technique taught in her seminar was similar to a type of intense pranayama exercise used by yogis to stimulate the spiritual energy/kundalini, and may cause people to remember deeply buried traumatic memories during the breathwork session. The intensive pranayama-like breathwork she did in the seminar triggered the energy before she was psychologically prepared. Unfortunately, in many types of breathwork seminars the instructors themselves may be unfamiliar with pranayama, yoga, or kundalini, and they may not have any idea how to deal with a kundalini awakening. Further, the instructors — or breathworkers, as they are sometimes called — in many of the courses are usually not fully trained psychotherapists and, consequently, have no idea how to help the participant deal with the traumatic memories or extremely emotional experiences that sometimes occur, nor are they able to provide any psychological follow-up and support.

In my work I have come across a number of people who have had experiences similar to Beth's with intense breathwork seminars. Another young woman, Jana, had a spiritual emergency when taking an intensive (and expensive) instructor-training course in a type of breathwork that involved swimming with dolphins. Jana, too, awakened her kundalini during the intense breathwork course.

During the swimming with dolphins breathwork course, while doing the intense breathing exercise, I suddenly started feeling rushes of energy up my spine. At first I felt bliss and expansion, but then I began to spontaneously unblock vivid and detailed memories of physical abuse in my childhood. I began to cry and sob uncontrollably. The instructor saw me crying and began to shout at me. She told me to "get yourself under control" because the class was "not a therapy session." This shouting pushed me even further into a crisis of tears, but the instructor only became increasingly hostile and angry with me.

As I came across more and more cases like Beth's and Jana's, I became increasingly concerned when I heard of "breathworkers" who were not fully trained in dealing with the emotional and psychological upheaval that can result from unblocking deeply buried memories. Many have no idea that they are working with a form of pranayama, and may not be aware of its potential effect on spiritual energy/kundalini. Even those who have some understanding of kundalini often have no awareness of the immense power of the awakened energies — and mistakenly believe that they can "control" or "suppress" the spiritual energy mechanism. In short, they may have no idea that they are toying with powerful techniques that were designed to awaken a spiritually transformative force — a force whose ultimate power is far beyond our control. Intensive breathwork techniques should only be practised under the supervision of a trained psychotherapist or knowledgeable spiritual teacher or counsellor who can deal with a possible psycho-spiritual crisis.

The experience of pranayama can, of course, be positive. A man I know whom I'll call Rubindar studied yoga under an excellent teacher in India. He had been doing yama and niyama, self-development and inner-growth work, for years before he began to practise pranayama and then awakened his kundalini. Here is Rubindar's story:

One day when I was meditating and practising intense pranayama at my guru's ashram in India, I began to experience strong rushes of energy up my spine, sensations of inner heat and inner light, and uncontrollable shaking of my body. The guru came over to me immediately, and sat calmly beside me. The guru began to speak to me in a calm, reassuring manner. As the symptoms continued, the guru told me that what I was experiencing was called kundalini awakening, and that the experience was not abnormal, but was a sacred experience. The guru then calmly explained how kundalini was well known in ancient yoga traditions. All the while, he continued to reassure me, telling me not to be afraid. He explained that kundalini was a powerful, but positive energy.

Although my dramatic spiritual energy/kundalini pulses up my spine and body shaking continued for several hours, the guru did not leave my side until they abated. After the kundalini symptoms eventually stopped, my guru advised me to eat some small sweets, which seemed to help balance my body and mind after the intense experience.

As a prepared spiritual aspirant, Rubindar did not unblock any traumatic memories during his pranayama/breathwork-induced kundalini awakening. The guru's wisdom and understanding helped turn what could have been an overwhelming and frightening experience into a positive one. Using the type of supportive technique similar to what a well-trained Western psychotherapist might, the guru spoke to Rubindar in a calm, reassuring manner. This reassurance, plus being given a context and vocabulary, being informed of the place of kundalini in yoga, helped Rubindar begin his journey of accelerated spiritual transformation, triggered by the awakening, on the right foot.

Unresolved Spiritual Guilt

A woman I'll call Minnie came to my office for therapy in a state of extreme depression and severe agitation. She, too, had awakened spiritual energy/kundalini through intense meditation practices, and her condition was made worse by deep-seated, unresolved spiritual guilt.

I began my intense spiritual practices as a means of trying to deal with a tremendous amount of inner pain. For the last four years I had been meditating and chanting for as much as two to three hours a day. However, about two months ago I increased the amount of time until I was meditating and chanting to most of my waking hours. My dedication to these practices had become so great that I was no longer able to work. Up until this time I had been fairly successful and had held middle-management jobs.

My reason for stepping up the intensity of my spiritual practices was an increasing depression. I felt as if there was a "black hole" in my soul that was trying to surface — and I was struggling desperately to keep it from coming up.

I had had a difficult childhood. My brother died young and my parents were cold and domineering and had a very unhappy marriage. When I was in high school, I was date-raped and became pregnant.

My parents and the doctors involved pressured me to have an abortion. I believed that abortion was murder. But, feeling powerless against my parents, I went through with the operation. In my mind, however, I made a secret pact with God: if God would forgive me, I would promise to never have another abortion as long as I lived.

Later I married a medical student and, while we were both still in university, I accidentally became pregnant. My husband insisted that I have an abortion and threatened to leave me if I did not, because he believed that having a child at that time would ruin his career. Again feeling trapped and powerless, I broke my promise to God and had the abortion.

This event marked the beginning of my depression. I separated from my husband shortly afterward, and I left the Christian church I had been raised in. I began to follow yogic spiritual practices, but when my depression persisted after trying this for a few years, I dropped yoga and became a Buddhist.

It was about a year after this that I had an intense kundalini awakening, and afterward the "black hole" I had so desperately been trying to suppress surfaced. I went into a deep depression.

Like many people, Minnie had had no idea that intensive spiritual practices, rather than helping her escape from reality, would eventually force her to face it. It is my opinion that the day-long meditation and chanting Minnie was doing up until the time of her breakdown had stimulated the spiritual energy/kundalini. Instead of blocking out the past, the awakening transformative energy had the opposite effect, and illuminated her repressed unresolved feelings. Her distress was related to the fact that she had never forgiven herself, or accepted God's forgiveness, for breaking her promise and having the second abortion.

Although Minnie's therapy and treatment may last a long time, she is gradually learning to deal with her traumatic past and let go of her spiritual guilt.

Spiritual Experiences Mislabelled as Psychoses

Fortunately, mislabelling of spiritual experiences as psychotic episodes does not happen as frequently as it once did. Standardized diagnostic criteria for the different types of psychosis now exist, and mental-health professionals who use them correctly are far less likely to create this kind of error.

Still, many people reading this book may have had profound STEs, mystical or psychic experiences that were labelled delusional by doctors or psychologists. I have seen three separate cases in my practice. All three were deeply spiritual women who are now either middle-aged or elderly. Many years ago, each one was hospitalized and labelled as psychotic after having profound mystical experiences. In each case their families and doctors thought the woman had been hallucinating, and the doctors believed her experiences were symptoms of psychosis. Since these women were, in fact, mentally healthy, had a good grasp of reality, and had sound judgment, they learned very quickly, in order to avoid psychiatric hospitalization, not to talk about their mystical experiences.

Although all three women went on to lead productive lives, they had to live with the trauma and stigma of being diagnosed with a psychiatric illness when they had been, in fact, mentally healthy. Further, they were forced to live "in the closet," keeping their rich spiritual lives and their mystical experiences a secret from those around them. They all found living this double life a tremendous burden. How much fuller and richer their lives — and the lives of their families — might have been if their STE experiences had been understood for what they really were.

Fortunately, most people having STEs and STEPs and undergoing long-term spiritual transformation of consciousness do not have to endure spiritual emergencies or psychosis, or being mislabelled as having a psychosis. But most STE experiencers do go through some challenging growth periods. It seems to me that this is a necessary part of the spiritual transformation process. The most pressing reason I had for writing this book was to help people undergoing STEs and other health-care professionals to become more aware of STEs, to know that they are not signs of mental illness, and to learn strategies that can help people integrate these experiences into their daily lives.

For this reason, most of the rest of the book is dedicated to providing more information on the long-term, accelerated process of spiritual transformation of consciousness, and on the techniques that can help us survive the challenging periods. I will also describe healthy balanced strategies to strive to achieve the true goal of spiritual transformation of consciousness and yoga, ongoing God-communion.

17

STRATEGIES FOR
LIVING WITH SPIRITUAL
TRANSFORMATION

MUCH OF MY PROFESSIONAL WORK has been dedicated to helping persons undergoing STEs, observing, researching, and sharing as much information as possible on how one can best survive the process of spiritual transformation of consciousness, and travelling widely to share ideas and learn from diverse spiritual teachers and other STE researchers. As many of the case histories in this book have shown, spiritual transformation of consciousness is a lifelong process of learning, healing, and personal growth, as well as a process of spiritual deepening. The transformation process can be challenging at times. There are, however, many strategies that can help decrease the number and/or intensity of the difficulties. In this chapter we'll look at a number of the strategies that I have found to be the most helpful.

Balance and moderation is a key concept. I believe that, if you want to travel as far as possible on your spiritual journey and make this journey as smooth as possible, you need to take good care of your physical, psychological, and spiritual health — and you need to pay equal attention to each.

Since I think that the spiritual transformative energy is, in fact, a biological-psychological-spiritual energy, it makes sense to me that we need to take care of all the areas in which this energy operates — the body, the mind, and the spirit. It is important not to forsake your body's needs while you are absorbed in the needs of the spirit, or become so intensely involved in emotional and psychological issues that you forget to take care of spiritual ones. My clinical experience has shown me that a balanced approach works best.

Promoting Physical Health Through a Balanced Lifestyle

The importance of promoting physical health is far too often ignored by those on the spiritual path. Some people get the idea that paying attention to the physical body is somehow "unspiritual." However, references to the importance of maintaining a healthy physical body can be found in many spiritual traditions. Several, such as Judaism, have dietary laws that were originally intended to help maintain physical health. Some traditions, such as hatha yoga, are even based on making the physical body a worthy vehicle for self-realization.

Balance and moderation are the best approaches to nurturing physical health. It is essential to have a well-rounded, nutritious diet, drink lots of water, get plenty of sleep, and get regular exercise, while avoiding drugs, tobacco, and other toxins. Physical and medical problems need to be heeded and attended to. As discussed in chapters 15 and 16 on spiritual emergencies and psychoses, ignoring the physical aspects of the spiritual process can lead to an increase in the number and intensity of problems, crises, and even spiritual emergencies. Conversely, clinical experience has shown me that paying attention to physical needs and balanced lifestyle can decrease problems and help stabilize the process of spiritual transformation of consciousness.

The following is a basic list outlining the features of a balanced lifestyle. As a medical doctor, I think a balanced lifestyle is important for everyone, but even more so for persons undergoing the spiritual transformation process.

The Basics of a Balanced Lifestyle

1. Develop and stick to a regular daily routine — have regular rising, bed, and meal times, and set aside several regular periods each week for exercise.

2. Get plenty of sleep and rest, and set aside regular times for daily relaxation and weekly recreation.

3. Do not skip meals. Eat a nutritious, well-balanced diet. You don't need to deprive yourself of occasional treats, but avoid junk foods in general. Eat in moderation.

4. Keep the amount of stress and hectic activity in your life to a minimum.

5. Communicate and share your thoughts and feelings with a supportive person daily, or as often as possible.

6. Keep your sex life moderate, and pay attention to your body if it seems to be telling you to cut down.

7. Spend time in nature; get some natural daylight every day.

8. Avoid toxins and self-destructive habits such as smoking and drugs; keep alcohol consumption to a minimum.

9. Get regular aerobic physical exercise, at least two or three times per week, ideally for at least thirty minutes. Try to go for an outdoor walk every day, for at least twenty minutes.

10. Spend a moderate amount of time each day in meditation, prayer, and/or a spiritual practice.

Since a healthy diet is central to a balanced lifestyle and to this process, I want to discuss it in a little more detail. A great many dietary modifications are promoted today as being necessary for true physical health. Some are even promoted as necessary for spiritual growth. An increasing number of people advocate the vegan diet — one that contains no animal or dairy products of any kind. Others favor lacto-ovo-vegetarianism, which allows eggs and dairy products but no other animal products. Some advocate eating meats, fruits, and vegetables, but no dairy products. Others say you should eat foods only in certain combinations, or only raw foods. One well-known diet promotes eating specific types of foods only at certain times of the day. Another advocates eating a vegetarian diet if you are a certain blood type and a non-vegetarian diet if you are another.

These and other diets and food fads indicate that there is absolutely no consensus among health-food advocates or spiritual teachers around the world about exactly what constitutes a healthful or a "spiritual" diet.

Further, different body types, medical conditions, cultures, food availability, and climates may necessitate different types of diet. Therefore, it seems to me that there are two sensible things to do: avoid any fanatical approach, and eat a nutritious, well-balanced diet. Learn to listen to what your own body tells you about your particular needs. My experience has taught me that different people function better on different diets; no one type of diet is right for everybody.

Find a well-balanced, nutritious diet that makes you feel good. If you feel sluggish after eating, lack energy in general, or are having difficulties with the process of spiritual transformation, try gradually changing your diet and see if this helps. You should be all right while you are experimenting as long as your diet still includes lots of fresh fruit and vegetables, whole grains, and adequate protein, and keeps fats and sugars to a minimum.

My own family provides a good example of how different people thrive on different diets. My former husband, an extremely athletic man who exercised a great deal and who had a different blood type from my own, knew that he felt sluggish and sleepy after meals that contain meat — especially red meat — and that his energy level was much higher when he stuck to a lacto-ovo-vegetarian diet that was high in carbohydrates. I feel bloated and weighed-down when I eat a meal high in carbohydrates, and my energy level and general well-being are much higher when my diet contains lean white meats, poultry, or fish, and lots of fresh vegetables and fruits, with a minimum of starches/carbohydrates. Our son seems to thrive on the same type of diet that I do. With these facts in mind, I would plan our family's meals so that everyone was getting the type of foods they thrived best on.

Grounding Strategies

The term "grounding" conveys the importance of mentally having one's feet on the ground and of remaining centred and connected to the physical world even when one is undergoing profound inner spiritual and psychological experiences. If one is overwhelmed by the inner experiences of spiritual transformation of consciousness, the intensity and frequency of STEs and associated symptoms can usually be decreased, and inner calm can be restored, by using grounding strategies. The following are some grounding strategies that have proven to be most effective:

1. Moderate the length of time spent in your daily meditation. In general, I recommend that sincere spiritual seekers strive to meditate for about forty-five minutes to one hour, every morning and evening. (See chapter 19, "Meditation — the Key to Spiritual Deepening.") If you are meditating longer than this daily, for a grounding effect decrease your meditation to a maximum of one hour twice daily. For a greater grounding effect decrease your daily meditation to a maximum of half an hour twice a day, or even to twenty minutes twice a day.

2. Keep prayers brief. Short prayers several times a day are more grounding than long meditations.

3. Decrease all forms of concentration.

4. Decrease amounts of reading.

5. Decrease stress and the hustle and bustle in your life.

6. Increase your sleep, rest, and relaxation time.

7. Try to follow a fixed daily routine.

8. Keep your eyes open while awake. Avoid closing your eyes and drifting in your imagination. Focus your attention on the world outside of you. Be fully here now!

9. Take several deep slow breaths, with your eyes open. Try moving your arms wide apart at your sides with each inhalation, and bringing them together in front of you with each exhalation, to increase your connection to your physical body.

10. Increase your daily physical exercise. Do some aerobic physical exercise daily, such as walking, jogging, cycling, or swimming. Walking outdoors in a peaceful natural environment is very grounding.

11. Try eating smaller, more frequent meals instead of three large ones per day. Never skip meals or fast during periods of intense STE activity, even if you feel an aversion to food. Eating frequent, light meals is very grounding.

12. Avoid caffeine (be aware that many foods besides coffee and tea contain caffeine — for instance, green tea, chocolate, and cola);

avoid junk foods; avoid excessive and regular intake of refined sugar. (Some people occasionally crave sugar during a STEP or a crisis and, in such cases, a small sweet snack sometimes seems to have a positive effect, but more nutritious foods should form the basis of your diet.)

13. Cut down or cut out alcohol consumption. Limit yourself to an occasional glass of beer or wine. Small amounts of alcohol can be very grounding; unfortunately, this can lead to an experiencer's using alcohol instead of safe techniques that contain no potential harm. Some STE experiencers have become alcoholics by unwisely "medicating" themselves with alcohol.

14. Increase your daily intake of protein, such as yogurt and other dairy products, nuts, legumes, chicken, and/or fish.

15. Cut out use of tobacco and all recreational drugs, including marijuana, if you haven't already done so.

16. Do light manual work, such as cooking, housecleaning, yard work, or gardening. Manual work where your hands touch the earth is particularly grounding.

17. Increase body awareness by rubbing your body or massaging your legs and feet; for an immediate grounding effect take a warm bath or shower, vigorously scrub your body with a cloth, sponge, or loofah, rub your scalp, and wash your hair.

18. Try having a vigorous massage to increase body awareness, but monitor the effect it has on you, as many types of massages may stimulate the flow of prana/life-energy.

19. Set aside time for contact with nature; regularly spend some time outdoors in a park or other quiet natural environment.

20. Be exposed to natural light daily (be careful about UV-ray exposure).

21. Take time off from work if necessary, and spend some time in a peaceful, quiet environment, such as a cottage or a retreat.

22. Spend some time walking or playing outdoors with your pets or young children. Looking after young children or pets will help to pull you out of your thoughts and keep you grounded.

23. Pay careful attention to how your sex life correlates with any difficulties you may be having and moderate your behaviour accordingly. If your sex drive is very high, having sex and orgasm with your partner may release sexual tension and have a grounding effect; however, if your sex drive is low, do not have sex or masturbate.

24. Visualize your energies withdrawing from your head region, moving down to the base of your spine, and staying grounded there.

25. Visualize your energies travelling down your legs to your feet, and focus on feeling your feet firmly planted on the ground; feel your energies linking you to the ground. Stamp your feet on the ground, and rub your hands in the earth, to physically feel your connection to mother earth.

26. Visualize your energies extending down from your body and projecting down to the centre of the earth. Feel your energy "hook" into or connect to the centre of the earth.

27. Find a creative outlet to express your energies, such as art, dance, music, or writing. Observe how these activities affect you and moderate them accordingly.

28. Try to flow with surfacing psychological or spiritual issues rather than trying to resist or struggle against them.

These grounding strategies help slow down or moderate the transformative energy and balance the body, mind, and spirit, and thus tend to lessen the intensity and/or frequency of STEs and the accompanying after-effect symptoms.

Promoting Psychological Health

Psychological health also needs to be nurtured as much as possible in order to facilitate a healthy process of spiritual transformation. Attitudes are important. We should all strive to think positively, practice gratitude daily, and be honest, forgiving, and compassionate. We must also deal with our unresolved psychological issues. I will talk about psycho-spiritual housecleaning in detail in chapter 18.

Good psychological health enables us to function at our highest potential in our day-to-day life and allows the spiritual energy to function smoothly. Part of being psychologically healthy involves nurturing healthy relationships, remaining active in society, and continuing to contribute to society in general and serve others in some small way. Ideally, the insights received during spiritual transformation will be translated in our daily life into healthier attitudes, increased responsibility for our actions and our growth, clarity of thought, and greater self-awareness.

When experiencers become reclusive or totally absorbed in the abstract aspects of their inner experiences, they miss out on the grounding — and humbling — effect that our daily interactions with others have. They can become so absorbed in their experiences that they lose perspective; they miss out on opportunities for "reality testing" and begin to lose contact with the here and now. Although some people may want to enter this purely mental and spiritual realm, most of us need to keep functioning in the physical world. We are not sadhus wandering through the woods, nor hermits or spiritual recluses on Himalayan mountaintops. We are regular people with families, jobs, and responsibilities, and we unfortunately live in a society that does not provide many places of sanctuary or have many roles for the person who is totally absorbed in the inner spiritual realm. I certainly have had to maintain my roles as mother, daughter, physician, wife, psychotherapist, medical teacher, and homeowner while I continued to experience spiritual transformation! And although temporary, brief periods of withdrawal from society to a retreat or to a natural setting may be helpful or even essential at some time during the transformation process, this is very different from becoming reclusive or completely absorbed in abstract spiritual matters.

As we have seen in the chapters dealing with spiritual emergency, when people begin to lose contact with the world around them they can develop serious psychological and emotional problems. And although most people undergoing spiritual transformation of consciousness are not in danger of losing contact with reality, all of us — like everyone who wants to grow — can improve our level of psychological health. This does not mean that we are psychologically "unhealthy"; it means that our insights into ourselves and our unconscious mental and emotional patterns can continue to develop and improve over time. The process of spiritual transformation of consciousness is also the journey to greater psychological self-awareness, to the healing of our wounds, and to self-realization.

The key to psychological and emotional growth is to get in touch with our emotional reactions, thought patterns, habits, unconscious feelings and attitudes, and our shadow or dark side — to discover unresolved psychological issues and unhealthy belief systems — and then to correct, heal, and/or resolve them. And we all have unresolved psychological issues and unhealthy belief patterns that need to be purified. Everyone involved in the process of spiritual transformation eventually discovers this. After many years working in the field it seems increasingly clear to me that what I call psycho-spiritual housecleaning is an absolutely essential — and unavoidable — part of the process of spiritual transformation of consciousness.

Promoting Spiritual Health

Spiritual health is ultimately the most important aspect of spiritual transformation of consciousness. The goal of this process is, after all, to live permanently in a state of deep ongoing mystical union while fully functioning in the world. The mystic in a unitive state lives as a vessel, a Divine instrument, manifesting the Divine will in the world in whatever small way Heaven designs.

Spiritual deepening moves the experiencer away from a life motivated by the desire to satisfy personal wants, toward a life of surrender, motivated by the spiritual desire to be in union with and an instrument of the Divine on the planet. A prayer that many people find helpful during spiritual transformation is derived from the *Grace Prayer* of the Unity Church: I call it "The Mystic's Prayer."

> *The Mystic's Prayer*
> *Please heal in me what needs to be healed,*
> *Reveal to me what needs to be revealed,*
> *Into Your hands I commend my spirit.*
> *Thy will be done, dear Father.*

Many of my STE patients found it very helpful and centring to repeat "The Mystic's Prayer" multiple times. Repeating this prayer helped them anchor their heart and mental focus onto the Divine. At times of stress or anxiety, repeating "The Mystic's Prayer" can help restore spiritual focus, serenity, and inner calm.

Spiritual health can be developed and deepened by a daily practice of prayer, meditation, gratitude, and surrender to the Divine. It can also be deepened through reading the holy books of the major faiths and reading other spiritually uplifting books. As so many spiritual Masters have said over the ages, those on the spiritual path are being propelled by the transformative energy to strive to develop love, honesty, compassion, humility, and detachment. Further, Spirit compels STE experiencers to use the insights gained from spiritual transformation to help others in some way and to make the world a better place.

It is also essential to keep our spirituality in balance and in perspective. It is not always easy to remember this. Once deep mystical experiences begin, many people begin to focus more and more exclusively on spiritual matters and may forget to take care of their physical and psychological health. As we have seen, this can contribute to a wide range of difficulties, crises, and spiritual emergencies. But mystical experiences are so extraordinary and lift us so far above the everyday, mundane world that some people are drawn toward immersing themselves in this aspect of life to the exclusion of all else. They may begin to strive to have more and deeper spiritual experiences. Frequently, they begin to meditate, pray, or engage in some other spiritual activity almost constantly.

When individuals begin to lose interest in their daily activities and to ignore their worldly responsibilities and focus only on the spiritual, it is called "spiritual intoxication" in some traditions. In such cases, people may forget to take care of the needs of the physical body or even deliberately ignore the physical body's needs because they think that the body is the antithesis of all that is spiritual. Some people in this condition may repeatedly perform some spiritual ritual that has come to have deep significance for them. In extreme cases, they may even wish that their spirit could leave the physical body so that they could remain permanently in a mystical state of consciousness. The spiritually intoxicated may feel a lack of connection both to the body and to the physical world. In short, they have lost their grounding.

People in this state may also become completely detached from how others react to them. As they lose this awareness, they may ignore social norms, and begin to exhibit inappropriate or completely bizarre behaviours, such as dancing in the street partially clad or even naked, oblivious to external stimuli.

Brief experiences of spiritual intoxication can be a temporary feature of an intense STEP. However, spiritually intoxicated individuals are in danger of being labelled psychotic if they are not able to integrate their spiritual experiences with everyday reality, and to function appropriately in everyday life again after a short period of time.

Even though most people undergoing STEs do not become spiritually intoxicated, it is still essential to keep spirituality in perspective. My clinical experience has shown me that people in spiritual transformation have far fewer difficulties and crises when they maintain a moderate, balanced approach to all aspects of their life, body, mind, and spirit. Ignoring any one of the three aspects puts us at risk of undermining the process as a whole.

Helping Someone Else in a Spiritual Transformation

You may well be reading this book not because you are going through the process of spiritual transformation of consciousness yourself but because someone you love is. Being the friend, sibling, parent, partner, or spouse of a person who is involved in this process is not always easy. It is particularly difficult when your friend, or whoever, is going through difficult periods, for instance, experiencing crises or emergencies, unblocking traumatic memories and trying to deal with them, or doing intensive psycho-spiritual house-cleaning. If you are sexually involved, tremendous stresses can be added to your relationship by your partner's fluctuating sexual desires. Fluctuating energy levels and mood swings can stress any type of relationship.

Further, you may be confused by your friend's changes in interest. The number of things you have in common may seem to be decreasing, and you may feel left out. You may even feel jealous if you, too, are on the spiritual path and are not having the types of profoundly moving STEs that your partner is. Of course, if you really are dedicated to your own path, you will soon become aware that each of us is moving at our own pace toward a goal that everyone will eventually reach. And, more important, the person who has more STEs and STEPs is not necessarily further on the spiritual path and they may not reach the goal any faster than you or anyone else. Undergoing STEs does not make a person "better," "more spiritual," or more "worthy" than anyone else in God's eyes.

If the person involved in the process of spiritual transformation is your life partner, you may be shocked by changing needs or values. For instance, your partner's need to take time off work may leave you with added financial responsibilities, or a decision to leave a high-paying job for a more spiritually satisfying one may force you to give up a lifestyle you enjoy. Tremendous stresses can be added to your relationship by your partner's fluctuating sexual desires. What's more — until you began to read this book — you may not even have believed that your partner's STEs were "real."

Communication is the key to dealing with your feelings about the changes in your relationship — just as it is in dealing with any type of problem in any type of friendship or relationship. Although admonitions about communicating openly and honestly have become so common that they sound like platitudes, the fact remains that they are true — especially when it comes to dealing with a life partner. You must begin to tell your partner, without acrimony or accusations, how the changes in your relationship are making you feel. You also can encourage your partner to talk about his or her inner experiences and how they are affecting him or her. If you can do this, you can begin to build a new relationship. And you may have to accept the fact that it will almost certainly be a new relationship. Your partner is involved in a process of transformation and is becoming, to varying degrees, a different person. Of course, all of us change to some degree throughout our lifetimes, and everyone who is growing is changing. If you are willing to accept the fact that your partner may be changing more rapidly than is usual, to accept the changes, and to make positive efforts to grow yourself, your partnership will have a good chance of surviving and emerging as a richer, deeper relationship. It is not necessary for you to have profound STEs yourself, but it is necessary for you to remain open and accepting.

The following are a few guidelines that are useful for helping those we care about who are experiencing STEs and spiritual transformation:

1. Support them by listening in a nonjudgmental way when they talk about their STEs and the meaning of those experiences.

2. Validate their experiences. Help them realize that others have had similar STEs. Accept their experiences as real. If you cannot accept them as real in an absolute sense, accept the fact they are real to someone you love, admire, and respect and, because of this, cannot be discounted or treated lightly.

3. Become better informed about STEs and help them do the same. Read — and suggest they read — books about mystical experiences, spiritual emergence, kundalini awakening, NDEs, etc. Do the same with the spiritual books from the major faiths. Suggest that they seek out, talk to, and learn from others who are undergoing similar experiences. Suggest that they go to educational conferences on these subjects. Attend yourself if you desire. However, while you are reading and attending conferences, etc., be discerning. Weigh ideas carefully — and test them against the teachings of the great spiritual teachers — before you accept them as truth.

4. Advise them to go to a qualified doctor for a physical checkup. It is essential to determine that none of the unusual symptoms are actually symptoms of an illness. Reassure them by letting them know that your suggestion doesn't mean you think their experiences are not spiritual; people can have STEs and also have serious medical problems just like anyone else.

5. Focus on the idea that STEs are positive, growth-promoting experiences. Remind them that many authorities think STEs are a normal part of human evolution. Remind them that they are involved in a long-term transformative process; changes do not occur overnight.

6. Respect their need to change their lifestyle temporarily or even permanently. Support their desire to decrease their workload and to decrease concentration. If this impinges on your lifestyle,

try to be accommodating and understanding. Remember that people going through these experiences are not being difficult "on purpose." They are not able to turn their STEs off and on.

7. Give them some time and space to integrate their STEs; understand that some degree of mental preoccupation with inner experiences is common, especially during periods of high STE activity.

8. Realize that there may be confusing changes in their sex drive and erratic fluctuations in their feelings about family relationships. Strain on relationships of all types is very common. Give them time and space to work through these issues.

9. Help them with self-empowerment. Encourage them to get in touch with their inner voice and to listen to the true higher guidance that they receive. Encourage them to pray and/or meditate about any problems. Encourage them to keep a journal and record any dreams, insights, or visions.

10. Encourage them to face their surfacing memories and to do their psycho-spiritual housecleaning. If they are in great emotional distress over surfacing memories, gently encourage them to seek professional support and help.

11. Support their desire to go for psychotherapy or counselling if they feel the need for help. Encourage them in this regard by helping them see their psycho-spiritual housecleaning process as a positive, growth-promoting step.

12. Reinforce their spirituality. Encourage them to find spiritual meaning in the STEs that they are going through. Encourage them to read uplifting spiritual books. If they belong to an organized religion, support their desire to attend meditations, services, masses, other events, or go on a pilgrimage to holy sites.

Regardless of whether it is you or a loved one who is undergoing the challenges that are sometimes associated with STEs and spiritual transformation of consciousness, it is helpful to remember that processes such as the surfacing of repressed memories and the accompanying psychological housecleaning usually come in waves. In other words, although psychological housecleaning is a process that may last a lifetime, the more difficult periods are temporary and they lead to deeper insights and understandings that can continually enrich our relationships and our lives. Further, all human beings have some degree of psychological issues that could benefit from some psycho-spiritual housecleaning, but persons in a spiritual transformation of consciousness process are simply being propelled to deal with their inner issues much more rapidly.

Counselling Patients Having STEs

At this point, I would like to say a few words to the doctors, psychologists, and other counsellors who may be reading this book. In my clinical experience, what people undergoing STEs really want is a professional person who will honour and respect their STE as something sacred, and not automatically label it as psychopathology. STE experiencers want to hear that they are not crazy, and that many other healthy, well-functioning people are having similar experiences.

Beyond this, most of the strategies outlined above can be used by doctors and other counsellors in helping patients who are experiencing STEs and spiritual transformation after-effects. The approach that I have found most useful in helping STE experiencers integrate their experiences and grow from them is based on the following four strategies:

1. *Support.* Listen to the story of the person's inner experiences in a nonjudgmental way.
2. *Validate.* Verify to the person that their experiences are real and not psychotic or hallucinations.
3. *Educate.* Help inform the person about the nature of STEs and spiritual transformation. Give them a non-pathological name for their STE experiences, such as a "mystical vision" or a "Near-Death Experience." Counsel them on balanced lifestyle, with attention to the needs of body, mind, and spirit.
4. *Facilitate.* Promote the psycho-spiritual housecleaning process by using standard and transpersonal psychotherapeutic techniques.

I sincerely hope that as more doctors, counsellors, and therapists around the world become familiar and experienced with helping people undergoing STEs and spiritual transformation of consciousness, STE experiencers will stop being mislabelled, and finally find the supportive professional help and guidance that they truly deserve.

18

PSYCHO-SPIRITUAL
HOUSECLEANING

RICHARD BUCKE, TEILHARD DE CHARDIN, and Gopi Krishna all believed that the eventual goal of spiritual transformation was the evolutionary development of a new, spiritually illuminated level of human consciousness. Ancient yogic theory, as put forward by Paramahansa Yogananda and other yogic teachers, also contends that humanity as a race is slowly evolving through successive stages, or "Yugas," toward a time when the bulk of humanity will live in a higher, more spiritual state of consciousness. The awakening of the spiritual energy/kundalini mechanism, combined with the spiritual effort of the aspirant, accelerates this evolution of consciousness. Before reaching this state of illumination, the transformative energy remodels and purifies the individual's psyche. Gopi Krishna once wrote that the future illuminati would be "chastened and purified by the fire of kundalini." I think this is a powerful description of what goes on during the process of psycho-spiritual housecleaning.

Samskaras and Psycho-Spiritual Blocks

To understand this from the yogic perspective, let's look at the concept of samskaras. Samskaras are mentioned in both the yogic and Buddhist traditions. Georg Feuerstein translates the word "samskaras" as "imprints," "tendencies," or "activators." He says they are not just marks or traces of our past actions but dynamic forces in our mental processes. He adds that one form of samskara is thought to generate the thought processes that reinforce ego-identity and propel us away from God-realization. Samskaras can also be thought of more simply as emotional imprints or scars and habits, left on our unconscious mind by our experiences and actions, from this lifetime and past lifetimes, related to our past karma.

For our purposes here, however, what is important is that in yogic and Buddhist traditions samskaras are thought to form impediments and blocks to the flow of prana and kundalini in our astral body. In some ancient texts they are metaphorically depicted as blocks held on the lotus petals at the chakras. In Tibetan Buddhism, they are sometimes described as knots that block the flow of the vital winds through the body.

Paramahansa Yogananda defines samskaras (also known as "sanskaras") as unconscious habits, urges, and tendencies — the impressions left in the conscious and subconscious mind by past thoughts and actions, and which create a strong inner urge for repetition. Yogananda points out that one can have both good samskaras and negative samskaras — thus the importance of striving to develop positive spiritual habits!

In Western interpretations, samskaras are sometimes characterized as our unconscious mental and emotional tendencies that are caused by un-resolved psychological or spiritual issues. In this sense, I think negative samskaras do indeed exist and that they may well represent impediments to the transformative energy as it goes about the business of remodelling and purifying consciousness.

Eventually, as our souls evolve, the psycho-spiritual blocks held in our unconscious, or held as samskaras on our astral body chakras, must be and are going to be removed and healed — whether we like it or not. I think this is part of what Gopi Krishna meant when he talked about the purifying and chastening effect of kundalini. I believe that the energies that course through the astral and physical bodies after a spiritual energy/kundalini awakening encounter these blocks. Because the blocks need to be cleared away, the memory of the original traumatic event and any unresolved emotions rise from the unconscious to the surface of our consciousness so that we can resolve them. As the samskaras surface we experience both the memory and the associated feelings. The inner drive to remove these blocks can be so strong that we may even unconsciously attract situations to our lives that force us to face and deal with the difficult issues associated with the blocks. We then have the opportunity for soul learning, either to repeat the past emotional habit, or to learn our soul's psycho-spiritual lesson, and break free from the habit, tendency, or wounding.

Sometimes when I am making presentations I use the metaphorical image of lotus flowers at the chakras to illustrate how I think this spiritual energy/ kundalini-driven cleansing process works. It is believed that our samskaras are held on the petals of our lower chakras. After a spiritual energy/kundalini awakening, as the energy rises to a chakra, it strives to open it, uncurling and opening the petals of the lotus bud. When a samskara (unconscious block) is encountered, the energy strives to cleanse it from the petal, so that the petal can unfurl and the lotus flower can open further. When the kundalini meets the block and begins to loosen it from the petal, it causes the associated memories and feelings to surface from the unconscious into conscious awareness, so that the related spiritual issues can be faced, the lessons learned, and the issues healed. This kundalini-driven cleansing is ongoing; it continues through the process of spiritual transformation until, ultimately (over many lifetimes), all our chakras are cleansed and our unconscious issues cleared. Our consciousness becomes like a vast, clear, and still ocean.

Our individual psyches and prana are gradually being cleansed and freed of impediments as we progress in the spiritual journey. I believe this is one reason why all of us must go through some degree of suffering in our lifetimes. This is the chastening effect of kundalini: suffering for the purpose of learning moral and spiritual lessons. When the psycho-spiritual lesson is learned by the soul, the suffering ends.

When some people suffer in life, they think that they are being punished by God for their transgressions. I do not believe an all-loving God punishes people to hurt them. But I do believe the purpose of our life journey is to learn spiritual lessons and grow — and we often must feel pain in order to learn and grow. Some yogic traditions contend that suffering can be the prod that turns people deeply toward God. God is not trying to hurt us. But it may well be that God, like an incredibly wise, loving, and patient parent, has structured the world in a way that allows us to learn and grow from the consequences of our mistakes.

When we begin to "know the self," we don't always like what we see. Taking personal responsibility or discovering — and then healing — the buried guilt we feel over things we have done and the anger and resentment we feel over things that have been done to us is not an easy process. Unblocking psycho-spiritual issues and learning our lessons is often very painful, regardless of whether the issue comes from this lifetime or a previous one. In my experience, real healing of deep emotional wounds and habits can only be done by turning our wounds over to God, by surrendering the feelings to the Higher Power and asking for help. Experiencing inner healing and learning spiritual lessons brings great joy and psychological release, develops inner strength and inner peace, and ultimately deepens our faith in the love and healing power of the Divine.

Spontaneous Surfacing of Memories

When the process of spiritual transformation accelerates, we sometimes begin to learn our spiritual lessons a little more quickly than we expect. As was discussed in the chapters on spiritual emergency, unresolved psychological issues and repressed traumatic memories often begin to surface spontaneously, intensely, and rapidly for people undergoing STEs.

Many other people involved in this field, including Dr. Bonnie Greenwell, have noticed this phenomenon. NDE researchers such as Dr. Kenneth Ring, Dr. Bruce Greyson, and Barbara Harris Whitfield, author of *Full Circle: The Near-Death Experience and Beyond*, have collected data showing that a high percentage of NDE experiencers unblock memories of childhood abuse. Based on this data, they speculate that early sufferers of abuse could have a higher predisposition for NDE and spiritual energy/kundalini awakening than the general population. I think, however, they may eventually discover that their data actually indicates that people who have NDEs — like people who have all types of STEs — are simply more likely to unblock repressed memories of childhood trauma and were not necessarily more frequently abused.

Regardless, the spontaneous unblocking of repressed memories seems to arise in a variety of ways. They sometimes burst into a person's conscious mind with no warning and without any obvious trigger. At other times they are triggered by a particular event or experience that relates in some way to the repressed memory. Sometimes the memories surface after we have offered a sincere prayer for help in understanding a problem that is troubling us. This happened to a woman in her midthirties whom I'll call Sally.

> I had been undergoing STEs for about four years when I came home from working out at the health club one afternoon and found that my husband was not home. Instead of accepting this as a normal occurrence, I suddenly began to get very upset and became overwhelmed by the suspicion that my husband was having an affair. I frantically began to look around the house for evidence of an affair, checking beside the phone for any scraps of paper that might reveal a number or some other incriminating evidence.
>
> Suddenly I stopped myself; I realized that I was behaving ridiculously. My husband had never done anything to give me reason to believe he was having an affair. I sat down and said a prayer asking God to help me understand why I was having such negative suspicions about my husband. Without warning, a memory that I had suppressed for years unblocked and flooded into my consciousness. I vividly recalled an instance ten years earlier in which I had been unfaithful to my steady boyfriend. Although I had managed to block the memory of the event, I realized I still felt a great deal of guilt about my actions that I had never resolved. It also became immediately clear to me that, because the issue was unresolved, I was projecting my own infidelity onto my husband.
>
> After meditating and praying on the matter for several days, I was finally able to accept God's forgiveness and to forgive myself for my actions. Afterward, my groundless suspicions about my husband's possible infidelity disappeared.

Blocked memories of unresolved psychological issues do not always float up as easily or as completely into consciousness as this one of Sally's did. Partial memories sometimes surface during the daytime as brief glimpses or "flashbacks," and a good deal of energy and effort is required before the pieces can all be pulled into place. Sometimes the flashes are not at first recognized as memories at all; until a moment of recognition occurs, they are thought to be the product of an overactive imagination. In some cases, blocked memories begin to surface — either completely or in bits and pieces — in vivid dreams or recurrent nightmares.

Blocked memories are sometimes held not only in our minds but also in our physical bodies. These are sometimes referred to as "body memories." They may begin to surface in the form of unusual sensations, sensitivities, or pains in different areas of the body — often an area that was traumatized during the original event. Body therapy on that specific region of the body may also trigger these body memories. A thirty-year-old patient of mine whom I'll call Betty provides a classic example of this.

> I have always been a devoutly spiritual woman. I have prayed and meditated daily since my teens. At the age of twelve or thirteen, I had been sexually abused by my older sister's husband. I knew the abuse had occurred but I had no memory of what had actually happened and held no conscious anger toward my brother-in-law.
>
> When I came to see Dr. Kason, I was complaining of recurrent symptoms, including outbreaks of herpes around my mouth, unpleasant gagging sensations, and sensations of pressure in my lower abdomen and pelvis.
>
> While doing a guided meditation with Dr. Kason, I unblocked the memory of my abuse. I recalled being vaginally raped and being forced to have oral sex on another occasion. During the meditation, my abdominal and pelvic pressures flared when I remembered the vaginal rape, and my gagging sensations became vivid as I recalled the oral assault. I also remembered that I first developed herpes soon after the oral assault.

Soon after Betty unblocked the full memory of her abuse, the physical symptoms of pressure and gagging rapidly decreased, and her herpes outbreaks became far less frequent. Betty was also able to begin the process of psychological healing through releasing and resolving her blocked rage with the help of prayer, meditation, and psychotherapy. As this healing occurred, Betty's process of spiritual transformation accelerated.

When either flashes of memories or complete memories begin to surface, they are sometimes accompanied by anxiety or other distressing emotions. Because these emotions are unpleasant or even frightening, people sometimes struggle to force the memory back down. Often they are not consciously aware that they are doing this and are puzzled by seemingly inexplicable attacks of anxiety, panic, rage, or depression. In some cases, the strong negative emotions that were associated with the original event are the feelings that surface along with the memories, and they, too, may cause the experiencer to struggle unconsciously to suppress the memory again. A good example of this was Beth, whose story of childhood sexual abuse was told in chapter 16. Beth felt a great deal of low-level anxiety most of the time. Each time she came close to unblocking the memory of her abuse, she felt increased anxiety, fear, and attacks of panic, and she tried to push the memories back down. She was even diagnosed by another doctor as suffering from panic attacks. Eventually she reached the point where she was ready to deal with the memories, and she allowed them to surface. With psychotherapeutic help she was then able to deal with the memories and begin the process of healing. Her "panic attacks" decreased dramatically and eventually stopped completely.

Once a memory surfaces, it must be dealt with and resolved. If it is not it will continue to cause psychological stress. Using the samskara analogy, we would say it continues to be a block to the flow of the transformative energy.

The resolution of surfacing issues is often accomplished only with a good deal of effort. The memories would never have been repressed originally if we had been able to deal effectively with and resolve the event and the associated emotions when they first occurred. For this and other reasons, many people undergoing the process of transformation decide to seek out counselling or to begin psychotherapy when memories begin to unblock.

Unfortunately, a surprising number of people are reluctant to ask for this kind of help. Even in this day and age, some people still think a stigma is attached to going for psychological help or to undergoing psychotherapy. They think it means something is "wrong" with them. Of course, nothing could be further from the truth. Seeking professional help is a sign that you are actively and enthusiastically involved in the growth process. Often it is the person who is the most "together" who seeks professional help first.

Whether you resolve traumatic memories alone or with a therapist, virtually all psychologists agree that you have to face the trauma and fully unblock the memory before you can begin to acknowledge, express, and eventually let go of the emotions associated with the original event. Only then can the psychological scars be healed — and the blocks be cleared away.

Strategies to Help Unblock Memories

If you feel that memories are trying to surface but are having difficulty making their way completely into your conscious mind, there are a number of techniques that can help. Before doing these or any other techniques, I recommend that you get under the care of a qualified psychotherapist or counsellor who can assist you in dealing with any memories that may surface.

1. First, make a conscious decision that you want the memories to surface and that, as part of your spiritual growth, you are willing to face any painful issues they bring up.

2. Pray to the Divine for help in unblocking the memories that you are ready for and that you need to face at this time to further your spiritual growth. Repeat this prayer occasionally throughout the day and again before falling asleep at night. You may receive help in flashes of intuition that occur during or right after a prayer. You may be led, for instance, to reread a passage from a certain book and, when you do, find it provides new, relevant insight.

3. Whenever you feel a memory begin to surface, focus on it. Don't push it away. If possible, take some time then and there to focus on the memory fragment and let it, and the associated emotions,

flow into your consciousness. Try to reexperience the memory as fully as possible.

4. Write down dreams that have an unusual impact, that are recurrent, or that are associated with childhood.

5. Have some bodywork done — massage, shiatsu, or acupuncture, etc. Enter a meditative state during the process and pray to unblock memories that are now necessary for your spiritual growth.

6. Visualize and focus on your inner child. See her or him as clearly as you can — your inner child often looks as you did in the full bloom of childhood. Alternatively, your inner child's appearance may bear clues as to your unresolved issues. Embrace your inner child with love. Ask if there are any memories that are causing pain or blocking his or her full expression in your daily life. Ask for help in bringing up these memories so that your inner child can finally be healed and free.

7. Meditate and visualize your heart chakra. Focus on any pain or area of darkness you feel or see in this area. Then, visualize light rising gently up from the base of your spine — or pouring down on you from above — and illuminating the darkness at your heart chakra. See the light flushing away at the dark areas, lifting the dark spots up, bringing them up to your conscious mind, and then flushing them away. Then focus on any images or memories that come to your mind. Some people like to visualize the divine power as a liquid light that flushes the spots of darkness out through the front of the heart chakra.

If, after trying these strategies, you feel you have memories that still will not surface but that you feel ready to face, do not force yourself! Wait a few months. There may be a good reason why these memories are staying repressed at this time.

Whenever a memory does surface, concentrate on it, and try to reexperience the incident in your mind. Try to expand upon the memory, and recall as many details about the event and surrounding circumstances as possible. Try to remember how you felt during and after the incident. Allow yourself to feel the emotions related to the incident. Give yourself permission to feel angry, enraged, sad, hurt, jealous, betrayed, or guilty, or to experience any other emotion you might be holding about the event. Then, in time, you can work toward forgiving yourself and/or the others involved and, finally, releasing the hold this event has had on you.

After repressed memories begin to surface, psychotherapy and a number of psychotherapeutic techniques can facilitate the healing of the painful emotions and scars left from earlier traumatic events. I have also found a number of techniques and strategies you can use to help resolve some of the wounds and issues that arise. However, many people find they need psychotherapeutic help in dealing with surfacing memories at some point in their spiritual journey — especially when the memories are surfacing very rapidly or are related to traumatic incidents such as violence or childhood sexual abuse. If the memories become overwhelming or if you simply decide you'd like to have some help dealing with them, don't hesitate to get it. In the meantime you may find the following self-help strategies helpful.

Dealing with Unblocking Traumatic Memories

1. *Keep a daily journal.* Set aside some time each day to write your insights, thoughts, and feelings in your journal. Include any upsetting incidents that may have occurred, or traumatic memories that may have surfaced since the last time you wrote. Make note of your reflections on these and any other memories or psychological issues you are working with, and record insights gained during your meditations. Also write down your dreams, especially those that recur, seem to have a message, provoke strong emotions, or are particularly vivid or "real." Sometimes the dream before waking is particularly significant.

   People who regularly keep a journal find that writing down thoughts, feelings, dreams, and reflections often helps clarify them and put them into perspective. Reflecting back on your journal entries can also help you gain insights and speed the process of resolving psychological issues.

2. *Use inner dialogue.* Sit in a quiet place where you will not be disturbed for a while. Close your eyes, relax, and focus your mind on a memory that has come unblocked. Allow yourself to re-experience some of the emotions involved in the original event; try to visualize the face of the person involved, or simply "imagine" that the person is sitting in front of you. Begin an inner dialogue with that person. If the person is someone who hurt you, tell them how what they said or did affected you, how it made you feel, and how it still hurts or affects you. Allow yourself to express the emotions you have about the original incident and its consequences. Don't be afraid to express all of the emotions — anger, rage, resentment, sorrow — you have felt or may have been holding back over the years. And don't be surprised if you actually reexperience some of these emotions quite strongly. When you have finished expressing your feelings, ask the other person why they did what they did. Then wait, and listen for the reply. Often this reply will give you a new insight and bring you to a new level of understanding regarding the incident. Respond to the reply, and continue this inner mental dialogue with the other person as long as you feel you need to and until you feel you have come to a level of understanding that allows you to put the incident more to rest and let go of some or all of the anger and pain. You can repeat this technique as often as you like.

If the memory you have unblocked is of you hurting someone, follow the same process but explain your reasons for doing what you did, apologize, and ask for forgiveness. Give the person a chance to respond, listen, and then continue with the inner dialogue until you feel it has reached a conclusion. Pray to be forgiven for your past hurtful action. Finally, pray for help to forgive yourself for having hurt the other person.

When using this technique, pray and meditate for help in healing the anger, pain, and/or guilt associated with the original incident or the aftermath — and for help in learning your spiritual lessons from this experience. "Ricky," one of my psychotherapy patients, used inner dialogue to resolve her anger. Ricky felt deeply hurt by her now deceased mother.

> On the day before I was to be married, my mother told my fiancé that he should consider putting off the marriage, because I would be such a difficult person to be married to. After this, I always felt that my mother disapproved of my husband and that my mother felt I was "bad" and unworthy of a good marriage.
>
> When I came for help to Dr. Kason, she suggested I try using the "inner dialogue" technique. I visualized my mother's face, and I told the image of my mother how terribly she had hurt me with the remarks she made before my wedding. When I asked mother why she had said such a thing, mother's image replied that she had always felt misunderstood in her own marriage to my father, as he had often been cold and insensitive, in contrast to her emotional sensitivity. My mother's image seemed to go on to tell me that she thought I was a very special, gifted person with deep emotional sensitivity. Mother seemed to explain that she had wanted to protect me from the kind of unhappy marriage she had had. Mother admitted that she had probably projected her own feelings about her own husband onto my prospective husband.

This answer that came in the inner dialogue session so surprised and moved Ricky that she began to cry, and was able to resolve much of her anger with her mother about the event. Ricky also began to come to a deeper realization of how much her mother had cared for her.

3. *Surrender your problems to the Divine.* Remember that the healing power of the Divine is far greater than the problems related to the memory — no matter how immense they may seem. Take a moment to reflect on the stupendous power that drives the

universe, how it fires the infernos of the sun and other stars and breathes life into the amazingly diverse plants and animals that populate our planet. Reflecting on this often helps us realize that the power of the Divine is immensely and unimaginably greater than the power any problem in our lives might have. With this in mind, surrender your problem to the Divine and pray for healing and guidance in resolving it. One image that I find helpful is that of putting your problems "at the feet of the Master."

4. *Focus on learning the spiritual lesson.* Instead of focusing your mental energies exclusively on your pain and suffering and on what other persons did to hurt you, focus your energy on discovering the spiritual lessons that you can learn from this experience. Remind yourself that life's hardships provide opportunities for learning and growth. Actively look for the lessons inherent in the problem you are facing. Pray, contemplate, and meditate and ask for help in discovering what your lessons are. Perhaps you made some errors, or poor choices. Or, perhaps your lesson is to work through your emotional reactions, strive for emotional equipoise, and forgive someone who mistreated you or others. Once you truly perceive and process your spiritual lesson, the trauma's negative impact will lessen in this light.

5. *Read inspirational and other self-help books.* Reading about others who have overcome traumas similar to the ones you have suffered can be a great help. Ask someone in the field to recommend a book or go through the self-help section of your library or bookstore and look for one or two books that seem to present a balanced view. Reading generally inspirational books can also be a big help. A few of the authors that I recommend and that represent a wide range of views include Augustine "Og" Mandino, Leo Buscaglia, Marion Woodman, John Bradshaw, Emmet Fox, Scott Peck, and Paramahansa Yogananda. And, of course, the holy books of the major faiths can provide great inspiration. The Psalms of the Old Testament have often provided me with tremendous comfort.

6. *Practise gratitude.* The old adage is that a half a cup of water looks half empty to the pessimist and half full to the optimist! Be a

grateful optimist. Rather than focusing on things you dislike or desire, practice expressing gratitude to the Divine for things you do have. During challenging periods, I recommend daily gratitude journaling — writing down five to ten things for which you are grateful every single day. The days it is difficult to feel grateful are probably the most important days to practise gratitude.

7. *Keep your problems in perspective.* Whenever you are feeling overwhelmed by your surfacing memories and problems, try to reestablish a realistic perspective. Reflect briefly on the terrible suffering and horrendous conditions other people have had to endure, such as war, torture, starvation, discrimination, unjust imprisonment, and concentration camps. Sometimes thinking of the hardships others are facing helps us see that our problems are far from being the worst in the universe and that we are more fortunate than many others.

8. *Talk to friends about your traumas.* The psychological burden of past trauma can be greatly lessened by telling a deeply trusted friend or relative about the traumatic memories you have unblocked. Those who know you and really care about you can give tremendous support and can often provide you with new and deeper insights. Sharing the burden does help speed the healing. In time, you may even be able to laugh with your confidante about yourself or certain aspects of your memories — and laughter, being such a powerful healer, can speed your emotional recovery even more.

9. *Join a support group.* Support groups are powerful because they allow you to share your experiences with people who can empathize and understand because they have gone through the same trauma themselves. Listening to these people can remove your sense of isolation and help you learn the strategies they have used for healing and growth.

Learning from Past-Life Memories

As discussed in chapter 16, I have found in my work that many people undergoing spiritual transformation begin to spontaneously unblock traumatic memories from what appear to be past lives. You might be having similar experiences and be concerned about them because some people think such things are "strange" or "crazy." But let me reassure you that many highly intelligent, mentally healthy people have described this phenomenon to me, and I, along with many other psychotherapists, am convinced that it is real. I have even experienced glimpses of past-life memories myself. The ones that have come to me have all been related to people I have known in this lifetime. The scenarios in the past-life memories, whether symbolic or actual, usually helped me understand at a deeper level some of the dynamics and difficult issues within my relationships. I have found the apparent past-life memories, when they occur, to be very insightful, aiding my understanding of complex interpersonal relationships.

During the process of my own spiritual journey, I have become very comfortable with the concept of reincarnation and have come to believe that we return to life on this plane again and again in order to learn spiritual lessons. People who find this concept difficult to accept should keep in mind the fact that Hindus, Buddhists, Indigenous Peoples, and members of a number of other religions accept the reality of reincarnation as a matter of course — and these people make up a huge percentage of the world's population. Jewish Kabbalistic teachings accept reincarnation, and some historians believe certain early Christians did too. Further, a 1981 Gallup poll showed that nearly a quarter of all Americans believed in reincarnation, and a more recent one showed that almost a third of all Canadians did, too.

Still, many people cannot accept the concept of reincarnation and, consequently, the reality of past-life memories. Some psychologists believe that what seem to be past-life memories are in reality historical images of others' lives that come from tapping into what Jung called the collective unconscious. Yet another theory is that apparent past-life memories are metaphors, symbolic images that are meant to make us aware of psychological or spiritual issues. According to this interpretation, apparent past-life memories can be seen as symbolic messages from our unconscious to our conscious minds, like many of the images in dreams.

Regardless, the fact remains that a great many people unblock traumatic memories from what they perceive to be or suspect might be past lives during the process of spiritual transformation. Often the memories are traumatic, and the psychological issues associated with them need to be dealt with and healed just as with other unblocked traumatic memories.

In my work as a psychotherapist, I have noticed that there are several similarities between unblocking traumatic past-life memories and unblocking ones from this life. First, the experiencers are usually ready, at some level, to face the memory — even if they are not consciously aware of it. Second, unblocking past-life memories often has the same — if sometimes less intense — impact on the experiencer as unblocking present-life memories does. Third, and most important, experiencers can gain great insight and undergo tremendous psychological healing when they try to work with the memory, reexperience the event, release the emotions associated with it, heal the unresolved emotions, and learn the spiritual lessons related to it.

Sometimes past-life memories that surface spontaneously actually warn us, or help us understand another person's behaviour toward us. It may seem as if the experiencer and the individuals involved in the memory are actually repeating the same type of unhealthy interaction that they had in a past life. When this awareness surfaces in a person in spiritual transformation, it often prompts them to react differently to the situation this time, or even to walk away from it in peace. This was true for Tom, a forty-five-year-old business consultant.

Tom had a Near-Death Experience when he fell into a severe drinking relapse during his recovery from alcoholism. After the NDE, Tom fully embraced his recovery, went into a spiritually based AA treatment program, and began intensive personal psychotherapy. He also found he now had ongoing kundalini symptoms, energy rushes up the spine, heat experiences, and light experiences. He underwent a profound spiritual transformation of his personality.

Tom had many unresolved issues relating to a relationship that had ended a year earlier. He was unhappy being single, and he longed to reconcile with his former girlfriend, Alice. Alice blamed Tom and his alcoholism for ruining her aspiration to achieve a high-income marriage. She was angry at his efforts to recover from his alcoholism, and abruptly ended the relationship when he insisted that he could no longer pretend there was no problem and drink alcohol with her at dinner parties. She felt humiliated and said that Tom made her look bad by his admission that he was an alcoholic. Alice expressed rage at how he had not lived up to her standards and expectations, how he did not help her fulfill her dreams. Tom felt profoundly guilty about this whole situation.

Tom had started praying to the Divine to help him heal this situation with Alice. About four months after the NDE, Tom started to get glimpses of what seemed to be a past life, coming to him in his meditations, in dreams, and then, finally, in his waking state. Within ten days the pieces of the past-life memory came together. The memory showed Tom that he had been an artist living in the 1700s, supported by a patron, a wealthy married woman — who seemed similar to Alice. An attraction and a clandestine affair developed between the two. The woman had plans for them to run away to Europe together and start a new life with her parents' wealth.

The memory went on to show that Tom had also been married, to another woman who lived in a town distant from the patron. Tom remembered a lifelong friend coming to see him at the patron's studio, telling him to come home, that his wife had had a baby and needed his help and support. In the memory, Tom realized his responsibility to his wife and decided to return home. His patron became enraged. She had no compassion for Tom's need to return home to care for his wife and child. She raged at him for shattering her dream of their happy life together in Europe. She complained that his leaving would humiliate her in her social circle. He pleaded for understanding, but she threw him out.

With the insights gained from the memory, Tom was finally able to make sense of his unresolved feelings about

Alice. He believed he had been so attracted to her because he unconsciously felt he "owed her something" from their past life together. He also saw that her behaviour toward him in both lifetimes was very similar. Alice was not supportive or understanding, and she was very angry when he did not fulfill her dreams and expectations. He also understood Alice's intense anger toward him — she had the anger of two lifetimes inside her.

With this understanding and with the help of prayer and psychotherapy, Tom was finally able to let go of his guilt over the ending of this relationship. Tom now realized that Alice would not be a healthy life partner for him, and that he needed a partner who would be supportive of his path of healing. Some time later, Tom met a woman who was also on a path of recovery, with whom he had a stable and happy relationship.

Tom's story shows how past-life memories usually relate to problems that are causing a great deal of pain and distress in this life. In cases like this, it is helpful to focus on learning the spiritual lessons involved. This is particularly true when the apparent past-life memories involve people with whom you are currently having emotional difficulties. As we saw in the story of Tom, the unblocking of the past-life memory often yields new insights and a new perspective on the problems you are struggling to understand.

In my clinical experience I have found that many of the lessons associated with past-life memories seem to be connected to our interpersonal relationships. Some people believe the reasons for this lie in the fact that a certain degree of continuity exists from life to life and that we encounter some individuals again and again. If this is the case, it is plausible that deep unconscious memories concerning an individual and an associated traumatic event might well affect the way we relate to that person in this life — and might also be a factor in some dysfunctional relationships. I have come across a number of people who, after unblocking and dealing with traumatic past-life memories, were better able to understand the unconscious dynamics of a particular relationship and then either improve the relationship or find the strength to leave it.

One of the best ways to discover the unconscious dynamics is to compare the emotional patterns of the past-life situation to those in your present life. Try to discover the parallels between the two situations. The common denominator between the two will often provide a powerful clue to exactly what the spiritual lesson is. This was true for "Olivia," a university professor and STE experiencer who started unblocking past-life memories relating to her current marital problems.

> My husband Jake and I were having serious marriage problems. Jake had already left me twice, and I let him return to our marriage because I loved him, and because we had two small children. Further, I am very religious, and I considered marriage to be a lifelong commitment.
>
> After a particularly difficult argument with my husband, I sat in meditation and intense prayer, asking God to help me, to guide me. To my surprise I immediately slipped into a vivid visionary experience, where I both saw and felt myself to be a woman in another lifetime, in India, and married to Jake, as now. Jake abandoned me in that past lifetime too, and left me alone with several small children. In that time and culture it was very shameful for a woman to have been abandoned by her husband. I reexperienced the intense pain and shame I endured, plus the extreme financial hardship I and our children suffered for the rest of that life.
>
> After this past-life memory came to me, my anger toward my husband Jake increased at first. I was enraged that he seemed to be repeating the pattern of abandonment of me and our children. I prayed deeply for God to help me get clarity, to show me the right attitude. To my surprise I once again slipped into a deep visionary experience. This time I again saw and reexperienced what seemed to be another past life long ago, when I was a beautiful young woman in an Arab's harem of many wives. My current husband Jake was a young handsome

tribesman in that lifetime. Although I was forbidden to have contact with any men other than my Arab husband, in that past life Jake and I fell in love and had a brief illicit affair. To my horror, in this apparent past-life memory our affair was discovered with disastrous consequences. Jake of the past life was sentenced to death as punishment, and he was beheaded in front of me. Within the harem I was cast down to the lowest servant role, but I was not killed. I reexperienced powerful emotions; my intense horror, shame, and remorse, plus tremendous guilt that I had been allowed to live, while the man I loved had been brutally executed.

After this second past-life memory came to me, my attitude toward Jake changed dramatically. I stopped constantly feeling that I was an innocent victim in our current marriage difficulties. I felt that Jake and I were souls who had loved each other over many lifetimes, but our relationship had always had traumatic endings.

Jake and I separated for the last time a few months later. After one year of intense grieving, I began therapy with Dr. Kason. With much reflection, prayer, and meditation, I began to realize that in order for me to learn my soul lessons from my marital breakdown, I needed to focus on me and my own shortcomings, rather than continually focusing on Jake and blaming him for his shortcomings. With this shift in focus, I rapidly learned what my soul lesson was, which was to forgive Jake for being imperfect. After all, I am imperfect too. This realization turned the corner in my healing process.

Olivia's story is interesting because it shows how — in a therapeutic sense — it makes little difference whether a perceived past-life memory was a real event from a past life or a symbolic message from the unconscious. In either case, the issue was the same; emotional healing, and learning the psycho-spiritual lesson for your soul.

When dealing with apparent past-life memories, you might want to consider the possibility of a karmic link between yourself and a person who has hurt you. It may be that this person's actions in this life are his or her response to your actions in a past life. It may even be that this cycle of action and reaction between the two of you has been repeated many times. If this is so, the realization may give you greater insight into exactly what your role in the situation is, and, with prayer and meditation, you may learn how you can resolve the karmic link, forgive and move on, or perhaps even restore harmony and balance between yourself and the other person.

In general, I believe that examining and reflecting on the psychological and spiritual issues related to what seem to be past-life memories has tremendous potential for promoting growth. When the memory surfaces, don't waste time and energy debating the reality of reincarnation. Whether these memories are actually from previous incarnations or are symbolic representations of psychological issues surfacing from your unconscious, they are making you aware of valuable psychological and spiritual lessons. These memories — or powerful images, if you will — can be used as tools to assist in your psychological and spiritual growth.

However, it should be kept in mind that these images are often extremely powerful. Occasionally images involving abuse or injustice are so powerful and seem so real that experiencers have to be reminded to keep the memory in perspective. Treating the person who apparently carried out an injustice in a past life as if he or she had actually done it in this life, or retaliating against or acting out in anger toward him or her, would be completely inappropriate. It would also ruin the potential for forgiveness, reconciliation, healing, and spiritual growth that the unblocking of past-life memories brings.

Resolution, Transcendence, and Forgiveness

In order to achieve resolution, any unfinished business relating to current life events and unblocked traumatic memory needs to be dealt with. This may be done in a number of ways. Sometimes it can all be resolved in therapy. Other times people find they need to speak face-to-face with the person involved in the original incident, either to express their feelings or to ask the person why they did what they did. Other times people may need to ask another for forgiveness for their own actions, and make efforts to make amends. Other people, for instance those who were abused as children, may feel they need to press criminal charges. Of course, the means of resolving unfinished business in an appropriate way are as varied and individual as the people and situations involved. Once unfinished business is resolved, the next step is to transcend the experience.

To me, transcendence means rising above the negativity of the experience and using the energy generated by the trauma for a positive purpose. For instance, the anger and outrage you feel about a trauma you suffered might motivate you and give you the energy to use what you've learned from the experience in a positive way. You might decide to start a support group in your area or begin volunteering at a local crisis centre. You might speak at churches or schools about your experiences in order to help others. You might write an article about avoiding or dealing with the type of trauma you suffered. Some people write a book about their experience and healing in order to help others. Many find that this is a worthwhile, therapeutic, and cathartic process even if the book is never published. Regardless of the specific action you decide to take, the important element in transcendence is to rise above the negative emotions and to channel your activated emotional energy — along with what you have learned — into something positive and constructive.

Forgiveness is the final step in healing psychological traumas, whether we must forgive ourselves, forgive others, or both. Many people try to forgive others too soon, before they have even begun to come to terms with their own feelings. If so, they later discover that they haven't forgiven the person at all, and wonder why they failed to do so.

Pauline, a twenty-seven-year-old singer, prematurely tried to forgive her mother.

> Around age fifteen, while sleeping over at my older sister's apartment in another town, I was raped by my sister's live-in boyfriend. I was horrified, and afraid to tell anybody. Finally, a few days later I told my mom. My mom told me not to tell anybody else, and this rape was never acknowledged by my family. Four years later, my sister

married the boyfriend. When I refused to dance with the groom at the reception, my father insisted to know why, so I finally told my dad the story of the rape. My father was furious that I had never told him right when it happened. My mother did not remember she had told me not to tell anyone. My whole family was upset. My sister got very angry at me, claiming that I made the whole thing up in order to ruin her wedding.

I was furious at my mom. I felt that she was not standing up for me against my sister or my father. I hated Mom for this!

When I was about twenty-five, I rediscovered my faith, Christianity. I started to pray and read the Bible daily. I made a conscious decision to forgive my mom for siding with my dad and sister at the wedding. I convinced myself that Mom had needed to side with Dad for family unity.

I really thought I had forgiven Mom, until I started psychotherapy five years later. Suddenly I found myself feeling tremendous rage and resentment toward Mom. With psychotherapeutic help, I realized that I had not yet faced the real issue that I was angry about. I realized that I was angry at Mom for silencing me when I was fifteen, and for not having helped me more at the time of the rape. Once this rage had surfaced and I began to process it, I finally felt as if I could really begin to work to forgive Mom.

You can truly forgive only after you have faced the incident/memory, felt and honoured your repressed emotions, and begun to strive to heal and transcend those emotions. Once you have accomplished this, you can then attempt to forgive, and get on with your life.

How to Forgive

Forgiveness is the final step in emotional healing, when you let go of your past emotional reactions to traumas, and feel compassion in your heart for both yourself and the other person. Forgiveness allows you to calm the mind and heart, and reach emotional equipoise. In the yogic tradition equipoise, or even-mindedness, is thought to be an essential attribute, required for spiritual growth and deepening.

Forgiveness is sometimes very difficult to do. In my clinical experience, some patients told me they wanted to forgive someone who wronged them, but they felt unable to forgive because their anger or pain remained strong, and/or because the actions of the person who hurt them were extremely painful, immoral, or even illegal. It is important to realize that forgiveness does not mean condoning or accepting a betrayal, or an immoral, cruel, or illegal act.

When striving to forgive another person, I have found it essential to distinguish between the error in a person's hurtful actions, and forgiveness of that person's soul. For example, this distinction is clear in how a loving parent loves their naughty child's soul and forgives the child for a misdeed such as spilling their milk. At the same time, the loving parent also acknowledges the error in the child's misdeed, and appropriately corrects and disciplines the naughty child for their actions, perhaps making the child clean up their mess so that they will learn not to spill their milk. According to the yogic tradition and many other spiritual traditions, our loving Higher Power, our Mother/Father God, loves us in this manner with profound unconditional love, repeatedly forgiving the souls of all of us despite our repeated errors in our actions. However, the loving Higher Power does discipline us for our incorrect actions, as well. God corrects us, by giving us the opportunity to learn our spiritual lessons through reaping the consequences of our actions, through what yoga calls the law of karma. This distinction between forgiving the soul while acknowledging the reality of the misdeed of another makes forgiveness of others' errors much easier.

As part of spiritual transformation and psycho-spiritual housecleaning, everyone must strive to eventually forgive the souls of those who hurt them, even if the injustices committed were clearly wrong, in order to achieve inner peace and equipoise. It is possible to forgive and wish another soul well, while still acknowledging the truth of the error in their actions. At the same time, we can take comfort in trusting in Divine justice, that God will be the final judge, that God will ultimately balance the karma of all souls' merits and errors. This confidence in ultimate Divine justice may be particularly comforting if you have not been able to bring a particular traumatic incident to a just, peaceful resolution through your own efforts.

Forgiving another person's soul is easier when you humbly look at yourself, and realize that you too are imperfect, and have made many mistakes in your life that might require forgiveness from others. Sometimes the other person will repent for their hurtful actions, and wish to make amends to you, to atone for their error. In such a case, through the grace of forgiveness in your heart, a new, healthier relationship can sometimes be developed. However, if the person who wronged you does not repent or sincerely apologize for their hurtful actions, you can still pray for their soul with forgiveness in your heart. Pray that they learn their spiritual lesson, "… *pray for them which … persecute you*," said Jesus (Matthew 5:44).

I advise people that forgiveness is a three-step process: First, you must consciously decide to forgive, because you want to. You choose to no longer carry the hurtful incident's emotional baggage around with you, because you are striving for inner peace, for even-mindedness, for equipoise. You wish to centre your heart in love, and not be burdened by anger and hurt from the past. You therefore choose to forgive, and let go of your processed emotions and emotional reactions to past events.

Second, you actively strive to forgive the other person. This entails sincerely, and from the heart, praying for the other person and wishing their soul well. Ask the Higher Power to help you to forgive them. It is often helpful to visualize the other person's inner child — the innocent child of God that lays somewhere deep inside that person's psyche, perhaps lost under heavy layers of egotism or bad habits. Focus on that pure-of-heart inner child within the person who hurt you, and mentally or verbally say, "I forgive you!" Pray for the other person's soul or inner child, as a brother or sister child of God, sending them goodwill, spiritual love, and wishing them those experiences that will draw them quickly back HOME to God-realization. I find it helpful to also affirm, "God's Will be done."

Finally, after your conscious effort to forgive, you must intentionally let go of your past emotionality relating to the incident. Give it all to God! Let go, and trust that God in his/her infinite wisdom will bring ultimate justice and healing to all. Deliberately move on with your life, putting this event behind you. If your anger or hurt resurfaces at a later date, pray to God for help to heal your wounds, pray for help to truly forgive, then pray for the soul of the person who hurt you.

To clearly punctuate your act of forgiveness and letting go of the emotions relating to a traumatic life event, many people like to do a symbolic ritual of some type. For example, I have in the past travelled to Niagara Falls for this purpose, to invisibly "throw my problem over the falls." Another time, while I was in California, I went to the Pacific Ocean and threw symbolic pebbles into the ocean, symbolizing my release of the trauma/karma into God's hands forever. Other persons may wish to write their past problem that they are releasing and forgiving on a piece of paper, then burn the paper in a symbolic fire. Others find it helpful to release the incident by briskly shaking it off with their hands, or by sweeping the event's energy away from their body with a hand gesture while stating "I release you" several times.

Once we have forgiven ourselves and others for past errors, we can regain emotional equanimity and inner peace. With this inner tranquility we can now more successfully strive to deepen in our spiritual efforts. Paramahansa Yogananda quoted the *Mahabharata*, "One should forgive under any injury ... Forgiveness is the might of the mighty; ... forgiveness is quiet of mind."

MEDITATION — THE KEY TO SPIRITUAL DEEPENING

MOST STE EXPERIENCERS at some point develop a strong inner urge for deeper spiritual awareness and desire to have more spiritual experiences. Many people who have never had an STE also yearn to actively embark on the spiritual path, to seek deeper spiritual awareness and glimpse the mystical states of consciousness described in this book. I have therefore added this chapter on meditation to address those seekers.

Meditation is the key to spiritual deepening, according to diverse yogic and Buddhist spiritual traditions. My personal and clinical experience supports this. Meditation has the greatest beneficial effect on spiritual transformation of consciousness when it is practised in combination with the rest of the Eight Limbs of Yoga, including purification of the character, regular self-reflection, devotion to God, and selfless service to others.

In my forty years of researching STEs and spiritual transformation of consciousness, I have observed that regular daily meditation combined with following the moral precepts of the world's great faiths (in general accordance with the Eight Limbs of Yoga) is the key to progress on the spiritual path.

The West has become increasingly aware of meditation in the last twenty-five years. Most people in the West have now either heard about meditation through the media — books, magazines, or television — or have been introduced to meditation by their friends, doctors, or clergy. Many health-care facilities have introduced meditation courses to their patient-care options, to help patients deal with stress or anxiety, for pain control, or to lower blood pressure. Many churches, temples, and synagogues of diverse faith traditions have introduced meditation courses for practitioners of their faiths, such as Christian meditation, Jewish meditation, or meditation in Islam. Meditation has always been included as an aspect of the Hindu and Buddhist religious traditions.

Thus, meditation is a universal technique, which anyone, of any faith tradition, or a non-aligned individual, can use to benefit their health in body, mind, and spirit.

The True Goal of Meditation Is Illumination

In accordance with the ancient yogic tradition, and as detailed in the *Yoga Sutras of Patanjali* (which includes the famous Eight Limbs of Yoga, or Eightfold Path of Yoga), the true goal of meditation is to transform your consciousness, to be able to attain and ultimately sustain an expanded, unitive mystical state of consciousness, which is variously called samadhi, nirvana, illumination, or God-consciousness. Yogic sages of yore discovered the scientific methods to achieve the goal of Yoga, samadhi. Paramahansa Yogananda said, "Yoga [including yogic meditation] is definite and scientific. Yoga means union of soul and God, through step-by-step methods with specific and known results. It raises the practice of religion above the differences of dogma."

The second line of the *Yoga Sutras of Patanjali* reads, "*Yoga citta vritti nirodhah*," which, translated, means "[The final goal of] yoga is the restriction [cessation] of the fluctuations of consciousness." This means that the goal of yoga, unitive communion, can be achieved when one has completely stilled the mind of all fluctuations of thoughts and emotions.

Meditation techniques are the way that one can learn to still the mind, to cease the fluctuations of consciousness caused by thoughts and emotions. In the inner stillness brought on by deep meditation, the unruffled clear consciousness becomes like a still pond, whose still waters can clearly reflect the light of the moon. The still mind that is no longer restless and fluctuating can more clearly reflect and transmit the light, love, and wisdom of God. This is a mystical interpretation of the Bible's sacred teaching, "*Be Still, and Know that I am God.*"* Thus meditation designed to still our consciousness is the key to spiritual progress.

---

* Psalms 46:10.

Meditation Is Part of the Eight Limbs of Yoga

It is essential to remember that, according to the ancient yogic science, meditation is part of a holistic approach involving body, mind, and spirit. Spiritual learning, purification of character, and meditative deepening should always be combined with and balanced with nurturing health of the body and mind. As I described in chapter 9, "The Yogic Model of Consciousness and Kundalini," meditation is one component of the holistic Eight Limbs of Yoga. As a reminder, the Eight Limbs of Yoga are:

1. Yama — Moral conduct — the "Don'ts"
2. Niyama — Spiritual disciplines — the "Dos"
3. Asana — Right posture to keep the body subtle and strong, enabling one to sit in meditation with the spine straight and body firm and comfortable
4. Pranayama — Control of life-energy/prana through the breath
5. Pratyahara — Interiorizing the mind, detaching from the outer senses
6. Dharana — Single-pointed inner concentration
7. Dhyana — Meditation
8. Samadhi — Illumination, God-communion, oneness of the soul with Cosmic Spirit

The healthy, balanced way to slowly and gradually deepen, purify, and expand our consciousness is in accordance with the Eight Limbs of Yoga. Combining meditation with devotional spiritual practices and spiritual purification of character, Limbs 1 and 2, will enable meditators to safely increase and expand their capacity for spiritual transformation of consciousness. They may then begin to experience glimpses of aspects of the Divine in their meditations, such as glimpses of Divine peace, wisdom, expansion, love, bliss, or deep intermittent mystical experiences or sabikalpa samadhis. After many years or perhaps after many lifetimes of deep meditation and self-purification/Soul learning, the meditator's consciousness may ultimately expand into an ongoing mystical state of God-communion while able to fully function in the world — ongoing unitive consciousness, or nirbikalpa samadhi, the transcendental true goal of yoga.

Benefits of Meditation to the Body and Mind

Meditation practice brings many possible benefits to the body, mind, and spirit. Some people first learn meditation specifically for some of the body and mind benefits, such as to lower blood pressure, or to decrease stress and anxiety. The following are some of the many benefits meditation can have on the body and mind:

- Meditation can reduce stress.
- Meditation can slow down body functions, such as the heart rate, and the breathing rate.
- Meditation can lower the blood pressure.
- Meditation can calm the mind, decreasing anxiety, restlessness, and worry.
- Meditation can calm the intensity of emotions, such as decreasing anger, grief, and depression.
- Meditation can help you physically and emotionally relax, decreasing muscle tension.
- Meditation can decrease the intensity of physical pain in the body.
- Meditation can still the mind so that one can experience inner peace.
- Meditation can stimulate neuroplasticity and brain healing.

As with any skill that you might learn, meditation takes practice to learn and to improve. It takes time to learn how to meditate deeply, and to develop the capacity to meditate for long periods. Beginner meditators will usually not experience all the benefits at first. It is important for beginners not to be discouraged if their meditation practice does not seem to be giving any results at first. With regular daily meditation practice, most meditators notice progressive spiritual deepening as well as the other mind and body benefits developing over the months and years.

Yogic Understanding of Meditation's Effects on Consciousness

According to the yogic model of consciousness and kundalini, there is a scientific explanation for how meditation can accelerate spiritual transformation of consciousness, and may stimulate the awakening of the spiritual energy/kundalini mechanism. As Paramahansa Yogananda explains it, during the practice of advanced yogic meditation techniques, and to a lesser extent also during the practice of concentration and interiorization types of meditation techniques (see, below, the section on "Types of Meditation Techniques"), with the gaze and attention focused at the third-eye/ajna region of the forehead, the intense meditative concentration and focus on the astral spine and the ajna chakra region of the brain tends to "magnetize" them. This magnetization of the astral spine and astral brain attracts the prana/life-energy, and tends to make it withdraw from its normal outward flow from the astral spine into the physical body and organs for use in outer physical body activities. Instead, the prana/life-energy flow is pulled to reverse direction and flows toward the sushumna/astral spine and then up the astral spine into the astral brain.

This inward and upward flow of the prana/life-energy that can occur during deep meditation is said by yogic science to have several potential effects on the astral body and consciousness. First, upon reaching the third-eye/ajna chakra region of the astral brain, the upward flowing prana/life-energy enables deeper, expanded inner awareness of our true Soul Consciousness. As stated in chapter 9, "The Yogic Model of Consciousness and Kundalini," with the inward flow of prana/life-energy during deep meditation, the consciousness moves inwardly, as well. The inward-moving consciousness detaches itself from bodily functions and the physical senses, enabling the consciousness to perceive astral peace and astral light, as it withdraws into the astral brain.

Second, as the upward-flowing prana/life-energy travels up the sushumna/astral spine, it helps purify and remove blockages in the spinal chakras and the sushumna channel. This upward-flowing prana can help burn away or purify our samskaras/unconscious habit tendencies, and our karma/past-life unlearned soul lessons, that are said to be held on the petals of the chakras along the astral spine. The cleansing and purifying effects on the psyche of upward-flowing prana in deep meditation can be observed in the changing personalities of many long-time meditators, even if they have never had a profound STE or a kundalini awakening. Over the years, long-time meditators tend to become more peaceful persons, more calm and even-minded, less easily upset by the inevitable ups and downs of life. They may also gradually abandon previous bad habits.

Third, by opening the channel of the sushumna/astral spine and removing blockages, and by creating a strong magnetism in the third-eye/ajna chakra, deep meditation may sometimes coax the kundalini mechanism to awaken. The awakened kundalini mechanism then spontaneously sends additional bursts or even a steady stream of prana and ojas to the astral brain, which accelerates the brain/astral brain's spiritual transformation process, and can enable sudden, dramatically expanded states of consciousness.

Finally, with continued balanced meditation practice in accordance with the Eight Limbs of Yoga, and the practice of long meditations, the brain/astral brain's transformation deepens, and the meditator becomes able to hold their inflowing consciousness steady at the ajna chakra/astral brain region for longer and longer periods of time. Their consciousness may thereby gradually pierce through the several astral layers, into the causal layer of consciousness, resulting in much deeper, more expansive, mystical states of consciousness. Some yogic traditions describe this progressive spiritual deepening in the advanced yogi meditator as resulting from the consciousness and/or the kundalini energies gradually ascending the progressively subtler channels of the sushumna/astral spine, and finally ascending the brahmanadi/causal spine of pure consciousness, to reach the causal brain. The result is that astral samadhi in meditation deepens into causal samadhi, an even more profound mystical state of consciousness.

Types of Meditation Techniques

One does not need to understand, or even agree with, the extremely complex yogic science of consciousness and kundalini, in order to learn meditation and benefit from a daily meditation practice. Yogic science will need to be examined and verified by future consciousness research. In the meanwhile, there are many types of meditation techniques, which can be easily learned from various books, meditation teachers, spiritual teachers of diverse spiritual traditions, or from a guru. To simplify what can at first seem to be a confusing array, here is a comparison of some of the more common types of meditation techniques being taught in the West today:

1. *Interiorization-type meditation techniques.* These techniques correspond to the practice of step five in the Eight Limbs of Yoga, interiorization of the mind. These techniques often help meditators to more deeply connect with their love for others, their intuition, and the inner wisdom of the "Higher Self."

   a. *Visualizations.* Many beginner meditation courses teach a type of visualization meditation. Some common visualizations for starting to meditate include: visualizing your heart centre as radiating light and love to your community, then to your country, then to the entire world; visualizing your heart centre as radiating light and love to another person; visualizing a lotus flower blooming and opening at your heart centre; visualizing a lotus flower blooming and opening on top of your head; or visualizing your body as youthful and healthy, healed from any current illness or disability.

   b. *Guided visualizations.* Another type of common visualization meditation taught today, in which a meditation leader verbally guides the meditator through a visualization exercise. These guided visualizations vary considerably, but, as an example, the leader may guide the meditator to shut their eyes and gaze at the "screen of the mind" at the third-eye region, and visualize themselves walking along a path. The leader may then guide the meditator to see themselves starting to climb up a mountain, and to reach a waterfalls, or the peak, or perhaps a sacred location. The leader might guide them to visualize an encounter with an inner helper or spirit guide of some sort. The leader may also guide the meditator to ask some important questions or seek guidance from their inner helper. Meditators are usually taught how to do a similar guided visualization meditation on their own.

2. *Concentration type meditation techniques.* These techniques correspond to the practice of step six in the Eight Limbs of Yoga, inner concentration of the mind. These techniques require the spiritual seeker to interiorize the mind and concentrate on a single-pointed interiorized focus. These meditation techniques help meditators still the mind, relax the body, and enter the inner silence, the inner peace. In the inner stillness, intuition is much stronger.

   a. *Concentration on a sacred image.* In this, the meditator may begin with looking at a sacred icon, such as a picture of a saint or a spiritual Master. The meditator would then shut their eyes and concentrate on a mental image of the saint/ Master, in their third-eye region. During this concentration/ meditation on the mental image, the meditator might also strive to feel the divine love of the saint/Master in their own consciousness, or in their heart centre.

   b. *Concentration on sacred words — "Japa."*

      i. *Repetition of a prayer or mantra.* Many spiritual traditions include the practice of repeating prayers or mantras, and using prayer beads, a rosary, or mala beads to count the number of repetitions. Typically a mala has 108 beads (108 being believed in some traditions to be a holy number). The meditator moves his hands bead by bead with each prayer or mantra repetition, to ensure that they carry out the desired number of repetitions.

      ii. *Repetition of a song or chant, either out loud or mentally.* Some spiritual traditions teach their devotees to sing a chant or hymn repeatedly, for example the Gayatri Mantra, or the Guru Gita.

   c. *Concentration on the flow of the breath.* This type of meditation is sometimes called "mindfulness meditation," or

"Vipassana meditation." Many stress-reduction courses taught in health-care facilities today teach some type of this meditation, which involves concentration on the natural flow of the breath. In meditation posture, the meditator is usually instructed to begin by taking a few deep breaths, and to tense the entire body with the inhalation, then relax the entire body with the exhalation. The meditator is then instructed to breathe naturally, and to focus their concentrated attention on observing the breath in a detached manner. The meditator is instructed to ignore thoughts and emotions as they arise, and to repeatedly bring their attention back to observing the flow of the breath. Some traditions combine the detached observation of the flow of the breath with mentally chanting a sacred word or syllable with each inhalation and exhalation, such as chanting "Ah" with the inhalation, and "Men" with the exhalation, "A-men." Practice of meditation techniques concentrating on the natural flow of the breath can lead to deep relaxation, interiorization, and inner stillness. Some meditators have even slipped into mystical experiences through deep practise of this type of meditation.

3. *Yogic meditation techniques.* These techniques correspond to the practice of steps seven and eight in the Eight Limbs of Yoga, meditation and samadhi. These techniques are sometimes referred to as "scientific meditation techniques," because they have been tested by many long-time practitioners of yoga meditation, and they have been proven to be effective. They bring the desired result of spiritual transformation of consciousness. These more advanced meditation techniques involve deep, single-pointed interiorized focus and concentration on the astral spine and brain, inner astral sounds, astral light, astral energies/prana, the inner silence, or on an aspect of the Divine. I will outline these yogic meditation techniques only briefly, because according to yogic tradition these advanced meditation techniques should not be practised by beginners, and should only be taught to a prepared

student by a qualified spiritual teacher or guru and practised under the teacher's guidance.

a. *Meditative concentration on the inner astral sounds — "AUM."*

b. *Meditative concentration on the inner astral sounds of the Chakras.*

c. *Meditative concentration on an attribute of the Divine, such as omnipresence, omnipotence, omniscience, or unconditional love.*

d. *Meditative concentration on the inner silence between thoughts.* This is often practised after other concentration techniques, which are used first to still the mind.

e. *Meditative concentration on the inner astral light.*

f. *Meditative concentration on the inner astral currents/prana going up and down the astral spine.*

g. *Pranayama meditation.* This consists of meditative concentration on the inner astral/prana currents going up and down the astral spine, combined with pranayama — breath and life-force control techniques.

There are also other very advanced meditation techniques in diverse spiritual traditions, but these are beyond the scope of this book. It is not my purpose here to give a scholarly or in-depth study of various techniques of meditation. Rather, I wish readers to have a general understanding of the types of meditation techniques being taught today. This overview is based on my own personal experience of forty years as a regular meditator. I started meditating regularly in my early twenties. Since that time, I learned many different meditation techniques from diverse spiritual traditions and teachers, including from non-religious memory-improvement courses, stress-reduction courses, two Buddhist meditation teachers, and several different yogic meditation teachers. For the last about twenty years I have been practising the yogic meditation techniques as taught by Paramahansa Yogananda and his lineage, Self-Realization Fellowship.

Correct Posture for Meditation

It is very important to maintain a correct posture for meditation. This is necessary to keep the body comfortable in a fixed position for a long period of time. Correct posture also permits smooth flow of life-energy/prana through the body, astral body, and astral spine, and the smooth flow of spiritual energy/kundalini up your spine/astral spine during your meditation. Correct posture for meditation is as follows:

1. Sit with the spine straight and erect. One can sit with the spine erect either on a firm chair, or cross-legged on the ground, or on a small cushion on the ground.

2. Close the eyes. The eyes should remain closed for the duration of your meditation. Some yogic meditators prefer to meditate with their eyes half-shut. However, you should be able to hold the eyes still in this position, if you choose this method. Meditating with shut eyes is the easiest and most common method.

3. Fix the gaze of the shut eyes upwards slightly, to the third-eye/ajna chakra region, between the eyebrows, above the top of the nose. Keep the gaze fixed at this point throughout the meditation. With regular meditation practice the gaze will go to this third-eye region automatically when the eyes are shut during prayers and meditations. This third-eye/ajna chakra area is also where the gaze usually goes naturally when people visualize things, on the "screen of the mind." As one becomes more advanced in meditation practice, they may begin to feel their consciousness drawn or pulled into the stillness at the third-eye centre, perhaps drawn by the "magnetism" created there by regular meditation practice. The gaze of the eyes also goes to the third-eye/ajna chakra automatically during mystical experiences. Many pictures of saints in mystical ecstasy depict their gaze as going upwards, as they are gazing through the astral third-eye centre to perceive the astral spiritual heaven realms. If you tend to fall asleep during meditation, double-check that your gaze is turned upwards.

4. The head should be straight and level, with the chin remaining parallel to the floor.
5. The arms should hang relaxed at the sides, with the hands resting gently on top of the thighs, with the palms upturned.

Suggested Routine for Meditation

Many STE experiencers wonder how they can introduce meditation into their busy lives. Most people today have many responsibilities, and find themselves struggling to balance time required for their work with time for their family, friends, fitness, laundry, and home upkeep. However, with a little effort it is indeed possible to add regular meditation practice to a busy life. I, and many other long-time meditators, have been able to find time to meditate morning and evening, despite busy work and career schedules, plus additional responsibilities as parents, spouses, and homeowners. A key to developing a meditation routine is to not skip any of your daily meditations. If your schedule is particularly busy and you do not have time to do a full meditation on a particular day, do a shorter meditation that day, but still meditate. Firmly establish the habit of meditating twice daily.

I suggest the following, to establish a basic daily meditation routine:

1. Plan a daily routine in which you schedule yourself at least thirty minutes to meditate in the early morning before you start your work of the day, and again at night before you go to bed. Begin your meditation practice with twenty to thirty minutes twice a day, then gradually increase your meditation time to about one hour twice a day. Set your alarm for one hour earlier in the morning, to give yourself time for your morning meditation.
2. Pick a quiet spot in your home for your meditation area. Meditate in this spot every time. Try to make this meditation spot sacred, by only meditating there.
3. Put a comfortable firm chair for meditation or a suitable cushion on the floor in your meditation area.
4. Create an altar or sacred space in your meditation area. You may, for instance, put a sacred image, a holy icon, or sacred

objects in your meditation area altar. You may wish to have Holy Scriptures, and/or hymn or chant guides there also. Viewing these sacred images and objects when you enter your meditation area will help draw your mind to thoughts of God immediately.

5. You may wish to wear a light shawl while meditating. Since your body functions tend to slow down the longer you meditate, you may begin to feel cold during longer meditations if you are not wearing a shawl or light sweater.

6. Before beginning your meditation, stretch and relax your body to reduce muscle tension. Many meditators do a short practice of hatha yoga exercises or similar exercises before starting their daily meditation, to relax and relieve muscle tensions.

7. Begin each meditation with a prayer, asking the Divine and the spiritual Master of your faith to be with you, and guide you in your meditation.

8. Read briefly from scripture or an inspirational text after your prayer, to help turn your thoughts more deeply toward God.

9. You may wish to sing a hymn or chant after your sacred reading. Singing to God helps to stir your love and devotion to the Divine.

10. After the prayer, sacred reading, and hymn/chant is the time to be still and meditate.

11. Start your meditation with a technique to still your mind, such as watching the breath, or japa — repetition of prayers or mantras. Highly experienced meditators practise yogic meditation techniques after practising the mind-stilling techniques.

12. If you do not know a meditation technique, silently pray inwardly, or focus on an attribute of the Divine.

13. After the mind has become still, focus on the stillness, and sit in the silence. "*Be Still and Know that I am God.*"

14. At the end of your meditation period, pray silently for others in need.

15. End your meditation with a short prayer of gratitude.

16. When your meditation routine gets established, strive to do a longer meditation, for about two to three hours (if you are able), about once per week.

Four Main Types of Spiritual Paths

According to the yogic tradition, there are four main types of spiritual paths, which all lead to God-communion, no matter which spiritual faith tradition you are following; Christian, Jewish, Hindu, Muslim, Buddhist, Sikh, Indigenous, or others. These four types of spiritual paths are: Bhakti yoga — the heart path of love and devotion; Karma yoga — the path of service and good deeds; Jnana yoga — the intellectual path of spiritual wisdom and understanding; and Raja yoga — the royal path, which is a combination of the other three paths. The yogic tradition believes that all the types of spiritual paths ultimately lead to God-communion. Meditation can be practised with benefit on any of the four types of spiritual paths. Different people are drawn to different types of spiritual paths, even within one faith, based on their own personality and personal preferences. Here is a brief description of each of the four types of spiritual paths to God-communion:

1. Bhakti Yoga — The Devotional Path

Bhakti yoga is any type of spiritual path which focuses primarily on love and devotion to God. A bhakti or devotional path of any spiritual tradition includes many devotional activities, expressions of love for God. This may include singing devotional songs of praise, such as "The Lord is my Shepherd," "How Great Thou Art," "Oh Happy Day"; listening to gospel choirs; singing devotional chants such as the "Guru Gita"; yogic kirtan (combined chanting, dancing, and meditating); devotional dancing such as Sufi whirling; openly expressing love and devotion to God and the spiritual Master of your faith, by saying such things as "Praise the Lord," "God is Great," "Allah is Great," "I love you Divine Mother," etc.; devotional rituals; practising the presence of God at every moment; and walking with God and talking with God.

404

2. Karma Yoga — The Path of Service to Others

Karma yoga is any type of spiritual path which focuses primarily on drawing closer to God by serving others. A karma yogi of any faith focuses their spiritual life on doing good deeds, striving and praying to be God's instrument of love and kindness in all they do. They humbly strive to do kind actions, and to be of selfless service to others, especially to the needy and the unfortunate. The great Christian mystic St. Francis of Assisi exemplified the path of karma yoga in his life dedicated to serving the poor, ill, and outcast. He extolled the joy of the path of service in his famous prayer:

> *Prayer of St. Francis of Assisi*
> *Lord, make me an instrument of your peace*
> *Where there is hatred ... let me sow love,*
> *Where there is injury ... pardon,*
> *Where there is discord ... unity,*
> *Where there is doubt ... faith,*
> *Where there is error ... truth,*
> *Where there is despair ... hope,*
> *Where there is sadness ... joy,*
> *Where there is darkness ... light.*
>
> *O Divine Master, grant that I may not so much seek*
> *To be consoled ... as to console,*
> *To be understood ... as to understand,*
> *To be loved ... as to love.*
>
> *For it is in giving ... that we receive,*
> *It is in pardoning, that we are pardoned.*
> *It is in dying ... that we are born to eternal life.*

Mother Teresa was a more contemporary example of a karma yogi — a person dedicated to the path of service to others, in the Christian faith. Mother Teresa lived her monastic life fully dedicated to the service of others, with her remarkable charity work selflessly serving the outcast and poorest of poor in the slums of Calcutta, India.

3. Jnana Yoga — The Intellectual Path of Wisdom

Jnana yoga (or Gyana yoga) is any type of spiritual path which focuses primarily on the development of spiritual understanding, discrimination, and wisdom. A jnana yogi of any faith focuses much of their spiritual life on the study of Holy Scriptures of their faith, listening to and/or reciting the Holy Scriptures, and in deep contemplation of the truth and meaning of the Scriptures. Jnana yoga, the path of wisdom, includes meditation practice in which the spiritual seeker strives to inwardly discriminate eternal spiritual "reality" from temporary earthly "non-reality." The goal of the jnana yoga path of wisdom is gnosis, to draw closer to nirvana, or God, through personal experience of mystical wisdom.

4. Raja Yoga — The Combined Path of Devotion, Service, and Wisdom

Raja yoga is referred to as the Royal Path of Yoga. A spiritual seeker of any faith on a raja yoga–type spiritual path will focus on all three of the above mentioned foci, devotion, service, and wisdom, as part of their spiritual practice. Their spiritual life will combine devotional practices like a bhakti yogi, with selfless service to others like a karma yogi, with development of spiritual understanding and wisdom like the jnana yogi.

In the classic yogic tradition, in addition to practising the Eight Limbs of Yoga, bhakti yoga, karma yoga, and jnana yoga spiritual practices, a raja yogi will also practise some more advanced types of yogic meditation and pranayama, including techniques that are specifically intended to stimulate the spiritual energy/kundalini. It is thought by many that raja yoga is the most difficult spiritual path to follow, but it is also the fastest and most direct path to self-realization and God-communion.

Different yoga teachers and gurus in the world today teach slightly different meditation practices to their devotees. Some yoga teachers emphasize devotion with chants. Other yogic paths emphasize mainly japa — reciting holy mantras repeatedly, counting repetitions with mala beads.

Some teachers emphasize the karma yoga path more: service to others. Yet other yogic teachers will emphasize study of scripture combined with contemplation and meditation. Yogic science contends that all four types of spiritual paths can ultimately lead the devotee to God-communion, albeit by different routes.

Hatha yoga, which is the third limb of the Eight Limbs of Yoga, is designed as preparatory for meditation practices in Limbs 6, 7, and 8. Hatha yoga is beneficial when combined with any of the four types of spiritual paths. Hatha yoga keeps the muscles and spine flexible and aligned. Other postures are said to stimulate certain body organs. Hatha yoga also purifies and stretches the astral channels/nadis, and is said to aid the flow of life-energy/prana through the nadis, while some postures are said to stimulate certain chakras.

Spiritual Results in Meditation

Regardless of whether or not they have had any STEPs or STEs as part of their spiritual journey, most long-time meditators begin to notice definite effects brought on by their regular meditation practice. Meditators begin to notice changes in their consciousness in meditation. According to the yogic tradition, through regular meditation practice, the spiritual aspirant has gradually expanded their consciousness's capacity to be receptive to the Divine, and increased their ability to perceive glimpses of aspects of the Divine Higher Power behind the universe. Long-time meditators will often experience some of the following glimpses of Divine attributes in their deep meditations:

1. *Peace.* Meditators begin to feel a deep inner peace, a calmness that increasingly stays with them as an after-effect of meditations.
2. *Expansion.* Meditators may feel as if their consciousness expands during deep meditations, as if their consciousness has expanded from the confines of their head to become a vast inner ocean of stillness. This oceanic inner experience of consciousness-expansion may be associated with an inner perception of a deep royal-blue colour.

3. *Wisdom/intuition.* Advanced meditators in deep meditation may find their still consciousness to be highly receptive to intuition and Divine wisdom. New deeper understandings and clarity may come about important life issues, and life direction.

4. *Bliss and Love.* Advanced meditators may find that their expanded consciousness becomes permeated with bliss, joy, and/ or unconditional love in meditation.

5. *Communion.* Advanced meditators may find themselves increasingly experiencing a tangible sense of being directly connected with the Divine Higher Power. The feeling has been described like being a drop of water that somehow becomes aware that it is one with, and part of, a vast and powerful ocean of life and love.

These results in meditation, peace, expansion, wisdom/intuition, bliss, love, and communion, tend to increasingly linger in the meditator after the end of their meditation. This makes long-time meditators become more peaceful people, with more equipoise, less easily ruffled by the ups and downs of life. When they do become upset by life's challenges, they find that they can more rapidly return to a state of mental peace, especially by meditating. Feelings of enhanced intuition, expansion, bliss, and universal love may also endure for varying periods of time after meditations.

The beautiful results of meditation and the enduring after-effects are incredibly alluring. Most regular meditators come to treasure their daily meditation time. Meditation becomes both sacred time to be alone with their Higher Power, and a blessed method to find inner stillness and peace of mind in a tumultuous world. Meditators confirm the ancient yogic truth, through their own inner transformation of consciousness, that meditation is indeed the key to spiritual deepening.

20

FINDING OUR WAY HOME

PEOPLE FREQUENTLY WANT TO KNOW how they can best stimulate their process of spiritual transformation of consciousness, to most rapidly and safely find their way HOME, to self-realization. It should be clear by now that I believe moderation and balance and following the holistic Eight Limbs of Yoga, including meditation, are the essential ingredients in any attempt to further spiritual progress, no matter what your personal faith tradition or type of spiritual path. With this in mind, I will now provide a list of stimulants to the spiritual energy/kundalini, before going on to discuss some of the balanced, moderate approaches that might facilitate progress on the spiritual journey. Be aware of them, use appropriate ones only in a balanced and moderate way, and avoid overstimulating the transformative energy. If you are in the least tempted to begin the excessive practice of many of the stimulants, turn back to chapters 15 and 16 on spiritual emergencies and psychoses; read about the importance of balanced living, body, mind, and spirit; and consider the tragic consequences of throwing yourself into spiritual emergency, or worse.

The effect that any one stimulant has will, of course, vary from individual to individual, and some individuals will be far more susceptible to each of them than other people would be. In general, the longer each activity is done and the greater the intensity of the practice, the greater the stimulating effect. Most of the practices are not harmful in and of themselves, and many are beneficial when used in moderation as part of the Eight Limbs of Yoga. It is intensiveness or excessiveness that can make some of them harmful.

Although it will take extensive research to determine exactly which activities are the most stimulating to the spiritual energy/kundalini, I have tried to list them — based on my research and clinical experience — with the strongest stimulants first.

Stimulants to the Transformative Energy

1. Intensely focused kundalini-type meditation. These are yogic meditation techniques that involve visualizing and focusing on the spiritual energy/kundalini rising from the base of the spine to the brain, perhaps piercing and activating the chakras. Sometimes the image at the crown is one of a lotus bud opening into full bloom with the upward flow of the spiritual energy/ kundalini.

2. Pranayama. This is a yogic technique for controlling the flow of life-energy/prana through the breath. It may include techniques that strive to move the life force/prana up the astral spine.

3. Intensely focused meditation on astral currents and/or inner astral sounds.

4. Intensely focused meditation on the Divine. These yogic meditation techniques involve concentration on a particular aspect of the Divine; for instance, omnipresence, omnipotence, omniscience, or the silence.

5. Receiving shaktipat. Spiritual energy transmission from a holy person or saint.

6. Receiving dharshan/a spiritual blessing. By being in the presence of a holy person or saint.

7. Intensely focused meditation on chakra points. These are yogic meditation techniques in which energy, divine light, sacred images, or opening lotus blossoms are visualized, or astral sounds are listened to, at certain chakra points. Each chakra may be perceived in sequence, beginning with the first (root) and moving upward to the crown chakra — or a particular chakra may be focused upon exclusively; for instance, the heart chakra, the third-eye chakra, or the crown chakra.

8. Intense prayer and devotion.

9. Intense practice of hatha yoga postures.

10. Intense self-reflection, depth psychotherapy, or recovery work.

11. Going on pilgrimage to a holy site — visiting a site where a spiritual Master or saint lived, and which still holds their sacred vibration. Receiving a dharshan/spiritual blessing at the holy site.

12. Intensive, prolonged concentration or focus on spiritual topics. For example, lengthy reading of spiritual material, discussing and debating spiritual topics, contemplating spiritual questions, or attending spiritual conferences.

13. Tantric sexual practices.

14. Tai Chi and Chi Kung.

15. Bodywork, massage, shiatsu, etc. — especially if aimed at increasing or stimulating the flow of life-energy/prana.

16. Chanting, and spiritual singing.

17. Intensive, prolonged concentration or focus on any subject without breaks.

18. Intensive, prolonged periods of reading.

19. Having sexual relations with a person who has an active kundalini.

20. Being in the prolonged presence of others who have an active kundalini.

21. Being in a state of emotional and spiritual openness; surrendering to the Divine; hitting bottom in addictions and recovery.

22. Being close to death.

23. Being close to someone who dies.

Although most of these activities are self-explanatory, I have provided additional information below on those that some readers might not be familiar with. More detailed quick references for some can be found in *The Encyclopedic Dictionary of Yoga* and far more thorough explanations in Eliade's *Yoga: Immortality and Freedom*.

Pranayama. In yoga, pranayama, specific breath control techniques, are believed to have a number of purifying, rejuvenating, and curative effects. In yogic meditation it is also a primary technique used to direct the prana and spiritual energy/kundalini into the astral spine/sushumna to begin its ascent to the crown. The fourteenth-century *Hatha Yoga Pradipika*, the most widely used manual on hatha yoga, urges caution in using pranayama, saying, "Just as a lion, an elephant, or a tiger is tamed gradually, so should the life-force be controlled: else it will kill the practitioner."

Tantric sexual practices. Although Tantrism contains many divergent schools, most are centred around the concept of shakti — another name for spiritual energy/kundalini. According to Feuerstein, one of the three main approaches in Tantrism can be roughly equated with kundalini yoga; the other two are known as the right-handed, or conservative, path and the left-handed path. The latter contains the practices, such as ones involving sexual intercourse, that have tended to tarnish the reputation of Tantrism in general.

Some Tantric sexual practices use spiritual visualizations done to encourage the inward and upward release of sexual energy/ojas at the time of orgasm (urdhva-retas). It is believed by some that successful upward release at the time of orgasm may result in a burst of prana and ojas up the astral spine/sushumna to the astral brain's brahma randhra. This could induce an expansion of consciousness or a mystical experience. Lack of correct understanding has led some misguided, untrained Westerners to try to adopt and misuse these esoteric spiritual techniques to try to manipulate the sexual energy during intercourse, thinking it will bring about an intensely powerful sexual experience, "super-sex." People who are doing this are attempting to play with fire. I do not recommend any attempts to force the upward flow of spiritual energy/kundalini. The spiritual energy/kundalini will awaken spontaneously or with a guru's assistance when the time is right, when the spiritual seeker is ready, when their body, mind, and spirit have been properly prepared through practice of the Eight Limbs of Yoga and meditation.

Shaktipat. More properly "shakti pata," this practice refers to the transmission of spiritual energy from a spiritual Master or saint to another person, usually a student or a disciple. Usually done with a touch, but sometimes a glance, shakti pata is reported to activate spiritual energy/kundalini and in some persons send the recipient into expanded states of consciousness or even samadhi for a period of time. In chapter 11, I shared the example of young Paramahansa Yogananda's prepared shaktipat awakening, transmitted by the touch of his enlightened guru, Swami Sri Yukteswar.

Prolonged contact with others who have an active kundalini. This is one of the most interesting phenomena currently being observed but, unfortunately, one we know little about. One of the places this phenomenon has recently been observed is at conferences on subjects such as kundalini, STEs, and spiritual emergence, and at spiritual gatherings of advanced meditators. A significant number of people report having increased spiritual energy/kundalini activity during and immediately after attending these types of events. Although this effect could be caused by intense focus on spiritual topics, it seems possible that the high concentration of people with active kundalini who are drawn to such events may also be a factor.

Although this phenomenon might seem inexplicable or even unbelievable to some, related phenomena are recognized in the yogic tradition. For instance, sat sanga is the practice of associating with enlightened spiritual Masters and saints. Such association is believed, in and of itself, to provide a dharshan/spiritual blessing, which can purify, uplift, and stimulate the spiritual process.

It is my opinion that a scientific explanation for this may one day be found. I have speculated that the phenomenon might even be a kind of "tuning fork" effect in which a type of "resonance" that is created by the high spiritual vibration and spiritual energy/kundalini activity that emanates from Masters, saints, and to a lesser degree long-time meditators and STE experiencers with an active kundalini, might begin to stimulate similar higher spiritual vibrations in an individual in whom the transformative energy is ready to become more active. Future research might also find that this provides an explanation for the way in which shakti pata manifests.

The Moderate Path to the Evolution of Consciousness

Many people accept the fact that there is too much risk involved in trying to rush their spiritual progress, but they still want to know how they can accelerate their progress as much as possible in a safe and healthy way. Many also want to know, more specifically, how they can stimulate the awakening of spiritual energy/kundalini to some degree and still avoid the pitfalls inherent in trying to force the transformative energy into too much activity too soon. We all need to remember that the science of stimulating spiritual transformation of consciousness and kundalini was the work of a lifetime according to the ancient Indian yogis, and that the true practice of yoga affects virtually every aspect of life. You need to be prepared physically, psychologically, and spiritually before taking up those practices that are most stimulating to the transformative energy. Further, you need to remember that the amount of focused concentration most people do in their daily lives today may already be providing much stimulation. With all this in mind, I think the safest route to stimulate healthy spiritual transformation of consciousness and awaken the spiritual energy/kundalini might be summarized in this way:

1. Follow a balanced, regular lifestyle. Eat a nutritious diet; have regular meals; get regular physical exercise; get adequate and regular sleep; avoid drugs, tobacco, and alcohol; avoid excessive stress.

2. Do a light practice of hatha yoga or Tai Chi.

3. Pray briefly several times a day, and deepen your relationship with the Higher Power according to your faith tradition.

4. Strive to live in accordance with the moral precepts of the world's great faiths.

5. Self-reflect, and attempt to resolve any psychological conflicts or negative feelings that you harbour relating to your family and other interpersonal relationships. Don't hesitate to enter into psychotherapy if needed to help resolve deeply rooted issues.

6. Practise meditation morning and evening, in moderation.

7. Conceptualize yourself and all beings as Divine children, spiritual brothers and sisters, here in earthly form to express our innate divinity.

8. Participate in the world, but in a manner that is detached from ambitions for personal power, status, or material possessions; detach from selfish ego desires; focus your efforts instead on making the world a better place by contributing in whatever

way you can; spend some time each week being of service to others.

9. Work toward developing the characteristics of higher consciousness: compassion, kindness, humility, gratitude, calmness, and surrender to the Divine; pray to be a clear instrument of Divine light, love, and peace on the planet.

Gopi Krishna, when asked "How can the average person achieve higher consciousness and help in the evolution of the race?" gave the following reply:

> The surest way should be to voluntarily develop the characteristics of higher consciousness. For instance, to always keep in mind that there is no barrier, no distinction, no wall between man and man. Whenever we see another person, though we may act in the normal way toward him, at the back of our minds should be the thought that the same consciousness, the same Divine substance, that is talking, hearing and listening in me, is also talking, hearing and listening in him; that it is one substance, one cosmic medium, that is expressing itself in all human beings.
>
> This will be in accordance even with the saying of the Christ, "Treat thy neighbors as thyself." And it is also the teaching of the *Bhagavad Gita*, to treat all fellow human beings as your own self. This would be, perhaps, the most effective way to melt the barriers which are created by the ego — to always put oneself in the shoes of another....
>
> Another very powerful exercise is to keep before the mind's eye an image of Cosmic Consciousness. Or, if one believes in a God, to imagine that it is a Divine Consciousness, a presence, an immanence, an ethereal eye spread all over the universe — omniscient, omnipresent, and omnipotent.
>
> The third would also be a corollary to the first: that since you now think — and you believe — that all men

are yourself, having all the same feelings and emotions, and are also expressions of the same energy, you should act in ways that will help them, either by advice or by teaching, or by backing their prospects or by raising them up if they are fallen. Or by advising them where they are mistaken, trying to help them in the same way we would like to be helped when we are in distress. This would be an effective method.

A fourth exercise would be in the morning and evening or at any convenient time — to sit in contemplation of Divinity, Cosmic Consciousness, God, Brahma, or by whatever name you call it, and continue thinking and meditating on it, reflecting on it as you would think, meditate, or reflect on a very stubborn problem that needed to be solved. Try to build up the image in the mind, an image of an infinite extension, of an endless duration in time. And then dwell on these thoughts, and never allow the mind to become quiescent or to go into sleep. This exercise is given in many yoga manuals.

The mind should remain alert, just as it remains alert when we are solving a problem, when we are concentrating on a mathematical proposition, or when we are studying a subject. We should keep the mind alert and reflect on the attributes of God — once, twice, or thrice a day — in a devout mood, and offer this contemplation as a prayer to the Almighty to help us raise our consciousness.

The fifth would be to live a life in harmony with one's relatives, friends, and even strangers, in harmony with one's conscience and in harmony with the teachings of great religious prophets — not to be sanctimonious or prudish, but to have healthy instincts, to practise moderation and always to behave in a manner that is noble. High moral calibre goes side by side with an elevated state of consciousness, so all these disciplines are necessary, because the stage we are reaching for is composed of all these

attributes. If we voluntarily cultivate them we help the
evolutionary forces to build up the consciousness that will
be the heritage of the future man.

Throughout history countless people have awakened the transformative energy. But only a few rare individuals have successfully navigated
the journey and achieved the transformation of consciousness that leads
to the state known as perennial cosmic consciousness, perennial mystical
consciousness, Christ consciousness, Buddha consciousness, nirbikalpa samadhi, or the Sahaja state.

As we have seen from the stories told throughout this book, the spiritual journey can be fraught with obstacles that range from the distraction of
developing psychic gifts; to delusions about the importance of one's role in
the cosmic plan; to lust for money, status, or power; and problems from inadequate cleansing of the unconscious to unbridled egotism. When walking
the spiritual path one needs to step carefully, pay great attention, and make
decisions using intellectual discernment, while always heeding the higher
guidance from the Divine — which comes to us in our inner voice, prayers,
dreams, meditations, and in the scriptures of the world's great faiths.

As you've read through this book, you have become familiar with the
wide variety of types and degrees of Spiritually Transformative Experiences.
You may have compared them to your own STEs or those of people you
know, learned about the difficulties that can occur during the spiritual transformation process, considered the tremendous importance of psychological
housecleaning, and discovered how critical a balanced lifestyle is, as well as
regular daily meditation. Beyond all this, you may have wondered about the
particular spiritual path that you have chosen and whether it is leading you in
the right direction. Although no one can make that judgment for you, there
are a number of signs that can act as guideposts. If the path you are following
is, overall, positive and well-balanced and is helping you progress along the
spiritual path, you will eventually begin to notice positive changes in yourself
and in your outlook. The following are some of the most important signs of
a healthy spiritual transformation of consciousness.

Signs of Healthy Spiritual Transformation of Consciousness

1. You find yourself developing more noble traits of character, such as compassion, kindness, universal love, charity, patience, gentleness, truth, honesty, gratitude, and humility.
2. Your desire to be of service to humanity grows and may become a primary focus as your feelings of unity with all humankind and all creation grow.
3. You have an intense inner yearning for the Divine/Absolute.
4. You may at times experience a spontaneous flow of tears and/or powerful feelings of love or gratitude at the mention or thought of the Divine/Absolute.
5. You find yourself developing a more clear, discerning intellect, and deeper psychological insights, along with a higher moral fibre.
6. You become more peaceful and calm.
7. You find yourself repeatedly experiencing mystical states of consciousness in your deep meditations.

If you can honestly say that you are developing some of these characteristics, you can be confident that you are moving in the right direction. But, of course, even the best of paths can be travelled too quickly or too intensively. If you find you are having more difficulties than you can easily bear or are having crises or spiritual emergencies, take stock of your practices, your lifestyle, and your need for assistance, and make the necessary changes. Perhaps, eventually, you may be one of the rare and blessed individuals who reach the crown of perennial cosmic consciousness in this lifetime. Most yogic traditions contend that many lifetimes of active spiritual transformation of consciousness are necessary before a soul completes its spiritual growth and purification. But wherever we are on the mystical path, the Divine blesses us with many wonderful glimpses of union along the way!

Do We Need a Guru?

We can learn any advanced skill, such as advanced meditation techniques, only from somebody who has already mastered that skill. As I mentioned in chapter 19 on meditation, advanced yogic meditation techniques should be learned from a qualified and experienced spiritual teacher or a guru, and practised under their guidance and supervision. Similarly, we can be successfully guided to soul liberation, higher consciousness, only by someone who is already liberated, in higher consciousness.

Many STE experiencers may wonder "What exactly is a guru?" and "Do I need a guru?" The word "guru," as it is commonly used today, refers simply to a spiritual teacher who instructs students in yoga and meditation. However, in traditional yoga philosophy, the true guru is self-realized, in higher consciousness, enlightened, in a state of nirbikalpa samadhi — ongoing God-communion. Thus there are only a small number of spiritual teachers who are true illumined gurus.

Paramahansa Yogananda explained the guru-disciple relationship in *God Talks with Arjuna: The Bhagavad Gita*.

> A "siddha" is a perfected being who has attained complete liberation in Spirit ... he can then return to earth as an "avatara" — as did Krishna, Jesus, and many other saviors of mankind through the ages. "As often as virtue declines, a God-illumined soul comes on earth to draw virtue again to the fore" (Gita IV:7–8). An avatar, or divine incarnation, has two purposes on earth: quantitative and qualitative. Quantitatively, he uplifts the general populace with his noble teachings of good against evil. But the main purpose of an avatar is qualitative — to create other God-realized souls, helping as many as possible to attain liberation. This latter is the very personal and private spiritual bond formed between the guru and disciple, a union of loyal spiritual endeavor on the part of the disciple and divine blessings bestowed by the guru. Students are those who receive only a little light of truth.

> But disciples are those who follow completely and stead-
> fastly, dedicated and devoted, until they have found their
> own freedom in God.

The yogic tradition contends that when a person is merely exploring spirituality, God/Spirit will provide them with spiritual teachers. Early on the spiritual path, the spiritual seeker is said to have a "propelled heart." The spiritual aspirant will feel the need to explore, to search for spiritual truth, and will try out and learn from many different spiritual teachers and traditions. According to Swami Sri Yukteswar, this is a necessary and important stage on the spiritual path. However, once the spiritual seeker has finished their exploring and has found the spiritual path that resonates with their heart and soul, with a "steady heart" they should fully commit to this path, and deeply and faithfully follow this tradition.

The yogic tradition also contends that when a spiritual seeker is earnestly and sincerely seeking self-realization, God-communion, God/Spirit will bring them an illumined guru, one who can successfully guide them to liberation. If God/Spirit has not provided a sincere spiritual seeker a living illumined guru in this lifetime, the seeker should devotedly follow the spiritual teachings and spiritual guidance of the illumined spiritual Master of the faith tradition which resonates with their soul, whether that Master be Moses, Jesus, Mohammed, Krishna, Buddha, or another illumined Master. In such a case, your faith's spiritual Master is your guru. The illumined guru/spiritual Master of your path will invisibly guide and bless your spiritual efforts, whether your guru be currently incarnated in a physical body, or not. The guru-disciple relationship is held to be an eternal relationship, which continues lifetime after lifetime, as long as may be necessary to bring the disciple to full liberation in Spirit.

Illumination is Life's Highest Goal

Near-Death Experiences and other STEs give us a glimpse of life's highest goal, an expanded mystical state of consciousness — samadhi, nirvana, God-communion. If this enlightenment, or unitive consciousness, is indeed the goal of human evolution, we will all eventually reach this goal over the course of many years or many lifetimes. This fact helps us keep our spiritual experiences in perspective. No matter how profound our STEs might be, they do not make us better than anyone else, nor more loved by God than everyone else. We are all God's beloved children. And having STEs does not mean we are necessarily going to reach cosmic consciousness any faster than anyone else. I believe that this blessed state of illumination is ultimately a gift of grace from the Divine, crowning our years of personal spiritual effort.

Right now thousands, perhaps millions, of persons around the world are undergoing the process of spiritual transformation of consciousness. Within this planetary scheme, each one of us has our own small role to play. By working together we can change our society to one that is more just for all, and more conducive to and more in keeping with the needs of spiritual evolution. By embracing the part we have to play in making the world a better place, and by joining forces with like-minded souls, we can bring the human race as a whole closer to the Divine vision of a harmonious planet blossoming in mystical consciousness. For me, and for many, many others, this is the true meaning of the coming of the cosmic Christ — the coming of generations of humans who exist in a perennial state of Christ consciousness. Spiritually Transformative Experiences and the process of spiritual transformation of consciousness that we are individually experiencing now are but the first steps through a doorway that leads us HOME, to a bright and glorious future for us all.

ACKNOWLEDGEMENTS

I wish to thank Bob Grant and Brian Clegg, who risked their lives to rescue me, Sally, and Gerry — saving our lives after the plane crash in 1979. I also wish to thank Gerald Kruschenske, who skillfully piloted the falling plane, avoiding deadly trees to bring us down onto the semi-frozen lake. I wish to acknowledge and honour the memory of Jean Peters, who lost her life in that fateful crash.

I wish to thank my son Jason Hintermeister for his love, patience, and support as I focused intensely on writing *Touched by the Light*.

I am deeply grateful to Gopi Krishna, who introduced me and many others in the West to the reality of mystical experiences and kundalini awakening happening to many people around the world.

I am profoundly grateful to Paramahansa Yogananda, the "Father of Yoga in the West," who dedicated his life to a multi-faith vision of world brotherhood/sisterhood and to bringing awareness of the science of yoga and meditation to the entire world.

Finally, I wish to thank the many patients, colleagues, and friends who shared the stories of their Spiritually Transformative Experiences with me, and thereby ultimately made this book possible.

BIBLIOGRAPHY

The following bibliographic references that I've drawn on are listed in the order of appearance in each chapter.

Preface

Kason, Yvonne. *Farther Shores: Exploring How Near-Death, Kundalini, and Mystical Experiences Can Transform Ordinary Lives.* Toronto: Harper Collins Canada, 2000, and Bloomington, Indiana: iUniverse, 2008.

Kason, Yvonne, and T. Degler. *A Farther Shore: Exploring How Near-Death and Other Extraordinary Experiences can Change Ordinary Lives.* Toronto: Harper Collins Canada, 1994.

American Center for the Integration of Spiritually Transformative Experiences. aciste.org.

International Association for Neath-Death Studies. iands.org.

Kason, Yvonne. *Soul Lessons from the Light: A Doctor Reflects on Her Five Near-Death Experiences.* Pending publication, 2019.

Chapter 1: My 1979 Plane-Crash Near-Death Experience

Kason, Yvonne. *Farther Shores: Exploring How Near-Death, Kundalini, and Mystical Experiences Can Transform Ordinary Lives.* Toronto: Harper Collins Canada, 2000, and Bloomington, Indiana: iUniverse, 2008.

Kason, Yvonne, and T. Degler. *A Farther Shore: Exploring How Near-Death, Kundalini, and Mystical Experiences Can Change Ordinary Lives.* Toronto: Harper Collins Canada, 1994.

Kason, Yvonne. "Transforming Kundalini and Near-Death Experiences." Skeptiko, May 5, 2019. Podcast 76. skeptiko.com/76-yvonne-kason-kundalini-near-death-experiences/.

———. *Soul Lessons from the Light: A Doctor Reflects on Her Five Near-Death Experiences.* Pending publication, 2019.

Chapter 2: Types of Spiritually Transformative Experiences

Kieffer, Gene, ed. *Kundalini for the New Age: Selected Writings by Gopi Krishna.* New York: Bantam, 1988.

St. Teresa of Avila. *The Interior Castle.* In *Harper's Encyclopedia of Mystical and Paranormal Experience*, by Rosemary Ellen Guiley. San Francisco: Harper, 1991.

Harpur, Tom. *Life After Death.* Toronto: McClelland & Stewart, 1991.

Evans-Wentz, W.Y., ed. *The Tibetan Book of the Dead; or, The After Death Experiences on the Bardo Plane, According to Lama Kazi Dawa-Samdup's English Rendering.* London: Oxford University Press, 1960.

Rinpoche, Sogyal. *The Tibetan Book of Living and Dying.* San Francisco: Harper, 1992.

Budge, A.E. Wallis. *The Book of the Dead: The Papyrus of Ani.* New York: Dover, 1967.

Newman, Barbara. *Sister of Wisdom: St. Hildegard's Theology of the Feminine.* Berkeley and Los Angeles: University of California Press, 1987.

Jung, Carl Gustav. *The Psychology of Kundalini Yoga: Notes of the Seminar Given in 1932 by C.G. Jung.* Edited by Sonu Shamdasani. Princeton: Bollingen Series XCIX, Princeton University Press, 1996.

Yogananda, Paramahansa. Cited in Ghosh, Sananda Lal. *Mejda: The Family and Early Life of Paramahansa Yogananda.* Los Angeles: Self-Realization Press, 1980, 2000.

Barton, Chayim Douglas. "Jungian Psychology and the Mahamudra
in Vajrayana Buddhism." Ph.D. diss., Institute of Transpersonal
Psychology, 1990.

Blofeld, John. *The Tantric Mysticism of Tibet.* New York: Dutton, 1970.

Evans-Wentz, W.Y., ed. *Tibetan Yoga and Secret Doctrines; or, Seven Books
of Wisdom of the Great Path, According to the Late Lama Kazi Dawa-
Samdup's English Rendering.* London: Oxford University Press, 1935.

Lansky, Phillip, and Shen Yu. "Bone Marrow Chi Kung: By Infusing the
Bones with Vital Energy, the Ancient Chinese Learned How to Bolster
the Immune System and Develop Their Spiritual Essence." *Yoga
Journal* 93 (July/August 1990): 21–25.

Greenwell, Bonnie. *Energies of Transformation: A Guide to the Kundalini
Process.* Saratoga, CA: Shakti River, 1990.

Tweedie, Irina. *The Chasm of Fire: A Woman's Experience of Liberation
Through the Teachings of a Sufi Master.* Shaftesbury, UK: Element, 1979.

Kripananda, Swami. "Kundalini: The Energy of Transformation." In
Ancient Wisdom and Modern Science, ed. Stanislav Grof. Albany, NY:
State University of New York Press, 1984.

St. Romain, Philip. *Kundalini Energy and Christian Spirituality: A
Pathway to Growth and Healing.* New York: Crossroad, 1994.

Prayer Department, Unity School of Religious Studies. *Holy Spirit
Regeneration.* Unity Village, MO: Unity School of Christianity, 1993.

Guiley, Rosemary Ellen. *Harper's Encyclopedia of Mystical and Paranormal
Experience.* San Francisco: Harper, 1991.

Feuerstein, Georg. *The Encyclopedic Dictionary of Yoga.* New York:
Paragon, 1990.

———. *The Yoga-Sutra of Patanjali: A New Translation and Commentary.*
Rochester, Vermont: Inner Traditions, 1989.

Baba, Bangali. *The Yogasutra of Patanjali, with Commentary of Vyasa.*
Delhi: Motilal Banarsidass, 1976.

Eliade, Mircea. *Yoga: Immortality and Freedom.* New York: Bollington
Foundation, 1958.

Krishna, Gopi. *Secrets of Kundalini in Panchastavi.* New Delhi: Kundalini
Research and Publication Trust, 1978.

Underhill, Evelyn. *Mysticism.* New York: New American Library, 1974.

Chapter 3: Mystical Experiences

James, William. *The Varieties of Mystical Experience*. New York: New American Library, 1958.

Maslow, Abraham. *Toward a Psychology of Being*. New York: Van Nostrand, 1962.

Bucke, Richard Maurice. *Cosmic Consciousness*. New York: E.P. Dutton, 1969.

Jung, Carl Gustav. *Memories, Dreams, Reflections*. New York: Vintage, 1989.

Kason, Yvonne. "Exploring Spiritually Transformative Experiences: How Near-Death, Kundalini, and Mystical Experiences Changed My Life, and Transform Other Experiencers' Lives." Presented at Chicago IANDS, International Association for Near-Death Studies, Chicago, December 9, 2017.

Chapter 4: Spiritual Energy/Kundalini Episodes

Krishna, Gopi. *Kundalini: The Evolutionary Energy in Man*. Boston: Shambhala, 1970. First published 1967.

Jung, Carl Gustav. *The Psychology of Kundalini Yoga: Notes of the Seminar Given in 1932 by C.G. Jung*. Edited by Sonu Shamdasani. Princeton: Bollingen Series, Princeton University Press, 1996.

Avalon, Arthur. *The Serpent Power: The Secrets of Tantric and Shaktic Yoga*. New York: Dover, 1974. First published 1919 by Luzac & Co. (London).

Eliade, Mircea. *Yoga: Immortality and Freedom*. New York: Bollington Foundation, 1958.

Sannella, Lee. *Kundalini: Psychosis or Transcendence?* San Francisco: H.S. Dakin, 1976.

———. *The Kundalini Experience*. Lower Lake, California: Integral, 1987.

Grof, Stanislav, and Christina Grof, eds. *Spiritual Emergency: When Personal Transformation Becomes a Crisis*. Los Angeles: Tarcher, 1989.

Greenwell, Bonnie. *Energies of Transformation: A Guide to the Kundalini Process*. Cupertino, California: Shakti River, 1990.

Yogananda, Paramahansa. *Autobiography of a Yogi*. Los Angeles: Self-Realization Fellowship, 2007.

———. *God Talks with Arjuna: The Bhagavad Gita; Royal Science of God-Realization; The Immortal Dialogue Between Soul and Spirit.* Los Angeles: Self-Realization Fellowship, 1996.

Grof, Christina, and Stanislav Grof. *The Stormy Search for Self.* Los Angeles: Tarcher, 1990.

Grof, Stanislav. *Beyond the Brain.* Albany, NY: State University of New York, 1985.

Krishna, Gopi. *The Biological Basis of Religion and Genius.* New York: Harper and Row, 1972.

———. *Higher Consciousness: The Evolutionary Thrust of Kundalini.* New York: Julian, 1974.

Kieffer, Gene, ed. *Kundalini for the New Age: Selected Writings by Gopi Krishna.* New York: Bantam, 1988.

———. *Kundalini, Empowering Human Evolution: Selected Writings of Gopi Krishna.* New York: Paragon, 1996.

Kason, Yvonne. "My Kundalini Awakening." Presented at the IANDS, International Association for Near-Death Studies, 2018 Conference, STE Experiencers' Panel, Bellevue, Washington, September 2, 2018.

Jyoti. *An Angel Called My Name: A Story of a Transformational Energy That Lives in the Body.* Prague: Dharma Gaia, 1998.

Alcoholics Anonymous World Service. *Pass It On: The Story of Bill Wilson and How the A.A. Message Reached the World.* New York: Alcoholics Anonymous World Services, 1984.

Joy, W. Brugh. *Joy's Way: A Map for the Transformational Journey.* Los Angeles: Tarcher, 1979.

Chapter 5: Near-Death Experiences

Moody, Raymond A., Jr. *Life After Life: The Investigation of a Phenomenon; Survival of Bodily Death.* New York: Bantam, 1976.

———. *The Light Beyond.* New York: Bantam, 1988.

Kershner, Irvin, dir. *Star Wars Episode V: The Empire Strikes Back.* 1980; Los Angeles: Twentieth Century Fox.

Schumacher, Joel, dir. *Flatliners.* 1990; Los Angeles: Stonebridge Entertainment.

Pearson, Patricia. *Opening Heaven's Door: What the Dying May Be Trying to Tell Us About Where They're Going.* Toronto: Vintage Canada, 2015.

Burpo, Todd, and Lynn Vincent. *Heaven Is for Real.* Nashville: Thomas Nelson, 2010.

Alexander, Eben. *Proof of Heaven: A Neurosurgeon's Journey into the Afterlife.* New York: Simon and Schuster, 2012.

Moorjani, Anita. *Dying To Be Me: My Journey from Cancer, to Near Death, to True Healing.* Carlsbad, California: Hay House, 2012.

Neal, Mary C. *To Heaven and Back: A Doctor's Extraordinary Account of Her Death, Heaven, Angels, and Life Again.* Colorado Springs: Waterbrook, 2011.

Ring, Kenneth. *Heading Toward Omega: In Search of the Meaning of the Near-Death Experience.* New York: William Morrow, 1984.

van Lommel, Pim. *Consciousness Beyond Life: The Science of the Near-Death Experience.* New York: HarperOne, 2010.

Holden, Janice Miner, Bruce Greyson, and Debbie James, eds. *The Handbook of Near-Death Experiences; Thirty Years of Investigation.* Santa Barbara, California: Praeger Publishers, 2009.

Yogananda, Paramahansa. *Autobiography of a Yogi.* Los Angeles: Self-Realization Fellowship, 2007.

Greyson, Bruce. "Near-Death Experiences and the Physio-Kundalini Syndrome." *Journal of Religion and Health* 32, no. 4 (Winter 1993): 277–90.

Ring, Kenneth, and Evelyn Elsaesser Valarino. *Lessons from the Light: What We Can Learn from the Near-Death Experience.* Needham, Massachusetts: Moment Point, 2003.

Harpur, Tom. *Life After Death.* Toronto: McClelland & Stewart, 1991.

Kason, Yvonne. "Near-Death Experiences and Kundalini Awakening: Exploring the Links." *Journal of Near-Death Studies* 12, no. 3 (Spring 1994): 143–57.

Brinkley, Dannion, and Paul Perry. *Saved by the Light: The True Story of a Man Who Died Twice and the Profound Revelations He Received.* New York: Harper Paperbacks, 1994.

Storm, Howard, in *A Message of Hope: The Near Death Experience; Accounts and Perspectives.* Video by M. Taylor Bach. Ft. Thomas, Kentucky: The Counselling Institute, 1987.

Kason, Yvonne. "Defining Spiritually Transformative Experiences and Their After-Effects." Presented at the IANDS, International Association for Near-Death Studies, 2018 Conference, Bellevue, Washington, September 1, 2018.

———. "Purifying the Heart." Presented at the IANDS, International Association for Near-Death Studies, 2017 Conference, Denver, Colorado, August 5, 2017.

———. *Soul Lessons from the Light: A Doctor Reflects on Her Five Near-Death Experiences*. Pending publication, 2019.

Eadie, Betty and Curtis Taylor. *Embraced by the Light*. Placerville, California: Gold Leaf, 1992.

Tassell-Matuma, Natasha A., and Kate Steadman. "Of Love and Light: A Case Report of End-of-Life Experiences." *Journal of Near-Death Studies* 34, no. 1 (Fall 2015): 5–26.

Brinkley, Dannion. As quoted by Mary Beth Schweigert in "Dannion Brinkley Has Died Three Times — and Lived to Tell About It." Lancaster online, July 21, 2014. lancasteronline.com/features/dannion-brinkley-has-died-three-times-and-lived-to-tell/article_bad0578e-0e68-11e4-9a9f-0017a43b2370.html.

Atwater, P.M.H. *I Died Three Times in 1977 — The Complete Story*. Albany, NY: Cinema of the Mind/Starving Artists Workshop, 2010. Kindle.

Chapter 6: Death-Watch Experiences and After-Death Communications

Kason, Yvonne. "Death-Watch Experiences." Presented at the 2018 ACISTE, American Center for the Integration of Spiritually Transformative Experiences, Annual Conference, Keynote Speaker's Luncheon Presentation, Chicago, October 5, 2018.

———. "Defining Spiritually Transformative Experiences and Their After-Effects." Presented at the IANDS, International Association for Near-Death Studies, 2018 Conference, Bellevue, Washington, September 1, 2018.

———. *Farther Shores: Exploring How Near-Death, Kundalini, and Mystical Experiences Can Transform Ordinary Lives*. Toronto: Harper Collins Canada, 2000, and Bloomington, Indiana: iUniverse, 2008.

———. "NDE-Variants and Kundalini: Exploring Death-Watch and Death-Bed Experiences." Presented at the 1995 Kundalini Research Network Conference, Philadelphia, 1995.

———. "Near-Death and Death-Watch Experiences: Openings Onto the Mystic Path." Presented at the IANDS, International Association for Near-Death Studies, 1999 Conference, Vancouver, August 1999.

Tassell-Matuma, Natasha A., and Kate Steadman. "Of Love and Light: A Case Report of End-of-Life Experiences." *Journal of Near-Death Studies* 34, no. 1 (Fall 2015): 5–26.

Moody, Raymond A., Jr., and Paul Perry. *Glimpses of Eternity: Sharing a Loved One's Passage from This Life to the Next.* New York: Guideposts, 2010.

Peters, William, and Michael Kinsella. "The Shared-Death Experience: Profound Healing and Transformation for the Dying and Their Loved Ones." Presented at the 2018 ACISTE, American Center for the Integration of Spiritually Transformative Experiences, Annual Conference, Chicago, October 5, 2018.

Daya Mata, Sri. Quoted in *Awake: The Life of Yogananda,* based on the film by Paola Di Florio and Lisa Leeman. Los Angeles: Self-Realization Fellowship, 2015.

Guggenheim, Bill, and Judy Guggenheim. *Hello from Heaven: A New Field of Research; After-Death Communication Confirms That Life and Love Are Eternal.* New York: Bantam, 1997.

Holden, Janice Miner. "After-Death Communication." In *Connecting Soul, Spirit, Mind, and Body: A Collection of Spiritual and Religious Practices in Counseling,* edited by Ryan D. Foster and Janice Miner Holden, 3–11. Alexandria, Virginia: Association for Spiritual, Ethical, and Religious Values in Counseling, 2017.

Chapter 7: Psychic Experiences

McCartney, Francesca. *Personal Communication.* Mill Valley, California: Academy of Intuitive Studies, 1990.

Ring, Kenneth. *The Omega Project.* New York: William Morrow, 1992.

Fowler, Raymond E. *The Andreasson Affair.* Englewood Cliffs, New Jersey: Prentice-Hall, 1979.

Steiger, Brad. *The Fellowship*. New York: Ballantine, 1988.

Thompson, Keith. "The UFO Encounter Experience as a Crisis of Transformation." In *Spiritual Emergency: When Personal Transformation Becomes a Crisis*, edited by Stanislav Grof and Christina Grof. Los Angeles: Tarcher, 1989.

Kason, Yvonne. "Psychic Experiences are not always positive/spiritual," in "Defining Spiritually Transformative Experiences." Presented at the 2018 ACISTE, American Center for the Integration of Spiritually Transformative Experiences, Annual Conference, Chicago, 2018.

Chapter 8: Inspired Creativity and Genius

Newman, Barbara. *Sister of Wisdom: St. Hildegard's Theology of the Feminine*. Berkeley and Los Angeles: University of California Press, 1987.

Hildegard of Bingen. Letter from Hildegard of Bingen to Guibert of Gembloux. Excerpted in Barbara Newman, *Sister of Wisdom: St. Hildegard's Theology of the Feminine*. Berkeley and Los Angeles: University of California Press, 1987.

Yogananda, Paramahansa. *Autobiography of a Yogi*. Los Angeles: Self-Realization Fellowship, 2007.

Ghosh, Sananda Lal. *Mejda: The Family and the Early Life of Paramahansa Yogananda*. Los Angeles: Self-Realization Fellowship, 2000.

Harrison, George. Interview in *Awake: The Life of Yogananda*: based on the film by Paola Di Florio and Lisa Leeman, 33, 176. Los Angeles: Self-Realization Fellowship, 2015.

Shankar, Ravi. Interview in *Awake: The Life of Yogananda*: based on the film by Paola Di Florio and Lisa Leeman, 30. Los Angeles: Self-Realization Fellowship, 2015.

Jobs, Steve, as referenced by Hitendra Wadwa and Mark Benioff. Interview in *Awake: The Life of Yogananda*: based on the film by Paola Di Florio and Lisa Leeman, 229. Los Angeles: Self-Realization Fellowship, 2015.

Yogananda, Paramahansa. *God Talks with Arjuna: The Bhagavad Gita; Royal Science of God-Realization*. Los Angeles: Self-Realization Fellowship, 1996.

————. *The Second Coming of Christ: The Resurrection of the Christ Within You (A Revelatory Commentary on the Original Teachings of Jesus).* Los Angeles: Self-Realization Fellowship, 2004.

————. *Wine of the Mystic: The Rubaiyat of Omar Khayyam; A Spiritual Interpretation.* Los Angeles: Self-Realization Fellowship, 1994.

————. *The Science of Religion.* Los Angeles: Self-Realization Fellowship, 1987.

————. *Whispers from Eternity.* Los Angeles: Self-Realization Fellowship, 2008.

————. *Sayings of Paramahansa Yogananda.* Los Angeles: Self-Realization Fellowship, 1994.

————. *Scientific Healing Affirmations.* Los Angeles: Self-Realization Fellowship, 1990.

————. *Songs of the Soul.* Los Angeles: Self-Realization Fellowship, 1983.

————. *Where There Is Light: Insight and Inspiration for Meeting Life's Challenges.* Los Angeles: Self-Realization Fellowship, 2015.

————. *In the Sanctuary of the Soul: A Guide to Effective Prayer.* Los Angeles: Self-Realization Fellowship, 1998.

————. *Inner Peace: How to Be Calmly Active and Actively Calm.* Los Angeles: Self-Realization Fellowship, 2004.

————. *How You Can Talk With God.* Los Angeles: Self-Realization Fellowship, 1998.

————. *Metaphysical Meditations.* Los Angeles: Self-Realization Fellowship, 1998.

————. *The Law of Success.* Los Angeles: Self-Realization Fellowship, 2013.

————. *Why God Permits Evil and How to Rise Above It.* Los Angeles: Self-Realization Fellowship, 2002.

————. *Cosmic Chants: Spiritualizes Songs for Divine Communion.* Los Angeles: Self-Realization Fellowship, 2002.

Chopra, Deepak. Interview in *Awake: The Life of Yogananda*: based on the film by Paola Di Florio and Lisa Leeman, 42. Los Angeles: Self-Realization Fellowship, 2015.

Abell, Arthur M. *Talks with Great Composers.* Garmisch-Partenkirchen: G.E. Schroeder-Verlag, 1964.

Einstein, Albert. *Living Philosophies.* New York: Simon & Schuster, 1931.

————. *The World As I See It*. New York: Citadel, 1979.

Saraswati, Swami Satyananda. *Kundalini Tantra*. Munger, India: Bihar School of Yoga, 1992.

Chapter 9: The Yogic Model of Consciousness and Kundalini

Krishna, Gopi. *Kundalini: The Evolutionary Energy in Man*. Boston: Shambhala, 1970. First published 1967.

————. *Higher Consciousness: The Evolutionary Thrust of Kundalini*. New York: Julian, 1974.

————. *The Biological Basis of Religion and Genius*. New Delhi: Kundalini Research and Publication Trust, 1978.

Saraswati, Swami Satyananda. *Kundalini Tantra*. Munger, India: Bihar School of Yoga, 1992.

Yogananda, Paramahansa. *Autobiography of a Yogi*. Los Angeles: Self-Realization Fellowship, 2007.

————. *God Talks with Arjuna: The Bhagavad Gita; Royal Science of God-Realization*. Los Angeles: Self-Realization Fellowship, 1996.

————. *The Yoga of the Bhagavad Gita*. Los Angeles: Self-Realization Fellowship, 2007.

Kason, Yvonne. "Kundalini, the Forefront of Consciousness Research: Evolving Paradigms for the New Millennium." Presented at the 1997 Kundalini Research Network Conference, Watsonville, California, 1997.

Guiley, Rosemary Ellen. *Harper's Encyclopedia of Mystical and Paranormal Experiences*. San Francisco: Harper, 1991.

Eliade, Mircea. *Yoga: Immortality and Freedom*. New York: Bollington Foundation, 1958.

Krishna, Gopi. *Living with Kundalini: The Autobiography of Gopi Krishna*. Edited by Leslie Shepard. Boston: Shambhala, 1993.

————. *The Dawn of a New Science*. New Delhi: Kundalini Research and Publication Trust, 1978.

Newberg, Andrew, and Mark Robert Waldman. *How God Changes Your Brain: Breakthrough Findings from a Leading Neuroscientist*. New York: Ballantine, 2009.

Doidge, Norman. *The Brain That Changes Itself: Stories of Personal Triumph from the Frontiers of Brain Science.* New York: Penguin, 2007.

————. *The Brain's Way of Healing: Remarkable Discoveries and Recoveries from the Frontiers of Neuroplasticity.* New York: Penguin, 2015.

Ring, Kenneth. *Heading Toward Omega: In Search of the Meaning of Near-Death Experience.* New York: William Morrow, 1984.

————. *The Omega Project: Near-Death Experiences, UFO Encounters, and Mind at Large.* New York: William Morrow and Co., 1992.

Greyson, Bruce. "Some Neuropsychological Correlates of the Physio-Kundalini Syndrome." *Journal of Transpersonal Psychology* 32, no. 2 (2000): 123–34.

————. "Near-Death Experiences and the Physio-Kundalini Syndrome." *Journal of Religion and Health* 32, no. 4 (Winter 1993): 277–90.

Feuerstein, Georg. *The Encyclopedic Dictionary of Yoga.* New York: Paragon House, 1990.

Yogananda, Paramahansa. *God Talks with Arjuna: The Bhagavad Gita; Royal Science of God-Realization.* Los Angeles: Self-Realization Fellowship, 1996.

Feuerstein, Georg. *The Yoga-Sutra of Patanjali: A New Translation and Commentary.* Rochester, VT: Inner Traditions, 1989.

Krishna, Gopi. *Kundalini: The Evolutionary Energy in Man.* Boston: Shambhala, 1970. First published 1967.

————. *The Secret of Yoga.* London: Turnstone, 1972.

————. *The Awakening of Kundalini.* Toronto: FIND Research Trust, 1989.

Chapter 10: Researching STE Experiencers

Greenwell, Bonnie. *Energies of Transformation: A Guide to the Kundalini Process.* Cupertino, California: Shakti River Press, 1990.

Kason, Yvonne, Michael Bradford, Paul Pond, and Bonnie Greenwell. "Spiritual Emergence Syndrome and Kundalini Awakening — How Are They Related? The Kundalini Research Questionnaire Pilot Project Results, 1991." In *Academy of Religion and Psychical Research 1992 Annual Conference Proceedings.* Philadelphia, 1992.

Krishna, Gopi. *Living with Kundalini: The Autobiography of Gopi Krishna*. Edited by Leslie Shepard. Boston: Shambhala, 1993.

Lukoff, David, Frances Lu, and Robert Turner. "Towards a More Culturally Sensitive DSM-IV: Psychoreligious and Psychospiritual Problems." *Journal of Nervous and Mental Disease* 180, no. 11 (November 1992): 673–82

American Psychiatric Association. *Diagnostic and Statistical Manual of Mental Disorders*, 4th ed. Washington: American Psychiatric Association, 1994.

Brook, Marie Grace. "Recovering Balance After the Big Leap: Overcoming Challenges in Integrating Spiritually Transformative Experiences." Presented at the 2018 ACISTE, American Center for the Integration of Spiritually Transformative Experiences, Annual Conference, Chicago, October 5, 2018.

Greyson, Bruce. "Incidence and Correlates of Near-Death Experiences in a Cardiac Care Unit." *General Hospital Psychiatry* 25, no. 4 (July/August 2003): 269–76.

van Lommel, Pim, Ruud van Wees, Vincent Meyers, and Ingrid Elfferich. "Near-Death Experiences in Survivors of Cardiac Arrest: A Prospective Study in the Netherlands." *The Lancet* 358 (December 2001): 2039–45.

Holden, Janice Miner, Cody Lankford, and Leslie Holmes. "After-Death Communication and the Biblical Fruits of the Spirit: An Online Survey." *Spirituality in Clinical Practice* 6, no. 1 (March 2019): 15–26.

Benning, Tony. "When Kundalini Shows Up in a Psychiatric Clinic: Diagnostic Delays and Clinical Conundrums." Presented at the 2018 ACISTE, American Center for the Integration of Spiritually Transformative Experiences, Annual Conference, Chicago, October 6, 2018.

Chapter 11: Patterns of STEs and Their After-Effects Over Time

Kason, Yvonne. "The Modern Kundalini Hypothesis: A Bio-Psycho-Spiritual Model of Transformation of Consciousness." *Proceedings of the Sixth Conference on Treatment and Research of Experienced Anomalous Trauma*, Virginia Beach, 1994.

Underhill, Evelyn. *Mysticism.* New York: New American Library, 1974.

Yogananda, Paramahansa. *Autobiography of a Yogi.* Los Angeles: Self-Realization Fellowship, 2007.

Chapter 12: Physical STE After-Effect Symptoms

Kason, Yvonne. "The Modern Kundalini Hypothesis: A Bio-Psycho-Spiritual Model of Transformation of Consciousness." *Proceedings of the Sixth Conference on Treatment and Research of Experienced Anomalous Trauma*, Virginia Beach, 1994.

Kieffer, Gene, ed. *Kundalini for the New Age: Selected Writings of Gopi Krishna.* New York: Bantam, 1988.

Greenwell, Bonnie. *Energies of Transformation: A Guide to the Kundalini Process.* Cupertino, California: Shakti River, 1990.

Krishna, Gopi. *Living with Kundalini: The Autobiography of Gopi Krishna.* Edited by Leslie Shepard. Boston: Shambhala, 1993.

Yogananda, Paramahansa. *Autobiography of a Yogi.* Los Angeles: Self-Realization Fellowship, 2007.

Greyson, Bruce, Mitchell Liester, Lee Kinsey, and Steve Alsum. "Electromagnetic Phenomena Reported by Near-Death Experiencers." *Journal of Near-Death Studies* 33, no. 4 (Summer 2015): 213–43.

Blalock, Sarah, Janice Miner Holden, and P.M.H. Atwater. "Electromagnetic and Other Environmental Effects Following Near-Death Experiences." *Journal of Near-Death Studies* 33, no. 4 (Summer 2015): 181–211.

Kason, Yvonne. "Counselling Clients with Spiritual or Religious Experiences." Presented at the Centre for Addiction and Mental Health, Queen Street Site, Toronto, June 23, 1999.

Chapter 13: Psychological STE After-Effect Symptoms

Kason, Yvonne. "Deepening Connection to Spirit: The Kundalini Process and Spiritual Transformation." Presented at the Life Enrichment Centre, Edmonton, April 24, 1999.

Bragdon, Emma. *The Call of Spiritual Emergency: From Personal Crisis to Personal Transformation*. San Francisco: Harper and Row, 1990.

Greenwell, Bonnie. *Energies of Transformation: A Guide to the Kundalini Process*. Cupertino, California: Shakti River, 1990.

Chapter 14: Spiritual and Paranormal STE After-Effect Symptoms

Yogananda, Paramahansa. *Scientific Healing Affirmations: Theory and Practice of Concentration*. Los Angeles: Self-Realization Fellowship, 1998.

Harrison, George. Interview in *Awake: The Life of Yogananda*: based on the film by Paola Di Florio and Lisa Leeman, 33, 176. Los Angeles: Self-Realization Fellowship, 2015.

Besant, Annie. *The Ancient Wisdom: An Outline of Theosophical Teachings*. Adyar, India: Theosophical Publishing House, 1939.

Crabtree, Adam. *Multiple Man: Explorations in Possession and Multiple Personality*. Don Mills, Ontario: Grafton, 1985.

Peck, M. Scott. *People of the Lie: The Hope for Healing Human Evil*. New York: Touchstone, 1983.

Gray, John, Jennifer Love Hewitt, Ian Sander, and Kim Moses, executive producers. *Ghost Whisperer*. Television series, CBS Television Studios, 2005–2010.

Ravich, Rand. Writer and Producer. *The Astronaut's Wife*. Film. New Line Cinema, 1999.

Beatty, Warren. Executive Producer. *Heaven Can Wait*. Film. Paramount Pictures, 1978. Based on the play *Heaven Can Wait* by Harry Segall.

Yogananda, Paramahansa. "Where Are Our Departed Loved Ones?" In *The Divine Romance: Collected Talks and Essays on Realizing God in Daily Life, Volume II*, 289. Los Angeles: Self-Realization Fellowship, 1986.

Chapter 15: STEs, Spiritual Emergencies, and Psychoses

Grof, Stanislav, and Christina Grof, eds. *Spiritual Emergency: When Personal Transformation Becomes a Crisis*. Los Angeles: Tarcher, 1989.

Bragdon, Emma. *A Sourcebook for Helping People in Spiritual Emergency.* Los Altos, California: Lightening Up, 1988.

———. *The Call of Spiritual Emergency: From Personal Crisis to Personal Transformation.* San Francisco: Harper and Row, 1990.

American Psychiatric Association. *Diagnostic and Statistical Manual of Mental Disorders*, 5th ed. Arlington, Virginia: American Psychiatric Association, 2013.

Lukoff, David. "Diagnosis of Mystical Experiences with Psychotic Features." *The Journal of Transpersonal Psychology* 17 (1985): 155–81.

Sannella, Lee. *Kundalini: Psychosis or Transcendence.* San Francisco: H.S. Dakin, 1976.

Ghosh, Sananda Lal. "Discourses of Paramahansa Yogananda." In *Mejda: The Family and the Early Life of Paramahansa Yogananda.* Los Angeles: Self-Realization Fellowship, 2000.

Chapter 16: Who Has Spiritual Emergencies and Why?

Krishna, Gopi. *Living with Kundalini: The Autobiography of Gopi Krishna.* Edited by Leslie Shepard. Boston: Shambhala, 1993.

Feuerstein, Georg. *The Yoga-Sutra of Patanjali: A New Translation and Commentary.* Rochester, Vermont: Inner Traditions, 1989.

Eliade, Mircea. *Yoga: Immortality and Freedom.* New York: Bollington Foundation, 1958.

Yogananda, Paramahansa. *God Talks with Arjuna: The Bhagavad Gita; Royal Science of God-Realization.* Los Angeles: Self-Realization Fellowship, 1996.

Chapter 17: Strategies for Living with Spiritual Transformation

Harris, Barbara, and Lionel C. Bascom. *Full Circle: The Near-Death Experience and Beyond.* New York: Pocket Books/Simon and Schuster, 1990.

Kason, Yvonne. "EHEs, Spiritual Transformation, and Kundalini Awakening: A Clinical Perspective." In *Academy of Religion and Psychical Research 1993 Annual Conference Proceedings.* Philadelphia, 1993.

Krishna, Gopi. "Religion, Science, and Illumination." In *Gopi Krishna: Selected Interviews and Discourses, 1979–1983*. Transcription by Michael Bradford. Flesherton, Ontario: FIND Research Trust, 1992.

Breaux, Charles. *Journey into Consciousness: The Chakras, Tantra, and Jungian Psychology*. York Beach, Maine: Nicolas-Hays, 1989.

Chapter 18: Psycho-Spiritual Housecleaning

Yogananda, Paramahansa. *God Talks with Arjuna: The Bhagavad Gita; Royal Science of God-Realization*. Los Angeles: Self-Realization Fellowship, 1996.

Kason, Yvonne. "Counselling Persons with Kundalini and Other Spiritually Transformative Experiences." Presented at the 1997 Kundalini Research Network Conference, Watsonville, California, 1997.

———. "Understanding NDEs and Their After-Effects: Learning from the Kundalini and Chakra Model." Presented at the IANDS, International Association for Near-Death Studies, 1999 Conference, Vancouver, 1999.

Bragdon, Emma. *The Call of Spiritual Emergency: From Personal Crisis to Personal Transformation*. San Francisco: Harper and Row, 1990.

Greenwell, Bonnie. *Energies of Transformation: A Guide to the Kundalini Process*. Cupertino, California: Shakti River, 1990.

Saraswati, Swami Satyananda. *Kundalini Tantra*. Munger, India: Bihar School of Yoga, 1992.

Kripananda, Swami. "Kundalini: The Energy of Transformation." In *Ancient Wisdom and Modern Science*. Edited by Stanislav Grof. Albany, New York: State University of New York Press, 1984.

Woolger, Roger J. *Other Lives, Other Selves: A Jungian Psychotherapist Discovers Past Lives*. New York: Bantam, 1988.

Jung, Carl Gustav. *The Psychology of Kundalini Yoga: Notes of the Seminar Given in 1932 by C.G. Jung*. Edited by Sonu Shamdasani. Princeton, New Jersey: Bollingen Series, Princeton University Press, 1996.

Barton, Chayim Douglas. "Jungian Psychology and the Mahamudra in Vajrayana Buddhism." Ph.D. diss., Institute of Transpersonal Psychology, Menlo Park, California, 1990.

Chapter 19: Meditation — The Key to Spiritual Deepening

Yogananda, Paramahansa. *Autobiography of a Yogi*. Los Angeles: Self-Realization Fellowship, 2007.

———. "August 19." In *Spiritual Diary: An Inspirational Thought for Each Day*. Los Angeles: Self-Realization Fellowship, 1996.

Feuerstein, Georg. *The Yoga-Sutra of Patanjali: A New Translation and Commentary*. Rochester, Vermont: Inner Traditions, 1989.

Baba, Bangali. *Yogasutra of Patanjali with the Commentary of Vyasa: Translated from Sanskrit into English with Copious Notes*. Delhi: Motilal Banarsidass, 1990.

Yogananda, Paramahansa. *God Talks with Arjuna: The Bhagavad Gita; Royal Science of God-Realization*. Los Angeles: Self-Realization Fellowship, 1996.

Newberg, Andrew, and Mark Robert Waldman. *How God Changes Your Brain: Breakthrough Findings from a Leading Neuroscientist*. New York: Ballantine, 2009.

Doidge, Norman. *The Brain That Changes Itself: Stories of Personal Triumph from the Frontiers of Brain Science*. New York: Penguin, 2007.

———. *The Brain's Way of Healing: Remarkable Discoveries and Recoveries from the Frontiers of Neuroplasticity*. New York: Penguin, 2015.

Chapter 20: Finding Our Way Home

Feuerstein, Georg. *The Encyclopedic Dictionary of Yoga*. New York: Paragon House, 1990.

Eliade, Mircea. *Yoga: Immortality and Freedom*. New York: Bollington Foundation, 1958.

Krishna, Gopi. *Higher Consciousness*. New York: Julian, 1974.

Yogananda, Paramahansa. *God Talks with Arjuna: The Bhagavad Gita; Royal Science of God-Realization*. Los Angeles: Self-Realization Fellowship, 1996.

Yukteswar, Swami Sri. *The Holy Science*. Los Angeles: Self-Realization Fellowship, 2010.

Kason, Yvonne. "Purification of the Heart: Five Stages on the Spiritual Path." Presented to the Spirituality in Health-Care Network, Toronto, October 2, 2010.

Related Works on Kundalini and Other Subjects

Arundale, G.S. *Kundalini: An Occult Experience.* Adyar, India: The Theosophical Publishing House, 1974.

Aurobindo, Sri. *Lights on Yoga.* 9th ed. Pondicherry, India: Sri Aurobindo Ashram Press, 1981.

Berman, Phillip. *The Journey Home: What Near-Death Experiences and Mysticism Teach Us About the Gift of Life.* New York: Pocket Books, 1996.

Bruyere, Rosalyn. *Wheels of Light: Chakras, Auras, and the Healing Energy of the Body.* New York: Fireside, 1994.

Chaney, Earlyne, and William Messick. *Kundalini and the Third Eye.* Rancho Cucamonga, California: Astara, 1980.

Chinmoy, Sri. *Kundalini: The Mother Power.* New York: Agni, 1974.

Colton, Ann Ree. *Kundalini West.* Glendale, California: Ann Ree Colton Foundation, 1978.

Condron, Barbara. *Kundalini Rising: Mastering Creative Energies.* Springfield, Missouri: School of Metaphysics Publishing, 1994.

Danielou, Alain. *Yoga: Mastering the Secrets of Matter and the Universe.* Rochester, Vermont: Inner Traditions, 1991.

Devananda, Swami Vishnu. *Meditation and Mantras.* New York: OM Lotus, 1981.

Edwards, Lawrence. *The Soul's Journey: Guidance from the Goddess Within.* Putnam Valley, New York: Lawrence Edwards, 1996.

Fraser, Sylvia. *The Book of Strange: A Thinking Person's Guide to Psychic Phenomena.* Toronto: Doubleday Canada, 1992.

Frawley, David. *Tantric Yoga and the Wisdom Goddesses: Spiritual Secrets in Ayurveda.* Salt Lake City, Utah: Passages, 1994.

Goswami, Amit. *The Self-Aware Universe: How Consciousness Creates the Material World.* New York: Jeremy P. Tarcher/Putnam, 1993.

Greyson, Bruce. "The Physio-Kundalini Syndrome and Mental Illness." *Journal of Transpersonal Psychology* 25 (1993): 43–58.

Greyson, Bruce, and Nancy Bush. "Distressing Near-Death Experiences." *Psychiatry* 55, no. 1 (March 1992): 95–110.

Grof, Stanislav, ed. *Ancient Wisdom and Modern Science*. Albany, New York: State University of New York Press, 1984.

Harris, Barbara. *Spiritual Awakenings: A Guidebook for Experiencers and Those Who Care About Them*. Baltimore, Maryland: Stage 3, 1993.

Irving, Darrel. *Serpent of Fire: A Modern View of Kundalini*. Introduction by Gene Kieffer: "Two Interviews with Gopi Krishna." York Beach, Maine: Samuel Weiser, 1995.

Khalsa, Rama Karan Singh. *Sadhana Guidelines for Kundalini Yoga Daily Practice*. Los Angeles: Archline, 1988.

Kripananda, Swami. *Science of Meditation*. Bombay: New Darnodaya, 1977.

———. *The Sacred Power: A Seeker's Guide to Kundalini*. South Fallsberg, New York: SYDA Foundation, 1995.

Krishna, Gopi. *The Riddle of Consciousness*. New York: Central Institute for Kundalini Research and Kundalini Research Foundation, 1976.

———. *Yoga: A Vision of Its Future*. New Delhi: Kundalini Research and Publication Trust, 1978.

———. *The Real Nature of Mystical Experience*. Toronto: New Age, 1979.

———. *Kundalini in Time and Space*. New Delhi: Kundalini Research and Publication Trust, 1979.

———. *The Shape of Events to Come*. New Delhi: Kundalini Research and Publication Trust, 1979.

———. *Reason and Revelation*. Toronto: New Age, 1979.

———. *The Present Crisis*. New York: New Concepts, 1981.

———. *The Way to Self-Knowledge*. New York: New Concepts, 1985.

———. *From the Unseen*. Toronto: FIND Research Trust, 1985.

———. *The Wonder of the Brain*. Toronto: FIND Research Trust, 1987.

Lutyens, Mary. *Krishnamurti: The Years of Awakening*. New York: Avon, 1975.

Malik, Arjan Dass. *Kundalini and Meditation*. New Delhi: Manohar, 1994.

Moody, Raymond A., Jr., and Paul Perry. *Coming Back: A Psychiatrist Explores Past-Life Journeys*. New York: Bantam, 1991.

Mookerjee, Ajit. *Kundalini: The Arousal of the Inner Energy*. Rochester, Vermont: Destiny, 1991.

Muktananda, Swami. *Kundalini: The Secret of Life*. South Fallsberg, New York: SYDA Foundation, 1979.

Mumford, Jonn. *A Chakra and Kundalini Workbook: Psycho-Spiritual Techniques for Health, Rejuvenation, Psychic Powers and Spiritual Realization*. St. Paul, Minnesota: Llewellyn, 1994.

Narayanananda, Swami. *The Primal Power In Man, or The Kundalini Shakti*. 4th rev. ed. Rishikesh, India: Shri Narayana, 1975.

Paulson, Genevieve Lewis. *Kundalini and the Chakras: A Practical Manual — Evolution in This Lifetime*. St. Paul, Minnesota: Llewellyn, 1993.

Pearson, Patricia. *Opening Heaven's Door: What the Dying May Be Trying to Tell Us About Where They're Going*. Toronto: Random House Canada, 2014.

Rai, Dina Nath. *Kundalini Awakening: A Practical Guide*. Lucknow, India: Kundalini Yoga Research Institute, 1997.

Scott, Mary. *Kundalini in the Physical World*. London: Arkana, 1983.

Shivananda, Swami. *Kundalini Yoga*. Bangalore, India: Yogavedanta Forest Academy Press, 1994.

Svoboda, Robert. *Aghora II: Kundalini*. Albuquerque, New Mexico: Brotherhood of Life, 1993.

Targ, Russell, and Jane Katra. *Miracles of Mind: Exploring Nonlocal Consciousness and Spiritual Healing*. Novato, California: New World Library, 1998.

Tirtha, Swami Vishnu. *Devatma Shakti: Kundalini; Divine Power*. 6th ed. Rishikesh, India: Yoga Shri Peeth Trust, 1993.

White, John, ed. *Kundalini, Evolution and Enlightenment*. New York: Paragon House, 1990.

Whitfield, Barbara Harris. *Spiritual Awakenings: Insights of the Near-Death Experience and Other Doorways to Our Soul*. Deerfield Beach, Florida: Health Communications, 1995.

Whitton, Joel, and Joe Fisher. *Life Between Life: Scientific Explorations into the Void Separating One Incarnation from the Next*. New York: Warner, 1986.

Wilber, Ken, Jack Engler, and Daniel Brown. *Transformations of Consciousness: Conventional and Contemplative Perspectives on Development*. Boston: Shambhala, 1986.

Yogananda, Paramahansa. *Man's Eternal Quest and Other Talks*. Los Angeles: Self-Realization Fellowship, 1992.

———. *Journey to Self-Realization: Discovering the Gifts of the Soul*. Los Angeles: Self-Realization Fellowship, 1997.

———. *The Divine Romance: The Collected Talks and Essays, Volume III*. Los Angeles: Self-Realization Fellowship, 1992.

———. *The Yoga of the Bhagavad Gita: An Introduction to India's Universal Science of God-Realization*. Los Angeles: Self-Realization Fellowship, 2007.

———. *The Yoga of Jesus: Understanding the Hidden Teachings of the Gospels*. Los Angeles: Self-Realization Fellowship, 2007.

INDEX

ABOUT THE AUTHOR

Ronald Miller Photography

Dr. Yvonne Kason, M.D., M.Ed., C.C.F.P., F.C.F.P., is a family physician and transpersonal psychotherapist (retired), author, and public speaker, previously on faculty at the University of Toronto, Faculty of Medicine. Dr. Kason is a board member of IANDS, the International Association for Near-Death Studies, and a member of ACISTE, the American Center for the Integration of Spiritually Transformative Experiences. Dr. Kason is the person who first coined the phrase "Spiritually Transformative Experiences" (STEs), in 1994. This term has now been adopted by many professionals in the field, including at IANDS, ACISTE, and ETERNEA.

Dr. Kason had a powerful Near-Death Experience in a 1979 plane crash, which propelled her to later become the first Canadian medical doctor to specialize her practice in the research and counselling of patients with Spiritually Transformative Experiences. She has now had five Near-Death Experiences and multiple other STEs. She was a founder and board member of the Kundalini Research Network, the founder of the Spiritual Emergence Research and Referral Clinic, Canadian Coordinator of the Spiritual Emergence Network, and the co-founder of the Spirituality in Health-Care Network. In 2002, she chaired the University of Toronto's first international conference on Spirituality and Health-Care. Dr. Kason is the author or co-author of six books.

Dr. Yvonne Kason retired from the practice of medicine in 2006 for health reasons (traumatic brain injury). Following a dramatic brain healing in 2016, a "miracle of brain neuroplasticity," Dr. Kason has now resumed writing, public speaking, and giving media interviews. Dr. Kason has been a guest on numerous radio and television shows across Canada and the U.S., and has been featured online on YouTube shows, podcasts, and several internet radio shows. Her inspirational 1979 Near-Death Experience has been reenacted on "Sightings," as well as in two television documentaries. A renowned international expert on NDEs, kundalini, and other STEs, she is in demand as a speaker to professional and public groups internationally.

Book Credits

Acquiring Editor: Kathryn Lane
Project Editor: Jenny McWha
Copy Editor: Laurie Miller

Cover Designer: Laura Boyle
Interior Designer: Sophie Paas-Lang

Publicist: Elham Ali

🏢 dundurn.com   📷 dundurnpress

🐦 @dundurnpress   📌 dundurnpress

📘 dundurnpress   ✉ info@dundurn.com

FIND US ON NETGALLEY & GOODREADS TOO!

 DUNDURN